LEAVING A LEGACY

THE AUTOBIOGRAPHY OF

GORDON MOYES

Ark House Press
PO Box 163
North Sydney, NSW, 2059
Telephone: (02) 8437 3541; Facsimile (02) 9999 2053
International: +612 8437 3541; Facsimile +612 9999 2053
www.arkhousepress.com

Cataloguing in Publication Data:

ISBN 0 9752044 9 1.

1. Moyes, Gordon, 1938- . 2. Uniting Church in Australia - Clergy - Biography. I. Title.

287.93092

Printed and bound in Australia by Griffin Press
Cover design by Simon Ray and Nicole Danswan

To the love of my life and partner in ministry: Beverley;
To our family who have ministered with us:
Jenny and Ron, Michael, Rachel and Emma; Peter and Trina, Cassie, Jack and Indiana;
David and Leisl, Brianna and Chelsea;
Andrew and Rebecca, Tom and Scarlett.

Table of Contents

INTRODUCTION

Introduction

As a young teenager in The Box Hill Boys High School in the early 1950's, I was challenged with my class, by our geometry teacher, to work out the angles and make a polygon. Most of the boys decided to make a cube as that was easiest. Some decided to make an octagon. I decided to make a do-deca-hedron; a solid figure with 12 equal faces or planes. I calculated the angles, cut the pieces from very thin wood then sand papered, glued and painted the model.

To make it personal, I decided to paint each of the twelve sides with symbols of my interests. For example one side with a pair of running spikes represented my sport, athletics (I held every schoolboy record – 17 years from the 100 yards to 1 mile). One had the symbol of a swimmer representing that sport, another, music notes representing my interest in singing (I was a soloist in the Australian Boys Choir, singing in concerts and in radio broadcasts each week), another, a palette and paint brush representing my interests in painting, particularly watercolours. One side had a Bible for my interest in Christian faith, one a Kappa Sigma Pi badge for Christian leadership, another piles of coins representing business (I helped my widowed mother every night count the day's takings – she always hoped I would be a business man and take over the family business), one symbol was a gavel, a sign of politics (my mother catered each month for the political party which met in our tea rooms above the bakery and cake shop, attended by Mr Robert Gordon Menzies) and I think the remaining ones represented my interests in the stage (I was a soloist in Gilbert and Sullivan operas), a love heart with 'B' standing for my girlfriend Beverley, a book, symbol of learning and teaching and so on.

Many people believe that a minister of religion would lead a very dull and un-interesting life conducting church services and caring for people in a parish. I discovered just the opposite was true. That as a minister of religion a person could undertake to develop skills and abilities, to learn new insights and to attempt im-possible activities which would generate more excitement and enthusiasm than one could ever possibly imagine.

This book tells how each of these interests developed over the years and became part of my life. The minister of religion has a wonderful freedom to expand aspects of his ministry as he feels God is leading him. My life has been like a dodecahedron with 12 major emphases. Each of the following chapters pictures what happened in one of those 12 sides. But together they make for an exciting, blessed, effective, and growing ministry in the word of the Gospel and in the care of people needs. I never could imagine that such a satisfying and adventurous life could flow from a commitment to follow in the service of Jesus Christ.

Over the years this minister of the Gospel would be given many privileges. We would build, during the late 1980's, the largest building to be constructed in Sydney, Australia's largest city, permanently altering the city skyline. We would work as an advisor and friend with the Prime Minister for more than a decade, having immediate access to the most powerful office of the land.

I would be responsible for raising and spending in the last twenty-five years more than a billion dollars, more than any other church minister in the world.

We would be elected by a panel of distinguished judges, to be 'Entrepreneur of the Year', and on another occasion 'Father of the Year', and on another occasion, 'Australian Public Speaker of the Year.' We would be hailed by the nation's top financial newspaper, the nation's most successful movie producer. We would be honoured nationally and internationally with honorary degrees and fellowships in diverse fields. We would be made a Companion of the Order of Australia, Australia's highest Honour, an honour never before granted to a clergyman in active service or a politician in any Parliament.

We would have weekly national television programs and the most listened to religious radio program in the nation.

Over a million citizens gave me their vote to become one of the top twenty-one selected from 290 candidates for our oldest parliament. A Christian newspaper in 2005 polled Christian leaders for their list of most influential church leaders, and I was the only person named in every list submitted from across the nation. It has been a varied and interesting life.

I would acknowledge all of those who have helped me from the earliest days who have worked along side of me in the tasks of ministry and will mention many by name at the appropriate places. But above all my life partner from our earliest teenage years, wife and mother of our children, Beverley, has been an outstanding companion and without her none of this would have been possible. The expanded word and deed ministry has impacted on hundreds of thousands of people over fifty years. Nothing learned is ever wasted when it is given to God to use.

I would thank Goldie Down who came into Intensive Care when I was hooked up to life support after open-heart surgery to leave six books for me with the statement: 'These are biographies of the famous I have written. I am now starting one on you!' and who wrote the sell-out biography *'Gordon Moyes, The Man, The Media and The Mission'* (Open Book). She details all the aspects of my life.

I would thank my typist, Carolyn Holmes, who took my typing and patiently made corrections and additions, my Personal Assistant Blossom Vickers who made some time for me to write, to her husband, Michael, who proof read the text and to Matt Danswan and Emily McIntyre of Ark House Press who saw it through to the bookshops.

In the following pages I share my thoughts on the growth of a modern minister who has created many unusual opportunities to share the Gospel in the hope of encouraging others.

REV. DR. The Hon. GORDON MOYES AC, MLC.

EVANGELIST

Chapter One

From my earliest days as a teenage Christian, I wanted to be an evangelist.

1952 was a great year in the Melbourne Churches of Christ. They were host for the World Convention of Churches of Christ and 10,000 people attended the great public rallies in the Exhibition Building. Thousands of overseas visitors were accommodated in the homes of Melbourne church members. I was taken to the World Convention by two ladies, Jean and Maggie Perry, who worked in my mother's cake shop. They were devout members of Churches of Christ, they had first taken me to Sunday school and were part of all of my life from teaching me to sing to teaching me Chinese words and characters.

At the World Convention there were church members from about 120 lands, each with their own distinctive dress and skin colour and language. They came from every inhabited continent on earth. Many gave away little craft pieces they had made from straw or wood. Everyone shook hands. There were famous preachers from churches of thousands of members, especially in America and singing groups from the Pacific Islands, India and Africa. There were missionaries from a score of lands who told their stories of service to God. Dr Oldfield was there from the great hospital in Dhond, India and Garfield Todd, the New Zealand Missionary from Southern Rhodesia who had established primary and secondary schools all over that country.

Associated with the Convention was an evangelistic mission held with two visiting Americans, Mr Ralph Pollock, a song leader and Dr E. Ray Snodgrass the evangelist. The Snodgrass-Pollock Mission was conducted in Wirth's Olympia. This great circus arena was now filled with chairs and thousands sang the popular choruses and hymns. 'The Awakening Chorus' lifted the roof. There was hardly a dry eye as they learnt the beautiful ' Beyond the Sunset'.

All of the members of the Court St., Box Hill Church of Christ were attending the Snodgrass-Pollock Mission. They were great nights. Some of us thirteen-year boys climbed up the very highest row of the seats at the back and made paper planes from the hymn sheets and sent them circling down upon the heads of the crowd below.

One night however, I heard what Dr Snodgrass was saying. He was holding up five fingers and showing how first God required us to have faith in Jesus Christ. The second finger meant we should repent of our sin and indicate to God that we would try to live a better life. The third finger meant that we should privately confess to God our sin and publicly take a stand for Jesus as one of his followers. The fourth finger meant that we should be baptised as he commanded us as obedient believers. And the fifth finger related to the promise of the Holy Spirit, who was given to those who believed, repented, confessed and were baptised as Peter had promised on the Day of Pentecost.

I understood every word. Then he asked those of us who would follow the way of Jesus to come to the front for counselling. As the choir and the congregation started to sing, 'Just as I am, without one plea, but that thy blood was shed for me and that thou bidst me come to Thee, O Lamb of God, I come', I came. I walked in tears down the high rows of seats and along the sawdust covered ground of the circus ring to the front and stood with those who received Christ as Lord.

Two nights later, our minister and my Sunday School teacher, Jack Ferris, visited my mother to talk about my baptism. We had a Bible Study then a prayer time. For the first time in our new house, we knelt down together on the floor of our lounge room and prayed. My mother and I understood what was happening. It was arranged for me to be baptised the following Sunday night, 21st September 1952, at the Snodgrass-Pollock mission in Wirth's Olympia. Hundreds of us were baptised that evening, witnessed by some 5,000 people.

20 years later, when I was preaching as an evangelist in America, a remarkable event occurred. I had travelled through many states on my way to another Churches of Christ World Convention, this time in Mexico City. I had been booked to preach in Enid, Oklahoma. It was a huge church, the largest I had ever spoken in to that time. Several thousand people were seated in the congregation. The minister had told me with some pride that every week they had over 100 millionaires in the congregation.

Just as we were about to enter the platform, the minister indicated that he would get a gown for me to wear, as was their custom. From the cupboard he produced an old gown and apologised for it. 'This gown used to be worn by the previous minister of this church', he advised. 'He died a few years ago after a 25-year ministry here. His name was Dr E. Ray Snodgrass.'

I turned to my friend, 'Did you say Dr E Ray Snodgrass? I made my commitment to Christ under his preaching!' The minister confirmed that this was his gown. He put it on my shoulders and I felt the blessing of the old evangelist, much like Elisha must have felt when he took the prophet's cloak of Elijah. (1 Kings 19:19-21)

That morning as I preached in his old pulpit, I held up five fingers and told the way of salvation through faith, repentance, confession, baptism and the reception of the Holy Spirit as he had done. That morning at the door as I shook hands with the congregation, person after person wept with the joyful memories of their beloved pastor. One lady, in a big fur, said, 'When you were preaching this morning in that gown, holding up your five fingers, I could just hear Dr Snodgrass speaking!' And I replied, 'He was. He was!'

I was later to hear many great evangelists in different parts of the world, but I did not want to be an itinerant evangelist, going to different churches and communities all the time. I wanted to be an evangelist, settled in one place where I could come to know the people, help them to come to faith in Jesus Christ and then be there for the next few years to see them grow in their faith and service. I wanted to see the new Christians progress and become mature in Christ.

Every week of my life since I have preached in services, on radio and television, in public halls and theatres, Opera House and Town Hall, in the open air, in football stadiums and factories, but always I have given an appeal for people to commit their lives to Jesus Christ and untold thousands have.

While the evangelistic message is one, the methods of proclaiming it are many. Over forty years I have tried, with varying success different methods of proclaiming the Gospel.

The Dynamic Of Preaching

Mission begins with God. When Douglas Webster wrote his little booklet *Changing Missions - Biblical and Contemporary*, he commenced with these words: 'We begin then, where mission begins, with God.' The mission of the Church primarily, is the fulfilment of the mission of God to the world.

However, there is general agreement that in the Church, there is a crisis in the sense of mission today. There has been a wholesale drift of membership from the churches and a reduction of the number of churches serving in the inner city. Many church leaders, awakened by the crisis, are searching for cause and cure. Many are grasping at the mission of the Church, crying for renewal, reformation, restoration, or revival - the choice depending upon the theological assumptions of the speaker.

The mission of God is fulfilled in part by the Biblical task given to the Church of Jesus Christ. This task is upward toward God, inward in renewal and outwards in reach. The mission of the Church, is the Church as 'sent' into the world as light, salt, the servant, the prophet, the witness and any other of the descriptions given to the Church in mission, in scripture.

1. The Biblical Foundations For Mission

The root idea of mission lies in the concept of sending and it contains the four elements of:

a) The sender who is the one expressing concern;
b) The message which is sent expressing that concern;
c) The messenger who brings the message of concern;
d) The recipients who are the receivers of the message and the object of the sender's concern;

Both in the Old Testament and the New Testament these four phases of mission are emphasised. God is always the sender. The message of man's fulfilment and wholeness in relationship with God is always the same. However, in the Old Testament the messengers of God were the chosen people and prophets of God, whereas in the New Testament the supreme messenger is Jesus. The recipients in the Old Testament are the people of Israel, whereas in the New Testament the emphasis is upon the whole world as the recipients of God's message.

The Old Testament concepts of God's mission to mankind are fundamental to the total understanding of the theology of mission. It would be true to say that the method of mission in the Old Testament was centripetal. Israel, God's chosen messengers, were so to live under the blessing of God, that nations and individuals would be attracted to Jerusalem and hence to her God. Jerusalem is the celebrated city of God and she is to be the home city of all nations. Other cities and countries may be enemies of God's will, but the significance of the election of Israel is that the day would come when Jerusalem would be the centre of the world's allegiance to God. Throughout scripture we see this emphasis upon the centrality of Jerusalem with the coming of the Queen of Sheba to Solomon, the journey of the Ethiopian Eunuch to Jerusalem for worship, the coming of the Greeks to see Jesus and the gathering of all the nations on the Day of Pentecost. At the end of history, the book of Revelation informs us that it will be the new Jerusalem that will be the centre of man's worship to God.

The Old Testament is not often seen as the source of God's saving purpose. A study of the Old Testament revelation, particularly the concern of God expressed in Genesis 1-11, indicates that God's concern and mission was to be for the whole of the human race. The theology of mission must commence with God's concern for the whole of creation. God's mission did not commence with the Exodus but with his expressions of love and concern for all of mankind in the opening chapters of scripture. They are the pre-history of Israel as the people of God and these chapters give meaning and significance to Israel's history, calling and purpose. Israel is the means by which God's mission is to be expressed to the whole of mankind. The call of Abraham and the development of the history of Israel is the beginning of the move to restore the lost unity of mankind and of the broken fellowship between God and his creation. The history of Israel is the continuation of God's concern with all of creation and therefore the history of Israel is only understood in the light of God's continuing care and concern for his creation.
Israel, as God's chosen vessel to bear his mission to the world, discovers resources of moral and spiritual strength that unifies itself as a nation. It holds a deep consciousness of the unique covenantal relationship between itself as a people

and with God. That covenant not only reveals to them a knowledge of God as Creator and Lord, but reveals their own purpose as servants of God.

Israel with her emphasis upon ethical monotheism was in stark contrast to the rest of the world and her very preservation as a people, bearing the witness to God's mission, is in itself evidence of God's concern for the fulfilment of his mission. That fulfilment of God's mission would be found in Christ.

In the New Testament the emphasis is still upon God's mission to the world. However, the method of bearing his message to mankind is different. The failure of Israel as a nation to attract people to God as creator and ruler and her rejection of the messengers of God, led ultimately to God sending his only Son. The Parable of the Vineyard and the introduction of Hebrews, are two points in the New Testament that seek to link the method of the coming of Jesus with that of the fulfilment of Israel's mission.

While it is important to understand that the theology of mission flows through the entire scripture, it is also important to realise the distinctions in the Old and New Testaments in the fulfilment of this mission.

We have already indicated that in the Old Testament the commission to proclaim to the nation was seen in a centripetal sense. Israel was to so live that other nations would be attracted to her God. But in the New Testament the commission is to proclaim to all the nations in a centrifugal sense. The Church, as the chosen people of God to bear the message of God, was to take this message to the uttermost parts of the world beginning in Jerusalem, then widening out.

The function of the mission of God was transferred to the Church, as the New Israel (1 Peter 2:9). The Church, as the new Israel, was to bear the message of God brought through his Son. Jesus had this world vision and commissioned his people to take the message to the uttermost parts of the earth.

Jesus was the bearer of God's message of concern to all of mankind. The Church, as his followers, is to bear witness to that message into all the world. The ministry of Jesus demonstrated his concern for the fulfilment of the mission of God.

The Kingdom of God was the focal point of Christ's proclamation (Mark 1: 14-15). There are some sixty references in the Gospel to Jesus preaching the Kingdom of God. The Kingdom was seen as the fulfilment of the Old Testament promises and begins with the preaching of Jesus. In his preaching the Messianic character of the coming Kingdom of God comes into sharp focus. In Jesus the expectation of salvation is being fulfilled, the revelation of salvation is becoming clearer and the history of salvation is unfolding.

In his understanding of himself, of the Fatherhood of God and of his unique purpose in his atoning death and resurrection, Jesus was outlining for those who would believe, his sense of fulfilling God's mission to mankind.

These fundamental concepts are each centring round God's mission to all of mankind. They provide the fundamentals of the theology of the Church, which was to go to all of humanity bearing the message that the fulfilment of God's mission is found through faith in Jesus the Christ. Henceforth his people would have the task of proclaiming that fulfilment. This task was no less than the evangelisation of the world.

It is important to realise that there is no separate theology of mission. It is not an appendix to Biblical theology, but part of its very heart. For no understanding of God as Creator and Jehovah, no understanding of Israel's election and purpose, or understanding of the coming, the ministry and the uniqueness of Jesus, can be complete unless it is within the scope of God's saving purpose for the whole of mankind. It is easy to document from the Acts of the Apostles and the Epistles of the New Testament, how the early Christians took the message of God's salvation through Christ to the limit of their geographical understanding.

The rapid and far-flung spread of Christianity within the first few decades of the existence of the Christian Church is the best commentary on the zeal and purpose of the early Apostles. To follow them was to follow in a path of mission. Every church found itself in a mission setting in a very peculiar sense. Every church was surrounded by multitudes without God, without hope. Here was their first challenge, as Paul tells the church at Philippi (Phil. 2:12-16). Similar words are spoken to the churches at Corinth, Ephesus, Thessalonica and Colossae.

Again, Paul commends the churches at Rome and Thessalonica for their efforts in evangelising their communities and beyond their borders (Romans 1:8; 1 Th. 1:8). The Apostle admonishes the Church of Corinth to abound in the work of the Lord (1 Cor. 15:58), that is they are to excel, to go beyond their usual bounds, to spill over and do the unusual. The Apostle also praises the Philippians for having an active part in his ministry (Phil. 4:10). It must be remembered that the Philippian Church had a missionary out in the field (Phil. 2:25).

Paul expects that his own example will inspire others to follow in his train. He calls upon the churches to follow him even as he follows Christ (1 Cor. 11:1; 4:16; Phil. 3:17; 1 Th. 1:6; 2 Th. 3:6-7). He makes it clear that his supreme mission is evangelism (1 Cor. 1:17, 'For Christ sent me not to baptise, but to preach the gospel.' He speaks in no uncertain terms of his mission to evangelise. (1 Cor. 9:16-18). To follow Paul meant to pursue the path of evangelism.

The early disciples had an enormous task in taking the gospel to the whole world. It is well-known that they were ordinary, uneducated men without influential backing and that they came from a second-rate province on the edge of the empire.
If anyone had considered at the time the probabilities of the success in their mission even granting their enthusiasm, surely the odds would have weighed heav-

ily against them. Yet it was this overwhelming sense that they were fulfilling the mission of God through the command of Jesus that propelled them into every known part of the world. Michael Green in Evangelism in the Early Church stressed this enthusiasm for evangelism.

'The enthusiasm to evangelise which marked the early Christians is one of the most remarkable things in the history of religions,' he explains. 'Here were men and women of every rank and station in life, of every country in the known world, so convinced that they had discovered the riddle of the universe, so sure of the one true God whom they had come to know, that nothing would stand in the way of their passing on this good news to others. As we have seen, they did it by preaching and personal conversation, by formal discourse and informal testimony, by arguing in the synagogue and by chattering in the laundry. They might be slighted, laughed at, disenfranchised, robbed of their possessions; their homes, even their families, but this would not stop them. They might be reported to the authorities as dangerous atheists and required to sacrifice to the imperial gods; but they refused to comply. In Christianity they found something utterly new, authentic and satisfying. They were not prepared to deny Christ even in order to preserve their own lives; and in the manner of their dying they made converts to their faith.'

The early Christians believed that there were three elements for the fulfilment of this mission - the first is that they were to carry their message to the uttermost parts of the earth, to complete the arrested mission of the Old Israel. The second is that this task would be theirs until the end of the Age. The preaching of the gospel was one of the signs that God intended to create a new heaven and a new earth. Their proclamation must continue until God again intervenes in history. Third, that this mission which began with the outpouring of the Holy Spirit would continue in the power of the Holy Spirit until the end of this world, with the coming of the Day of the Lord.

Their effectiveness in fulfilling the mission of God can be seen in the estimates Bishop Stephen Neill made that by the end of the Third Century there was somewhere about 5 million Christians out of a total Roman Empire population of 50 million. Their mission was a fulfilment of their Biblical understanding of God's mission to men.

2. The Dynamics Of Mission

In spite of what has been said by some who are critical of the mission of the Church, we are not living in a post-mission era. Certainly that concept is not borne out in the scriptures, nor is it evidenced by the continuing need of the world, nor is it found in the expectations of the Third World churches, nor, I will contend, should it be part of the expectation of any Christian. The Christian lives in the most urgent era of the history of the Church. Only a full recovery of the dynamics of mission can enable us to fulfil our purpose as the people of God.

The centrality of Christ is fundamental to our theology of mission. That Jesus is central to the Biblical revelation needs no argument.

The coming of Christ, his dying and rising and ascension, are the central pivots in God's plan of salvation.

The Incarnation-Cross-Resurrection event is central to any Christian understanding of history, the salvation of mankind and the mission of the Church. This event is central to the divine history of salvation. For here the promise is fulfilled, sin is judged, forgiveness is offered, death is defeated and life and immortality are brought to light. At the heart of the Christian theology of mission must be the Incarnation-Cross-Resurrection event and the salvation that was made possible as a consequence of it.

There is a universality about the scope of that salvation, for Jesus 'the Lamb of God takes away the sin of the world'. That salvation however, is only potentially universal until it is actually appropriated by the individual who believes in Christ. Scripture bears records, however, that this salvation is far beyond human response and includes the completion of the restored cosmos. There is an ultimate cosmic fulfilment through Christ.

Jesus, himself, outlined the purposes of his mission in the Parable of the Vineyard (Mark 12:1-9). In this the relationship between God and his creation is outlined. Here Israel has a responsibility, which they failed to fulfil. So God sends his own Son and Messenger. But he is killed, delivering the message.

In John's Gospel (Chapter 9) there is an even more touching outline of the mission of Jesus. It has to do with John's exposition of the healing of the blind man. John sees Jesus as the light of the world and that his mission was to bring men into that light. Jesus searched for the man who had been made blind after he had been expelled from the Jewish Temple. Here once more the mission of Jesus in seeking, searching and saving, is outlined. The fulfilment of mission is found only when people see Jesus, discover him as the light of the world and continue to live in that light.

In all outlines of the theology of mission, Jesus Christ stands central. Through God's grace he is the bearer of the message of God's loving concern of whom the scriptures speak. The Apostles were gripped by God's great redemptive act through Christ.

The Disciples were convinced that they had been eyewitnesses of the great decisive redemptive act of God through Jesus. They believed that as a consequence of this act mankind could now enter upon the salvation offered since the beginning of the world. They believed that what was happening was in complete harmony with the teaching of God's mission as outlined in the Old Testament. They believed that this was to benefit all of mankind dependent only upon a receptive, faith-obedience to the gospel.

Hence they were willing to share their understanding of the completion of God's mission with everyone they met. 'We cannot but speak the things which we have seen and heard' (Acts 2:32, 3:15; 4:10, 33; 5:29-32). John, in his first Epistle, joyfully and confidently writes that what he has seen and heard he must declare to those who read his word (1 John 1:1-3). Here was the essence of reality-experience. Paul is an even clearer example of the way the early Apostles were motivated to proclaim the fulfilment of God's mission. Johannes Blauw writes of Paul:

'There is no doubt, however, that Paul's reflection of the gospel is the fruit of his missionary activities (1 Cor. 15:10). The 'irregular' apostle has done more work than all the other apostles, even though he does not give himself credit for it but ascribes it to "the grace of God that was bestowed upon me." The eccentricity that is characteristic of Paul's apostleship has a deep meaning also for the missionary task of the present. Just as to Paul the light arose over the mystery of the salvation of all humanity (Eph. 3:4-6) which had not been known to previous generations, so the Church of today will not be able to understand the 'divine economy' (Eph. 3:9) in any other way, nor preach the mystery (Eph.3:9) in any other way than by its continued "preparation of the gospel of peace" (Eph.6:15). Missionary work is like a pair of sandals that have been given to the Church in order that it shall set out on the road and keep on going to make known the mystery of the gospel (Eph. 6:10). Only thus will this mystery be revealed more and more to the Church itself. Serving among the Gentiles enabled Paul to serve the Church; the Church lives mainly on his missionary epistles!'

The dynamic that motivated the Apostles and centred their preaching upon Jesus as Christ, lay in the equipping of the Holy Spirit. From the foundation of the world the Spirit of God has been brooding over mankind. On the Day of Pentecost, the Spirit of God equipped and empowered the disciples to fulfil their mission to the world in a new way.

However, Pentecost is not merely an historical event in the history of the Church. The Holy Spirit did not merely come on that day. He came to abide and to continue the fulfilment of the mission of God. Through the presence of the Holy Spirit the mission of God has a new dynamism. The 'come' of the Old Testament, is replaced by the 'go' of the New Testament. The Holy Spirit was the power that made the men go in mission. A close study of the book of Acts reveals that all major steps of expansion were initiated, inspired and empowered by the Holy Spirit.

It was through the Holy Spirit that the religious barrier was broken when Philip went to Samaria, Peter went to Cornelius, when Christians from Cyprus went to Antioch and when Paul and Barnabas set off on the first missionary journey. It was the Holy Spirit who equipped the early Christians with power and boldness to proclaim the gospel and endured them with courage in the midst of obstacles and persecution. Christians believe that the Holy Spirit is the guide in the formation of churches, the dynamic behind the ongoing spread of the gospel and the inspiration of Christian mission.

From what has already been said it is obvious that the cutting edge of the theology of mission comes at the point of proclamation. It is not just enough to have a Christian presence within the world; there must be a Christian proclamation of the great salvation act.

For the last two decades it has been popular to speak of the Christian presence within the community and some speak of the Christian presence as though the serving, healing and comforting witness of the gospel is sufficient in itself to fulfil the mission of the Church. However, the emphasis in the New Testament is on evangelism by the direct proclamation of the message of God. More than 140 times the New Testament uses such words as 'to announce', 'to tell', 'to spread good news', 'to talk' and 'to herald or proclaim'.

Any church engaged in the fulfilment of the mission of God must have the dynamic that comes through the proclamation of the gospel, supported in turn by the presence of a witnessing, loving and serving community. There remains a sense of urgency in the fulfilment of the mission of God. Throughout the scripture there is stress laid upon the imperative of the task, which is given to the Church. (John 9:4, 4:35; Matt. 9:37-38). The urgency was accepted by the early Christians who believed that now was the acceptable time and now was the day of salvation (2 Cor. 6:1-2). Christians, therefore, must live both in their private and public lives with the sense of urgency to fulfil the mission of God.

3. The Church As God's Agent Of Mission

Johannes Blauw has indicated that there is no other church than the Church that is sent into the world and there is no other mission than that of the Church of Jesus Christ. If one understands the election of Israel as an election for service, then we have already begun to see the role of the new Israel, the Church of Jesus, chosen for the service of bearing the message of salvation to the entire world.

The Church has been chosen as God's agent for mission. She is to perform for the world the service of being a witness to the Kingdom of God, which has come and is coming in Jesus Christ. It is impossible to separate the Church from mission. The Church is only the Church when it is the Church in mission. The Church is God's agent on earth through which God expresses himself to the world. God has no other redeeming agency than the Church.

The Church is at the very centre of God's cosmic purpose and is the means through which God fulfils his mission to men. The Church is the earthly agent of God's cosmic reconciliation and to witness to that mission is the primary task of the Church. Dr Martyn Lloyd-Jones has said,

'So I would lay it down as a basic proposition that the primary task of the Church is not to educate man, is not to heal him physically or psychologically, it is not to make him happy. I will go further; it is not even to make him good. These are things that accompany salvation; and when the Church performs her true task she does incidentally educate men and give them knowledge and information, she does bring them happiness, she does make them good and better than they were. But my point is that those are not her primary objectives. Her primary purpose is not any of these; it is rather to put man into the right relationship with God, to reconcile man to God'.

If the proclamation of the gospel in the fulfilment of the mission of God is the primary task of the Church, it ought not to be only proclamation by word. It must also be proclamation by deed. Christ gave us an example not only of preaching, but of service; not only of worship but of witness; not only to individuals, but to society. The witness is evangelical and social, private and public, individual and corporate. In the Prayer of Christ recorded in John 17, Jesus prays for his Apostles and all those who will believe 'in me through their word'. His commission is 'as you sent me into the world, so I have sent them into the world' (John 17: 18-21).

For me starting to fulfil the mission of God as an evangelist began in the slums of Melbourne as a teenager in 1957.

Pastor To The Slums

When I was studying to be a minister of the Gospel, my student churches were two adjacent wooden churches in the inner slum areas of Melbourne. For seven years during the 1950's and 1960's the people of those inner slum areas were my parish. During that time as student minister, then part- time minister and finally as a full- time graduated and ordained minister, my work as Pastor to the 'Slums' was still that of an evangelist, with a strong emphasis upon social care.

During my first eight years as a Pastor to the slums of inner Melbourne, I was involved in a great deal of social work. We were helping people with food, clothing, finding accommodation, helping drunks and derelicts and particularly working as Parole and Probation Officer with young offenders. I spent as much time going in and out of the courts and the jails as I did any other place. But always there was ringing that ordination charge, 'Do the work of an Evangelist'.

In the slum ministry I sought to do this by preaching a Gospel message every Sunday night regardless of the size of the congregation. The first time I ever preached was a Gospel service and fourteen people were present, eleven of them my friends and relatives who came visiting the little inner suburban church to give me encouragement. Every Sunday night of my life in the nearly fifty years since then I have preached a Gospel message and invited people to commit their lives to Jesus Christ.

Billy Graham came to Melbourne in 1959 and the thought of preaching evangelism in the style of Billy Graham influenced many of us, but I also felt that the better way was to train and equip members of the Church to be evangelists themselves. So for four Sunday afternoons while I was working in the slums I brought together a group of rather unwilling church members and taught them how to witness to their faith and how to lead others to Jesus Christ. Then for four Sunday afternoons in a row we encouraged them out of the church building to go and visit friends and relatives and share the Gospel with them. It was a miserable failure. After four weeks not one life had been committed to Christ through the evangelistic witness of our members and so the program was quietly dropped.

Every Sunday night I would preach a Gospel message from the centre of the platform asking people to commit their lives to Jesus Christ as Saviour and Lord. A few did and there was great rejoicing at their baptism. At most baptisms, I prayed in Paul's words, 'Woe to me if I preach not the Gospel.'

They became seven incredibly happy years. Beverley, the love of my life, who had started there as my seventeen year old girlfriend had become my fiancée, two years later my wife. Three years later she became the mother of our first child. Our baby daughter was the delight of all of the people in the church. With so many elderly people in both congregations, the coming of the first full-time minister in forty years and the first baby to be born into a church manse in the two churches in that century, created a great deal of delight for the elderly members. We used to think that Jenny had one hundred grandmothers.

An evangelist in the slums, I witnessed over a hundred local residents committing themselves to Jesus Christ and being baptised into the Church. By 1963 I had graduated both from the Federal College of The Bible of Churches of Christ and from Melbourne University and the time had come to move on.

I had cherished the idea for seven years that I should do some post graduate study in the United States of America and after writing to many various universities and colleges I decided that I would seek admission to the Christian Theological Seminary in Indianapolis, Indiana and work at the University of Indiana toward a Doctorate in Christian Education.

The idea behind all that I did was that I might equip myself to one day ministering in a large city church teaching Scriptural truths by the most efficient and effective means to large numbers of people. I wanted to be an evangelist who would teach the truths with integrity and insight.

An Australian minister of Churches of Christ was the senior pastor a very large church in Indianapolis. He wrote offering me a position on his staff while I completed postgraduate studies and the thought of becoming Associate Minister at the Norwood Christian Church under Rev. Dr Theo Fisher was a tremendous opportunity. Theo had become a leader of integration between the black and white communities of Indianapolis. He had marched with Martin Luther King into Selma, Alabamha and had succeeded in taking the Church with him down the road to integration. In those days of intense civil rights campaigning, Theo Fisher was a man of great courage and I looked forward to working in ministry with him.

The second part of the picture fell into place when the Christian Theological Seminary offered me a postgraduate scholarship. The letters flew backwards and forwards across the Pacific and it became a matter of great excitement as we looked forward to leaving Australia on Boxing Day 1963 to commence our new life in the United States of America.

We had spent more than seven months getting ready to depart in 1963. We had been advised to gain a non-quota immigrant visa because I would be working as well as studying in the United States of America. So we both had completed the long series of medical checks. Now, armed with our chest x-rays, certificates of clearance about smallpox, venereal disease and a host of other unwanted conditions, with our taxation clearance and church authorisations we waited upon the Consul for our visa.

We filled in endless forms which were sent backwards and forwards across the Pacific to Washington DC for official approval for our immigration. The people at the Consulate were quite nice but the queues were inordinately long and we had to stand with baby daughter in arm for hours before we would have our certificates and applications processed.

We packed all of our belongings. It broke our hearts to give away many of the gifts that we had been given for our engagement and wedding but it was not possible to take everything with us. In the centre of the lounge room we had a huge wooden crate five-foot square and three foot-deep. It weighed half a ton and it was the maximum that we were allowed to take on the ship. We sold some of our furniture and gave most of the rest of it to other young couples. Inside that wooden crate was placed all of our blankets, sheets and towels on the bottom and around the edges to protect the rest of the contents, all of the clothes that we intended taking, all baby Jenny's requirements, the crockery, special wedding gifts, family photographs, typewriter, books, sermons, university transcripts and everything else that would be needed to establish us in our new life were packed into that crate. They went in with loving care, everything wrapped in towels or linen to protect them on the long sea journey. Eventually the wooden lid was closed and the whole lot bound in hoop iron and carted by truck to the wharves to be loaded on the S.S. Monterey. We had saved for three years to get enough money for our fare and it was a proud moment on the last day when we went to Macdonald Hamilton Pty Ltd and paid our fares, two adults and one child, Sydney to America, with airfares from Melbourne to Sydney and from San Francisco to Indianapolis.

That day we sold the car and the last of our Australian possessions were on board the ship sailing to Sydney, where we would join it on Boxing Day after our final Christmas with Beverley's mother. The day of our final appointment came as we went to the American Consulate to get the last approvals on our visa.

The queues were long and we waited patiently for several hours. Suddenly the Consulate seemed to go berserk. Members of the Consulate ran to one another talking in excited whispers. People broke out into stares. Men wandered away from their desks and met in huddles. Someone locked the outside door of the Consulate and no one was to be admitted. Those of us who were being processed were just left as if we were not there or were invisible. Someone turned a radio on and people could hear. The news broke upon all assembled. 'President John F. Kennedy has been shot. He has been assassinated in Dallas, Texas. No news of his condition is yet available officially, but it is believed that he is dead.'

The Consulate went into a tailspin and with it the world. Minor details like our visa applications were literally wiped off the Consul's table. World events caught us up in their confusion. Immediately the American Consulates everywhere in the world were placed onto terrorist alert. The Consuls were recalled to Washington DC. Somewhere, there on the floor, or on a bench, or in a waster paper basket were our visas with our photographs and everything required except the official stamp.

The Consul's office remained closed for several days. The new President was sworn in and then the Consul's office returned to normal. Now, with only days to go before our departure, we once more lined up with extra long lines of people wanting to be processed. It was Christmas Eve and the staff of the Consulate were harassed. They could not find our visas. We pleaded with them to commence new applications. We sent telegrams across the Pacific asking for cabled permission to leave without the visa. The legal minds in the Consulate argued that new visa applications could not be processed while present applications were pending.

Then it was time to break for Christmas parties and the Christmas holidays. My mother and friends went to Sydney to farewell us on Boxing Day. Some friends drove up to Sydney at the passenger terminal to wave us goodbye. Beverley and I and baby Jenny slept on the floor, owning nothing except our toothbrushes. Even our hand luggage had been taken on board and placed in our cabin on the S.S. Monterey. Christmas Day left us feeling utterly bereft without money, clothing, furniture, car, job or house.

On Boxing Day the Consul gave the dreaded news to us from his home. 'I am sorry but there is nothing I can do. We will just have to process a new visa application for you when the office opens in January.'

In Sydney the S.S. Monterey sailed out into Sydney Harbour and standing at the shore was my mother and friends with no one to wave goodbye to.

Back in Melbourne Beverley and I and baby Jenny were still sleeping on the floor. It would be another six months before the visas would finally be approved, before new x-rays of our chests were completed and we were guaranteed pure from infection of tuberculosis, smallpox, venereal disease and all the other unwanted conditions. New taxation clearance certificates had to be obtained but by then I had missed the start of the university year. I could not wait in Indianapolis and I could not be unemployed in Australia. President Kennedy's assassination had affected our lives completely. I needed some work in order to keep us and so became Chaplain in a mental hospital and minister to a small country church. My time as a Pastor to the Slums loomed into life as a bush padre.

A Country Parson

Our furniture was duly unloaded in San Francisco. Our luggage went on to Indianapolis. It would be more than two years before, eventually we would get all of our hand luggage returned and get the crate back to Australia. We lived with borrowed everything during that period of time, gradually replacing our necessities and re-establishing our lives until the time came when we could once more take up the interrupted journey.

Two years later, with another baby on the way, the hoop iron crate arrived back in Melbourne. How excited we were and how long were the delays of getting it out of the bond store. Eventually, with duties paid the truck delivered it to our country parsonage. With great excitement we burst open the iron bands and levered up the wooden lid. We peeled back the layers of blankets and bed linen still surrounded with mothballs. And inside lay all of our earthly possession. The kitchen saucepans were all out of shape from the pressure of the crate being dropped by a crane. The typewriter was bent in the middle; the lecture notes and books had mildewed pages. The clothes looked terribly old fashioned and out of date and nothing seemed to fit. Things were broken. In fact as we unpacked and unwrapped everything complete despair settled upon us. Most of those things went back into the crate and the whole lot was sent to the tip. But the call to be an evangelist was still thrashing in my veins.

In 1965, I had only been in Ararat for one month when I realised that there was a desperate need to do something to help the teenagers of Ararat. My experience as a Parole and Probation Officer was already being called upon and I recognised that too many young people were going before the courts. The life in a small country town is not very exciting and many young people found the most exciting things happened when they broke the law.
I was contemplating the problems of the young people in the community one night in bed. It was incredibly hot and I was awake, unable to sleep. Eventually I got out of bed and seeking something cooler went out and sat on the front steps of the manse. Only those people who have lived in the inland of Australia know how hot some of those summer nights can be when the north winds continue

to blow from the inland across the Wimmera. I guess it was well over a hundred degrees and after midnight, as I sat on the stone doorstep at the end of the long passage that ran through the wooden manse thinking about the problem of young people in the small country town.

While I was sitting there a drunk ambled past, grasping hold of our front fence to steady himself. He looked up and saw me and wished me good evening. I said 'Good evening to you' in return. Suddenly discovering an audience in the otherwise deserted street the drunk opened the front gate and staggered up the front path and collapsed on the front step beside me. He placed his arm around my shoulder and thrust his stubbly beard close to my face and with strong alcoholic breath said, 'What's troubling you mate?'

I explained to him that I was not able to sleep because I had been thinking much about young people in the community and that there did not seem to be much in Ararat for them. This was a signal for him to start on a long discourse about the needs of youth in the community. He had grown up in that country town and there never had been anything for him and for other young people. 'The community does nothing, the council just sits on its backside, the school teachers are only thinking about their promotion to another bigger town and the churches only thought of wanky things for kids to do.' As the drunk continued on this long discourse about the needs of youth an idea began to firm in my mind.

What if we did organise a big occasion in Ararat and brought to Ararat the leading sportsmen in Australia, the leading bands, the leading teenager singers and television personalities? What if I brought to Ararat some of the best known people in the country and the best youth preacher I could find and see if we couldn't give them good entertainment and at the same time a strong Christian challenge to find purpose in their lives? What if I could get the whole town involved in organising this youth emphasis? What if I could get all the stores to display youth fashions and the sports stores to put on special sporting displays and the community service groups like Rotary and Lions and Apex and the Country Womens Association to focus their activities and fundraising in support of some on-going programme for young people in Ararat? What if we started it off by getting every young person who lived in the Shire together? What if I had a special 'Teen Week'? While my drunken friend kept talking meaningless rubbish about his own youth and telling me the story of his life, an idea began to formulate for what was going to become a week in the life of Ararat that is talked about to this day. Forty years later, I was invited back to Ararat to open a new church building, which was a direct result of 'Teen Week'!

After an hour or so I managed to get my drunk friend back on his feet and out the front gate and off again up High Street to his destination. I went to my study and wrote down thought after thought as ideas tumbled out of my mind.

With no money, no organisation, I gathered together a group of young adults and launched the idea of Ararat's 'Teen Week'. Soon we had a committee of twenty and we were setting up a new approach to youth evangelism.

I realised with young people that we had to get to them personally so I rounded up about twenty young people from the streets and asked them to come to my house and bring with them their Ararat High School Year Books going back over the previous ten years. The kids sat around the lounge room floor with the Year Books before them and discussed what had happened to every person in the class photograph. We took each year and each class in turn and gave a name and address to every child. Someone got the Shire voting rolls and we traced down the addresses of every teenager who lived in Ararat and the surrounding Shire.

I then recruited twenty young typists to sit at a long row of manual typewriters and write to 2,000 young people a personal letter inviting them to a series of activities. At the same time I asked my colleague ministers if I could have the opportunity of addressing their congregation and inviting representatives to form a Teen Week Committee. Soon we had prayer groups meeting each week in four churches and I set myself a timetable of four months to prepare for this massive Teen Week. I visited the Apex, the Rotary, the Girl Guides and Rangers, the Country Womens Association. In fact there were 110 adult groups or committees in Ararat and we contacted them all. We set up a catering committee for the biggest youth tea that the community had ever seen, an administration committee, a hospitality committee, a finance committee and a prayer committee.

We then set to work drawing up a list of the most famous people in Australia and I wrote to them inviting them to come to Ararat. The Prime Minister wrote back commending what we were doing and sending his photograph. The *Ararat Advertiser* began to run front page articles in every edition about the progress of Teen Week. To have the photograph of Prime Minister Menzies on the front page commending the unique Teen Week in Ararat certainly brought the attention of the whole community to what we were doing. Then the Premier of Victoria, Mr Bolte, decided to pay a visit and indicated that what we were doing in Ararat was beyond anything he had seen in any other community in Victoria.

On Thursday, 16 July, 1964, the front page read 'Sydney Church Leader Commends Teen Week' and reads 'Rev. Alan Walker of Sydney, who was awarded the Order of the British Empire by the Queen for his church work in Australia, has commended Ararat's Teen Week'. It then went on with a commendation from Alan. Neither Gordon Powell nor Alan Walker would come to Ararat at the invitation of a 25-year-old minister in a small country church but at least they sent their encouragement, which was featured in the *Ararat Advertiser*. Incidentally that was the first correspondence with those two great church leaders, which led to a 25 year friendship with both.

We scouted round all of the League footballers who were heroes in those days and all of them agreed to come and be part of the unique Teen Week. We got together with Olympic athletes, top entertainers, television personalities and others designed to bring young people together with a great sense of challenge to Christian commitment. Television stars who ran the teenage programmes of that day gave us a day and, of course, all of the politicians and community leaders quickly recognised that this was an opportunity to be seen and they too came to town. The motels and private houses were booked out with outstanding personalities.

We took over the Ararat Town Hall to launch our Teen Week with a free meal for young people, explaining what would be on during the week. The meal was catered for by church ladies groups and the Country Womens Association. A banner headline ran across the *Ararat Advertiser* for Tuesday July 28, 1964, reading 'Teen Week Launched by 600 Teenagers'. It told the story of how 600 teenagers gave Ararat's unique Teen Week a spectacular launching. More than a thousand attended the opening night's programme. Each day and each night in the schools, in the Town Hall and in the main community centre outstanding personalities spoke about the need for purpose, direction and goals in life.

I invited a well-known youth speaker, Jack Calder, to wrap up each session with a call to commitment and a challenge to young people to live in Godly ways. The result was beyond our estimation. The buildings were crowded; the programme was paid for. Hundreds of young people came into contact with the Christian message. Four thousand five hundred of them attended in one week in a community that had only 5,000 people in it. For weeks afterwards the paper produced photographs in every edition of football stars meeting with young people, of young people becoming involved in community service projects, of youth groups that had new vitality, of YMCA classes that were brimming as all of the church youth groups and community youth activities provided special on-going programmes.

But Teen Week was not only a time of celebration and fun, it was a time of Christian challenge to living the way of Jesus Christ. I made sure that we gathered the young people together in order that we might present to them in a clear fashion the Christian gospel. A national paper the following week reported, 'The Victorian country town of Ararat was the scene of a thrilling adventure with youth from July 26 to August 2. A number of churches co-operated in this effort to reach the teenage section of the community and the results were staggering. A galaxy of talent drawn from across Victoria was used including League footballers, TV personalities, international singing stars, instrumentalists and vocalists. There was an attendance of 4,500 people in this small country town with over 1,000 in the final meeting in the Town Hall, there were 261 commitments to Jesus Christ.'

That national report brought enquiries from all over Australia. In fact we had the closest experience in the four little churches of Ararat to a revival that we had ever seen. How do you cope with 261 commitments to Christ in one week?

The Presbyterian Church set up membership training classes as did the Catholic, Anglican and Methodist churches and at the Church of Christ we had more than 100 new members in training. For the next eighteen weeks I conducted training classes for church membership and baptisms of families and groups. The little church with 36 members was suddenly packed out. The membership had increased by more than 300%. Now we needed to keep up the momentum and a new monthly program called 'Teen Meets' was established. Hundreds of young people gathered for roast suckling pig cooked on a spit. Bible studies became crowded and our old buildings were inadequate. We immediately started to demolish the buildings and to rebuild a huge new youth hall and kitchen. I drew up plans for new halls, kitchen and a rebuilt church. It took time to build these over the next year and I was called to open the rebuilt church forty years later! Young people gave of their money and their time in the most remarkable way. Rabbiting parties were set up to clear farms of rabbits and then their carcasses were sold with the money going to the church. Mid-week home groups were established and groups of more than 600 met for special activities in the Town Hall.

The young people put their newfound Christian faith into practical service cleaning overgrown gardens and houses for elderly people, washing windows and mowing lawns for those who were sick in the community. Groups adopted wards in the mental hospital and started visiting the patients. In the midst of our greatest achievements the preacher on those occasions, my friend Jack Calder, announced he had terminal cancer. He was dead within six weeks. He had only had one mission in his life and it was our Teen Week. Hundreds of people crowded his memorial service and thousands attended his funeral. 'That one week' said his widow, 'meant more to him in his life than anything else he had ever accomplished.'

When we go back to the country town of Ararat we still meet people who talk about that remarkable week. Recently in the Darling Harbour Convention Centre a fine young man who was present at an international convention greeted me warmly, indicating that he was one of the young men I had baptised following that Teen Week. The fruits still live on and it all started on that hot summer night when we sat out on the front step with a drunk talking about the needs of Ararat's youth.

Suburban Minister

On the night of my ordination back in 1959, I knelt in prayer as hands were laid upon my head and representatives of the Federal Conference of Churches of Christ in Australia laid their hands upon me in the act of ordination. I always remembered the ordination charge given to me: 'Do the work of an evangelist'. That phrase continued with me throughout every year of my ministry. I have never forgotten that I was called to 'do the work of an Evangelist'. No matter what other activities I have been involved in always there has been this ordination charge ringing in the back of my mind 'do the work of an Evangelist'.

I spent thirteen years as a suburban minister of the Cheltenham Church of Christ in Victoria. They were busy years with all the demands of a very large parish that was growing from strength to strength. In the first couple of years we overcame the inertia which was in the church, changed some of the leadership from the very tired and elderly people who were in positions of power, removed the debts that were strangling the church and affecting all aspects of growth, saw our offerings rise incredibly as additional people came into the membership of the church, extended property and added staff. In the midst of running the church sporting teams, playing football, training with the young fellows and putting into practice almost every kind of social welfare programs you could imagine, I still had ringing in the back of my mind the old ordination charge 'Do the work of an Evangelist'. I managed to quieten this call for several years because I received a large number of invitations to be a visiting Evangelist for state-wide Church Evangelism Crusades.

For many years I went to Western Australia each year where all the Churches of Christ in Perth and the nearer country areas came together for a state-wide Evangelism Crusade. Each night for fifteen nights I preached in the huge theatre attached to the main Perth City Church. Scores of people made commitments to Christ in each of those evening rallies. During the day time I spoke on radio, gave lunchtime lectures at the Universities and Teachers Colleges, spoke to women's and men's morning teas, breakfasts and dinners and at youth barbecues. It was an exhausting round to be capped off every night by an evangelistic rally.

Then for two and a half months I toured New Zealand on behalf of the Churches of Christ in New Zealand conducting evangelistic crusades up and down that nation, never pausing for breath and having every single day a Crusade Day, starting with a new city every Monday after finishing late Sunday night at a prior place. I was fortunate to have as a working partner and crusade director, Alan Avery, another Churches of Christ minister from Melbourne. He made sure everything ran well.

After two and a half months away from home I met my wife for a delightful one-week holiday where to my surprise I found that I had been booked in to a wonderful hotel on Mt. Cook but left to pay the bill myself. There were similar crusades in Tasmania where we visited every church in that state, conducting crusades each running for a week. Then came Crusades in New South Wales and Queensland under the leadership of Kevin Crawford.

Looking back on those years as a visiting evangelist I realised that I was away far too much when my children were young. I was always tired and weary from speaking usually about thirty times each week with large public crusades each night and all day filled with half a dozen other speaking engagements or appointments with elderly citizens' groups, nursing homes, many secondary schools, radio stations, editors of local papers, men's breakfasts, lunches and dinners and family barbecues.

EVANGELIST

The life of a visiting evangelist is weary from constant moving, living out of a suitcase, sleeping poorly in some person's home, skipping meals or else having the meal at a function where more often than not it was sandwiches and sausage rolls. All the time the visiting evangelist is encouraging the local minister, listening to his problems, giving advice and counsel to individuals whose marriages were falling apart or whose children were off the rails and then leaving behind young Christians who had committed their lives to Christ during your visits. But I was never really confident that the local church would care for them and see them nurtured and grafted into the congregation. It was at this time I learnt the meaning behind the Apostle Paul's statement when he listed all the things he was doing in various churches throughout Turkey and Greece and concluded, 'and all of the time I have the burden of the churches upon my heart.' The work of a visiting evangelist is not easy and if properly done is the most exhausting ministry imaginable. And then because of the wonders of aircraft flight I would literally finish an extensive six week non-stop campaign, get on a plane and two or three hours later be back at home where the mail would be piled high, where there would be recorded dozens of messages to contact people urgently and where every problem of the past six or eight weeks in the local parish demanded instant attention. It was not surprising that upon returning home I often suffered from heavy chest infections and hoarse voice.

When I was not a visiting evangelist I always felt my ministry was that of a pastoral evangelist, particularly to men. In most churches women outnumber men. Today Wesley Mission is one of the few very large churches in the land where there are more men than women and where the average age of the membership is only thirty-one.

I had a concern to reach men in the Cheltenham area and therefore visited people in their homes of a nighttime, particularly wanting to talk to the husband and father. More often than not I found whenever I asked a man a question about his own personal spiritual life and his relationship with God that before he could utter a word of reply his wife would jump in with some kind of defensive statement. I realised over a period of months that every man I had spoken to directly had his wife answer for him. I realised that many men were not at home in their own homes. In their own home the wife inevitably dominated the conversation and if I wanted to speak to men I had to get them while they were in their garage or outside their own homes. Most wives did not know how to make a place where a man can really call his house his own.

So I started what became a habit for many, many years of making an appointment to visit one man every Tuesday lunchtime at his work and to have lunch with him wherever he ate his lunch. I only had two rules - one was that I would eat wherever he ate and the other was that no one would ever buy me lunch. I was not visiting for a free lunch but I was there to talk to the man about the significance of his work, of his role as a father and a husband, of any problems he had in his own life, of how he saw his relationship with God at the moment and if he would let me outline to him the facts of the Gospel, the necessity of baptism and taking his place within the membership of our church. Visiting those men every lunchtime became a sacred duty and a wonderful opportunity of sharing the Gospel. Almost every lunchtime or at least once every second week I had the joy of seeing a man make a commitment to Christ and frequently this was then followed by other members of his family whom we baptised together. I was doing the work of an evangelist.

Sometimes I had lunch at the bar of a pub, out of a paper bag sitting on a footpath with my back to the factory wall, in a Board room with the finest silver and crystal, in a works canteen or in a restaurant, but wherever that man had his lunch I would sit with him and share the Gospel, doing the work of an evangelist. One by one I saw men and more often than not other members of the family coming to faith and into the membership of the church.

The greatest change in this approach to the work of an evangelist came about when I was sitting in a little South Yarra Italian restaurant having lunch with Jack Fawcett. Jack had been divorced and was presently running an advertising agency. He had his eye upon another young woman and was talking about getting married. As we sat together having lunch in the restaurant, he with his glass of red wine and I with my glass of lemon squash, I shared the Gospel with him. Step by step I took Jack through the outline of what it means to become a believer in Christ and to become a member of our church.

I outlined to him some eight verses of the Gospel and slowly walked him through, with him understanding and agreeing to each proposition until in the end I led him in a prayer of commitment of his life when he for the first time bowed his head and prayed out aloud in front of someone else. His response at the end of that prayer was wonderful. 'I'm a Christian. It's wonderful. I am feeling different already. You know I secretly always wanted to be a believer and know the truth of Christ. I am amazed it is so simple. I just didn't know where to look when I looked at the Bible in the past. Oh, thank God, I know I am saved and I feel quite different. I want to thank you for just showing me how I could become a Christian. If you hadn't spent this hour with me over lunch I would never have found out how. Oh, I feel wonderful.'

On the spur of the moment I said to Jack Fawcett something that ultimately was the most inspired question I had ever asked a man. 'Jack, if you feel so different and you have realised what it means to become a Christian in just this little time sitting down together looking at these Bible verses, why don't you come with me while I explain this to other people as I have to you and learn so that you yourself can then go and share with others?' Jack Fawcett readily agreed and thereafter began a pattern of training and working as an evangelist that would change every Tuesday night of my life. We met the following Tuesday night and we had prayer together in the church's boardroom before going out to visit a married couple. I told Jack that all I wanted him to do was sit and listen to the way I would share the Gospel verses, learning from me as I led the discussion, then at an appropriate time I would ask him to explain the difference Christ had made in his life and I wanted that to be brief and to the point.

At the first house we visited the husband was a metal fabricator. He employed a number of men and made car trailers, horse floats and the like. He was a big strong man and his wife was open and friendly. I led the discussion in the same way as I had shared with Jack in the restaurant in South Yarra and at the end of the time asked the father if he would commit his life to Christ and membership in our church. I felt overjoyed when he indicated that he would and turning to his wife said, 'And I am sure you'd like to become a committed Christian and member of the church, also, wouldn't you?' She agreed and so it was in that first visit two people confessed Christ as Saviour and came into membership of the church. The following Tuesday night when we went visiting another two made commitments for Christ. Then came a very important decision. I asked Val Adcock, a wonderful Christian lady who was terribly crippled and unable to get out of the house, if she would set up appointments for us each Tuesday night.

Henceforth I would give her a list of people with whom I had some contact either because their children were associated with our Children's or Youth Programs in the church or else whom I had met through some avenue of activity in the local community and she set up an appointment asking the same question each time, 'Would you please receive Mr Moyes and one of our younger men who would like to visit you this coming Tuesday night at 7.30pm to speak to you about your faith in Christ and membership in the church?'

Val started making appointments and Jack and I would go and visit them. After four weeks of training I then asked Jack if he would lead the conversation using the scripture passages and I would keep silent except for a word of testimony. On his first night Jack led two to faith in Christ and an agreement to be baptised and become members of our church. He was overjoyed. After four more weeks he had led about seven people to faith in Christ and membership in the church and this all occurred before he was baptised. At the end of eight weeks of training, I then asked Jack to take Trevor Adcock and train him in the same way as I had trained him and I would take another person. In asking for two more people to come visiting with us I discovered an interesting fact, that a number of people said they would pray for us but they couldn't go visiting and talking. So I asked them to take upon themselves the same discipline of those of us who were going out visiting, that is, they would give up their Tuesday nights, we would all meet together in the boardroom of the church for prayer and then while half of us kept praying in the Board Room the other half of us would go out and visit, coming back to report to them at the end of our visit.

That really put some impetus into their prayers and some focal point because they kept praying for the people whom we were visiting. While we were in the house sharing the Gospel with others, we kept remembering that back at the church these other faithful people were actually on their knees praying for us by name. That gave us courage in our witness. The first night we returned to our prayer partners and revealed that two or three more people had committed their lives to Christ. There was great enthusiasm. The people who were praying felt they were really part of the action. After another eight weeks there were four of us now trained in sharing the Gospel and all four of us had led others to Christ. We then chose another partner and added more to the prayer team. Then another round of eight weeks' visitation began. At the end of those eight weeks, the eight of us all took another eight partners and another team was added to the prayer partners. Soon we had sixteen people visiting each Tuesday night and Val Adcock had the task of organising eight homes where we might visit each week. The prayer partners were alive with their enthusiasm and every Sunday night we witnessed more baptisms as adults came to faith. The church membership grew rapidly.

Over the next years each Tuesday night was spent visiting and each Sunday night was spent taking the public commitment of those who had made their commitments to Christ with us on the Tuesday night. They would go through a short period of training in Christian faith and the meaning of church membership before being baptised. Over the years it was my privilege to baptise hundreds of adults who came to personal faith in Christ through our Tuesday night visitation evangelism. I was again doing the work of an evangelist.

City Superintendent

Rev. Dr Alan Walker was an evangelist who came to prominence through the Methodist Church's Mission to the Nation in the 1950's. He conducted many other missions in Australia and around the world in the next forty years especially through the World Methodist Council's World Evangelism program. He preached in more than 140 countries and with his wife, Win, was a constant traveller and preacher. Alan was a prophet to this nation, opposing all the forces of evil and corruption, especially Australia's involvement in war and capitalistic exploitation. He used the media well and in his last program of development established the Pacific College of Evangelism, now called the Alan Walker College for the training of church leaders from Asia and the Pacific. I describe him as the greatest Christian minister in Australia of the twentieth century. He was a model travelling evangelist.

Alan Walker was impressed and invited me to lecture staff and Board members on how to grow the Central Mission at a staff retreat at Vision Valley and a members conference in Wesley hall on what was his own vision. This was in 1977.

I was in my thirties but had studied church growth across America, had practiced it in Melbourne and had made a special study of Alan Walker's concepts. I was amazed that so few of the staff of Wesley Central Mission really understood the big picture. They understood one piece of the jigsaw that involved them, but few had any idea of the integrated theology of mission.

EVANGELIST

Perhaps only Dr Jim Pendlebury, Harold Henderson, Stan Manning and Dr Keith Suter who had just started at the Mission, understood the big picture. Everyone else had his or her favourite bit of the jigsaw and was pleased when Alan Walker promoted that, but they were either tolerant or critical of some of his other emphases. One leader of the fundraisers in the 1970's complained that Alan's left wing political involvement and comments were the reason why it was so hard to raise money for the Mission.

Alan was impressed that I was able to express his concepts simply and cogently. I expressed them as five policy points and they guided my leadership over the next quarter century. For in 1977 I was appointed his successor. I had written a 500 page thesis entitled, *Transforming the City Church* in which I acknowledged Alan Walker's vision and this book became the blueprint for all we did over the next twenty-seven years. It encapsulated the vision of how to develop a city ministry. What we are today is due to the fact that we followed the blueprint I had written. My 500 pages included the summary I had made of Alan Walker five policy points for Mission development. For twenty-seven years, every new staff member heard from me in a Staff Orientation lecture.

The original thirteen centres and services that Alan had grown to twenty-three when I arrived, have grown now to over 490 centres and services. Those principles that Alan Walker enunciated and I have followed, work. We have today the world's most viable city ministry.

Wesley Mission has become a great social welfare and evangelical organisation, not by accident, but because we have consistently lived by our policy points.

No theological college in Australia teaches urban mission – the role of the Church in the cities. Wesley Institute now has an accredited Master's degree in this subject. Again, we are on the cutting edge. I have been teaching this subject every year in America since 1980. In 2002, the Trustees of Emmanuel School of Religion where I have taught Urban Mission over more than a decade, honoured me by appointing me Adjunct Professor of Church Ministries.

Different Approaches To The Work Of An Evangelist

As an evangelist I felt there was a unique opportunity in the heart of a great nation to speak to the whole nation, using unique methods and the media during both Easter and Christmas. The aim of Holy Week is to present as many people as possible with the true story of the meaning of Easter. Each year, we reach 20, 000 people face to face with the message of Easter. The Easter Sunrise Service, screened nationally on television, is seen in all capital cities of Australia and the larger regional centres and is watched by a million people.

Likewise at Christmas time An Australian Christmas was a bold attempt to put the true meaning of Christmas into one out of every five homes in the nation. A tightly structured Christmas service was presented before a congregation of

50,000 people, each with their candle and carol sheet. The start of summer in our hemisphere is a good time for a great outdoor gathering. The Christmas story was told by about 2,000 members of the cast and choir who became the people of Bethlehem. Craftsmen, potters, carpenters and weavers set the scene, all in costume. The Shepherds arrived with their flocks of real sheep. Mary and Joseph arrived on her donkey. The Wise Men arrived on their haughty camels in splendid attire, much to the delight of children. The colour and pageantry caught the imagination of the country as we retold the true meaning of Christmas. Handel's 'Hallelujah Chorus', sung by the full choir and accompanied a symphony orchestra brought the evening to a climax and as 'King of Kings and Lord of Lords' was sung a massive fireworks display burst into the heavens. Each presentation each year is an awesome experience! Mary Lopez Productions produced the show for us. Mary also produced the annual Schools Spectacular. Leading Australian television artists such as Mark Williams, Maria Venuti, John Foreman, Marty Rhone, Adrian Ross and Francine Bell were just some of the leading performers. A full orchestra was under the baton of Maestro Tommy Tycho.

I had the privilege every year, in-between the colourful pageant of telling the Gospel message in its theological context. A million people watched. As part of this presentation, viewers were asked to contribute to the needs of those homeless with whom we minister. Thousands rang to make a donation or talk to our counsellors and to speak about the coming of Christ.

The cutting edge of evangelism must be present in any effective city ministry and Wesley Mission has demonstrated over the past century that it is not enough for a church to just worship or serve, but that there must be the gospel of hope presented to those in the city streets. Consequently, the evangelistic program of Wesley Mission means its services of outreach are designed primarily for the person who is not a Christian. Special effort is made to reach these people with the good news of the gospel. These services are so arranged that those people who are not Christians can understand what is happening and feel at home during them. Conversions are recorded. Lives are changed. I have been true to the command of the Master to disciple people in his name.

In 1979 I conducted my first Easter Mission in Sydney. I continued the tradition that Rev. Dr Alan Walker had established and simply followed his pattern adding a few things of my own. The Palm Sunday feature in Hyde Park went well, as did the breakfast and lunches. They weren't really evangelistic outreaches because I discovered that all the people on the mailing lists were deeply committed Christians but it certainly did give them encouragement as we met together at Easter time. The Good Friday afternoon service featured the premiere of Chuck Colson's film *Born Again* and the theatre was packed with 1,400 people. The evening rally saw many commitments to Christ. My diary says, ' I launched Easter Mission and spoke at 36 functions during Holy week. It was a great week and a very successful mission, especially our newly instituted Feast of Tennebrae on Maundy Thursday and a television service from the North Ryde Drive in Theatre.'

I was determined that Easter Mission would be upgraded instantly. By 1980 the men's breakfast began to change. A deaconess working for us, Beryl Bradley, accosted me quite stridently. 'Aren't women in business too? Why aren't women invited to the breakfast? The idea of a men's breakfast is just sexist!' Beryl was right and from that moment on we have simply had an Easter breakfast and an Easter lunch with both men and women coming to whichever they preferred. The Tennebrae service developed and grew into more than 8 Tennebrae services that are now held using the same material and background concepts throughout Wesley Mission centres. And after that first year at the North Ryde Drive in theatre we negotiated with the Sydney Opera House. We knew that our Sunrise had the potential to be seen oversees if produced well and the Opera House was the natural site for not only a national telecast but one which would be seen internationally. I had appointed Rev. John Graham as my colleague. John had been a very talented producer and director of television programmes for the Christian Television Association in NSW. He came on to my staff and immediately started to develop a much better concept of telecasting from the Sydney Opera House. For the next 20 years Martin Johnson was on my staff as senior manager of Communications and was responsible personally for the production and direction of our great telecasts every Easter from the Opera House and at Christmas time from Darling Harbour.

We also began to upgrade the street marches. Instead of motley collections of Christian carrying palm branches heading around the streets to Hyde Park we now have the whole programme conducted by our Wesley Institute for Ministry and the Arts, with hundreds of vibrant students, with broadcast music, singing and dancing as they wave their palm branches and travel round the streets behind the escort police vehicles with Jesus riding on a donkey in costume, surrounded by his disciples. The grove of palms is an ideal site and people from all around Hyde Park gather around as our choir and special speakers tell out the Easter message.

A similar thing happens on Good Friday. With all the city shops closed and the streets full of people it is an ideal time to have a Christian witness to what happened on the way to the cross. About 100 actors and singers all in costume form up in Martin plaza. Then Christ in full costume, bloodied and bruised, carrying a heavy wooden cross, staggers out between armed guards, to the beat of muffled drums. The procession is sombre as it slowly moves up through Pitt Street with thousands of people watching from the footpaths. The television cameras from all networks beam this in their news services across the nation.

When the procession on Good Friday moves up Pitt Street and comes to Wesley Centre, the whole procession, together with hundreds of other people from the footpath, go into Wesley Theatre, completely filling the thousand seats. This is followed by a production of Christian drama and music featuring on the significance of the day and concluding with the disciples in costume passing the elements of the communion to everyone present.

Throughout the week about 20, 000 people attend Easter Mission and I am now joined by some of my colleagues in proclaiming the significance of the death and resurrection of Jesus. Easter is a tremendous time for people to understand what God is doing and how we can respond to him.

In recent years on Easter Sunday afternoon commencing from Hyde Park and marching down to the forecourt of the Opera House we have joined with Christians of many churches, 'marching together in the Aussie awakening.' Tens of thousands of people have gathered in the forecourt of the Opera House and we have joined with other Christian leaders in giving the message of Jesus to all those who were present.

Whenever there has been time available we have used our resources of Wesley Theatre to screen Christian films so that there is an ongoing programme all day everyday during Holy week. Teams of young people knock on doors of all the central business district office blocks and apartment buildings giving people Easter brochures and literature about what Wesley Mission is doing. The whole week is an opportunity for Christians to actively present the key events of the life, death and resurrection of Jesus and how that impacts on our life today. Each year millions of people see some part of our witness and hear some part of the Gospel message.

The use of special Christmas and Easter times to do the work of an evangelist was preceded by an earlier evangelistic method that proved to be successful in small rural communities. That involved concentrating on one age group.

For more than two decades I worked as an evangelist in other churches, conducting as many as 35 three-day crusades each year. Every Thursday evening after work I flew off to some remote country church, taking a dozen or more meetings by Sunday lunchtime, then flew back to Sydney for the afternoon to midnight Sunday programme at Wesley Mission. It was with a great deal of regret that I laid aside my personal evangelism in local churches in 1993 to rely on the media.

But the doctors had made it clear. I was to stop working 100 hour weeks following the heart attacks and surgery, especially with the stresses of a hundred air flights or more a year, with the handling of heavy luggage, frustration with not finding car-parking spots and the ever present time deadlines for flights. But across the nation there are some four hundred country towns where I had preached as an evangelist.

A further aspect of my work as an evangelist was when I became part of an international team to join with a great evangelist. When Billy Graham first came to Australia in 1959 he had a tremendous impact upon Christian people in the community in general. His crusades were well attended everywhere he went.

The crowds in Sydney filled both the Sydney Cricket Ground and the Sydney Show Ground. In Melbourne the largest crowd that had ever gathered until that time gathered in the Melbourne Cricket Ground, with 120,000 people present. They were allowed to not only pack every seat in the grandstands but also in the grass and far surpassed the previous highest attendance, which was during the 1956 Olympic Games.

While Billy Graham was in Melbourne he had a special school for evangelists. I had seen this advertised some months earlier but I was only a Bible College student and didn't qualify. However, I wrote to the Head Office of the Billy Graham Evangelistic Association in America and requested that I be granted permission to attend the School of Evangelism. I explained that while I was not an evangelist at that time and was only in my third year of training, the fact was that one day I would be an evangelist. It was my ambition to preach the Gospel to many people in public buildings, open air rallies, on radio and maybe even on television. I wanted to take advantage of what Mr Graham would have to teach us. I was overjoyed when I received a letter indicating that I could attend. I was the youngest by far and in that gathering were all the well-known identities in church leadership and evangelism in Victoria.

At the end of one of his lectures on evangelism I dared ask Mr Graham a question. I explained that I was only a young man learning to be an evangelist and asked him what are the things about which I should be aware in my life as an evangelist. Billy looked on me kindly and replied, 'There are three great dangers. The first is women. You should make sure your life is morally pure and never get engaged in any entanglements with women nor even give the impression that you are friendly with anybody else except your wife. The second great danger will be money. You should always be scrupulously honest in the way you handle money. God will enable a lot of money to pass through your hands, if you allow none of it to stick there. The third danger is pride. If you manage to avoid the first two dangers then you will probably fall into the trap of pride.' I have never forgotten Billy's answer and I have always kept his warning clearly in my mind.

Twenty years later, Billy Graham again came to Australia and this time when he came to Sydney, I was the newly appointed Superintendent of Wesley Mission. By this time the Billy Graham Evangelistic Association had already come to know of some of my evangelistic endeavours during the 1970's and therefore I was invited earlier in the year to join with members of the team to give a lecture to 800 clergy in the Billy Graham School of Evangelism. Again I was among the youngest in the audience and to be lecturing these 800 New South Wales church leaders and evangelists on how to do their own work was a great responsibility and one that could easily have put me off side with so many who were more senior and experienced than I was.

The Sunday of the opening crusade meeting I held a morning service in the

Lyceum Theatre with Billy Graham's special soloist Evie Tornquist. She was a gorgeous blond with a marvellous singing voice and the Lyceum Theatre was packed with 1,300 people present. I had asked Dr T W Wilson to speak, an associate evangelist of Billy's and a man who had become my close friend back in 1959. More than 40 years later we were still exchanging letters and cards with each other. The Sunday afternoon that Billy spoke at the first crusade meeting proved to be a gorgeous day. The stands at Randwick Racecourse were packed and I had been given the privilege of saying the opening prayer which was heard not only by the 50,000 people present but which was part of the world wide radio broadcast and part of a television programme that would be screened to millions of people world wide. This was a great honour and I thoroughly enjoyed the exposure.

After that service I received the message that Mr Graham would like to see me during the following week. That one meeting turned into three private meetings. Billy Graham asked if I would like to join their team as a special lecturer in the Schools for Evangelism. He had heard reports and had heard me personally and asked if I could come four times a year to wherever he was conducting a major programme anywhere in the world to give some lectures to others on evangelism.

This was a great honour and I was deeply moved. I wrote in my diary on the 18th of May, 'I have met privately with Billy three times. His friendship was warm and genuine. Every member of the team has been very encouraging. Billy has discussed with me his invitation to be a major lecturer in his Schools for Evangelism Church Growth and Nurture to each of his four major crusades around the world each year. This invitation deeply moved me. The generosity of the travel conditions will be very useful to Wesley Mission and thus should open the way to world contacts with Christian leaders. This is unquestionably a great opportunity and one I want to share with Beverley to the uttermost.'

However I was not to accept his invitation in all the details. The work at Wesley Mission in those days was precariously balanced with a great deal of financial trouble. It really needed a consistent and steady hand and to be away four times each year would be too much. I wrote and thanked Mr Graham for his invitation and indicated that I would be honoured to once a year go to a major centre where he was conducting a crusade to give the lectures.

The first such invitation came in October the following year 1980 and it couldn't have come at a worse time.

Thanks to the help of Professor Alf Pollard I had the Mission's finances well structured and therefore to take a week away in America fitted in to the diary quite well. I travelled via San Francisco to San Jose. This is in the heart of Silicon Valley and I was to preach in a number of preliminary crusade meetings before Mr Graham arrived. On the day Billy Graham arrived I was having breakfast with about thirty members of the team. Billy came in to the room, greeted some old friends and went and sat at his place at the head table. After grace he looked up saw me in the distance and came over and asked me to come up to the head table where I was given a position between himself and Cliff Barrows. My first appointment as an associate evangelist was to speak in the San Quentin prison. Hundreds of prisoners sat there listening to the musicians that were with the team. They were a couple of cowboys called the Agajanian Brothers and could play country music incredibly well. I didn't have a great impact on the prisoners of San Quentin although scores of them spoke to me afterwards with words of appreciation. I gave three lectures, in the large Bethel Church of San Jose. There were 2,000 ministers gathered there from around the United States to listen to my lectures on evangelism and those of other dignitaries that travelled with the Graham team. I made some very good friends there that have lasted until now. The most recent of these lecturing assignments was in 2005 with a School for Evangelism conducted in conjunction with a Festival of Faith conducted by Billy's son, Franklin Graham.

People who work with Billy Graham and Billy himself, live a life under threat from crazy gun toting people who believe if they can shoot the evangelists they will get a lot of notoriety. On one trip I preached in one large church seating 2, 500 people to two packed services one after the other. I was met in the car park in Memphis and immediately told by some people to get out of my car and come with them immediately and someone would park the car for me. They whisked me into the back door of the church at a speed of knots that astounded me. I was taken up back stairways until I came into the church vestry. There were several armed guards in the foyer of the church and one outside the door of the vestry. I was told that the police had been notified that that morning an attempt would be made to shoot the preacher during the telecast service. I was the preacher! Only one of the services was to be telecast but on this occasion they were going to telecast both services and I had been asked to prepare two different addresses, one of which would be used on a subsequent week. It was not known when the attempt on the life of the preacher was to be made but it would be during one of the two services.

When the time for the service began I had prayer with the elders and the other ministers and walked onto the platform and sat in the pulpit while other people led the opening exercises of the service. There was a large orchestra accompanying the organ, piano and the magnificent choir of some 250 voices. The church was packed for both services. Sitting in the pulpit with me was an armed guard holding a firearm. Immediately in front of the pulpit facing the congregation was another armed guard. I preached the sermon surrounded as I was with such armed protection and at the end of my sermon was immediately ushered out through a back door of the pulpit and into the protected vestry. I was not allowed to meet people at the front door of the church or greet anybody. Obviously nothing happened that morning but it was an illustration of the queer events that surround us when we proclaim the gospel. Needless to say I was not shot at either service.

Another unusual thing that happened to me during the Billy Graham Crusade in San Jose had also to do with security. I was assigned a car driver and a security man. The security man was a senior police official from the San Jose County who had volunteered his time and like other members of the force were given security tasks of caring for various speakers. This meant that whenever I went on an official function I had to have a security guard travel with me. The other was the driver who drove a big American limo. I was not allowed to walk to the crusade entrance or to go in through any of the gates, I had to be driven and we were taken in by a different entrance which was a high security entrance and driven to the back part of the platform from which we spoke. I obviously understood how Dr Graham had to live in this tight web of security but I didn't understand why one of his associates or helpers should have to also have that high degree of security. But unfortunately the number of people in America who are crazy enough to make an attempt on the life of such a person in such a public place is sufficiently large to warrant such security. I became close friends with my senior police security and also with my driver.

One day when I was travelling in the limo with my driver I said to him, 'Now I know you are a volunteer doing this service but it is obvious you are not a taxi driver. What were you doing before you started doing this work of driving as a volunteer for the Billy Graham Association?' He looked at me and said, 'I was in prison.' 'Why were you in prison?' I asked and he replied, 'Because I had failed in my Christian duty. Because I became swelled up with pride. Because I forgot the Ten Commandments. And because I was guilty of a serious crime.'

Later that night we had coffee together and he filled me in on the details. He was the son of a judge in an affluent New England State. He had a privileged life and it was expected he would go into law. He went to Harvard Law School and graduated with the highest possible honours. He was immediately made an associate of one of the most distinguished judges in his home state. He had a career path clearly set before him and it would be possible that he could have become a judge of the Supreme Court of the United States. He was intelligent, extremely dedicated to the law and highly competent. He married a very fine woman from one of the best and well connected families in New England. In law or politics his future was guaranteed. He had a large home, horses, a farm and a beachside house. He used to invite people there for holidays and it was there he found some of his guests involved in taking cocaine. After a period of time he succumbed to the temptation to try cocaine and began to sniff cocaine himself. Then some of his friends had difficulties in getting quantities of cocaine. They needed large sums of money to buy the cocaine in the purity and quantity that they needed. Within a matter of a year or so he had financed several very large importations of cocaine from South America. That returned enormous amounts of money to him and he enjoyed the benefits of being so wealthy.

Of course, eventually, he got caught. He and learned lawyers connected with his father put up a spirited defence but he was a convicted felon, convicted on the grounds of importing and distributing prohibited drugs. He went to prison. It was while he was in prison he was converted through watching a Billy Graham televised Crusade. Other Christians within the prison helped him grow in his faith. At the end of his prison sentence upon release, the Billy Graham organisation accepted him as a volunteer and gave him the task of driving me around during the San Jose crusade.

I kept in contact with him over the years that followed and eventually rejoiced when for the first time in history the bar association in his state accepted him back into practise as a lawyer, even though he was a former convicted felon.

That story had an interesting sequel. About six months later, I was preaching in a large Anglican church in Sydney when I met an intelligent and competent man who told me he drove taxis for a living. I told him that having listened to him speak to me during our discussion that he had an education and a background that didn't fit in with his occupation as a taxi driver. He told me he was a lawyer but had been disbarred. I told him about my friend in San Jose and within a week or two had offered him a job. It was my privilege some years later to help support an application for him to be re-admitted to the bar. God's grace is seen constantly in the changed lives of people who give themselves to him in total commitment.

On the Sunday morning of the San Jose crusade I was invited to speak at the Crystal Cathedral with Dr Robert Schuller. I had met Dr Schuller several times before, the first being back in 1972 and then subsequently when I spoke on the platform with him at some Church Growth and Evangelism workshops in Australia. Dr Schuller very generously invited me to share his platform. His interview guests that day were Bonnie and Jack Wraither. They were millionaire film producers from Hollywood. Gathered with us was Roger Williams, the pianist. Bonnie Wraither was the producer of all of the 'Lassie' films and Jack Wraither had produced the series *The Lone Ranger* and many other television specials. He was the man who had purchased the famous 'Spruce Goose', the largest wooden plane ever to be flown by the eccentric multi millionaire Howard Hughes. Jack had also purchased the 'Queen Mary', then the largest floating vessel in the world and tied her up to a wharf near the Spruce Goose. Together they owned the Disneyland Hotel and had a million acre ranch in Western Australia about which they wanted to talk to me.

Schuller explained his current problem. Veterans day was coming up and he wanted to buy a 32-foot American flag. He was saying that financial pressures were so great that he wasn't able to afford the $6,000 price tag. I instantly recognised what Bob Schuller had in mind and opening my wallet took out a $20 US note and put it down on his desk and said to Jack and Bonnie 'Why don't we buy Schuller the flag together. I'll put a deposit on it and you can handle the instalments.' Jack Wraither laughed and promised Schuller he would pay him the remaining $5980 on the flag upon which I had placed the $20 deposit. So together Schuller stated his need, two men used their resources and the problem was solved. Schuller has his flag and you will see it in every telecast each Veterans and Memorial Day from the Crystal Cathedral.

However, things were not happy at home. When I had left to go to San Jose for the week, Beverley was very troubled about her sister Gwen. Gwen lived in Melbourne with her husband Jim. They didn't have children and were Uncle and Aunt to our children, whom they loved dearly. Gwen had developed cancer in the pancreas and very quickly became weak. She was quite ill the day I left for the San Jose Crusade but in the first three or four days that I was away she went downhill quickly. Beverley spoke with her every few hours on the telephone but the disease rapidly advanced throughout her body. While Beverley was talking to Jim on the phone Gwen quietly died. Beverley immediately left Sydney and flew to Melbourne and my secretary, Fay Overton, shifted into our home at Roseville to care for the four children. Gwen had been a wonderful sister and she and Beverley had been as close as two sisters could be. Gwen was a tremendous friend to us all, an ideal sister and a wonderful Aunt to the kids. I was so shocked to hear on ringing the family that she had passed away so quickly.

I rang Beverley in Melbourne and immediately made inquiries of Qantas to get the first flight back home. But there was no way in which I could get a plane back home in time for the funeral. I not only lost a day flying back across the International Dateline but the difference in time between America and Australia meant I couldn't have arrived in time for the funeral. It was a most unusual experience that night at the crusade in Spartan Stadium. I was sitting next to Mr Graham at his request. Cliff Barrows had announced that my wife's sister had just died in Melbourne and in the opening prayer Gwen's life and death were remembered. Billy Graham preached a powerful sermon that night to 25,000 people present. Some 980 came forward in commitment to Christ. But the point that I will never forget was that while I was on the platform and Mr Graham was speaking in San Jose, Beverley and our loved ones were in Melbourne attending Gwen's funeral. My eyes were filled with tears as across the miles and across the ocean our hearts were united. Our faith had united our hearts. I wrote in my diary that night, 'It was a sad time. I was in tears often. Billy started speaking at 8pm, which was 1pm Melbourne time, the exact starting time of the funeral. I imagined the church, the people in it, the family and friends gathering and every moment that went past I imagined what was happening back home. I prayed and shared in the events half a world away. It was a queer experience to be on a Wednesday night 8pm in a stadium in California when in Australia it was Thursday afternoon 1pm and all of my loved ones were in a church mourning the death of my wife's sister.'

I was to meet with Billy Graham on many other occasions in other crusades. It was also a privilege on his behalf to attend a number of Schools on Evangelism, Church Growth and Nurture and to lecture students at Wheaton College and on behalf of the BGEA to speak in great churches in Memphis and Fort Worth and Norfolk Virginia.

Mr Graham followed those lectures with an invitation to lecture in 1984 in Amsterdam to 10,000 evangelists who gathered there for the first International Conference on Evangelism. This was followed by another such conference in 1986 when another 10,000 evangelists from around the world gathered. On each occasion I was asked to speak on the theme of 'The Social Responsibility of the Evangelist'. It was a privilege to meet with leading evangelists from around the world and a network of friendships developed between these men and women who give their lives to proclaiming the gospel in every corner of the earth. I interviewed all of these great people for my radio and television programs back in Australia. However I never saw myself as an itinerant evangelist. I was the pastor to the people who met at Wesley Mission and the Superintendent of Wesley Mission, exercising a ministry of social responsibility as well as preaching the gospel in a settled place.

My personal knowledge of over forty years is that in Billy Graham we have seen one of God's great preachers, one who has honestly and fearlessly proclaimed the gospel and fulfilled in the most honourable of ways the work of an evangelist. Now in frail health we still honour Billy Graham, not only a great evangelist, but also a good man. Thirty years after starting to teach other evangelists, I am still doing the same with his son, Franklin.

Another aspect of my work as an evangelist has been seen every week in Wesley Theatre, on television and radio, which has changed people's lives. Letters and messages come to me every week telling me of the changes. A taxi driver who picked me up at midnight outside 2GB told me that one Thursday night he was in despair. His marriage had broken up and his wife and children had left. In a small flat after work at 4am, he decided to blow his brains out with a shotgun. He loaded the gun and took two cans of beer out of the fridge for a last drink. While he drank the cans he idly switched on the television and by chance, it was my program that is repeated in the early hours of the morning. I was saying, 'It does not matter how deep the hole is that you are in or how dark the outlook. If you ask God to tackle your problems together, you will overcome them. 'That is all he heard or remembered. But that was the voice of God speaking to him that night. He put away the gun; he went to sleep and has been strong ever since he asked God into his life to help him. God speaks through the evangelist.

Let me tell you about two special friends of mine. Jayke Zedras and his girlfriend, Samantha walked into the Sunday Night Live service in Wesley Theatre a few months ago. Samantha is extremely attractive and vivacious. She is a hairdresser with hair that only a hairdresser could hope for. Jayke is also a hairdresser, but most of his head is shaved except for an intricately shaped top piece. He has very broad shoulders, typical of a man who pumps iron. He has a barrel chest and I was not surprised to know he was a wrestler of some international note.

A couple of weeks later Samantha and Jayke were baptised. They have been part of one of our Bible study and prayer groups and a new members class. At his baptism Jayke said, 'I would like to thank everyone in this congregation for their prayers that have made me the man I am today. This is one of the greatest achievements of my life. Before I became a Christian and long before I met Samantha I was a sinful man, wicked and a very selfish individual. I took other peoples lives for granted, treading on them for my own gratification. This carried on for most of my life, however when I turned 21 it was all taken away from me just when I thought I had achieved in my own vision everything that I wanted which was success in night clubs, use of drugs. God swept my life away and I was basically left for an ambulance crew to salvage. I have been reconstructed from my hips down and it took seven years for me to recover from that fatality.

'I also took God for granted and by the time I had recovered I went back into the night clubs, took more illicit drugs and returned to abusing my body and the people around me. This pattern continued for many years.

However I have since learned that during this time the Lord knew what was in my heart, he knew that deep down inside I needed something else but in his own precious time he gave me my past life to learn from and use as wisdom today.

'Much later in life God blessed me with Samantha, my soul mate. She's my everything. I would not be here today if she did not pray for me. God knew that Samantha was the perfect partner for me, that I would listen to a person such as her. She took me to see *The Passion of the Christ* movie. I can't explain to you what it's like to see someone not only suffering but being tortured for hours and that it was done for me and all of you.

'Jesus did it to save us so that we might have a chance of eternal life. And through Samantha taking me to that movie we came to Wesley Mission and with no hesitation gave our lives back to Jesus and to God right there. Dr Gordon Moyes blessed us, which is when we decided and realised Jesus is our saviour. He forgives no matter what you do in life; no matter how bad you are and no matter how down you get in life.

'I have also discovered that when you are down your salvation is actually up before you. Grab it when that little voice inside you, that many people a call conscience, but which is the voice of God, speaks. You will be richly blessed as Samantha and I and our families and our friends have been.'

Jayke has consistently witnessed to his faith to his old friends and already several have now become Christians. That really is new beginning…new hope! Recently a meeting of the International Wrestling Federation was held in Sydney and Jayke was invited to speak about how the amazing change in his life had occurred.

An evangelist is never off duty. Many a time the passenger in an aircraft has turned the chitchat into a discussion about salvation. Once I was driving to

Newcastle. At 6.45 am, I was at Swansea. I saw a green garbage bag stuffed with garbage by the side of the road only a metre from my wheels. As I drove past I thought it must have fallen from a truck, but a casual glance revealed a legless bare pair of men's buttocks sticking out the open end of the garbage bag covered with human excreta and bloody fingermarks.

I could not believe what I had seen! I drove on, shaking my head in the early morning light. Then the conviction grew that that is exactly what I had seen. Then I turned the car and drove back. It was a pair of bare human buttocks, covered with excreta and bloody finger marks! They were stiff and cold. But there was no bulge in the garbage bag where a head should be! I thought I had found the remains of a dissected corpse. I carefully rolled the bag over to see if there were any legs. They were curled up inside the bag in a foetal position. The rest of the body then groaned and moved.

He was a 25-year-old man, severely battered about the face and covered with blood. He fell there after being pushed out of a moving car while drunk. During the night he crawled into a plastic garbage bag to get out of the rain. He curled up tight inside the bag and had pulled his trousers down to relieve himself. The blood on his buttocks was from his own fingers as he tried to pull up his trousers while he lay there. I pulled the garbage bag off and checked if he was all right. How he did not suffocate with his head curled underneath his arm in the end of the garbage bag I do not know. He immediately swore at me and threw a punch at my face.

He argued with me to leave him where he was. I helped him off the road into the bushes where he pulled the green garbage bag over his head again. I then drove on towards my speaking appointment at a businessmen's breakfast. I drove on relieved but not happy. So I drove back again and found him where he had curled up again inside the garbage bag. I called to him to get out of the bag and helped him up. He threw another punch at me and said, 'You're the second person to wake me up!' I pushed him over to my car to take him to hospital.

I took him with me to the Apollo Motor Inn where I was met by a surprised waiting crowd. In the gents' toilet I helped him clean up, dropping his soiled underwear into a bin and having to dry him off under an electric hand dryer! I took him upstairs and introduced him to some of the men as my friend John. He had cups of black coffee to sober him. Some of the businessmen surrounded him with interest and support.

As I was talking later about how society does not really see the homeless, he interrupted to tell his story. He was homeless. He was terminated as a ladder maker and had gone to find a cheap caravan to live in near Newcastle in the hope of finding work. He had a wife and six year old daughter somewhere in Sydney.

They had been separated since he lost his job. He had been drinking with friends until a fight developed and they dumped him bleeding by the side of the road. He sheltered from the freezing rain in the garbage bag. I had called him out of the garbage bag, which had almost become his tomb. In fact, he was almost as good as dead. Unless his life changed, he was headed straight back into the tomb be it in a caravan or a plastic garbage bag. Unless he turned to Christ, he was dead!

Only Christ could give him life! The Christian businessmen determined to continue to help him, until in a clear mind they could present the claims of Christ. Only Christ gives to the alcoholic and the homeless and the city a life that is meaningful and eternal.

As I presented a Gospel message to the crowd that morning in the Apollo Motor Inn, he shouted out as mentioned to me to let him tell his story. That was a big risk, but I did. He told most of what I have just told you. When he finished, the Belair Baptist Church minister said he could stay in some temporary church accommodation until things worked out and a businessman present said he owned an aluminium extrusion factory and he would give him a job. Jesus Christ still saves lives in a permanent and wonderful way. The work of an evangelist is full of wonderful experiences.

MINISTER

Chapter Two

I have always been blessed with a number of key laymen who taught me how to be a minister. What I had learned in theological college and university were only the tools for the job. The real teaching came at the hands of the mentors around me.

The earliest man of great influence was my first church secretary, Basil Sterling. My student churches were two adjacent wooden churches in the inner slum areas of Melbourne. For seven years during the 1950's and 1960's the people of those inner slum areas were my parish. I had started preaching in those two little inner area churches before I even went to theological college. My first sermon in a church was just after my 18th birthday. Before I even commenced university studies and theological college studies I was already preaching every week. It was most unusual for someone so young to be appointed as a student minister. In fact I was consistently reminded that I was the youngest ever to be so appointed and that if I did not perform consistently well in my studies then the church work would be withdrawn from me.

However I was totally committed to the idea of being a minister and therefore worked very hard both at studies and at being a student minister. I had won a scholarship to Melbourne University and I was committed to studying full-time at the College of The Bible in Glen Iris. The College regulations prohibited me from taking any further studies but I wanted to get as much completed in as little time as possible. So, without telling the College authorities, undertook additional subjects in classical Greek, a language I had never previously studied. I hoped my six years of Latin would help me.

In one year I attended a private coaching college plus evenings with a private tutor and decided to sit both for Year 11 and Year 12 exams at the one time. Commencing without knowing one word of Greek and passing at the matriculation level of Year 12 all in one go was going to demand a lot of effort. I carried Greek verb endings around on pieces of paper in every pocket and made translations of the simplest speeches of Plato and Socrates in the back of other books.

I wrestled with the reading of the history of Heroditus and the marvellous wars and marches of Thyucides and Xenophon. At the same time I was heavily involved in athletics and playing several sports. My girlfriend Beverley, with whom I had been going steady since we were 13, used to ring me faithfully every day during my lunch hour and I would slip away from lunch to spend a delightful 15 minutes in the telephone box away from the prying ears of the 60 other students in the College.

We only saw each other on weekends and she helped me by typing up sermons, essays and long university dissertations. At age 19 we were engaged and planned to get married just after our 21st birthdays. Our birthdays came within one week of each other. The four weeks at the end of 1959 were probably the most hectic in our lives. I was completing my final year at theological college and desperately trying to beat a record - of receiving honours in every single subject. Although I would not be Dux of the College in my theological subjects, my aim was to attain first class honours in every subject, which was something that no other had ever achieved.

That was accomplished at the same time I was doing university exams in classical Greek. These were the exams that the College did not know I was sitting for. I sat for Year 11 and Year 12 simultaneously and the results caused a great deal of mirth among my two tutors for I failed Year 11, but passed the much more difficult Year 12 for which obviously I had done more work.

In the middle of these 1959 exams we celebrated our 21st birthdays; I was ordained in a most moving ceremony attended by about 700 people andwe had a hectic round of parties and kitchen teas, which culminated in our marriage. If any series of activities were designed to cause a breakdown, that series of exams, marriage preparations, 21st birthdays, ordinations and the like would be it.

Yet what happened immediately after our wedding was to surprise us all. I became seriously ill on my honeymoon and returned to hospital and surgery! Being a full-time student I had very little money. In fact, as I was to discover a few weeks later, I possessed absolutely nothing at all except for a car, a new bride, a host of kitchen tea and wedding presents, a theological certificate, a university scholarship not yet fully taken, an ordination certificate and a marriage certificate. We started with absolutely nothing else except boxes of books. The hospital wiped the debt by describing me officially as 'pauper'.

Our two student churches at Ascot Vale and Newmarket were excited for their young couple and people showered us with good wishes and gifts. A coffee table made by the Church Secretary, Basil Sterling, survived 20 years in our home until four children later, the legs eventually gave way under the onslaught of childhood frolicking and shifts into four manses.

I was now an ordained minister and was continuing in part-time ministry with the two little churches. I had enrolled in an intensive university course in the Summer School during January and February to increase my proficiency both in New Testament Greek and in classical Greek and to take up the rest of my university scholarship until graduation.

One of the hard lessons I learnt in those early days before ordination when I was a student preacher aged only 18, was that my bright ideas for church development and growth were not well received by older people in the church. The fact is that the churches in these areas had been there for decades and so had the people.

The church was an important part of their life. It was the one stable thing that did not change in a world that saw slum reclamation programmes, the bulldozing of nearby homes and the building of huge concrete State Government housing projects. In that world of change and decay it was important that in the church things did not change. On the other hand coming in as a very idealistic and enthusiastic 18-year-old first year Bible college student, I wanted to see change, growth, development and new people coming to the Lord and joining our church.

I did not realise that every new person that came into the church was a threat to many of the older people already there. They did want to change but did not want their positions of authority to be challenged by new people, particularly the younger people and university students we were beginning to attract.

The point of this tension always arose in the church board meetings. These were the half dozen people elected by the congregation year after year to provide the oversight of the church. These deacons and elders had the responsibility of the leadership of the church and they were sure nothing was going to change.
At our Bible college our theological studies had not yet included any lessons on church administration and without any training I was thrown into the fray of trying to lead innovation and change a church that was declining and refusing to change.

The most powerful man on our Church Board was the Church Secretary, Basil Sterling. He was a good-hearted fellow with a good sense of humour, but he was completely immovable on matters of church policy. He had married the Church Secretary's daughter 35 years earlier, had spent his life in the welfare of the church and the Sunday School and was our most dedicated layman. His work was merely the opportunity to earn money to enable him to give more into the work of his church. He knew precisely what he wanted in the church's life and ministry and change was not on his agenda. All of the others opposed change, were suspicious of new youth programmes, did not like outreach for new people and enjoyed their positions. Over the years they had seen student ministers come and go, all of them having come with enthusiasm but sent on their way with their enthusiasm dampened and with their tails between their legs, knowing well that theological students were the lowest form of church life.

The Church Board was dedicated to the slogan 'Come weal, come woe, the status is quo!'

At 18, I decided early in the piece that the way to go was to change the structure of church administration. What we needed was additional people forming the Board with fresh insights and new ideas. I did not want to throw the older people out because they were faithful, but I wanted to have their conservatism mixed with the new ideas of youth and with the attitudes of people who had recently come to Christ from outside the church.

I wanted more young people involved in church administration and more women and more people from the edge of the church. I discussed this with the love of my life, my 18-year-old girlfriend Beverley. She took an active part in everything I did and we discussed long into the night before I left to go back to college, how we should handle the problem. Eventually I came up with a new programme of church administration.

It was going to be called the Functional Church Board. We took the major functions of the church: its worship life, evangelism, stewardship, social activities, education, youth ministries, finance, missionary outreach and the like and created a separate committee for each function. One member of the Officers' Board would be on each committee and each committee would appoint three representatives to a central committee that would meet monthly. Each committee would be totally responsible for its area of work.

The Missionary Committee, for example, would promote the interests of missions in the life of the church, publicise the mission fields, encourage prayer for missionaries, letter writing and parcel sending and invite visiting missionaries to be speakers at special meetings.

The Education Committee, for example, would run the Sunday School, adult classes, teenage groups, develop curriculum, promote its group activities, enrol teachers and conduct teacher training programmes, organise its own budget and work out a master plan for educational facilities.

The old Board would not meet at all but would be dissolved among the membership of all of these other functional committees. When we came together three representatives from each committee would compose a much larger board and would include more women, younger people and the enthusiastic new Christians who were joining us.

I shared this vision with Beverley. I knew the Board would be totally resistant but Beverley encouraged me to go ahead with the planning. So we called a special church meeting for a Sunday afternoon to discuss the new system of 'functional church government'. This I was sure would capture the imagination of the large number of people who would attend and break the monopoly of the small group who resisted every change.

But God was on their side. The Saturday morning before the Sunday church meeting I felt an agonising pain in my right side. It grew so bad that I had to limp off to our family doctor, Dr W.A. Kemp. His broad and strong fingers probed into my side, causing excruciating agony. He looked up at me over his glasses, 'You have a burst appendix there, my lad. It has to come out straight away. You haven't even got time to go home. I want you in hospital immediately and I will operate within an hour.'

Before I knew what was happening I was being wheeled into the little surgery of the house that served as our local hospital. It only had three or four rooms and probably could not cater for more than eight or ten patients at any one time. The old matron had been there for years and had delivered almost every baby in the community, including myself eighteen years earlier. I remember Dr Kemp switching on a movable lamp above the operating table, placing a wire mask over my face, then pieces of gauze and cotton wool and then dripping ether onto the gauze. He asked me to repeat my name and address and count backwards and very soon I was unconscious.

My next impression was waking up and round the bed stood my widowed mother, my girlfriend Beverley and Dr Kemp. He was waxing enthusiastically about how successful the surgery had been and how I had been saved in the very nick of time. Dr Kemp leant over me and in my hazy mind I could hear him saying, 'Don't you worry about your church services tomorrow morning. I will come and see you early in the morning and then I will go out and preach for you.' And the doctor who took out my appendix went the following morning and filled the pulpit for me.

'But what about the church meeting? Who can explain my ideas?' There was only one person who knew all that I had in mind - my 18-year-old girlfriend, Beverley. 'Will you? You know it. You can do it.' Beverley looked askance. It was one thing for me to take on the entire church board in a public meeting but it was really asking too much for her to do it. But her love and loyalty in that emergency overcame her reticence.

That morning at church Dr Kemp explained my predicament and absence, preached a good sermon and encouraged everybody to stay for lunch and for the public meeting in the hall that afternoon. The hall was filled with enthusiastic people. There was one group, however, who were less enthusiastic. In my absence the meeting was chaired by Basil, the Church Secretary. He opened with what must have been the deciding statement of the entire meeting, 'You all know why this meeting has been called - to discuss some new hair-brained scheme of church government. I want you all to know I do not agree with that suggestion.

There is nothing wrong with our Board as it is. We have the right system, but Mr Moyes wants you to discuss it. His girlfriend Beverley will now explain it all to us.'

Beverley read the letter that I had sent to all the members outlining the plan of participation. She then expounded the various functional committees and explained how each one would work, each under a chairman with a committee of new people round about the chairman.

After a long and careful explanation Basil said, 'Are there any questions?' And then, without pausing to wait for any said, 'Is there anyone in favour?' And then, without pausing to wait for anybody to comment, indicated it would be put to the vote. I have no doubt that the people there that day felt intimidated. Basil continued relentlessly on. Beverley felt defeated, humiliated, rejected. She sat down in tears. Basil was triumphant; there would be no change to the Board.

The taking of the vote was a mere formality. However, immediately the meeting was closed a number of old people who had been around for a long time and not so much intimidated by the Church Secretary came up to Beverley and were quite defiant, 'It is a good idea. It is time we had some changes in this church.' And of course many of the younger people stood around in groups talking to each other in quiet tones. Gradually the people drifted out. The Board was in control. Nothing would change.

But then the greatest surprise of all occurred. Basil was not happy with his victory. His victory over an 18-year-old girl seemed quite empty. He went over to Beverley and said, 'How are you going home? Are you going home by train as usual? You are not going to travel 15 miles by yourself. You can't do that. I'll drive you home.' Basil had never driven Beverley home before. He only knew that she travelled every Sunday to come to worship with me by train those 15 miles from the other side of Melbourne. Beverley protested, 'But it will take you a couple of hours to travel out to Mount Albert.'

'No', said Basil, 'Let me do it, I owe it you. You are a good girl and a brave one. I admire you.'

Beverley visited me later that night in hospital. She was in tears. It had been the worst experience of her life. She had tried to present faithfully what was a good idea but ran into the opposition of the years, which were determined not to move.

That idea of 'functional church government' died forever. But something was born in the church through that meeting that day. The people believed in us and what we were trying to do. Beverley had actually won the day although not the vote. For Basil changed. He realised our sense of commitment and desire to help their church grow. He started to support us.

Not long afterwards Beverley and I became engaged and Basil led the church in celebrating our engagement. Three years later we married and he and Dorothy came to our wedding as proud guests bearing a most beautiful hand made coffee table as their gift for us.

It was not long after the Functional Church Government programme was defeated that Basil moved a motion at the Annual Meeting of the church that they make a special appeal to the Federal College of The Bible to allow me to continue ministering in that church for another two years. Then after another year, he moved another motion asking if we could be appointed after ordination for another two years and then another two years. We remained more than seven years and the part-time student church became a part-time preaching appointment of an ordained man, then a full-time appointment with students assisting and behind that development and growth was Basil. We never did implement the Functional Church Government programme. We did not change the church government structures at all, but we did change the church. And leading the church was the man who had opposed it for so long.

We now saw growth and development, the purchase of new properties and the renovation of old. We raised more money than ever before and appointed new people to positions of authority. In fact we saw something of a revival of life that the church had not seen for decades and it went from decline and certain death to renewal and continues to this day as a healthy, vigorous church in that community. And I think the most telling feature was the change that occurred when Basil won the vote but lost his heart to a courageous 18-year-old girl.

God had funny ways of bringing about change. Perhaps if we had won the vote that day we would have had Basil as an opposition member to everything that we did. As it was we lost the vote but we won all of the people.

Basil became our most stalwart supporter, not just while we ministered there, but ever since. When I started the national television program, Turn 'Round Australia, Basil became a monthly financial supporter, which he continued for the next twenty-seven years. Now close to one hundred years, Basil lives in retirement in Queensland. I regularly write and telephone him. He proudly tells everyone that he taught me everything I know. And he is right. He was a great mentor.

My second mentor was Charlie Ferris. The Cheltenham Church of Christ, where I ministered from 1966 to 1979 grew to become one of the largest congregations in Australia and Ice Cream Charlie was the ideal man for a period of growth and development. He was the State Manager of a large Electrical firm and used to making sound business decisions. It was one of our children who called him 'Ice Cream Charlie'.

But in those thirteen years of ministry the real mark lay in the number of buildings that were built around the Cheltenham Church of Christ. A new manse was constructed; a new office for the church, a twenty-three unit Christian retirement centre was constructed and opened in the presence of fourteen hundred people. We then built Greenways Village, which went on to have ninety seven units and a nursing home and then the Christian Retirement Centre stage 2 of thirty six new units plus two new tennis courts, then Pine Lodge with sixteen more retirement units, three houses to be demolished for car parking and another to be built as a centre for administration. The church was developing and growing, adding to its properties and going out in faith in multi-million dollar developments. When the time came to announce my retirement I indicated that I wanted to stay for one more year - our thirteenth - so that in that year we could completely clear any debts on the entire property, leaving the multi-million dollar campus in pristine order with new buildings, a regular maintenance program and no debt.

During all of this time my wife Beverley was active in four different women's organisations and as pianist for two choirs. Our children were engaged in Sunday School activities, girls clubs, boys clubs, Christian Endeavour, Christian Youth Fellowship, Teens Club, tennis and netball teams.
Looking around on the final service after thirteen years of ministry I invited more than four hundred people present whom I had welcomed into membership of the church to stand. Many hundreds had been baptised over that thirteen years and one thousand people had been buried. I had united in marriage more than two thousand individuals and seven out of every eight members of the church had joined during my ministry. The church was throbbing with life and was in good heart.

Together we bought houses, many of them around the church in order to get land for new developments. We built $5 million worth of buildings and paid for all of our debts. By this time the income of that church had the highest weekly offering of any church known in Australia and Ice Cream Charlie was the most competent treasurer you could imagine.

He had his finger on the pulse of church finances. He was able to talk in round figures with positive vision: 'This is going to cost us $750,000 but I move we go ahead. We have a vision for growth. We will have to lift our income by 15% next year but we can raise it. The people here have got the capacity to give. We have a good programme going that is bringing honour to God. Do not worry about the money. Fulfil the mission of the church and the money will come.'

His speeches convinced many a special business meeting called to discuss some new project. What an absolute delight to have a Treasurer with a vision like that! Charlie not only kept the books for what had come in and gone out with accuracy, but he had a vision of where we ought to go in the future.

It was one of Charlie's regular visits to come to our home on the night before Christmas and personally thank my wife and myself and our children for the year's ministry. He always had our holiday pay made up in advance and always a bonus for last year's service and, as well, an additional week's payment as he said, 'To buy the kids an ice cream.'

It was always his favourite saying and that extra week's salary to buy the kids an ice cream was something that meant more to us as a touch of his love and concern than almost anything else.

Often during a hot summer's January day he would stop one of our kids in the street and say, 'Has your dad bought you that ice cream yet?' The kids could always reply with enthusiasm that we had a special treat at the end of each year knowing that it came from the church in appreciation of our ministry as a family. What a mentor Charlie Ferris was and although our young children did not realise it, they were being encouraged in positive attitudes to the church anddiscovering how their parents were appreciated.

My Third Mentor is Dr Jim Pendlebury. Jim was born in Cessnock. He was educated in primary schools in Cessnock and Griffith and attended Cessnock High School where he won an exhibition to Sydney University and a Teacher's College scholarship.

Over the next years he graduated Bachelor of Science with Honours, Diploma in Education, Master of Science with Honours at Macquarie University and then later Doctor of Philosophy at Macquarie University. He was amongst the first Master of Science graduates and the first Ph. D. in Chemistry to graduate from Macquarie University. All the time he was studying in post graduate work, he never gave up his Christian commitment to his home church at Bexley or to Wesley Mission. He declined an opportunity to do academic research in America in order to continue his service in the Churches of Sydney.

He has won many awards and scholarships including an International Teacher Development Program scholarship that led to him travelling to study in the United States. He has been made a life member of the New South Wales Science Teachers Association and was granted the meritorious Service Medal from the Sydney College of Advanced Education. He was honoured by the Queen with the Medal of the Order of Australia and has been recognised both by the community, professional associations and church associations with their highest honours.

Dr Pendlebury has written many scientific, educational and research science articles and is the author of several books. Dr Pendlebury has provided leadership within the Methodist and Uniting Churches for more than 50 years. With his wife Thelma, he has held all the leading official positions within their home congregation at Bexley Uniting Church.

In 1968 he became a member of the executive Board of Wesley Mission and has continued for almost forty years. For over 34 years he has been the Honorary Treasurer of Wesley Mission and has seen the Budget grow under his oversight from $1 million to $150 million per annum, all while he worked with us in an honorary capacity.

He has held many positions within the Uniting Church Presbyteries and Synod and for the past fifteen years has been Chairman of the Council of Wesley Institute for Ministry and the Arts. He has also served as a Board Member for the Alan Walker College for Evangelism.

For the past 27 years of my leadership, he has been a close colleague, mentor and advisor on every aspect of Wesley Mission's growth and development and with his wife, Thelma, have become our closest friends.

The fourth mentor was Professor Alf Pollard. Professor Pollard was an actuary and regarded as one of the world's leaders in that field. He was born in Melbourne, grew up on Norfolk Island and educated in Sydney. He was the most brilliant student in NSW in the Leaving Certificate in his year. At Sydney University he won 12 scholarships and prizes and the University medal as the best student of all facilities. He graduated Bachelor of Arts, Master of Economics and Doctor of Philosophy. He then graduated as Master of Science and Doctor of Science. He held many Fellowships. He was at various times an expert in technological science, mathematics, acoustics, astronomy and statistics. He became expert in psychology, demography, divinity, economics and actuarial studies. He was the foundation professor of actuarial studies and economics at Macquarie University. He was the author of ten books and over 50 research papers and the editor of Economic Trends published monthly from 1966 – 2002. He was an Officer in the Order of Australia and consultant to the Federal Government on matters of economics and superannuation.

Alf was granted nine international awards and honours. He was a doyen in the insurance industry. He loved sport and played tennis for seventy years on a daily basis, playing over 12,000 sets against the same singles opponent and like any statistician, has kept every result. He was a fully committed Christian, active all his life in the Methodist and then Uniting Churches. In 1979, at my request, he became Honorary Secretary of Wesley Mission Sydney. He served the Wesley Mission Board and Parish Council faithfully as an Officer of the Mission, taking part in making every key decision. He was responsible for taking Wesley Mission from a financially shaky church, to probably Australia's strongest and most endowed charity.

Alf deeply loved music and all his life sang in choirs. For some years he was the conductor of the Wesley Mission choir and the choir at Lane Cove Uniting Church. He was Chairman of the Radio Community Chest, which produced the Messiah in Sydney Town Hall every year, the Sydney Cultural Council which ran the Sydney Eisteddfod and the Lane Cove Musical Society. He was not only a singer, but also a pianist and composer. He was trustee to many important trusts. I learnt many of my management skills at his feet as well as the more formal instruction from three of the best management colleges in the nation.

My fifth mentor is Dr David Greatorex. Professor Greatorex, like Professor Pollard and Dr Pendlebury was an academic. Like Professor Pollard he was an officer in the Order of Australia. He had graduated from Sydney University with BA honours and a Masters degree in Commerce and Administration. He was a charted accountant who went on in his business studies and completed a PhD. He worked for many years with IBM in Australia New Zealand and the United States of America, being fast tracked for senior advancement.

He had been director of a number of very important Australian companies and financial institutions but after his time as a senior manager with IBM became the Managing Director of Capita Finance Group Australia, the Chairman of the State Bank of NSW and visiting professor over many years of Business Studies at Macquarie University. He was also the financial backer of a significant number of start-up companies in medical and computer equipment. His voluntary service to the community included the Sydney Dance Company, The Centennial Park Trust, The NSW Cancer Council, The Girl Guides Foundation and the Salvation Army. He became Chairman of the Westmead Millennium Research Institute to develop facilities and research functions on the cutting edge of medical technology and has been a director over many years of the Macquarie Graduate School of Management. He is a fellow of many significant associations including The Australian Institute of Management and the Australian Institute of Company Directors.

I got to know David well in 1987 when Professor Pollard brought together a cross section of people to have Friday lunch together at the Australia Club. This included a significant number of academics and outstanding businessmen. David was a member of that group and I immediately developed a good friendship with him. He was a member of my Rotary Club and so we had another area of close association. David had been an outstanding sportsman in his youth to national standard and had a strong Christian background. After a while I invited him to join the Wesley Mission Board, which he did so enthusiastically. His business expertise was outstanding and helped us immensely.

Although I had in Professor Pollard and Dr Pendlebury two of the most outstanding honourary leaders any church could have as Mission Secretary and Mission Treasurer, I always believed that we should look to the future in terms of risk management and have someone standing in the wings in the event that either of the other two should become incapacitated or die. I brought to my to colleagues Dr Greatorex as a possible replacement for either of them and David received their unanimous support. Later, when Professor Pollard did unexpectedly collapse following one of his usual vigorous tennis matches, I asked David Greatorex to become Wesley Mission Honorary Secretary, a post which he accepted with enthusiasm. Since that time David and his wife Deirdre have become very dear friends on a personal level and David has become a very astute advisor to me in financial and managerial matters. In 2000, Prime Minister John Howard presented his firm SecureNet with the 1999 Australian Exporter of the Year award, capping a remarkable 12 months for the three-year-old company.

He is Chairman of six emerging companies, of which SecureNet is the most advanced. One is an outsourcing consultancy, another is in telecommunications and yet another is health insurance. This outstanding businessman and academic, like Alf and Jim, has not only become one of my three closest personal friends but an outstanding mentor and advisor. With my wife Beverley we enjoy the company of these three men and their outstanding wives. With their support I could withstand any social pressure and with their guidance achieve beyond my natural capacity.

I would encourage every minister to build a long-term network of mentors, to whom they are absolutely accountable, to whom they owe transparency of conduct and thinking and from whom they are prepared to learn. My three friends know everything about my life. I have listened to them. I am accountable to them. I am indebted to them.

The life of a minister can have some real highlights. I was always interested in playing sport and meeting with athletes. From the early 1980's, I supported a Baptist Minister, Dr Mark Tronson, in developing chaplains in all the major sports. I was too involved in ministering to Wesley Mission to become involved in being a chaplain to a sporting team and as the chaplains were appointed to all the major sporting teams across Australia, I hung back, knowing that was not part of my own core ministry.

But Mark then came up with another idea. He asked if I would be their appointed chaplain to the national Olympic team. It was short term andto the Winter Olympics in Calgary Canada, 1988. It was right at the time of us moving from our Pitt Street premises into the new George Street premises, but I jumped at the chance. I discovered how young most Olympians were and how devastating it was for them when after carrying the hopes of the family, friends and country, they became part of the 96% of all Olympians who would win no medal. I was thrilled to be a part of the experience, meeting some fabulous people within the Olympic Family and helping others in various ways. Whilst in Calgary I addressed a number of Christian organisations and Christian youth organisations.

Incidentally, this gave me some ideas that I took to the Premier of New South Wales to help in the Sydney 2000 Olympic bid. He insisted on absolute secrecy so other cities would not copy the idea. Then at Monte-Carlo, the Sydney team announced their surprise. A committee had been established, of which I was the Chair, to find home hospitality for 10,000 parents of athletes. We also made specials fare arrangements for those parents and tickets for the events. We would supply bed and breakfast for them all, free of cost. I used all of my Rotary and church contacts, with some amazing organisation by outstanding Rotarians. It was this, said Premier Fahey, which tipped the balance in favour of Sydney among the Olympic voters.

During those same Sydney Olympics of 2000, we hosted 200 American Christians who helped us in our daily street outreach and our evening rallies that featured some of the world's greatest athletes in Wesley theatre. Every night Gold medal winning athletes gave testimony to the power of Jesus Christ in their lives. My special addresses each night have been continuously accessed on the Internet ever since.

However, that led to another interesting expansion of my ministry. Would I be willing to be nominated as Chaplain to the Office of the Prime Minister? I would be available to meet with the Prime Minister at his request for any personal ministry, undertake to specifically pray for him and his family and be willing to attend those functions where a chaplain might be required. Then nomination was made and I was accepted by Prime Minister Bob Hawke as his Chaplain. That led to a remarkable expansion of ministry with some amazing people.

Prime Minister Bob Hawke had been a deeply committed Christian as a youth but his adult behaviour did not measure up to Christian standards. I got the feeling that he wished it did. Beverley and I suddenly found ourselves on the Commonwealth Government's VIP List for all sorts of functions. I was invited to say grace at dinners attended by the Royal Family, to meet and have discussions with the Queen and Prince Phillip, The Prince of Wales and Diana and to be guest at important functions in Sydney and Canberra. I would drop the Prime Minister a private note from time to time telling him that I was praying for certain difficult decisions he was facing.

Once while walking with Prime Minister Hawke down a passage, he drew me aside into an office of some other person and waved his minders away. He told me of some concerns he had with two of his children and gave me details that should not be included here. Then he was weeping. He was to weep openly on television later, but this was the first time I think he wept in public. I held his arm and I prayed for him and each member of the family by name. He was not then the Prime Minister, but a father, overwhelmed with family cares. He was utterly sincere and concerned for them. The tears were real.

This special chaplaincy seemed to be so well received that I was asked to expand my ministry to the person of the Governor General. Governor General Bill Hayden accepted the appointment enthusiastically andI discovered that in the highest office of the nation was a man with spiritual hunger. He responded to me with great warmth and extended invitations to dine at Admiralty House. On one occasion he and I were walking ahead of security men following his opening of the next stage of the Alan Walker Village. We got into a lift and he waved the security men back. He wanted a moment of private conversation. A great storm had enveloped Carlingford and at that moment as we were in the lift, lighting struck and took out the main supply station for the whole area. Our lift stopped mid-floor. The security men yelled at us not to panic. We stood for a while and as the time dragged on, sat on the lift floor. 'I want to talk to you about Jesus' said the Governor General. We had a long and pointed discussion that led to me presenting the claim of Jesus on his life. I urged a public announcement of his commitment to Jesus. He indicated that was not possible while he was in office, but could occur afterwards. He later rang and asked me to bring the videos I had made in the Holy Land on the life of Jesus and to talk further. I did so.

He and Dallas then decided to quietly and without announcement go to a church near their private home in Queensland. That visit was a disaster. He rang me to ask why the church members behaved as they did. An over-enthusiastic Pentecostal group stressing, 'being slain in the Spirit' was too much for a seeker of Christ. A gentler approach by someone he trusted would have made all the difference.

I had known Prime Minister John Howard for many years. He is a committed Christian. One of the most amazing things I have witnessed was the Prime Minister kneeling down at an Aboriginal Praise Corroboree, being surrounded by Aboriginal ministers who laid hands upon him and prayed for his leadership. I have prayed for him through his tenure. He always greets me most warmly and has suggested Federal Government help for a number of our ministries such as our suicide prevention service, our drug and rehabilitation services and a special donation of $10 million to update all of Lifeline's telephone equipment. He has attended many services in which I have been the preacher. When two to three thousand people attended a dinner to celebrate his thirty years in Parliament, I was asked to be one of those making a tribute to his leadership. That made the local liberal politicians who sat with me in the Legislative Council sit up and take notice!

Dr Peter Hollingworth had a depressing and degrading time until he was forced out of office as Governor General, the first ever to do so. Since that time, we have spoken and I continue to pray for him. He was the one who invested me as a Companion of the Order of Australia, our highest national honour. We have been invited to dinner at Yarralumla and he has called me since. General Michael Jeffreys A.C. and his wife Marlene are outstanding Christian people and I appreciate their friendship.

General Douglas MacArthur in World War 2 had an objective: to expand the area of the allies' occupation and to push back the forces of Japanese expansionism until victory brought peace. He achieved this by island hopping developing beachheads on small islands throughout the northern Pacific, building landing strips and ancillary services, establishing partnerships with local communities to strengthen the offensive and pushing on towards his goal, the defeat of Japan.

None of the islands of itself could accomplish this. But together, the movement would win a permanent development and a spread of democratic governments. MacArthur was Supreme Commander of the Allied forces in the Southwest Pacific. In 1943, MacArthur's forces drove the Japanese from New Guinea, western New Britain and the Admiralty Islands. By September 1944, MacArthur had also recaptured western New Guinea and Morotai. On October. 20, 1944, MacArthur and his forces landed on the Philippine island of Leyte. His troops landed on Mindoro in the central Philippines, then invaded Luzon. He retook the southern Philippines and Borneo before Japan surrendered in August 1945. The process of island hopping and beachhead penetration followed by rapid support with ancillary forces and partnerships with the local community was a successful strategy of penetration and goal achievement. It is this military tactic that provides Wesley Mission Sydney with its strategy, which will enable the fulfilment of its vision throughout Australia and beyond.

Wesley Mission has goals as outlined in our Vision Statement and in the sixty or more performance indicators our industry groups have identified. 'Wesley Mission Sydney is a strategic city church committed to the proclamation of the Gospel of Jesus Christ and a ministry of word and deed throughout Australia, ministering to human need, utilising the media and providing personal and family care.' That is a big vision. Some would say it is an impossible task. How can one city church achieve such penetration and growth?

The strategy I suggest of beachhead partnerships is similar to that used by General Douglas MacArthur. One area of our work will expand into a rural or regional community, establish partnership with the local churches there, bring in reinforcements while we have a brief occupancy with an employment service or disability service, or other government funded operation. Then quickly, with our new local partners, we introduce other ministries, suicide prevention, credit counselling, prison ministries, mental health services, eating disorders programs, student ministry, evangelism visits, homes for hope, homeless people, street youth programs, drug education, foster families, home care programs and so on.

We are already well-known in every area. For the past 21 years we have telecast into every community in Australia, mentioning week by week, various parts of our work. I have written twice to every church in every community in NSW where we plan to work. They know us. They have heard of what we do elsewhere.

Now, in about 80 communities we had a beachhead opening up. We moved quickly to establish relationships and start bringing in other services. Some examples come quickly to mind. We established Serenity Farm at Horsley Park and established good relationships with nearby Fairfield Uniting Church. Their members became a support group for our staff and for the recovering alcoholics we were helping. They continued even when the farm turned into our various lodges.

From that Creditline leased some of their vacant premises. We have been providing preachers for their services. Fairfield Employment Services opened just around the corner. They began a meal service to the poor and we used our media to promote them. The Fairfield Uniting Church now has Presbytery approval to sell a property, redevelop their church hall andformally link with Wesley Mission. Staff members Noreen Towers, Nerida Dunkerley, Keith Suter, Wayne Koivu and Graham Towle have been part of this process. The story could be repeated with other staff in many other places: the Central Coast, West Wyalong, Castle Hill, Richmond, Penrith and so on.

To influence a whole country is a large vision, but through our media (videos, internet, radio, television and travel), we discover we are now influencing areas far from our shores. Our books and Bibles by the tens of thousands are distributed in Siberia and China. Our work-parties have built houses in Fiji and later this year, the first library and community centre in Rotuma.

Some of us may wonder what we can do to help considering the vastness of the problems facing our state, our country and our world. Hunger in Ethiopia and the sub-Saharan area is such a vast international problem that many people think it can never be solved. We grow pessimistic due to the size of the problem.

Our pessimism leads to paralysis. Because we cannot do everything we cease to do even the something we can do. One does not need to travel overseas to come face to face with hunger and homelessness, disability and unemployment, drug and alcohol abuse. But can one church and one person achieve much? Who can forget that nameless Chinese man clutching his plastic shopping bag running out before the row of lumbering tanks in Beijing, forcing the front one to turn aside and then to stop? He waved his plastic shopping bag and forced the whole menacing row of mighty tanks to halt. Defeated by courage and a plastic bag!

In this lucky country we are sick of people suffering from cold homelessness and grinding poverty. The only thing that prevents our significant economic problems being cured and the poor being helped is that politicians are paralysed by the size of the problem. It appears too much so nothing is done. Rural problems in Australia are large. The Uniting Church is doing little or nothing. Corporate Australia is withdrawing, but rural and regional Australia is Wesley Mission's biggest opportunity for growth, as we exercised the strategy of beachhead partnerships.

In 1979, I preached to the growing numbers of Chinese people in a Chinese service I had started in Wesley Mission on the theme, 'It's God's Time In Asia.' Later, I was to put Rev. James Mau and Rev. Fu Cain Chen onto the staff to minister to the growing number of Chinese we had in our congregation. Later, when we began the International Congregation with Dr Tony Chi, most of the Chinese attending came from Singapore. More than 1000 Asians were attending by 1990.

But when I asked Rev. Wilfred Chee to join us it was with the intention of better serving the Mandarin and Cantonese speaking Chinese. Because I have always had a burden in my heart for the Chinese people hearing the Gospel, especially those who were poor and unable to speak English, in 1979 I announced I would be starting a worship service for Chinese people. I had completed some research that indicated there were approximately 40,000 Chinese living in Sydney. By ringing all of the major churches and denominational headquarters in the city I established that a total of about 38,000 Chinese did not go to any church. This I regarded as a mission field.

So I established a ministry of outreach to the Chinese, started services where my preaching was translated in Mandarin and Cantonese and then sought these two outstanding Chinese Ministers to take over.

I was admiring the fact that these Chinese in Dr Wilfred Chee's service are affluent, educated and professional in their outlook and qualifications. The numbers of doctors, teachers, lawyers, accountants and professors is really outstanding. Mercedes cars crowd our car park. They are Chinese of competence and ability who have really established themselves in this country but I knew there were many poor Chinese here. So not long after Rev. Dr Wilfred Chee joined our staff I said to him, 'Are there any poor Chinese in Sydney?' Wilfred replied, 'Yes, there are many poor Chinese.' I asked him, 'How many? Where do they live? Where do they work?' Wilfred replied, 'We do not know many but they probably work in the kitchens of Chinese restaurants.'

I thought for a moment and then said. 'Wilfred, I want you to lay aside for the next 2 months or for however long it will take you, all your regular responsibilities. We will get other people to cover for you on those but I want you to visit every Chinese Restaurant in Central Sydney. Visit every Chinese laundry and any other places of business, which might employ Chinese. Do not go in the front entrance and do not speak to the proprietor. Instead go up the back lanes. I want you to meet the poor Chinese who do not speak English. I want you to enter the restaurant by the back door and speak directly to the workers. Find out who they are and what their needs are.'

Dr Chee undertook a backdoor, back lane visitation program throughout the Central Business District. He reported that most of the people he met were illegal immigrants. They were mostly illiterate and frequently financially exploited. He estimated there might be upwards of two thousand such illegal, illiterate and exploited Chinese.

We had discovered a hidden people group where our normal methods of reaching Chinese would not work. We decided upon a strategy and Wilfred personally visited and invited many of these kitchen hands to an evangelistic mission. We conducted the evangelistic mission in our George Street complex near China Town, used only Chinese musical instruments and old well-known Chinese hymns and conducted the mission commencing at 12 a.m. (midnight) to 2 a.m. The reason why we ran the mission in the early hours of the morning was that this was the only time when the kitchen hands were free from work. 26 men made commitments to Christ in that evangelistic mission.

We established a church fellowship and worship service for them. Sundays were not suitable for worship for them because they worked long hours on Sundays in order to feed wealthy Chinese Christians who love to go to restaurant after the service. Our worship service for kitchen hands were held on Wednesday afternoon at 3.30 p.m. - the time most were free. We then discovered we had to establish English-speaking language classes and these were held early Saturday morning.

We then realised that most kitchen hands were locked into very boring and mundane work with no chance of improving themselves or their income. So we established with suitable translators work skill programs training these Chinese as specialised chefs and as front of the house waiters. We established also The Evangelical Chinese Library to provide elementary Christian books on theology and very soon we had scores of Chinese learning the language, learning new work skills and visiting our church library, often staying for hours. 4 or 5 mature Chinese Christians developed the library as a ministry, talking with them, providing literature and a telephone ministry seeking better employment.

While working with this hidden 'people group' we found there was a sub group of illegal workers. These were far from illiterate. They were mainly University Students who had overstayed their government approvals. They were illegal immigrants without work permits they were also working in positions where they were easily exploited. That group of students were likewise encouraged to attend special services for them at a time suitable and in a format that was close to their traditional culture. English speaking classes were established, work skill programs were commenced, books at their advanced level of understanding were purchased and the government was approached seeking amnesty for all of these over stayers so they would be free from prosecution. I approached the Immigration Department to regularise their stay upon their admission of overstaying. This was done.

To help students feel at home, important cultural festivals like 'the Moon Festival' were held, except on these occasions, all the normal cultural emphases were made with a Christian message.

At the first Moon Festival attended by more than 800 Chinese students I preached on the theme that Christians do not look to the Moon - but to the Son of God. The audience grasped the difference instantly. The quality of musical performing skills, of singing and dance were absolutely outstanding.
We followed this up with a number of 'Love China' programs to support the students who had been rejected by China's government because of their associa-

tion with Tiananmen Square. On the first anniversary of commencing this work among illegal students we had a new congregation with more than 120 baptised members. At the second anniversary we had 250 baptised members present.

The development of these Chinese congregations from the hidden peoples group is a classic example of how a city church can minister to sub groups within the heart of the city. Most have since gone on their way, to other places, have graduated from the university and the restaurant kitchens. We need to find others whom we can serve, including new arrivals from Hong Kong.

God is preparing people for us to meet. He prepared my first close Chinese friend when I was three years of age. She was a three-year-old girl named Rosemary Woo. Her parents ran a Chinese laundry. Thirty years later, a member of a Chinese family knocked on my door and said, 'Mr Minister, would you come and bury my sister? She is a Buddhist and we have no Buddhist priest.' Of course I would. That family have remained friends with us to this day. I conducted the wedding service for their daughter. In their immediate family, many members are now active Christians.

When I stepped as a little boy through the doorway into the Chinese laundry I was beginning a journey that has made it possible for our family to step into a wonderful friendship that is rich to this day with hundreds of Chinese Families.

God prepares others for us, but we have to step over the threshold. The Chinese congregations are very important to Wesley Mission.

Ministers in the Uniting Church are not all happy with their experiences as a minister. I recently rang ministers across Australia who have been in public conflict with denominational officials. Most felt forced out of ministry and deprived of their livelihood and calling. None of these ministers were guilty of any moral lapse or public offence. Every single one complained of the denominational process, of what they defined as lack of justice, of indifference, callous treatment, secret trials and unfair process. John Mark Ministries states there are now up to 10,000 former ministers in Australia, the majority of whom feel they have been failed by the denomination, which they served. This is a scandal of wasted resources, officious bureaucracy and a lack of mediation skills. To be a minister of religion today is to be an endangered species. Denominational officials seem to delight in targeting any minister who gathers large numbers of people to worship.

The Church was given the ministry of reconciliation (2 Cor. 5:19). This includes reconciliation within marriage and between fellow believers who have deep disagreement. (1 Cor. 7:10f and Matt 5:23f.) The qualities that should be found in the reconciliation process include conflict mediation that is biblically based, open, affirming, inclusive, accepting, personal and non-judgmental.

The way forward will involve at least five steps:

1. There must be a recovery of doctrinal integrity. Mainline church members must pray and dedicate themselves to the renewal of their denominations. Within the Uniting Church a group called The Covenanters have committed themselves to daily prayer for the denomination. There is a need to recover core New Testament values and reconsider the role and authority of the Scriptures.

2. There needs to be an accountability of church officials within the ecclesiastical bureaucracy, not within their own circle, but in the accountability process that includes outside observers and parish participants. Church officials should receive training in conflict resolution and management training before their appointment.

3. There needs to be a commitment to restructure top-heavy administration with a downsizing of expensive bureaucracy. Many denominations have brought in outside experts to make recommendations to solve such issues but then keep the implementing of the recommendations to themselves. Hence no real changes are made. Within the Uniting Church thousands of dollars have been spent on outside mediators, without the results of the mediation ever being reported or implemented.

4. There needs to a fresh approach to the management of church resources. Within the Uniting Church there is not one official known to me, with post- graduate qualifications in management. There is little concept of benchmarking and achieving world best practise. Many of the tasks fulfilled by people trained in pastoral responsibilities would be better outsourced to appropriate organisations outside the church. There is a role for church administration and it is best kept to areas of policy making, setting standards of service delivery, research, setting visions, creating flexible regulations, overseeing ministry training and quality assurance.

5. There needs to be an emphasis on the kingdom of God not just denominationalism. Para-church organisations are not to be feared or snobbishly rejected, but incorporated into the denomination's evangelistic and service thrust.

There is probably no greater waste of the resources provided by faithful members in the pews, than what occurs within the church structures themselves. There is no greater denial of the doctrine of reconciliation than that evidenced by church officials who cannot cope with conflict. When we get our doctrine of reconciliation right, our practice will improve. Ministry is the highest profession open to a Christian. It is a pity that those so called and ordained should, find in such large numbers, that there is no place for them in the congregations of the church due to the interference by those who do not have accountability to any congregation. Many people have little idea what a minister does, apart from conducting services on a Sunday. I was visiting a member of the Cheltenham Church of Christ at his work many years ago, as had become my custom and I was intrigued to see Ray Verity an accountant and efficiency expert, completing a time and motion study on people who worked in his particular industry. Over lunch I asked him if he would be interested in doing a time and motion study on myself. He researched the papers on the subject and declared later that a time and motion study had never been conducted on a clergyman. So we set up a program where over a period of 36 days I carried a time book with me and noted every 15 minutes exactly what I was doing, the distance travelled if in the car, the people met, the type of work I was undertaking and so on. I thought this would be relatively easy but it was a huge task and a travelling alarm clock going off every 15 minutes in my pocket kept me up to the task.

At the end he analysed on a huge matrix all of the activities undertaken, the amount of time spent over the 36 days and then analysed what I was doing in the light of expectations drawn up from a survey by ordinary members attending the church, other people in the community selected at random and the Elders and the Deacons of the church who had the responsibility of oversight of ministry.

Then he asked 30 penetrating questions. In answering some of those questions I changed the practices of my life entirely. For example, he had indicated that I had spent 17 hours over the 36 days on writing letters, producing church papers, orders of service, printing, folding new sheets and the like. His question was penetrating. Are you paid to do this work? Have you been trained in the efficient use of such equipment and so on. I decided from that time on I would, 'stick to my knitting'. That is, I would do the work of ministry and I would raise funds to employ people with gifts and expertise in all of these other support activities. I would encourage every minister to do the same kind of analysis. It made me a much more effective and efficient person and built up significantly the staff who would work with me. When Ray Verity completed that time and motion study on my life I was the only employed person in that church. Within seven years of that date we were employing fifteen staff, had increased dramatically the numbers of people attending by five fold and had increased our church income many more time than this.

Basically my diary has followed the same pattern. I try to keep Monday free for recovery after six non-stop days, including all day Saturday and Sunday. We have had for more than thirty years our own home, which required gardening, building and maintenance on this day as well. Although our children were at school for most of this time, this was a time when Beverley and I were able to do those things about our home which all married couples do. However, since being at Wesley Mission, one in every four Mondays has been taken up making television programs which involved the preaching of four sermons, conducting four interviews and hosting a very demanding television schedule. The days off have always also been the time when I started my sermon preparation for the following Sunday, wrote the manuscripts for books, radio and television programs and other extra activities. On the mornings of each week day my primary responsibility was teaching school classes. Throughout most of my life I have taught secondary school children with over 900 being taught every week for 15 years. During my rural ministry I also taught an additional five classes in primary schools each week. School classes commenced at 8.30 in the morning and ran till 12.30pm and also involved the lugging of heavy projector equipment from classroom to classroom. At Cheltenham I was unable to do primary school teaching and my wife, Beverley, taught in my place teaching many classes in the primary school. This was another voluntary task she did in the life of the church, apart from playing for the choir, church services, weddings and funerals and raising funds for our work. She was never paid for any of this activity yet worked more than 80 hours a week in an unpaid capacity. Today many minister's wives have to go to work and the Church misses out on the tremendous contribution that is then made over the generations by the wives of ministers, using their skills and abilities in running meetings, auxiliaries, clubs and activities in a voluntary capacity.

Each week day morning began early mostly before 6.00am with Bible study and the writing into a wide margined Bible insights into the scripture passages that would be used the following week. We would also use this time for prayer for church members and people suffering from illness or family crisis. In more recent years Beverley has had her own special prayer time where she kept a daily diary of those people for whom she prayed and the consequential results of those prayers. In our first three ministries I had the advantage of mostly having lunch with my wife – the most private time in the entire week. But usually during this period of time I would also be dashing off orders of service, selecting hymns and writing paragraphs for the weekly newssheet.

At Wesley Mission three mornings a week would be taken up with conducting meetings of Management committees, Aged Care committees, Senior Staff meetings and the like.

Week day afternoons are always spent in pastoral visitation. As early in the week as possible, I would always visit everybody that we knew who was in hospital or a nursing home or in some specialised Aged Care facility to remind them of the love and concern we had for them. I would conduct communion services with frail and shut in people, taking some of the bread and wine from the previous Sunday's services. I would always visit every day about 5 homes to meet with members who are home at that time. These were always made by appointment, unless I had some spare time, in which I would call into the nearest available to the last person I had visited.

With over a thousand funerals during thirteen years at Cheltenham most afternoons also had at least one funeral. Every home I visited was listed in a large ledger carried in my car which included the name of every member and contact of the church and then running across the page the dates of every visit I made to that family home. Listed were also the names of children and any other person who might be in that home to jog my memory. I can tell you now for any given year even thirty years ago who I visited in which week. The names of people visited were listed for each monthly meeting of my elders and people who needed further support from elders and Church carers would be mentioned. It was always my aim to visit one hundred homes each month and to be able to report to the elders the names of every home visited. It was important with this pastoral visitation to also visit the homes where death had come or those persons who were frail and sick.

I tried to keep every Friday morning clear for sermon preparation and with Monday, Friday and some time on Saturday night, I would always see that at least 20 hours had been spent on those sermons. Evenings were always filled with activities. Tuesday and Thursdays before evening meal I would be training with the church sporting teams. Other days I would be counselling people who came in after their work. Evening meal was a good family time but unfortunately always interrupted by telephone calls from people who knew that we would be there at that time. Most mid-week evenings saw home group studies, elders and deacons meetings and every Tuesday night was spent visiting the homes of non-members. Even after the auxiliary activities were completed late at night the minister is usually the last person to check that the church is secured, that all the halls are locked, that the chairs are stacked properly, the floors are swept and things made ready for the next day. At Wesley Mission on more than three hundred days, I opened a new office or a new building and on three hundred days attended a fete or fundraising event.

Saturdays are inevitably full of activities. Most of my Saturday mornings throughout my life have been spent on maintaining the church gardens, working in church working bees, doing maintenance on the church and manse properties, working with various fetes and fairs and, of course, conducting weddings. Having married more than two thousand individuals, I had lots of Saturdays taken up with wedding services and receptions. This inevitably clashed with sporting matches. I was frequently having to leave a sporting match halfway through to drive furiously home where my wife will have laid out my clothes on the bed and after a quick change run into the church with gown flapping and church registers under my arm to arrive before the bride arrived. In spite of hundreds of weddings I was only beaten to the church by a bride on one occasion when an astute taxi driver kept driving around the block until I arrived. At many a wedding, if a guest had walked onto the platform and lifted up the leg of my trousers, red, yellow and black football socks would have come into view. Saturday nights throughout my whole life have always been spent in the final typing and printing of sermons for Sunday. Some time during the week had to be found for letter writing, producing church papers or magazines and doing all of the other administrative tasks such as writing reports that are required by a church.

Ray Verity's time and motion study showed that I was working 116 hours each week on the job. But even going to bed late at night when Beverley and I finished our day by having our Bible reading, devotional time and prayers for church members and the wider community, our work did not stop. Frequently during the night, particularly in our early years, sleep would be interrupted by a telephone call to tell us that some member of a family had been taken to hospital or was close to death and a visit was immediately required. I used to get out of bed and put some day clothes on over my pyjamas, particularly in the winter. I would return home after spending an hour or maybe more in a hospital or a home, hang up my clothes and be back into bed in pyjamas that were still warm. Ray Verity's 116 hours a week outline forced me to face more effective and efficient ways of using my time and I have always appreciated that assessment.

Why do people come to church? My basic answer is because of the pastoral care given to the people who associate with that particular church. Recently in 2002, the elders asked all people attending the Sunday evening services at Wesley Mission why they attended the 7pm services. There were some suggested answers and then people were invited to give other reasons. There were 26 reasons given in total with eight of the reasons receiving multiple votes. People were attracted to our evening service primarily because they were invited by someone else who always attended, but others came because of our radio and television programs. However most people indicated they continued to come due to the fact that, 'The uncompromising Word of God is preached in an interesting, inspiring and different manner by Rev. Dr Gordon Moyes.' The second reason given by most was 'The praise of the Lord in a Christian atmosphere of love and acceptance of all people regardless of colour, social status and friendship.' And the third reason given was 'Interesting, enjoyable worship style, with different approaches to church services than what you usually find in a church.' The role of ministry is one of the most exciting and varied lifestyles that can ever be undertaken and I'm thrilled to see that the same major emphasis are being made by my son and son-in-law as they continue their ministry today.

Recently, our minister son David, pastor of Belconnen Baptist Church, one of the largest Baptist churches in the nation, was leading a seminar of senior pastors in Sydney on developing churches. They were using as a resource a book called *Breakout Churches by Thom Rainer* (Zondervan). In the words of the author, 'This book is the story of churches and leaders that broke from the shackles of mediocrity to become great churches and great leaders'. The Rainer Research Team conducted surveys of 50,000 churches and leaders, drawing on analogies from the book *Good to Great* by Jim Collins and recommends the type of leader needed to move churches from stagnancy to growth and from mediocrity to greatness.

Here is a summary from *Breakout Churches* (p44) of the various levels of leadership.

Those ministers who could be described as a 'called leader', who know of God's call to ministry and who have responded to that call were 98% of people surveyed. Those ministers who could be described as a 'contributing leader', who take time to do well the basics of Christian ministry such as preaching, teaching and prayer, were 22% of all surveyed. The 'outwardly-focussed leader' who seeks to lead church and self to ministry beyond the walls of the Church, were 14% of all surveyed. The 'passionate leader' who exudes a contagious enthusiasm for ministry so others gladly follow, were 6% of all surveyed. The 'bold leader' who is willing to take risks, where success is only possible in God's power, were 3% of all surveyed. The 'legacy leader' who has a burden for a successful ministry beyond his own lifetime, were less than 1% of all surveyed.

The study group of senior pastors reflected on the 1% of church leaders that have made an impact on Australian churches over the past decade. Only a few names came to mind among the group.

David sent me some comments from the group and wrote, 'You are certainly in that 1%. Proud of you Dad.'

PREACHER

Chapter Three

I first started preaching in Melbourne's slum areas. Looking back on it I guess I must have looked very much like a boy preacher. I started preaching during my 17th year but I had been preparing for it for some time. All my first sermons were preached to a congregation of none in the quietness of the lounge room of my mother's house. My first pulpit was an upturned banana box on top of a piano stool. It held my notes and I took turns in leaning upon it, leaning over it, holding onto it and thumping it as I went through my sermon manuscripts.

No one had taught me to preach. I had not read any 'teach yourself to preach' books. All I knew was that the example of preaching that I had been hearing for many years in our own local church in Box Hill was not quite the kind of preaching that I wanted to emulate.

I wanted preaching to be vital and alive, full of interesting comment on events that were happening at that moment in the newspapers and magazines and bringing to bear insights from the Bible.

Not knowing where to turn for material and not having much water in the bottom of my well, I had been cutting out articles from magazines like *Reader's Digest* for some time. I rewrote these into a style that suited myself, placed carefully some Biblical quotations and insights and thought that that made a sermon. My ignorance was only surpassed by my confidence. I put together those sermons, wrote out pages of notes and standing in the empty lounge room with the upturned banana box in front of me, preached to imaginary congregations.

The first sermon I really clinched originally came from a sermon written by Dr Peter Marshall, who was quite in vogue at that time following his tragic death. Dr Marshall, who was the subject of the film *A Man Called Peter*, was the Chaplain to the United States Senate. A book of his sermons called *Mr Jones, Meet The Master* had just been published and a condensed version of one of his sermons entitled *Disciples in Clay* had featured in *Reader's Digest*. I took this *Reader's Digest* condensed version of his sermon, adapted it and worked it over and over.

PREACHER

Just after my 18th birthday I was invited to take an evening service in the Newmarket Church of Christ. I organised friends from my home church and some relatives who lived near Newmarket to attend that night. I looked forward to that first sermon with tremendous enthusiasm and practiced preaching it on the upturned banana box in my lounge room until I was very familiar with every part of it. I even wrote out every word for conducting the rest of the service including the prayers, the reading, a poem I had found, the welcome to people and the announcements and all the other bits and pieces that went to make an interesting evening service.

What my banana box did not prepare me for, however, I discovered thirty seconds after walking out onto the platform before the congregation was that there was a microphone in the pulpit. I had not been prepared for the microphone and it rather mesmerised me. Knowing how offputting it can be for people to move in close to a microphone and then far away from it, all that first night I maintained a steady distance from the microphone in order to give the listeners the right level of microphone help. I need not have bothered. I found out later that it was not plugged in! It was not even a microphone for amplifying my voice through loud speakers, but a microphone to amplify the sound into some sets of hearing aids for deaf listeners, none of who were present anyway!

I should not have been overawed by the congregation. True, my friends had come from the Box Hill Church of Christ willing to help out a young student in his first sermon and my Aunty and Uncle and a couple of cousins were there. Together my friends and relatives swelled the congregation. The fact was, there were 14 people in the church that night including myself and eleven of them were my friends and relatives!

I preached Dr Peter Marshall's sermon *Disciples in Clay* with tremendous enthusiasm.

On the way out of church that night, one of the two Newmarket people who were there, a young girl about 16, came up to me and without batting an eye, said, 'I really loved that sermon. That was a magnificent presentation tonight. It really moved me, I really loved that sermon.' My ego swelled up and my head nearly burst at such praise. Then she went on, 'Yes, I really loved that sermon. In fact it was one of the best *Reader's Digest* ever published!'

Talk about being deflated. The air went out of me quicker than a balloon that has been let go. From that moment on I learned to avoid *Reader's Digest* and I have never used anything in *Reader's Digest* subsequently as a source for likely sermon insights.

Other students also had problems with their preaching. I remember a student friend of mine, a former farmer named Cliff Perkins. He was a big, strong, rugged fellow but he had problems with some of his words. He would frequently use a wrong word, which sounded something like the right word, sometimes with disastrous results. He was preaching in the other little wooden church at Ascot Vale one day close to Easter and he was telling the story of how the Apostle Peter betrayed Christ on the night before his crucifixion. Cliff made the point quite clearly that Peter followed Jesus into the courtyard of the High Priest and stood round the fire as it was burning in the centre of the courtyard. Using a touch of dramatic realism he said 'And there stood Peter, in the High Priest's courtyard, warming his hands on the brassiere.' From that moment on none of the women in the congregation could stop laughing and several of the men guffawed out loud. Poor Cliff's sermon was lost, but I am quite sure that he learnt what the distinction was between a brazier and a brassiere.

Many people ask me when I first started to preach without being dependent upon notes. The source of that habit came by accident. I was preaching one day in the little wooden church at Ascot Vale. The pulpit was beside a wideopen window, which had been opened to catch a breath of fresh air on a stifling hot summer Sunday. I was not long into my sermon when a gust of wind blew in the window and twelve pages of typing slid off the pulpit and fluttered down in all directions and in complete disorder onto the floor beneath. I suddenly realised that every eye in the congregation was riveted upon me wondering what I would do next.

Nothing could have been done to catch people's attention more than it was at that moment. I instantly thought, 'All of these people are wondering what I am going to do and they are waiting to laugh as I go down out of the pulpit, pick up all the pages, sort them into order and then go on.' Then I had a second thought, 'If I cannot remember it when I am preaching it, how can I expect people to remember what I have said when they go home?'

At that moment I decided to take the risk and preach the rest of the sermon without going down to pick up my notes. Everybody's attention was upon me, waiting to find out when I would stumble and stop having run out of material. I kept my eye fixed upon everyone and there was magnificent eye contact for the duration. I finished the sermon as I had prepared it and made all the points that I felt necessary and not for one instance did anybody's attention wander away.

I had discovered the secret of communicating with people by looking them in the eye. Although I have often used notes since in more than 15,000 sermons I have prepared, always on the most of important occasions I preach without notes in order to keep that eye contact.

After that day I ventured down from the pulpit, preaching beside it, then a little away from it and then finally preaching in the centre of the platform without notes and without any pulpit and with no barrier between the people and myself. The further I got away from the pulpit the more intense was the contact. Ever since I have typed out my sermons in full and generally speaking, preached without notes.

PREACHER

Later that year was my first Christmas service. It was an important occasion because all the churches of the area gathered together in a large Christmas service. The combined churches packed out the huge church in which we all gathered.

I had been asked to preach the Christmas Day sermon and I was shaking with fear during the hymn prior to my sermon. My nervousness must have been very obvious because the elderly Baptist minister reached across and placed his hand on my arm in a steadying influence and said something absurd, which broke the tension and greatly relieved my fear. In the midst of this enthusiastic hymn, while everybody was singing about shepherds watching their flocks by night, the Baptist minister said to me 'People have funny faces when they are singing, don't they?'

As I gazed down from the high pulpit I suddenly realised the truth of the matter and began to chuckle. My nervousness ceased and I commenced that sermon with a totally relaxed frame of mind. After a little while in those two wooden churches I realised that preaching was the most important thing that a man could ever do because it has eternal consequences. A person can be made right with God eternally through the foolishness of what we call preaching. I printed a sign upon the top of my pulpit where no one else could read it, except myself that said, ' No man can at the same time present himself as important and Jesus Christ as Lord.' I have read that quotation thousands of times and I have sought to follow it in practice.

The task was to present Jesus Christ as Lord. That became the main feature behind everything that was said and preached. And over the next few years people did become Christians. That girl who had read the sermon written by Peter Marshall made her commitment to Christ, then her sister and friend; a whole group of boys who were on probation made their commitment to Christ and changed their entire lifestyle. Then some men who came on parole from prison made their commitments to Christ and some parents of children who attended the little Sunday school and a whole host of teenagers from high school where I used to conduct classes. Then the young man with whom I had lunch once a week for two or three years discussing the faith, a young science graduate with his Masters degree in science and later his PhD completed, confessed faith in Christ. He too was baptised and came within the fellowship of the faith.

The pulpit may have been of polished wood but it was the old upended banana box standing on the piano stool that became the first pulpit from which the riches of Christ and his salvation were proclaimed.

I wish to discuss preaching from the perspective of my ministry of nearly fifty years, within the evangelical tradition. Here is my philosophy of preaching. I will outline nineteen aspects of preaching that we have found to be blessed of God in the setting of a local pastoral ministry. At Wesley Mission, Sydney, we have been through one of the greatest periods of church growth in the history of our nation.

Here is *Principle #1*. Preaching is effective if you communicate the Gospel in a contemporary manner. Some evidences of that growth would include such things as:

* In the last fifteen years we have established 14 new congregations and 12 daughter churches, most of which are selfsufficient and no longer part of our ministry;
* We increased our annual income from $5 million p.a. to $150 million per annum, by far the largest church congregational budget in the world;

*We have raised the funds and appointed new fulltime staff at a rate of two additional staff every single week for the first thirteen years, three per week for every week of the next three years and six per week for the past 2 years;

* Since 1988 we have established the Wesley Institute of Ministry and Arts, with 400 fulltime students currently enrolled and 3000 completing parttime courses;

* We have built, at a cost of $100 million, buildings to house homeless people, care for dying people, provide psychiatric treatment for depressed, purchased a fourth hospital, housed children and families in crisis and the like, with none of this money coming from governments.

* We have seen more than a dozen people commit their lives to Christ every single week, with many people entering the ministry and missionary service. One Sunday I preached on the significance of overseas crosscultural missionary service. I gave an appeal for men and women who would commit themselves to fulltime missionary service. Twelve people did so, including a doctor and two nurses. Later the same day in a service I repeated the same message and gave the same appeal and fortyone committed their lives to missionary service. Later the same night I repeated the same message for the third time and two others made commitments. On that oneday 55 commitments were made to fulltime service in crosscultural evangelism. On another Sunday another forty people committed themselves to training for fulltime Christian ministry or missionary service.

* We have increased our national coverage by television and radio and in purchasing and running two of the most famous radio stations in Australia. I served as Chairman of the Board of both radio stations for a decade.

* We have conducted some of the largest services ever held in Australia, with 35,000 attending our largest Christmas Service in openair gatherings featuring over one thousand singers, dancers and actors telling the Christmas Story.

* We demolished all of our church head office and worship facilities and constructed a new Wesley Church, Wesley Theatre and Lyceum, college and parish areas, restaurant and four level shopping arcade, undercover car parking for 400 cars and a 38 storey office tower, all leased and we have opened the whole com-

plex at a cost of $320 million, with 35,000 people attending the opening celebrations. We opened the whole complex debt free!

* In the last eighteen years, we have demolished and rebuilt, purchased and leased more than 350 buildings for the ministry of just one city church and have increased our net asset worth by more than $250 million dollars.

And the primary reason for this amazing growth of a church has been the fact that we have concentrated on communicating the Gospel by word and deed.

Here then is *Principle* #2 of preaching from my experience: Preaching is successful if the church demonstrates that the Word of the Gospel and the deed of practical care are ministered together.

The Apostle Paul was the greatest church planter and Gospel communicator in history. How did he go about his work of planting new churches and communicating the Gospel? He never left us a manual, but he did leave us clues in his letters and his addresses and the accounts of his travels recorded by Dr Luke in 'The Acts of the Apostles.'

Paul explained the characteristics of his ministry and gave a pattern for our preaching ministry today when he was closing his Letter to the Romans. Here are the distinctives we must follow in communicating the Gospel today. These distinctives indicate how we must communicate the Gospel. Note from Romans 15:1419 a framework for communicating the Gospel.

1. The Gospel Starts With Grace of God. (vv. 1415)
'I myself am convinced, my brothers, that you yourselves are full of goodness, complete in knowledge and competent to instruct one another. I have written you quite boldly on some points, as if to remind you of them again, because of the grace God gave me.'

When he was Saul of Tarsus, the crusading rabbi, Paul knew little of the grace of God. He persecuted the church and sought to destroy it. When Paul met Jesus Christ on the Damascus road, he experienced the grace of God. God's grace saved him. God's grace called him and made him an apostle. 'We have received grace and apostleship, for obedience to the faith among all nations, for His name.' (Romans 1:5) Preaching starts with the grace of God.

Here is *Principle* #3: Preaching must start with the grace of God.

There is much shallowness in preaching today. Too many ministers think they are called to be entertainers or poppsychologists, or else they give summaries of what new social concept the church must accept. The focus has shifted from God to humankind. Preaching is too much us and not enough God. Too much entertainment and not enough evoking a response. For all their words the Word of God is not being clearly heard.

Dr John Piper in his book *The Supremacy of God in Preaching* (Baker, p20) says, 'If God is not supreme in our preaching, where in this world will the people hear about the supremacy of God? The vision of a great God is the linchpin in the life of the church, both in pastoral care and missionary outreach. Our people need to hear Godentranced preaching. They need someone, at least once a week, to lift up his voice and magnify the supremacy of God.'

Piper says the goal of preaching is the glory of God. 'My burden is to plead for the supremacy of God in preaching that the dominant note of preaching be the freedom of God's sovereign grace, the unifying theme be the zeal that God has for his own glory, the grand object of preaching be the infinite and inexhaustible being of God and the pervasive atmosphere of preaching be the holiness of God. Then when preaching takes up the ordinary things of life family, job, leisure, friendships; or the crises of our day: AIDS, divorce, addictions, depression, abuses, poverty, hunger and, worst of all, unreached peoples of the world, these matters are not only taken up. They are taken all the way up into God.' (p.20)

The Gospel must start with the glory of God. I have conducted more than 400 small evangelistic campaigns in local churches, mainly in rural Australia. On each occasion I proclaimed the Gospel of God's grace and Christ's redemptive love.

Here is *Principle #4*: Preaching can be the work of a visiting evangelist conducting a special crusade, short or long, with one church or many, proclaiming the grace of God .

For over fifteen years I spent over 35 weekends every year conducting a small evangelistic crusade from Friday night to Sunday morning with the churches in some small rural community, returning Sunday afternoon to an evangelistic ministry in my own church and through television and radio. That was an exhausting and bodynumbing approach to preaching. It is a valid form of evangelism, but probably not as effective as the effort warrants. The proclamation of the Gospel, however, must always start with the grace of God.

2. The Gospel is the Centre of Our Ministry. (v.16)
'Because of the grace God gave me to be a minister of Christ Jesus to the Gentiles with the priestly duty of proclaiming the gospel of God, so that the Gentiles might become an offering acceptable to God, sanctified by the Holy Spirit.'

Paul had a 'priestly duty of proclaiming the gospel of God'. He used two different words for 'minister' here. One translated 'minister' is the word from which we derive the word liturgy lietourgon. Paul used this word to describe himself.

Other times he used the common term doulos to indicate a 'servant' of Jesus Christ, or diaconos, a 'minister.' But here he chose lietourgon because he saw his preaching like that of a priest offering sacred worship to God.

His priestly offering was not a lamb but his Gentile converts: 'that the Gentiles might become an offering acceptable to God, sanctified by the Holy Spirit.' Though he is involved in the tough, mundane business of travelling the ancient world on foot, suffering from exposure, threats, beatings and rejection, in his heart he sees himself in priestly garb in the Temple, lifting up the souls of men which then ascended as a sweetsmelling fragrance to Christ. They were a 'spiritual sacrifice' to the glory of God.

Here is *Principle #5*: Preaching is the presentation of the Gospel as a 'priestly duty'.

Note that Paul does not use the expression in connection with any liturgical practice but explicitly with 'the gospel of God'. He is affirming that the proclamation of the gospel is a solemn and sacred act. This insight into ministry certainly adds dignity and responsibility to our service. How we perceive ourselves greatly determines how we live our lives.

Psychologists remind us of the importance of selfimage. Imagine what this priestly selfperception did for Paul. His ministry was to him intensely sacred. The most mundane daily occurrences were holy.

However ignominious his treatment, he was garbed in imperturbable dignity as a servant of God. Everything was done to please God. All of life was a liturgy. If only we could see our service as such, our lives would be transformed. A friendly word to a homeless man becomes an offering to God. A child held and loved is a liturgy. An unemployed person treated with dignity is a gift to God. This sacred view of life was characteristic of the missionary Paul. (*Romans,* Kent Hughes, Crossways. 1991 p288). This high view of the priestly ministry leaves no room for the minister of God to live an immoral life, or live in homosexual or adulterous relationship or any other life style that is not holy and acceptable to God.

During my early ministry in a rural community, I faced an argumentative, rundown and divided church of 35 members. We decided that the best way the church could pull out of being selfcentred was to become centred on communicating the Gospel to a township of 8,000 people.

Here comes *Principle #6*: Preaching is a whole community event.

We ran a oneweek mission from Sunday to Sunday. We first worked hard to contact every person in the community. In four months of preparation we visited every family we could and 27 adults from outside the church families made commitments to Jesus Christ and were baptised. Then eleven laymen went visiting some more and 32 adults made commitments to Christ and were baptised.
Then we contacted all 8000 people in the town by mail, visit and through the newspaper and 4,500 attended in one week, with 261 making commitments to

Christ! The membership of that small church increased by 300% that week because the whole community joined in the preaching of the Gospel.

Communicating the Gospel has been the centre of my ministry. Following that, for the next 13 years, each Tuesday night I met with a small band of people for prayer. Then half the band would go out two by two to appointments previously made to 'discuss faith in Christ and membership in our church.' The person who came with me was learning to witness and share the Gospel message. During this period, going out each Tuesday night, I led over 800 people to Christ in their own homes!

Here is *Principle #7*: Preaching is a weekly event, involving laymen and personal contact.

At my very first church sermon I preached in the slums of our city, only fourteen people were present. Yet I gave a Gospel appeal. In the subsequent seven years I stayed at that church scores of people made commitments because the church knew I was serious about preaching for commitment and they supported that.

Here is *Principle #8*: Preaching starts with the preacher's commitment.

At Wesley Mission, Sydney, we preach for commitment to Christ every Sunday, without exception and legend has it that there has not been one Sunday in 120 years that has not seen at least one person coming forward in at least one of our services to commit his or her life to Christ. In our other services and through our media response to our telecounsellors about a dozen commitments are counselled each Sunday at services conducted by myself or my colleagues. I never stand up to preach without praying for conversions and people making public their commitment to Christ. We pray every week that God will give us disciples, not just decisions. Converted, changed, repentant lives are the objective in our preaching.

Here then is *Principle #9*: Preaching is the means of conversion.

Communicating the Gospel involves reaching hidden people groups and crossing ethnic boundaries. Twentyseven years ago I announced I was planning to commence a Chinese service. I would preach each week at a separate time, have a Chinese interpreter, finish with Yum Cha and seek to minister to those without English. One Chinese man and his wife, Mr and Mrs Ping Hui, agreed to start with me. Ping brought his brother Andrew and his wife Mabel. They brought four more. Soon I was preaching with both Mandarin and Cantonese translators. Today we have 3,500 Asians attending and three Chinese pastors.

In the same way we identified with Chinese students in Australia at the time of the Tienamin Square massacre. Over 800 students looked to Wesley for protection from Chinese Embassy officials and we became involved with programs concerning immigration, visas, education, English classes, Bible studies and the like. We stood in solidarity with them in a very trying time.

We have visited China and made a film of both the Three Self Patriotic Movement and the Underground Churches. We are establishing a Chinese Internet web site and three of my books have been printed in Chinese in China and used widely by the underground church. More than a million copies have been purchased.

We have Indonesian groups, Tamil and Singhalese, Tongan, Fijian, Rotuman and Samoan. I have on my staff ministers from the Pacific, Asia, Sri Lanka, Singapore, Malaysia, America, Samoa and Rotuma to minister to people within their own culture. We preach multiculturally and are translated where appropriate. We have Bible readings, prayers and choral items in languages other than English.

Here is *Principle #10*: Preaching requires reaching multiculturally to people groups.

3. The Gospel brings Glory to God. (v.17) 'Therefore I glory in Christ Jesus in my service to God.'. The word translated 'glory' carries the idea of 'boast.' Paul used it seven times before in Romans. He was not bragging about his ministry, he was boasting in what the Lord had done. Paul did not serve and suffer as he did just to make a name for himself. He wanted to bring glory to Jesus Christ: 'That in all things He might have the preeminence' Colossians 1:18

When we go out in faith and take risks for the Gospel, in communicating the word boldly through the media and serving needy people in Sydney, even though the task is too big and our money is too limited, we bring glory to God.

Yet many churches are afraid to take risks. Their main objective was what Kennon Callahan calls 'Protecting their place on the face of the cliff.' He means that in mountain climbing, sometimes climbers find themselves on the face of a cliff where they cannot find a handhold or foothold. In that predicament many people freeze. They cling for dear life. They fear any move could mean the abyss below. Many churches become frozen on the face of the cliff. They cannot find anything in their history that would save them. They cannot see anything hopeful ahead. They became preoccupied with maintenance, membership and money. (Leadership, Carol Stream, *Christianity Today*, Spring 1991, Illinois, USA.)

That is what I call *Principle #11*: Preaching is bringing glory to God by reaching out in faith and taking risks for God.

Fourteen years ago I stood on our major city street. We had just demolished the finest church office in Australia, upon which we still owed a million and a quarter dollars. Ahead of us was a two acre hole that was eight stories deep. I said to our General Manager of Corporate Services, Richard Menteith, 'Dick, if we are wrong in this and this all falls over, you and I will have the grandest burial site in all of Australia!'

Developments for the work of God always involve reaching out in faith and taking risks. Any time I stand in a public park and preach the Gospel, every time I face a business convention, every time I speak on radio or television, I am going out on a limb, risking in faith. The press likes to ridicule an evangelist. The journalist likes to find the dirt of immorality. The local minister likes to repeat gossip about his colleague. The public likes to cut down tall poppies. It is risky communicating the Gospel.

Speaking at a football oval one night, the roar of motor cycle engines drowned out everything else as a large number of heavily tattooed 'bikies' roared into the oval. They rode their motorbikes up to the front of the platform. The atmosphere turned ugly. I was about to preach on Isaiah 6, which states, 'Here I am Lord. Send me.' I looked at my colleague minister and thought, 'Here I am Lord. Send him!' But God had called me to be the preacher. I changed my introduction, the bikies listened on their motorcycles and when I gave the invitation, one rolled his bike forward.

Since 1963 I have been on television. We have taken risks to bring God glory through consistently communicating the Gospel on the media. Twentyseven years ago I started Turn 'Round Australia the most widely watched Christian television program in Australia. Twentyone years ago I started broadcasting on commercial radio. Ever since I have broadcast for four hours every Sunday night on 'Sunday Night Live' to the largest audience in the country for a Christian broadcast. I always preach the Gospel and ask people to respond to the call of Christ and speak to our telecounsellors. It is risky because speaking on the media invites people of all attitudes to sue over something said. Ours is a litigious society.

For years some network or another has telecast our 'Discovering' Series, made in 150 locations around the Mediterranean Sea. Our Christmas and Easter specials are seen nationwide in prime time.

Our videos are screened in a dozen countries in several languages. Colleges and schools, not only in English speaking countries, but in Spanish, Italian and Korean countries also study with our videos. 96,000 people hit our web site for sermons every week of the year. Our print magazines, national Christian news broadcasts, press releases on social issues, are read by hundreds of thousands weekly.

Here then, is *Principle #12*: Preaching is taking the modern highways of communication to reach into every corner of the world.

4. The Gospel is Empowered by God. (v 18-19)
'Therefore I glory in Christ Jesus in my service to God. I will not venture to speak of anything except what Christ has accomplished through me in leading the Gentiles to obey God by what I have said and done by the power of signs and

miracles, through the power of the Spirit. So from Jerusalem all the way around to Illyricum, I have fully proclaimed the gospel of Christ.'

The Holy Spirit empowered Paul to minister and enabled him to perform mighty signs and wonders. The miracles God gave Paul to do were 'signs', in that they came from God and revealed him to others. And they were 'wonders' in that they aroused the wonder of the people. But their purpose was always to open the way for the preaching of the Gospel. The Spirit of God empowered Paul to share the Word and to 'leading the Gentiles to obey God.'

This then is *Principle #13*: Preaching is the exercise of spiritual gifts empowered by the Spirit of God.

The ministry of miracles, signs and wonders are outside the New Testament purpose, unless they are directed towards helping people accept the Gospel. Making people disciples must be the aim. So many in the ministry of signs and wonders seem more intent on confirming believers and comforting themselves than making disciples.

Nothing would convince unbelievers more than documented and verifiable miracles. At Wesley Mission, we do not claim to lengthen legs and remove tumours but by word and deed, in counselling, nursing, providing medical and psychiatric treatment we share the love of God with the lost around us. Changes in conduct and character are just as much miracles as the healing of the sick. God empowers our work through his Spirit.

This then is the important *Principle #14*: Preaching must be in the context of care.

This has been at the heart of the work of the Salvation Army for more than a century. Wesley Mission has likewise built a ministry of caring for people: the outcasts, the poor, homeless, drug addicted, psychiatrically ill, the prisoner, the dying AIDS sufferer, the stroke and cancer sufferer, the child in crisis, the family desperately strapped for cash, the hungry, the unemployed and so on.

Today we have over 4,000 fulltime staff in over 500 centres of care in the name of Christ. The communication of the Gospel is empowered by God when it is done for his glory, using the spiritual gifts of people and is ministering to people with loving words and practical care and concern.

5. The Gospel Is Spread ccording to to God's Plan. (v20-22)
'It has always been my ambition to preach the gospel where Christ was not known, so that I would not be building on someone else's foundation. Rather, as it is written: 'Those who were not told about him will see and those who have not heard will understand. This is why I have often been hindered from coming to you.'

God had a plan for Paul to follow: he was not to preach where any other apostle had ministered. This is evidence that Peter had not founded the church at Rome, for this would have prevented Paul from going there. Peter did not arrive in Rome until after Paul.

'From Jerusalem all around to Illyricum' (Yugoslavia) is more than 2,000 kilometres! What a tremendous achievement despite dangers and hardship. Paul 'fully proclaimed the gospel of Christ' by preaching in all the strategic centres and establishing churches there. Paul was the pattern of a pioneer missionary.

This is my *Principle #15*: Preaching is taking the Gospel to peoples and places where Christ is not known.

Crosscultural missionaries are still needed, but a trained national is best. Skilling the trained national uses the person who has the best language skills, the closest cultural identification, prevents the brain drain to the West, gets the best result for the invested missionary dollar, avoids the problems of visas, furloughs and closed doors and gives encouragement and trust to the national church.

Through my Chairmanship for many years of The Overseas Council For Theological Education and Mission, we have trained national pastors in national seminaries and given funds for theological training, professor support, building and library acquisition for a score of countries. We start at the bottom with lowly village pastors. We are committed to culturally relevant, training of nationals to evangelise their own communities.

Principle #16: Preaching must be culturally relevant, building up the local body to evangelise their own communities.

Paul had a tough and disciplined ministry and every evangelist must be tough and disciplined, especially in his commitment to a sacrificial salary and a holy and blameless life. Many concerned with ministry and evangelism have disgraced us all by their lack of personal discipline concerning money, pride and sex. Their falling from grace has damaged every ministry, made a mockery of our commitment to lives of purity, holiness and simplicity and reminded us all, that but for the grace of God 'there go I.'

This is *Principle #17*: Preaching is living a life of holiness, disciplined by the scriptures.

No church in Australia had more involvement than Wesley Mission in supporting the socially needy in our community, nor has a reputation for speaking on economic and political issues of social justice, yet we emphasise the priority of evangelism by living a life of holiness and discipline by the scriptures. We have been tough on our staff who have violated the standards of personal holiness in defiance of the clear instructions of the scriptures and outspoken about those churches that condone adultery, homosexual liaisons and immoral relationships, especially among church leaders. It is not wrong to enter into another man's labours (John 4:38), but Paul avoided 'building on someone else's foundation.' This was Paul's own calling: he is not saying that this is what all Christians should do. He is well aware of differentiation of function in the service of God. Some plant and others water and they both work together with God. 1 Cor. 3:69

Some lay the foundation and others build. 1 Cor. 3:10ff He is simply saying that his own calling is to plant the seed or to lay the foundation. Others will work later, but Paul establishes new churches and this means going into areas where others have not been. He is to preach the gospel to those who have not heard. To go to those who have heard would be to renounce his calling from God.

Principle #18: Preaching must build up the body of Christ and cooperate with others engaged in the ministry of growth.

Everything Paul did was with the aim of preaching the Gospel of Jesus Christ. Other great missionary hearts that have followed in Paul's footsteps held the same objective. Raymond Lull, brave missionary to Islam, lived by this famous refrain: 'I have one passion it is He, it is He.' Charles Wesley sang, 'Thou, O Christ, art all I want, more than all in Thee I find.' It was said by Alexander Whyte of his long Saturday walks with Marcus Dods, 'Whatever we started off with in our conversations, we soon made across country, somehow, to Jesus of Nazareth.' Martin Luther said, 'We preach always him'. This may seem a limited and monotonous subject, likely to be soon exhausted, but we are never at the end of it.' So it was with Paul. He would travel anywhere to preach the Gospel of Jesus Christ.

Dr David Livingstone was cut out of the same mould as Paul. When Livingstone volunteered as a missionary with the London Missionary Society and they asked him where he wanted to go he replied, 'Anywhere, so long as it is forward.'

We are living in times of the Gospel closing round all known groups of people. The Gospel starts with the grace of God, is the centre of our ministry, brings glory to God, is empowered by God and is spread according to God's plan. Nothing is more important than working together to communicate the Gospel of Jesus Christ.

Principle #19: Preaching is working together to close around all who have not yet been evangelised.

God's only Son brought the good news. There is no calling more fulfilling nor with such eternal consequences than the work of ministry, in communicating the Gospel in a way that our contemporaries understand and which encourages them to respond.

One of the world's great business entrepreneurs is John Sculley, who was then the President of the Pepsi Cola Company. He masterminded the Pepsi Generation. Another great entrepreneur is Steve Jobs, the man who developed the Apple Computer and then the Macintosh Computer which revolutionised the computer world. John Sculley and Steve Jobs are friends and Steve Jobs wanted John Sculley to leave Pepsi and work for Apple.

Steve said to his friend, 'You're the best person I've met. I know you are perfect for Apple and Apple deserves the best.' But John Sculley replied, 'Steve, I'd love to be an adviser to you, to help you in any way, but I don't think I can come to Apple.' Steve Jobs hung his head in disappointment and after an uncomfortable pause issued a challenged that haunted John Sculley for days. He said to John, 'Do you want to spend the rest of your life selling sugared water or do you want a chance to change the world?' (*Odyssey*, John Sculley, Harper 87. p90)

Here is *Principle #20*: Preaching is the highest calling from God.

That is a question Jesus would ask of men and women whom He would challenge to follow him in the ministry of the Kingdom of God today: 'Do you want to spend the rest of your life selling sugared water or do you want a chance to change the world?' Because after the ministry of communicating the Gospel of Jesus Christ, everything: medicine, politics, law, business, sales, insurance, professional sport, public service, nuclear physics, computer programming. Everything is selling sugared water! Only the communicating the Gospel gives you the radical chance to change the world.

Preaching In The City

Today the greatest movement in the world is into the cities of every inhabited continent. One hundred years ago in 1900, only 8% of the people of the world lived in large cities. Most people lived in villages in rural areas. In spite of the growth of industries, 92% of people were still engaged in agriculture.

But two world wars, transportation and a growing population able to be sustained in a city, saw within one hundred years more than half the people on earth living in cities. Over three billion people now live in large cities. Urbanisation has been the greatest story of the twentieth century. We have a missionary gospel to spread into the cities of the world.

Yet many church denominational leaders still behave as if nothing has changed. They still organise the life of the church based upon state lines and a village parish system. The denominations have not learned how to use the media to penetrate the city and possess no strategy to penetrate the security of highrise apartment blocks. They give token support to developing multicultural congregations and have no policy for influencing the social, political and economic systems of our modern community. This is rank failure by the Christian Church in the Western World.

Yet the city is the most important factor impinging upon the future of the church. In the next ten years we will add another billion people to the planet and most will live in our cities. Christianity will be successful only if it learns to capture the cities of the world.

Nations are changed by people who capture the streets of the city. The ideology of globalisation is today being fought in the streets of large cities. The people of Manilla overthrew the Marcos regime from the streets; the people of Selma, Jackson and Washington marched behind Martin Luther King Jr; the people of India filled the streets of Calcutta behind Mahatma Gandhi; the people of Paris overran the Bastille; The people of Beijing crowded Tienamen Square. So on throughout history. You can change history by changing the minds of people in the streets of the cities.

Only after his death and resurrection did the people of Jerusalem realise that Jesus was the Messiah of God, an ideal King, a victorious conqueror, a humble hero and a suffering servant.

He had come not to bring political victory, but a reign of peace and righteousness with justice for the poor and humble. How they wished they had greeted him with more commitment! I have always been captured by a line in the musical Jesus Christ Superstar. The Palm Sunday crowd is singing 'Hosanna' and waving to Jesus and as Jesus passed by they called out 'Christ, you know I loved you. Did you see I waved?'

Many in the crowded city that day waved. But Jesus wanted devotion, not greetings, commitment of the heart, not waving of the hand. Even those who wept for him later that Holy Week were told not to weep for him but for themselves. Jesus did not want tears of sorrow, but the toil of discipleship of those who would follow him. The crowd needs to be confronted with the accurate picture of who Jesus is, if their waving is to be turned to commitment. The missionary Gospel has tough demands.

That is why in my ministry I have sought to enter the city at every available point through the secret accesses of radio, as people listen in their bath or bed, their car or campervan. Every day. Every week. You would think such a successful media program would be supported gladly by the Church, but our media programs have been vilified by NSW Synod of the Uniting Church in Australia because it is evangelical and firmly based on scripture and not one cent of support has ever been given.

Through television I seek to enter every city and town in our nation, into lounge rooms and kitchens, bedrooms and classrooms. Every week. Through our magazines I enter the waiting rooms of doctors, dentists and lawyers. In our books we enter the libraries and homes to sit upon shelves and beside beds. Through our videos we stay by the video machines in the schools and homes. We preach in eight languages every week to reach the major ethnic groups. Our Bible based sermons are heard by more Australians every week than any other, perhaps by more people than are in all the churches of our nation put together.

Through our 56 church worship services we conduct each week in our central church we challenge the people of our city by lifting high Jesus Christ and saying, 'Who is this?' I am never proud of the fact that across our land I am listened to by more people than any other preacher in our nation. That is not a matter for pride: Jesus has entered many cities on the back of a donkey! But even a donkey can be used to take the Master into the city! We spend ourselves to bring Christ to the city so that people will say, 'Who is this?' Then seek the answer.

Modern people in many of our cities accept Christianity, but they do not become members of the church. We have to convert believers into belongers! But some people who belong to the church are not really committed. We have to convert these belongers to believers! Jesus Christ does not ask for your admiration. He wants your commitment! Jesus does not ask for acknowledgment he wants your commitment. Do not say, 'Christ, you know I loved you. Did you see I waved?' Say instead, 'Jesus Christ, my Master, I'll take up my Cross and follow wherever you lead me.' And join the crowd that follow him. Jesus was a carpenter and today this church needs 'joiners'!

A wave changes nothing. Jesus wants to make disciples who will be committed to turning the world upside down. He wants our city confronted, changed, turned around, converted! That means you! Turn to him now! Stop waving, start following! Preachers have to learn to speak the language of the city. We have to listen to what the streets are saying and learn to communicate with people our message in the language they understand. Too often the church talks to itself in its own language and the people outside in the city do not understand. By this I do not mean the language of the gutter, but the language of the culture of the city. Preachers will get a shock if they print verbatim copies of what they say and get a cross section of society, including youth, to cross out whatever they do not understand. John Wesley did this with the girls who milked cows and so improved his ability to communicate.

Paul communicated the Gospel intelligently when he entered the great cities of the Mediterranean world in the first century. He spoke to the citizens of each city in their own culture.

At the time of Paul's visit, Athens was in the twilight of the Greek civilisation. She would never recover her glory. Athens has been continuously inhabited for 3,000 years, but it was in the centuries before the Roman Empire that Athens reached her height.

In the 5th century BC, the days of the marvellous buildings of Pericles, Athens became the mistress of the world and the mother of Democracy. Great writers like Aeschylus, Sophocles and Euripides, joined with historians like Herodotus and Thucydides and thinkers like Plato and Socrates. Their Classical Greek is acknowledged as the world's most perfect expression of human speech in all history.

Great art, sculpture and architecture flourished. The Parthenon, commenced in 447BC, even to this day, remains one of the world's most pleasing buildings. All about were other temples, theatres, the agora or marketplaces and the magnificent colonnades of the Stoa of Attulus. It is probable that Paul walked through these columns debating with the Epicurean and Stoic philosophers, as was typical of the teaching method of the time.

He certainly climbed nearby Mars Hill and spoke to the Areopagus Council. In great cities of the world we copy the architecture of Athens and many of our public buildings reflect those of Athens; we lecture on Greek philosophy and Classical Greek, unspoken for 2,000 years by any community, is still taught in some of our colleges and universities.

If you examine the sermon of Paul (Acts 17) to the Jews of Antioch in Pisidia, you would find that Paul starts with the history of the Jews in Egypt, covers their development as a nation, their expectation of the Messiah and points to the death and resurrection of Jesus and our need to repent and believe. Yet when Paul entered Athens his approach was totally different from that at Antioch in Pisidia. He appreciated their culture and spoke their language. He marched to the beat of their drum. He first spoke to Jews and Greeks who worshipped God. Paul commenced with those who would give him a favourable hearing. He joined the philosophers in their debates and with people who just passed by. In the time of Paul there were two schools of philosophy: the Epicureans and Stoics. They debated him. The Stoics' aim was to attain personal supremacy over all areas of life and to control human passions. The Epicureans' aim was pleasure, the happiness the mind finds in freedom from physical excesses. The Stoics and Epicureans walked through the Stoa of Attulus, arguing with each other, for the benefit of crowds of people who followed them to hear some word of insight. Paul was not afraid to talk about his beliefs in the context of other philosophies and faiths.

He indicated up front his own religious beliefs. He preached 'about Jesus and the resurrection.' As the philosophers debated Paul, 'some of them asked, 'What is this babbler trying to say?' The word for babbler is spermologos. It means a pickerup of scraps, a guttersparrow that picks up little bits of rubbish or seeds. They said Paul picked up bits of wisdom, scraps of thoughts from here and there. The philosophers despised him because he did not argue in the conventional form.
Paul acknowledged their religious attitudes. He was not flattering them, but was stating a fact about Athenian life, dominated as it was by so many beautiful temples to many gods. 'I see that in every way you Athenians are very religious.' He indicated the statues dedicated to gods. 'As I walked through your city and

looked at the places where you worship, I found an altar on which is written 'To an Unknown God.' That which you worship, then, even though you do not know it, is what I now proclaim to you.'

Several such altars have been discovered although the inscription is usually in the plural 'To the Unknown Gods'. Epimenides, who lived in Athens in the sixth century B.C., urged the building of such an altar so as to include any god not honoured with a Temple to avoid any calamity from a wrathful god. Paul said the god they did not know, was known to him as the Father of the Lord Jesus Christ. Paul started with what they knew.

Paul preached from a point of agreement. The city fathers nodded in agreement. Every city alderman likes to be told that he has a fine, respectable city. All of the Athenians would accept that God was the Lord of heaven and earth as the Stoics argued and that such a God did not live in the beautiful temples surrounding them, as the Epicureans argued. Paul went on, 'The God who made the world and everything in it is the Lord of heaven and earth and does not live in temples built by hands. And he is not served by human hands, as if he needed anything, because he himself gives all men life and breath and everything else.'

This pleased the Stoics. Paul said God created the world. That refuted the Epicureans who declared that the universe came by chance. Paul also agreed with Plato that God is a spirit. But then Paul went on with the devastating words 'From one man he made every nation of men, that they should inhabit the whole earth; and he determined the times set for them and the exact places where they should live. God did this so that men would seek him and perhaps reach out for him and find him, though he is not far from each one of us.'

He moved from local interests to the everlasting God. The Creator and everpresent provider for them all, demands from us righteous living and has fixed a day of judgement for us all, calling upon us to turn from our wicked ways. Paul is now at the crunch of the gospel but to show them how close God is to them he does not quote Old Testament poets. Greek city councillors are not going to listen to Hebrew poets.

When he spoke to Jews he quoted Hebrew poets, but when he spoke to Greek city aldermen he quoted Greek poets. 'For in him we live and move and have our being.' As some of your own poets have said, 'We are his offspring.'' He quotes two poets including Aratus who came from the same area of the Empire, as did Paul.

'Therefore since we are God's offspring, we should not think that the divine being is like gold or silver or stone an image made by man's design and skill). In the past God overlooked such ignorance, but now he commands all people everywhere to repent. For he has set a day when he will judge the world with justice by the man he has appointed. He has given proof of this to all men by raising him from the dead.' Resurrection! That shocked them.

That is the heart of the gospel: God made us, loves us, redeems us and will judge us by Jesus Christ, the same Jesus slain upon the Cross, but now raised from the dead. The Greeks had argued about resurrection. Aeschylus said when a man dies, his blood seeps into the ground and there is no resurrection of the body. They believed in the immortality of the soul, but not the resurrection of the body. Christianity is based upon resurrection, not immortality. God gives a new life and a new body, incorruptible and eternal in the heavens.

He found a typical response. Some scoffed, some wanted to hear more and some believed in Jesus Christ. It is ironic, that of all the famous philosophers and debaters in the Royal Stoa that day, only three names are known in history and they were the three believers in Jesus Christ: Among them is Paul, 'Dionysius, a member of the Areopagus, also a woman named Damaris and a number of others.'

Dionysius became the first bishop of Athens. Damaris became a Christian. Their names are remembered while the names of the philosophers are forgotten. For all their wisdom the Greeks had not found God. Paul's teaching survived while the philosophers were picking up crumbs of human wisdom. We all will be judged by Christ. We all can be saved through faith.

That is why he was successful. Paul taught us to be relevant to our own city's culture and to speak to it the Gospel. We are all influenced by our culture. That cultural influence impacts even our Christian faith unknown to most of us. Some cultural influences today are setting the tone for our community values and political policies.

We are dominated more by economic policies than anything else. For the last two decades the defining principle in our culture has been that we improve our quality of life by improving our standard of living. Our focus has been on material benefit and expecting from governments policies that would deliver us a better standard of life. Governments hold as a top priority improvement of economic standards. Yet people say their top priorities are not prosperity but quality of family life, security of employment and personal care when in ill health. Culture tells us there is an economic solution to our problems. Experience tells us the supposed solution is actually the problem. Some cultural influences in the Church today are more insidious.

I listen carefully to church leaders. Some refer to cultural mores being essential Christianity rather than to Biblical mores. Recently I heard two leaders speaking not of Christianity but spirituality. That is a cultural expression that has become politically correct. They were promoting spirituality not Christianity, Jesus not the church. These church leaders are speaking as if we can divide spirituality from Christianity and Jesus from the church. They obviously have not thought through their statements.

Jesus did not come to improve the quality of our spirituality. This is new age philosophy. God was not incarnate among us to improve our spirituality, but to save us from our sins. He incorporates us into his body, the Church. You cannot have him without his body the Church and spirituality, without Christianity, is an empty shell.

I have heard one deriding those who stress the uniqueness of our faith saying we should accept the beliefs of all people as being equally valid. This is pluralism. But pluralism is the enemy of Christianity. It denies the words of Jesus John 14:6 'I am the way and the truth and the life. No one comes to the Father except through me.' It denies the truth of the Apostles who said, 'Salvation is found in no one else, for there is no other name under heaven given to men by which we must be saved.' It denies the significance of the Cross and his shed blood for the sins of the world. It denies the authority of Scripture.

All religions are not equal. We do not all worship the same God and we are all not heading for the same destination. You cannot be a Christian and a pluralist at the same time. But this is a culturally accepted concept. These viewpoints are opposed to traditional Christian faith, but are exposed by churches accepting liberal theology.

I heard another church leader say the church needs to be inclusive of all people and their behaviour. One person said we have to accept, within church leadership, people regardless of their culture, behaviour, whether they were gay or straight, immoral or people with HIVAids. Everyone agrees that such people are welcome in the church where they can hear Biblical teaching and the Gospel that can change lives, but we cannot welcome into church leadership such people without any changes in their behaviour. The whole Biblical concept of being born again, of being saved from sin and of living a life of holiness, was ignored.

I have heard our culture is one of whatever anyone thinks or feels is valid for that person, regardless of the Body of Christ as a community of faith. Their philosophy of individualism denies the discipline of the community and promotes as true whatever an individual may think or feel.

One church leader said we must accept the lifestories of people as basic for the way our church is ordered. What was important was their experience should be heard and become the basis of our church order. But the church's order and faith is under the authority, not of people's feelings and experience, but of Scripture. It is not surprising to learn that the church leader espousing these views, was herself a lesbian living in an immoral relationship!

There is a need today for Christians to stress Christianity as our key commitment not spirituality. We need to stress the uniqueness of our faith rather than the pluralism of others' beliefs. We need to stress our openness to all other people without the acceptance of their standards of behaviour. We need to stress the sense of the Church as a community rather than the priority of individualism. We need to stress the authority of Scripture rather than the authority of a lifestory.

We come from distinctive cultural backgrounds and we must learn the difference between what stems from our cultural heritage and what is essential to our faith. What is essential will abide and what is cultural may change. You may have grown up at a time when it was said you could not be saved unless you abstained from using makeup, avoided picture theatres, ballroom dancing and billiards! Other people add their own cultural ideas.

But there is a difference between faith and culture. We need to learn that lesson. We Christianise our culture. We take our behaviour patterns and baptise them, saying, 'That is Christian.' But there is a difference between what is essential to the faith and what is simply cultural.

When Paul entered the great cities of the Mediterranean world in the first century, he spoke to the citizens of each city, understanding their culture. The early church faced the issue constantly as the Jewish culture tried to contaminate the essence of Christianity. They insisted Jewish cultural traditions had to be observed by Christians. This included having all baby boys circumcised, not eating shellfish and pork and having all food kosher killed. When Christianity spread into the areas we today call Turkey, Greece and Rome it faced a new set of cultural demands.

This included the acceptance of slavery, Emperor worship and oaths of loyalty to the state. Paul had clarity of vision when it came to seeing what was essentially Christian and what was merely a reflection of the culture of the times. We need Paul's clarity of vision today.

How wise of Paul, to adapt his message to the city in which he was speaking, to direct his address to the mindset and philosophy of his hearers, to scratch them where they were itching. How much wiser is he than some contemporary church leaders! He refused to dilute the gospel of Jesus Christ to the cultural traditions and standards of his day. He did not give away the essence of the Christian faith in the hope that compromise and change would increase their spirituality. Instead Paul stressed Jesus and the resurrection – the missionary gospel.

We must hold to the cohesion of Christian culture rather than dilute the faith with the passing trends of modern culture. We understand our culture and to speak to it. Like the Athenians, some will scoff at us; some will want to hear us some more; and some will believe. That's the response in the volatile city. But we have communicated the missionary Gospel to the city.

I have never felt alone in the streets of the city. Jesus Christ has been there before me and he has made the city my home. He loves the city. He wept for the city. The missionary gospel to the city is of Jesus and his resurrection. I must take that message to the people of the city.

The Methodology Of Preaching

People often ask me to explain how I prepare a sermon. I briefly outline the process.

1. I start two years before I actually preach a series of sermons by defining what I will seek to do, by gathering some key resources, by indicating what my Bible resources will be. I then start reading through the Biblical text, word by word, a little every morning, making notes on the background as I go. With major books of the Bible, I read one or two of the best commentaries, making notes of key insights.

2. One year before I preach a series of sermons I break the passages down into small portions - one a week for fortyeight weeks. These pericopes are usually the length of a single thought or paragraph. I write the theme of that passage, consider a title that fits then print a leaflet with each week of the coming year, the theme, the title of the sermon, the Bible reference and an over all title for the series and a couple of paragraphs on why this is relevant to us today.

3. The printed brochure is then posted to several thousand people indicating time, place and date of each sermon. Hundreds of people use this as a guide for their weekly Bible study prior to my preaching. We also run weekly groups where each passage is studied. We have some groups, which meet after the sermon is preached, which then discuss any issues raised. These groups give me good feedback or raise important questions. So the congregation is involved.

4. After some sermons, I stand and answer immediate questions from the audience.

5. Two weeks before preaching a sermon, I start out typing it, adding in bits and pieces that have occurred during the months previously. Often the computer has a dozen or more thoughts that have been placed under the title months earlier.

6. In one sentence I write what I believe this sermon should achieve. Everything subsequently must be within the limits of that core purpose. I then write the conclusion, then the major argument. I add illustrations, always taken for the news of the current week. Finally I write the introduction.

7. I always type my own manuscripts. 8 pages takes 28 minutes to preach - the time allocated by the television and radio programs! My typed manuscripts may be 35 or more pages, but I can use only 8. So, delete, delete, delete. This takes longer than anything else. If a deleted idea or illustration was good or could be used in future I file it under the appropriate sermon to be prepared later. Soon only 8 pages are left. These are printed, corrected, reprinted and sent to the Internet. My sermons are on the Internet before I preach them. Over 96,000 people

access them every week. I include in each my sources to which I am indebted and my references used. A print copy is made for everyone coming into the congregation. Many people for whom English is a second or third language follow the text as I preach it. Others mark relevant or meaningful passages.

8. Significant points of interest to a wider audience are caught up in a press release and sent to newspaper editors and radio and TV stations. Local papers particularly reprint these press releases.

9. Over the next few weeks counsellors will be busy responding to the telephones from people who hear the sermon via media. Office girls handle written queries and send out thousands of printed copies.

10. This whole process is repeated for each of the different regular services in which I preach. The printed sermon of this week - will be used with a fresh introduction and illustrations one year from now in one of my lunchtime services. Suitable groups of sermons will be turned into manuscripts for a book.

I spend a lot of time, at least twenty hours, preparing each sermon, but I get lots of miles out of each one. It may be thought that forty years of preaching the gospel limits a person, but I wrote in my diary how I felt about that at the end of 1997:

'I am enjoying preaching the gospel now more than ever and in so doing I am trying to take the 7pm congregation from a group of people who had been used to socially orientated topical sermons on the issues of the moment to a deeper appreciation of the eternal issues of scripture. For 18 months I preached on Romans, dividing the Epistle into small groups of verses but maintaining their place in the overall outline. Most of these sermons in fact all of these sermons were doctrinal with our evangelical cutting edge.

During 1998 I have prepared an outline of 46 doctrinal sermons on the Holy Trinity. I will follow the outline of the Nicean Creed. It is a good discipline to concentrate on the great doctrines of the faith and at the same time remain contemporary and relevant. I am deliberately raising difficult intellectual issues and trying to give students a handle on their faith. At the same time I am broadcasting them to a large secular audience and seeking to interpret difficult doctrine to simple and often antagonistic minds. The most part of the radio audience is agnostic but prepared to listen to something so long as it is interesting, relevant and entertaining! Who said preaching wasn't a challenge?'

More Miles Out Of Each Sermon

A preacher not only writes his or her sermons, but many other things as well. Sometimes I thought of describing myself as a writer. I never studied journalism but from the age of 18, I started to write editorials, essays, booklets, newspaper columns, books, film scripts, short stories without number. It all started in an unusual way.

LEAVING A LEGACY

My first years in the slum churches saw a weekly production of 'Focus', a church newsletter which contained an editorial designed to make people think. My university essays, papers and dissertations probably influenced those editorials greatly. I also wrote a 'newsy' column about people. I soon discovered people love to read about people. Today those papers, bound into years, occupy about a metre of shelf space.

But the real influence upon my life as a writer began a day or two after my accidental start as a country parson in the country town of Ararat, Victoria, after we were prevented from sailing to USA to take up my position at the Christian Theological Seminary in Indianapolis.

A day or two after I arrived a journalist from the *Ararat Advertiser* called to see me. News was always hard to find in a small country town and he had to work hard to find interesting stories. Often the most interesting thing that would happen in a country town would be in the courts. He would listen for a phrase from Mr Alan Vanstan, the local magistrate who would fine a young man for speeding around the community. He would make a comment such as 'There is too much speeding by reckless drivers in our community these days. This is the second case I have had this week.'

Sitting in the court the young journalist, Chris Fisher by name, would write up a story which would headline in the next day's paper, 'Epidemic of speeding, says Magistrate.' The front page would be full of interviews with people about the recklessness of young drivers speeding in Ararat streets.

The fact was, nothing much happened in Ararat and so a journalist had to work mighty hard to beat up a story. Chris Fisher was about 23 years of age, with a mop of blonde hair, big frame and an engaging smile.

He was sitting in my study wanting to know why I had come to Ararat. I explained to him that with the assassination of President Kennedy, the Australian U.S. Consulate had gone into a terrorist alert and on that terrible day documents were accidentally lost, including my visas. This meant my wife and I missed our ship, which sailed to the United States a couple of days later, with all of our luggage on board but without our stamped passports and visas. I had borrowed a car from my stepfather who ran, among other things, a car wrecking business and he had a blue Mark 8 Jaguar, which he had put together from pieces from wrecked Jaguars. At least that was a temporary vehicle for us. Chris took the photograph of Beverley and I and our nineteenmonthold daughter, Jenny and went on his way.

I was amazed to see on the following day that we had made the front page and the second page and the third page. That story had run out into a whole series of articles under the heading 'Missed Boat to U.S.A. 'Pastor for Ararat'. I suddenly discovered I was described as, 'Brilliant Church of Christ minister, Pastor

Gordon K Moyes, BA, has taken up an appointment in Ararat for twelve months before starting four years theological studies in America, which is planned to lead towards a Doctorate.

'An authority on the decline of churches in Melbourne's inner suburbs, Mr Moyes is only in Ararat because arrangements for his U.S. trip were not completed in time for the American university year.'

On and on the story ran. Chris developed a great theory on my expertise in pastoring to the slums and then wrote a paragraph on my postgraduate studies on the scholarship at the University of Indiana in Indianapolis and added to my dreams and plans.

There was then a major feature on the blue Jaguar with, 'It is not every Pastor who has a father with a Jaguar works.' The old car wreckers yard had suddenly been transformed into a 'Jaguar works'.

We were overwhelmed with embarrassment with the fulsomeness of the articles. While most of the facts were true they had been expressed in a way which greatly exaggerated their significance. I suddenly realised the power of the press, as people called to see us and rang up and sent invitations to speak at functions.

The power of the press, even in a country town, was enormous, as I soon discovered. So I went back and closely examined his style. I then bought the leading Melbourne papers and closely examined their style of writing. I was used to slowly working into a subject, explaining why I wanted to talk about this matter, giving reasons for it and background and then logically working up to a conclusion.

I discovered that journalists started with the conclusion. Their sentences were short, unlike those of a speaker. I counted the words in every sentence and counted the sentences in every paragraph, noted the number of words in a heading and in a subheading. I realised that stories put the facts in the first paragraph and interpretation later and that often the last three inches of a story would be simply cut off because there was not enough column space available.

Chris Fisher had so much success with his first story that he was around the second day to get a follow up story. Things were slow in Ararat and he wanted a few more ideas.

Ideas were something that I had in abundance. I gave him a few ideas and that started a romance with the press which has never finished. Soon two and three articles in every single issue of the *Ararat Advertiser* were about our work, achievements and ideas. Within a matter of weeks thousands of people were reading what we were doing. I studied closely the journalist's style, had lunch with a major Melbourne editor and asked him to teach me quickly what he wanted. He gave me a dozen rules for writing for newspapers and I wrote them down at the lunch table on a paper serviette.

I then submitted articles to him and discovered that they were being printed in Melbourne papers completely unedited. That Melbourne editor eventually published 20,000 column inches of articles without ever editing one aspect of those columns.

I was soon asked to write special columns for Easter and then Mothers Day and Christmas. I wrote those and soon they were picked up by other local papers. Before long the columns were being syndicated through more than a dozen papers. Without meaning to I had started on a career in journalism. Those newspaper columns became a weekly feature for the next twenty years of my life and when Chris eventually became a newspaper proprietor himself, owning a stable of newspapers, my writings were featured in columns, which he syndicated across his own network.

But in the church other things needed to be written. Every week I had a major article I wrote for a church paper, youth studies had to be written, studies for camps and studies for adult Bible study groups.

Soon the number of studies began to mount up, all duplicated and used widely by other groups and churches. I was then asked to write a booklet explaining the doctrines of the Christian faith and then a booklet on the meaning of church membership. Soon that booklet was spread throughout Australia and all adults coming into membership of Churches of Christ completed their membership studies with the same booklets.

Then the Joint Board of Christian Education of the Presbyterian, Methodist, Congregationalist and Churches of Christ asked me to write Sunday School lesson material and dozens of lessons for teenagers and young adults were written and in thousands of Sunday Schools across Australia those lessons were taught by faithful teachers.

Perhaps the biggest surprise came when I was aged 25. After 50 years of writing a continuous column in The Australian Christian Randall T. Pitman, one of Australia's greatest classical scholars, retired and the editor asked me to take up the column in his place. So I wrote each week a scholarly article on a significant New Testament Greek word and its theological insight. I wrote on the one hundred most significant New Testament words and their theological meanings. It has been a thrill to find even to this day, those columns filed among ministers' resources throughout Australia and New Zealand.

I then started writing a column each week for a leading church magazine on Christian doctrines and on one occasion the same column was being printed among Methodist, Presbyterian, Congregational and Churches of Christ papers with the same articles being printed within all four churches. I then wrote a series of columns for several years on insights found in the New Testament through new translations. Over the next years 3, 000 columns for church magazines came from the typewriter.

At the same time I was continuing my studies in pastoral and clinical education and in counselling people. I realised how many people in my work at the Aradale Mental Hospital were suffering from depression, schizophrenia, anxiety and stress. I took some of the psychological knowledge I had gained from my own studies, added it to case studies I was finding in counselling in the mental hospital and in my own study and added to that the insights from the Scriptures.

Soon a series of booklets began to be printed covering such issues as *How to Overcome Fear, The Answer to Anxiety, How to Love, How to Use Suffering, Mastering Failure, Making The Most of Growing Old, How to Overcome Frustration* and so on. Those booklets were used by many groups of people suffering from depression and the booklet *Defeating Depression* was printed more than 100,000 times. Mr Albert Graham of Ballarat printed all of these booklets and Mr Tom Frazer was the untiring distributor and salesman.

I then found numbers of people needed books to guide them in family life and so books like *Equipped For Marriage, How To Find Lasting Friendship and In Time of Death* began to appear. Then a series of small books on Christian doctrinal matters such as *The Existence of God, How Were We Created?, What Happens to Me When I Die?, How to Overcome Sin and How to Grow From Doubt To Faith.* The one In *Time of Death* has been reprinted scores of times and hundreds of thousands of copies have been distributed by Funeral companies to grieving families.

These booklets received widespread sales across Australia and in turn created demand for more books. My first book on church growth, *How To Grow An Australian Church,* is still a best seller and although it is now more than thirty years since I first wrote it, it sells several thousand copies every year and has become a basic book for church development, found in every church library. I then wrote in the field of evangelism and contributed two chapters to books produced by Billy Graham on *The Calling of The Evangelist* and *The Work of The Evangelist.* Those books have been studied and used all over the world and tens of thousands of copies have been sold, thanks to the influence of Billy Graham's name. I then wrote a series of books on motivation. The first, *The Secret of Confident Living* was used by Norman Vincent Peale on his television program in America when he stated, 'This book has the thoughts, substance and motivational quality to make it a truly indispensable aid to successful living.' His reading of that book commenced a lifelong friendship with that great American and this book, with his help, soon sold out.

Other books such as *Be A Winner* were bought by businessmen, salesmen and insurance executives. The books *Twelve Steps to Serenity* and *Confident in Time of Trouble* brought letters from people all across Australia and overseas who have been helped in their time of need.

Good books on youth leadership are always hard to find and so very quickly followed two books on youth leadership. Then came chapters in other people's books.

At the same time I was writing scripts for radio spots of 30 seconds and 60 seconds length on Christian matters. Four and a half thousand radio scripts were written and broadcast over the last thirty years.

Then came three books to accompany a series of films I made. *Discovering Jesus* has had a phenomenal use in many countries of the world. Today that book is used by more than 4,000 secondary schools in Australia as a textbook and by churches as an adult study book. It was followed by *Discovering Paul* and *Discovering The Young Church,* which was my 36th book. These were printed in Chinese in China and over a million copies have been purchased. Chinese Christians have used these books widely and I was thrilled to visit Chinese Universities and to hear from students on how much my books were valued by them. Who knows what the end of this influence for Christ will be.

Beyond this has been my interest in films and the scripts of thirtyeight documentary films were written both on religious and secular subjects. I found people loved listening to stories, so I wrote and broadcast over 400 short stories. Many of these were published and others recorded as volumes of cassettes. Every week, without fail, someone tells me they love hearing my stories.

Many of my films are now on DVD and are sold worldwide. Every week I had written editorials in *The Christian Sentinel* and subsequently *Mission Talk.* I have about 2, 500 editorials filed.

In 1979 I took over the editing and writing of articles in *Impact* a monthly magazine. Within three years we had 60, 000 readers each month. Then another, smaller magazine *Frontlines,* which features my editorials. In India, a Christian monthly magazine similar to *Reader's Digest* reprints each month one of my 3000 word articles, which are read by very large numbers of people. In 2003, Beverley and I purchased a magazine, *Marriage Works,* designed to help young people improve their marriage and family life. This bimonthly has a growing subscriber base and I write an article in each edition.

But we are now living in the Internet era. So apart from having 3000 manuscripts of sermons available, I also have about 3000 management talks, conference addresses and papers on strategic planning on the world wide web. About 100, 000 hits each week are scored on these sites from all over the world.

Each week we not only have printed copies containing my editorials, but Internet based Wesley Family News going to thousands of members, staff and donors. Likewise I edit and write for several thousand members and supporters of the Christian Democratic Party's the 'CDP e.mag,' which contains the manuscript of my 'Cross Bench Comments' in a weekly political editorial that I also broadcast. Enquiries and appreciation flow in from all parts of the globe, but I am particularly thrilled with local people who are blessed through the Internet. One reader wrote:

'Dear Gordon, I just wanted to say thank you for your esermons. They are always very interesting and encouraging, mainly because of your positive attitude which you spoke about in your last sermon. Sermons at my church seem to have the attitude that whatever you are doing, you are not doing well enough. This has a very discouraging effect on me.

You have been an encouragement to me for years. You are a strong uncompromising Christian who is 'in the world' (in very big ways including chairman of the inquiry into health) but most ardently 'not of the world'. All this from the Uniting Church too! (Which I left as a young adult because of what I perceived as a lack of adherence to biblical teaching).

God has blessed you and because of your willingness to serve, we have also been blessed, Thank you again. C.W.'

And another:

'Gordon, I'm deeply touched by your kindness and generosity you have consistently demonstrated towards me. The benefit I find is that you genuinely serve others, comfort the weary and actively motivate me to lead in your example.

I share also the appreciation that 'I have always felt most welcomed when attending Wesley Mission lunchtime services in the city' no matter of what diversity or background parishioners come from, in meeting their individual need.

I also find the Email sermon facility to also achieve great rewards in delivering a concise sermon to people who are unable to attend church service for whatever reason.
I have found this outreach to be most practical and fruitful in assisting to deliver God's word in other ways. This is another prime example of an effective strategy by Wesley Mission reaching modern community, which is not limited by geographic boundaries in utilising today's technology.

Ultimately we are seeing God's hand at work in ministry.

Again please accept my appreciation of the fellowship of your team of ministry staff and you provide at Wesley Mission. Regards, George Gohari, Superannuation Administrator, Sydney Water Corporation.'

And another:

'Gordon, I noticed your name in one of the Prime Minister's press releases where he spoke at the opening of the Alan Walker Village at which you also spoke. This led me to do an Internet search which found the Wesley Mission where I ended up reading some of your sermons. I found the sermon, 'DO ALL PATHS LEAD TO GOD? Who He Really Is' very interesting.

I've been somewhat disillusioned by the 'Church' in Australia mainly due to the publicity given to some of the modern approaches the Uniting church is adopting to homosexuality and popular left wing views that I consider are undermining the traditional values of our society. So I was pleased to see your comments regarding these matters. And I found the points you made regarding other religions and the relativism that is prevalent nowadays to be reassuring and topical. I was also pleased to see your involvement in the campaign to protect marriage. By the way, I first met you back when you were the Minister at the Cheltenham Church of Christ many years ago! Anyway, I've put my name down to receive your future sermons via email, so I look forward to receiving those. Regards, David Looke, MicroWay Pty Ltd, Australia's Major Distributor of Programming Tools.'

Over all this I have written the scripts for more than two thousand television programs and on my shelf measuring more than 15 feet in length are the typed manuscripts of about five thousand sermons. These are always typed by myself, not by a typist.

Looking back, then, over my career as a writer I realised the old typewriter which had served me faithfully gave way to a new manual typewriter, which gave way then to a newer and more efficient typewriter, which in turn gave way to a series of electric typewriters and then to an IBM golf ball and then to Olivetti electronic typewriters and eventually to my beloved Olivetti topof therange hard disk word processor, then Compaq computers and laptops.. I have always enjoyed sitting down at the keyboard and it has certainly taught the elements of spelling, punctuation and grammar to a man who had trouble with all of these at school and University.

A visiting Professor from Milligan College, USA, Dr Richard G Phillips, was doing some lecturing and research here in Australia when he came upon my book *Discovering Jesus*. He took that back to the States with him and set it as a textbook for students in his class. He gathered other books that I had written and then on behalf of the College wrote and asked me if I would come to lecture the students. I accepted the invitation and then was greatly honoured when I discovered that he had taken a series of my books and submitted them to the Academic Committee of the University and that they had approved his recommendation. So it was, I spoke at the Milligan College Graduation.

Long rows of students in their academic gowns and mortarboards came up onto the platform to receive their degrees from the Chancellor and the President of

Milligan College and to shake my hand as their visiting graduation speaker. At the end of the long line of graduates, I in turn stood before the Chancellor and the President. The years of writing were being recognised and a new doctoral hood was placed on my shoulders as the University granted me a Doctorate of Letters for my written work.

This is one of the rarest and oldest of graduate degrees and recognises proficiency and experience in work that has been published widely.

Forty years ago on a hot summer's day in the country parsonage at Ararat, Chris Fisher called from the *Ararat Advertiser* and introduced me to the world of journalism and writing. I had missed the boat to USA and had never gotten round to studying there for that doctorate. But later that was conferred on me. 'God works in mysterious ways his wonders to perform.' Communicating the gospel is done primarily through preaching, but writing the message can communicate to even more people.

Chapter Four

CHURCH LEADER

The process of becoming Superintendent to the Central Methodist Mission in Sydney was a very protracted and onerous one. I discovered I had to be patient. There was much waiting in this game.

During 1977 I had been to the Central Methodist Mission in Sydney on a number of occasions, at the request of the then Superintendent, Rev. Dr Alan Walker. He asked me to address about 100 ministers during January 1977 at a conference held at Vision Valley. I was then back to speak at the Mission Anniversary in May 1977. That was a significant occasion because Alan Walker had indicated to the congregation that after 19 years of ministry, he was planning to retire at the end of that year. A new Superintendent would have to be appointed.

The process of appointing a new Superintendent has occurred at the Mission only every 20 years or so. There were not many who really knew how the process worked. To make matters worse, Rev. Dr Alan Walker was retiring at the time when the then Methodist Church moved out of existence and became part of the new Uniting Church in Australia (a union of the Presbyterian, Methodist and Congregational churches). This involved a whole lot of new regulations and new processes.

The process went something like this: a Settlements Committee was established by the Mission to find a new leader. I understand that over a period of months they listed the names of some 45 people including some in overseas countries who could be suitable. Those people had their credentials closely examined. At the end of 45 possible candidates for the position, one, an outstanding Methodist minister in South Africa was the leading candidate. Others had heard of my ministry in Melbourne and I had recently been heard by all the members of the Settlements Committee when I preached on four occasions during the Mission's May Anniversary. Consequently seven of them came to Cheltenham one Sunday to observe what was happening. They tried to mix unobtrusively among members of the five congregations that I was addressing that day. They then had lunch in our Manse and spent about three hours in discussion with Beverley and myself.

Then there were other meetings held back in the Mission. I am not sure how many were held but they were times of apparent anxiety. The leading candidate from South Africa and I were ultimately the only two candidates to be voted upon and the arguments in favour of one or the other ran hot. The ballots were almost equal. Then came the final ballots and I received the majority vote. One member of the Settlements Committee telegrammed me: 'Vote close. Mission hopelessly divided. Strongly advise you to decline.' He was one apparently supporting me and he wanted me to avoid a hopeless situation.

Just because the Officers and the Board of Wesley Mission had voted in favour of me, it did not mean that I would receive the invitation. The candidates again had to be discussed and their recommendation of myself had to be agreed to first of all by the Mission Council, a larger body of about 80 people and then at a Parish meeting (a much larger gathering of all of the members including many hundreds of people). My understanding is that as each meeting went by I received more affirmation from those attending and consequently the decision was made that I should be invited to be the next Superintendent. However, because the Central Methodist Mission was the most obvious part of the new Uniting Church in Australia anywhere in the nation and because it was the largest parish of the Uniting Church in the nation, there were a number of other complications as a large number of groups and individuals felt they should have a say on the successor to Australia's most visible minister.

The Pastoral Relations Committee of the Presbytery of Sydney discussed the matter at great length. Because I was a minister from another denomination and also from Melbourne (that most unlikely of places for a successful minister), the debate then had to be referred on to other councils of the Church. The congregations of Wesley Mission, meanwhile, were anxious that I should be invited and reply. The Pastoral Relations Committee of Presbytery referred the matter to a full Presbytery meeting where for some hours the position of the successor to Alan Walker was discussed. They agreed that I should be invited. That then raised the question of whether my credentials were acceptable to the Uniting Church. Consequently the matter was passed over to the Synod Ministerial Education Committee to examine the matter in detail.

The irony was that for more than 20 years I had been doing courses and equipping myself as a Churches of Christ Minister, to be the most effective Minister that I could be. I had never once dreamed of working within the Uniting Church and certainly never becoming the Superintendent of the then famous Central Methodist Mission. But all of the courses and programs that I had taken were equipping me to take the place of Alan Walker and some of the courses I had undertaken were in the Uniting Church's Theological College.

I had been properly trained at a Theological College and graduated with honours in every subject. I had subsequently completed a university degree and graduated. I had undertaken some post-graduate study for the London University Bachelor of Divinity. But apart from this, I had undertaken many additional courses. It had been my habit to undertake at least one major study program every year over a period of some 20 years. Some of these were in the field of psychology and counselling and others were in the field of theology. I had sat in various schools of theology, including the prestigious Ormond School of Theology at Melbourne University, under such visiting scholars as Professor Alan Richardson of Great Britain, Dr Hans Kung, the distinguished Roman Catholic scholar from Switzerland, Professor James S. Stewart from Edinburgh, Professor Edward Schweitzer from Switzerland, Dr Leon Morris, Dr Colin Williams, Dr Philip Potter (leading Methodists), Rev. John R.W. Stott, Dr Edwin Robinson, Bishop Stephen Neill (leading Anglicans) and Dr Koysume Koyama, of Japan.

I had also completed other programs such as with the Church of England Chaplaincy Department in the Royal Melbourne Hospital in clinical pastoral education. I had completed a sensitivity training program with the Victorian Council of Churches, Christian Education Department; a professional counselling course at the Cairnmiller Institute and a two-year program on the rehabilitation of alcoholics and drug addicts with the Victorian Department of Mental Health. In the two years prior to my call to Sydney, I had undertaken a course in Transactional Analysis and Gestalt Therapy. (two psychological methodologies supported by internationally trained experts to help people confront themselves, take control of their lives and to make the changes required)

What had given me a great deal of satisfaction however, was being part of a group of ministers and theological lecturers around the world known collectively as 'a panel of scholars' who prepared, every four years, papers for study and discussion at the World Convention of Churches of Christ. I also worked with the Churches of Christ Christian Union Department studying the Proposed Basis Of Union of the Uniting Church in Australia and how it would impact upon local congregations. It was our desire to see Churches of Christ become part of the Uniting Church, of which we were then official observers.

As an author, I had, on behalf of the Federal Conference of Churches of Christ in Australia, written A Guide To Church Membership, which was a six- week training course for adults in church membership, used in churches throughout the nation. Tens of thousands of people undertook this course. I had also written many lessons published by the Joint Board of Christian Education for the member churches of the Uniting Church. Methodist, Presbyterian and Congregational ministers and Sunday school teachers had used my lessons with young people. I had published two books, one of which had sold at that stage 12,000 copies and a further 120,000 copies had been purchased of a series of 20 booklets on 'Christian Living' that I had written. Every fortnight for eight years I had written a scholarly article in a national magazine on some 200 New Testament Greek words, their doctrinal and theological background and their implications for Christians today.

CHURCH LEADER

As a young minister I had always been heavily committed to communicating the good news to young people. For many years at Cheltenham I had spoken every week to more than one thousand teenagers in youth gatherings. These weekly presentations meant I had a lot of experience in communicating with youth. As an evangelist I had conducted crusades for groups of churches in every state of Australia. As a pastor I had been ministering for the twelve years previously in what had grown to be one of the largest congregations in Australia. As a person interested in the Uniting Church in Australia, I had with the Department of Christian Union explained to Churches of Christ who were interested in what was happening with the proposed Uniting Church in Australia. This had led to a number of Methodist, Presbyterian and Congregational churches inviting me to address their congregations on some of the confusing aspects of the proposed union. I knew the Uniting Church regulations better than most ministers who would enter the Uniting Church.

I had also had the privileged position in Melbourne of being well-known because of nightly appearances on television. I had made more than one thousand television presentations on GTV on the Nine Network and my television experience went back to 1965 when I also started radio. Hence my experience as a minister suitable for the Central Methodist Mission in Sydney was considerable and beyond that of any of the other ministers currently working in the Methodist, Presbyterian or Congregational churches in Australia. There was one other desirable feature; I was securely married with four young children to a wife who was extraordinarily competent and able and both of us were still in our mid thirties. No other candidate matched the credentials.

Let me assure you that did not convince the Synod Ministerial Education Committee. They required me to come to Sydney and spend a whole day in theological debate and discussion. It was an enjoyable experience. They spent most of the day asking questions about the issue of adult baptism by immersion. This was not only a practice from the New Testament days which I understood and repeated, it was also an area where everything that I believed and practiced had been substantiated and authoratively supported by theologians from within the traditions that made up the new Uniting Church. As a result the Synod Ministerial Education Committee recommended me then to the Synod Settlement Committee. The Synod Settlement Committee then spent much time in discussion and then finally made a recommendation to the Council of the Synod of the Uniting Church in New South Wales. That Council met in an all day conference at Wesley College at the University of Sydney. I was obliged to attend and stood outside the meeting waiting for the call to be examined by members of the Council of Synod. I was given a time and duly made my appearance on time and ready. The Council of Synod discussed important business, discussed me and the position at great length and left me waiting outside alone for more than three hours, a demonstration of a lack of grace and courtesy. Eventually I was invited in and the position was confirmed, but I was learning patience.

There was one requirement, that I should attend the United Faculty of Theology in Melbourne and undertake some further studies in church sacraments and in the new Uniting Church polity. I did not mind that at all. I would be meeting with my friend Professor Norman Young under whom I had taken studies previously and in studying the regulations and practice of the new Uniting Church I was merely studying what I had already been lecturing to Methodist, Presbyterian and Congregational churches in Melbourne. I spent a year with young students doing this required course, although they all thought the requirement stupid. Many of them asked me to help them in their student studies and in their understanding of the issues. The lecturer was quite keen to have my understanding on the issues of Bishops and the Concordat with South India, two proposals that were rejected.

Shortly afterwards I was asked to meet one of the staff leaders of the New South Wales Synod. This meant another trip from Melbourne to Sydney. The time was set and I duly came to the Mission Settlement building in Castlereagh Street where his office was situated. These were buildings previously built by the Central Methodist Mission. There was a long history of more than a hundred years of conflict between the Methodist Conference and its huge, cantankerous and successful child, the Central Methodist Mission. Now the Uniting Church in Australia had taken over the former Methodist offices and it was anxious to show the newly appointed Superintendent of the newly named Wesley Central Mission who was boss. Once more I sat outside the office of this church leader. He was a very committed and careful man. He duly worked through mountains of paper work. I sat outside his office waiting for an hour. His secretary bought me a cup of tea and apologised for the waiting, saying he was extremely busy. I waited another hour. Because I was sitting waiting in the passage, which leads in and out of his office, I observed that no one came or went. He was busy with papers and wanted me just to wait because of his busyness. Again a lack of grace and courtesy I had never experienced in the world of academia or commerce.

I began to realise something I had never before experienced: that keeping people waiting is actually a power game. Keeping other people waiting is a means of indicating who has got the power. I then remember that whenever I had rung any of these church bureaucrats I was always kept waiting before they answered the phone. Some poor secretary would keep coming on the line apologising while I was just kept waiting.

Waiting was a power game and one which I have never joined. It is my habit to answer the phone as quickly as possible and if there is someone in the foyer waiting to see me, I will go and welcome them personally to my office or else if I do have someone there and the new comer has come without an appointment, I go and explain the situation, ensure that they have some refreshment and be as quick as I can.

There was one other aspect to this matter of waiting. During this period of time throughout 1977 and 1978 before I commenced in Sydney, the Board of Mission invited me to lecture all the other Uniting Church ministers on the issue of church growth. I had conducted church growth seminars in every state of Australia to over 15,000 church leaders. Now I was to speak to hundreds of ministers and church leaders in St. Stephens Macquarie Street with my friend and acquaintance of some ten years, Rev. Dr Robert Schuller of California. That was a mistake. The problem was I was 20 years younger than most of the other contenders. Here was I, an outsider from Melbourne, teaching my elders and betters how to suck eggs.

The problem was that at these meetings there were present most of the ministers who were among the more than 40 or so contenders for my position who had been rejected. A dozen or more of these ministers, who knew they had been rejected, took time out to meet me personally and give me some advice.

Each of these were prominent Methodist ministers who had been the leaders of the largest Methodist churches in the country and especially in New South Wales. They were on the list of possibilities who could have been chosen but they had been rejected and knew it. Now they came to give me inside information. I was taken to a series of small coffee breaks where over a cappuccino the message was given: 'Don't get your hopes up too high; no one can follow Alan Walker; everybody expects the successor to fail and rather have one of the more successful New South Wales Methodist ministers fail, they consider a Melbourne based minister from another denomination would be less damaging. Then a proper appointment could be made of a more suitable candidate. We doubt that you will be here long. Don't be disappointed.' I had that message six times so I knew the matter was being discussed widely.

Well, I had been kept waiting so long I now knew that waiting was part of the process. I was to remain twenty-seven years as Superintendent of Wesley Mission Sydney. The work has grown for more than 25 consecutive years and is today bigger and stronger than at anytime in its history. If those same more suitable candidates are still alive, I guess I have kept them waiting!

The Role Of The Superintendent

This ministry at Wesley Mission Sydney is unique in many ways. I believe there were several emphasises to be made if this was to become one of the world's most amazing ministries.

1. Minister Of The Gospel

Wesley Mission is a church, a large city church committed to the ministry of word (preaching, celebrating sacraments, communication of the gospel, teaching the faith) and deed (works of charity, social welfare, rehabilitation, medical care). Its leader must fulfil each role.

It is essential that the leader of Wesley Mission be an ordained Minister of the

Uniting Church to fulfil sacramental, property and trust obligations. The senior minister is designated Superintendent Minister. That ministry is one of both word and deed and these two cannot be separated from each other. In some similar missions, the ministry of the word has been delegated to a minister of the church and the ministry of the deed has been delegated to a lay manager of social welfare. In every case the total work has declined and in most has ceased. Without the ministry of word and deed together, the impetus for good works is lost.

2. Initiator Of Programs
Each of eight Sydney Superintendent Ministers has developed a ministry of powerful preaching, attracting the largest sustained membership of any church in Australia's history (now covering 190 years). Each such long serving Superintendent has also initiated a variety of Christian welfare programs to meet the social needs of each era, namely 'homes for waifs and strays'; 'support for fallen sisters' and 'Institute for the Inebriated' in the nineteenth century. During the post World War 2 period: psychiatric hospitals, geriatric services, aged care hostels, nursing homes and Life Line Telephone Counselling Service were established.

I, in my turn, wrote a 500-page treatise in 1977 before coming to the position outlining my intentions and approach to the city ministry. It included 160 published potential new developments that would require research and if such research sustained the concern, would be established to meet community needs.

Almost all subsequent developments at Wesley Mission have been the outworking of these initiatives. They include: Gamblers Anonymous and addictive gambling counselling; Christian Educational Institute; national weekly Christian television program; cassette ministry; estate planning division; television commercials; major Easter/ Christmas ministry to the nation; development of investment land; Asian student outreach; computerised mail fundraising; cross divisional seminars on social issues; unemployment retraining programs; child abuse programs; monthly supporters luncheons; home domiciliary support services; clothing collections via street bins; tele-counselling; staff birthday celebrations; emergency family accommodation units; friends of WM fundraisers; art sales; school vacation programs for the underprivileged; rebuilding the existing city property; relocating Life Line; building retirement villages on equity participation basis; publishing a well-researched history of Wesley Mission; building a Day Hospital for community based elderly; pre-school centre for intellectually disabled; Printing prestige Annual Reports; a volunteers division under paid staff; youth Hostel; magazine subscriptions; establishing a Chinese ministry; founding a Creative Ministry School; developing a new worship format using video clips and promotions as worship; joint staff/elders planning retreats; management training for all senior staff at Mt Eliza Management School, establishing a financial counselling service to aid people in credit-card debt; establish an institute for ministry in evangelism, and so on.
Only a few of the 160 concepts have not been implemented. All of the above are

now significant additions to Wesley Mission. With the exception of a dementia program, no major developments at Wesley Mission have been generated by staff, although every one of the above have been developed and conducted by competent staff recruited for the task. The Superintendent initiates new programs. I doubt if any minister has ever come to a new ministry with a 150, 000 word strategic plan to cover the next twenty years.

3. Interpreter Of Christian Doctrine
The role of the Superintendent involves initiating responses to community need, based upon a theological understanding of Christian response. The response of Wesley is never just a practical response. It is a theological response. That is: this is what we know God wants us to do in this situation. To guide me on these issues I have always consulted the church's statements. But often the media wants personal opinions and they want them immediately.

Bio-ethical decisions, human rights issues, gender issues and social conscience matters proceed from a doctrinal basis. Doctrine determines practise. Our response to social need does not follow government awareness of need. It usually precedes both awareness and funding by the government.

The Superintendent interprets the Church's policy on such matters and provides the logic and impetus for such decisions, using published Uniting Church policies where relevant. If an official statement is required I always refer inquirers to Moderators or Presidents.

4. Accountable Person to the Community
Ministries like Wesley Mission depend ultimately upon public support and funding. An important principle in fundraising at the level of millions of dollars a year lies in the axiom that people give to a person they trust. The response is to a person, not an organisation. Every year I send a full audited financial statement to over 20, 000 donors, corporations, church boards and government departments. We are transparent.

The Superintendent must come under public and press scrutiny on matters of morality, accountability and credibility. Where charities do not have a human face, they do not grow. Hence 'The Fred Hollows Foundation' grows, as does the World Vision Famine relief, which always has the face of a starving child.

Missions grow strong on the sustained personal accountability and leadership of the Superintendent.

5. Communicator
All Superintendents who have been effective have been great communicators through preaching, writing, use of the press, radio and television.

Unlike a business that has a manufactured product or service to sell, the Mission exists because it communicates effectively its plans to meet human need in a Christian fashion that deserves the practical and voluntary support of the person to whom the communication is addressed.

Most business executives prefer a low profile whereas a Mission's success is in direct proportion of the profile and communication skills of the Superintendent. Paid public relations staff and image creators have never been accepted by the public. The public expect the authoritative leader of the work to communicate the truth using all means of media.

6. Image Creator
The public responds emotionally to human need. It does not respond according to intellectual awareness. Do governments get elected on the basis of a rational community response?

The Superintendent is required to create the image within the bounds of authenticity and credibility of the Mission as a centre of compassionate care and sensible service. The Superintendent embodies the traditions of the Church over the centuries while at the same time being on the cutting edge of care.

The role of Superintendent, when reduced to that of either a manager or a Chairman of the Board, results in a lowering of public perception and support.

The giving of money for practical social care came from people covenanting to give: 'a penny a week and a shilling a quarter.' We teach the lessons of gaining, saving and giving, which enabled Wesley's poor to grow in self-esteem and dignity.

The greatest need in the Church today is for competent, visionaries and inspiring leadership. Most denominations operate in a leadership vacuum. The cry of ordinary members as they see our denomination in decline and fragmenting over moral issues, is 'Where are our leaders? Why are they silent?'

TIME Magazine recently named and profiled the 'twenty most influential leaders and revolutionaries of the past 100 years'. If the Church were to do the same in Australia, our list would include some great and inspiring names, but as far as the Uniting Church is concerned, they would all be long retired or dead.

A good test is to ask public commentators, journalists and radio talk back personalities whom they regard as leaders of The Uniting Church. The answers I got included Archbishop Peter Hollingworth, Rev. Tim Costello and Rev. Fred Nile. One is an Anglican, the next a Baptist, the third a politician.

The words of Karl Jaspers have an ominous ring for us today: 'The power of leadership appears to be declining everywhere. More and more of the people we see coming to the top seem to be merely drifting.' It is a problem wider than the

Church. Ted W. Engstrom writes: 'Solid, dependable, loyal, strong leadership is one of the most desperate needs in our world today. We see the tragedy of weak men in important places, little men in big jobs. Business, industry, government, labor, education and the Church are all starving for effective leadership. So today, perhaps more than ever before, there is such a need for leadership.'

When we decry the scarcity of leadership, we are not talking about a lack of administrators or managers. We have plenty of people to send out memos, formulate regulations and attend committees. We need administrators to undertake serious management studies to improve their skills. The Uniting Church In Australia has over a billion dollars of assets yet I cannot think of one administrator in the UCA, outside of Wesley Mission, who has completed advanced management training and who holds graduate qualifications. Wesley Mission believes in training leaders. Currently 80 staff are doing advanced leadership training and another 1,600 are doing skill enhancement courses and management courses.

To be good stewards of God's resources we expect administrators to be good managers. Some could become good leaders. Leaders can be made. Leaders read the signs of the times, look with vision, speak with skill and gather people together to get the job done effectively. Leaders do not wait for things to happen, they make things happen. Leaders take disparate people and make them a potent force. John Wesley was such a leader. He wrote, 'We act at all times on one plain uniform principle - we will obey the rulers and governors of the Church, whenever we can consistently with our duty to God, whenever we cannot, we will quietly obey God rather than men.' That was the leadership spirit of Apostles Peter and John.

I believe that ministry and mission are not two different things, but that mission is accomplished by the ministry of all the people. Churches of Christ had a traditional plea: evangelisation of the world through the unity of the Church which could be retrieved by restoring the principles and practises of the New Testament Church as a basis for unity.

As a young Churches of Christ minister, I set out to review the validity of each aspect of that heritage over a period of twenty years. I published Rethinking Restoration– the most thorough review I have seen made in Australia of the Restoration principle. My conclusions were regarded as too radical, even though they were published. In the 1970's I was committed to Unity between the fractured parts of the Church and I wrote and lectured on how the proposed Uniting Church in Australia needed the evangelical witness of Churches of Christ and how Churches of Christ needed to move from observer status to that of a negotiating denomination if it was to fulfil our plea that a united church could strengthen our witness in evangelism. But at a Federal Conference, the Christian Union proposal to join in the Uniting Church in Australia was rejected. Over the next few years I was invited to explain to Churches in the Uniting denominations their own Basis of Union. I decided then I should be true to my commitment to Christian unity and join the Uniting Church.

At the Churches of Christ Federal Conference January 14th 1979, before 3000 people on the Sunday night closing rally in the Melbourne Town Hall I preached on the theme 'Salvation in Christ'. I pointed out that evangelism was our primary purpose, to win the world for Christ. We had to become totally committed to the mission of the Church.

But the following week after that Federal Conference in the Melbourne Town Hall, I was inducted into being the senior minister of Wesley Mission, a church that in 1884 had changed its name from 'Church' to 'Mission', because that was to be its main emphasis. I believe in a missional church and have argued for 35 years that the Church is only the Church when it is the Church in mission.

If the churches want managers instead of evangelists, at least they should insist that they are trained in graduate management. Currently we have millions of dollars of assets under the control of unqualified people. The training of people to be ministers of the faith is quite different to the training of managers. When I look at the head office of the UCA Synod of NSW, I see a revolving door of senior staff coming and going because other senior staff do not have graduate management qualifications. If a minister wants to also manage, he or she should immediately start doing management courses at the Australian Graduate School of Management at the University of New South Wales, or the Mt Eliza School of Management at Monash University, each are acknowledged as the best in their business and are places where I have trained since 1967. At least they should be doing regular management courses run by the Australian Institute of Management or the Australian Institute of Company Directors, two other institutions where I have trained in management and company governance.

If you want a church led by managers, churches should start putting in some key performance indicators for each state to identify key result areas, publish them and quantify progress. Some denominations have appointed as a church leader, a CEO. However, the role of a CEO is not to manage; a CEO appoints managers. A CEO provides strategic directions and thinking and is the chief communicator to the people and the world outside the Church. In any large organisation it is the CEO who should head strategic direction and who should be the chief communicator with both the members and the community. Leadership, not management is the key requirement.

Because I have credentials with the United Methodist Church (U.S.A.) associated with the UCA, I speak each year in their churches and in one main centre have given regular lectures on urban mission. The United Methodist Church have, more than any other denomination, moved to a management model. Under the management model, the United Methodist church has lost 1,000 members a week, every week, for the past thirty years.

CHURCH LEADER

Some people say the denominational structures are dead and that the modern church does not need national structures. Try telling that to the Pentecostal churches who have put vast resources into their new national structure in the past two years. The Australian Christian Churches are now the third largest denomination in Australia. They have learnt how to become an effective lobby group nationally to gain government funds and twenty church members recently stood for election to the Australian Parliament late in 2004.

Church bureaucrats are always interested in one question: 'Where does the money come from?' Their answer is to close churches and sell properties. Reductionism to save money always leads to diminishing ministry and mission. Huddling together in slow decline is not the way of the future. Never talk about reduction. Always talk about ways to raise more money. Churches must live by faith, taking risks. Money will always flow to a vision of service to people in need. It is never a money problem, it is a vision problem and that is what church bureaucrats rarely have.

In a not-for profit organisation, the CEO should also be the major fundraiser. I have built up a team of people to carry out the functions of fundraising, but I sign the thousands of letters, I meet with corporate business executives, I conduct the negotiations with the Prime Minister and various Federal Ministers and with the Premier and various State Government ministers in seeking extra funding. The Chief Executive should be accountable for his performance in all areas of his activities, including fundraising. The Chief Executive of a not-for-profit organisation never depends upon levies and fees imposed upon constituent bodies or church, but on generating extra finance from outside the membership. Church leaders always think in terms of extra taxes on congregations' areas of service to the needy. If increasing funds are not made available, then that Chief Executive should make way for someone else who can raise the funds.

There are enormous amounts of money available from believers, but believers give to a trusted leader who has developed accountable reporting systems and a visionary plan that is communicated well and that meets the real needs of people. Wesley Mission every year pays over three quarters of a million dollars to presbyteries, synod and Assembly to pay for services of the bureaucrats who do little ever to help the poor and needy.

Money is never the problem- vision and strategic goals are; communication and accountability are. Because people do not restrict their money being given just to denominational work any longer, this means our market for finding financial support is now broadened enormously (there are more of them than us) and because companies are becoming socially responsible, there are hundreds of corporations that will help denominational work if it has strategic vision, communicated by trusted leaders who account well for its expenditure and who meet real needs. I am amazed how many community organisations now support the Seventh Day Adventist Church Aid programs for overseas developments, for example.

Church leadership must grow out of discovering what is the minimal structure needed to effectively carry out the mission of the Church. Structure is the product of strategy. Form follows function.

In such a debate, people often accuse the other viewpoint of being hierarchical and top-down authoritarian while their viewpoint is grass roots, people-centred and relevant. If you want to have a model, it is neither top to bottom or bottom to top. Rather it is shaped like an arrow, with flutes, shaft and point. Like an arrow it is missional directed towards an objective target. The flutes that keep it flying true are the members, in whose counsel is wisdom. I would always try in any church organisation to have a place for large crowds of people who attend inspirational worship and who, by their participation, accept ownership. These large-scale celebrations of the church would rotate around the major population areas. It is these people who are the true stakeholders, not church bureaucrats.

The shaft represents the daily work of church agencies, specialised, as there is need. These are responsible for accreditation, effective service and achievement of strategic goals of the Church.

The arrow point is its leadership. Here lies the strategic thinking, the oversight of policy and the most able communication. If the direction is right, the arrow hits its target.

From 1970, I saw the need for training new leadership within the churches. Waiting for others to do something rarely accomplishes much, so I planned to run a course for church leaders and ministers. The Summer School for Successful Ministry began. This was a big venture, as I wanted to bring together outstanding leaders in the field of growing Christian congregations from across Australia. From 1970 I planned for the people of Australia. We advertised in all of the church papers around Australia and indicated that we had secured the services of Australia's outstanding church teachers as guest lecturers. They came from every denomination.

In the first program Reverend Alan Walker from Sydney attended and a host of others. People like Bishop Jack Dain, Reverend Bill Adams, Mr Kevin Crawford, Reverend Michael Dennis, Doctor Bruce Peterson, Reverend Doctor Dudley Ford, Jay Bacik, Reverend David Cohen and a dozen more joined our lecturing panel. Bishop Chandu Ray came from Singapore and spoke about contemporary Evangelism in a pluralistic society. Doctor Alan Walker spoke about Evangelism in the local church, Bishop Jack Dain on committed to ministry and we had other sessions on using the media, developing an Australian theology, how to improve communications skills, strategy of church growth in the eighties, harnessing youth power in Evangelism, reaching children in worship services, conducting a ministry to single adults, releasing the power of tired people and so on.

The idea was to provide throughout January an experience where ministers and church leaders from across Australia could live in the homes of our church members, attend lecture programs each day in small groups around our Cheltenham complex, share meals together and then at night listen to some great preaching from some of the finest preachers of all denominations in Australia. The first Summer School for Successful Ministry was an outstanding success. Over five hundred people attended the course and we were packed out in each of our mid-week preaching sessions.

That developed friendships with ministers across Australia from various denominations who had never met each other but whose names were well-known. The following January and then for the next four Januarys I ran these Summer Schools for Successful Ministry, with the final one being conducted in Sydney with three hundred ministers and fifteen hundred church leaders attending. It was the first time in Australia that such a course in in-service training for people in ministry was ever conducted.

I had recently written a book, *How to Grow an Australian Church,* which took off like wildfire and in the first year approximately ten thousand copies were sold. Over the years several thousand copies a year were purchased. This was the first handbook on church growth in Australia to be published and there was obviously an important market for it. Even though it is now dated, (thirty years old) it still covers all basic principles and *How to grow an Australian Church* has become a byword in church growth literature. In 2005 I was again asked to update and republish it. It was republished in Britain and Canada and it had a new life in those areas. People then wanted me to lecture on the principles in the book and so a whole series of probably three or four hundred lecture programs in every state of Australia was held using the material that I presented in that book.

Church leaders need a vision of the future and a fresh commitment to Biblical values at the start of the twenty-first century as never before. The mainstream denominations are in strife. The Uniting Church in Australia is in crisis. Membership is rapidly falling and together with that decline, a financial downturn. Hundreds of thousands of former members have left and UCA members and ministers are to be found in other denominations. The UCA bureaucracy in the NSW Synod want a better return on investments in aged care properties, to rationalise church properties and to sell off properties to fund administrative costs: i.e. their salaries.

The Uniting Church in Australia is not in good shape. It has the oldest average age of any denomination. Two thirds of our members are females over 60 years of age. In spite of all the talk about our ethnic congregations, we have the highest percentage of Anglo members of any denomination. In spite of all the rhetoric, we are not a multi-cultural denomination.

Many people are despairing of their own church. Many others are leaving to join other denominations. In 2004, 6,500 members who left were officially quantified.

Many are simply being lost to the faith altogether. We have the lowest retention rate of young adults of any denomination. We know of the immoral lifestyles led by people in leadership in the Assembly, Synods, its boards and agencies, including its centres of ministry training. The details of such immoral life-styles have been reported to the appropriate moderators and General Secretary of Synod. Immorality among paid staff of Assembly and Synod, their boards and agencies has been named in letters to Moderators concerning complainants who have come to me.

I have publicly fought this fight against the morals found in some parts of the liberal wing of the Uniting Church for over twenty years. Mostly, it was a lonely battle. I called the first evangelical summit of leading evangelicals from every state of Australia that met at Vision Valley in 1997 when over fifty evangelical leaders spent three days together. There was a unanimous commitment to seek to change our church. Unfortunately this mostly resulted in more prayer but no action. We are better at the struggles in prayer than the struggles with power.

I have been quoted in the media frequently concerning our church, but I have only responded to public material about the Uniting Church, mostly material generated by the Uniting Church's public relations people and the decisions that resulted. I have never initiated one single attack on the Uniting Church or any of its staff and have raised concerns only after complainants have come to me.

Once the church or its staff enters the public arena then I regard the issue as being open for public discussion. Many fine evangelicals are standing up for Biblical truth today. Many attended and spoke powerfully at the National Assemblies in Perth, Adelaide and Melbourne. There are also many evangelical organisations seeking revival, renewal in our prayer-life, changes in UCA direction, more support of missions overseas, greater emphasis on indigenous and ethnic congregations in Australia, Christian education programs for youth and in schools and a more conservative theological approach to ministry training and the like.

Yet all of us are working hard in our own areas. Most of us are without the support of like-minded believers and most without any sense of co-ordinated effort. More significantly, the concerned members do not have all the resources of the Synod and Assembly that are used to defend their positions.

This is an urgent time in the history of the Uniting Church that requires the prayerful and intellectual contribution of concerned members and organisations who/which desire to: change the power structures of the Church; reclaim a conservative reading of the Bible for the Uniting Church; develop alternative ministry training for candidates; question legal issues involving retention of church property; make present church leadership more accountable; find better ways using parish financial contributions; recall our people to Godliness in personal living; discover a new sense of national mission and so on.

CHURCH LEADER

One of the constant troubles within the Uniting Church in Australia is the left wing political ideology that comes up on every issue. Some bureaucrats behave as if they were failed politicians. The grassroots membership constantly complain about these political emphases. Some, who have no direct accountability to any congregation, seem to delight in stirring the more conservative members by their support of every radical, social, left wing view on issues such as abortion, euthanasia, same-sex marriages, liberalisation of laws curtailing brothels, pornography and X rated films and videos. With great predictability those left wing bureaucrats respond in such a way to outrage the church's membership. I would have respect for these church bureaucrats if they were consistent in their claims to represent the poor, but they live in North Shore homes, drink wine and champagne and demand salaries beyond that of parish clergy.

Many church members do not realise that more than one has had failed political ambitions that are now guiding their church decisions. The NSW Synod's most high profile left wing bureaucrat is Rev. Harry Herbert. According to Senator Graham Richardson, he met Herbert as an active member of the ALP branch at Monterey. Harry was an aggressive ALP member with high hopes. But the arrival of Graham (later Senator) Richardson neutralised Harry Herbert's extreme left wing political views. 'From the time Richardson joined the branch my reign of glory ended,' Herbert is quoted. Frustrated in his political ambition by the powerful 'numbers man' of the ALP, Herbert continues to promote his political views within the Synod where there is no equivalent of 'the fixer' to stymie his reign of glory. For a number of UCA leaders, failed political ambition, not a Biblical evangelical commitment, determine their direction in the Church.

There is virility and growth among the Uniting Church ethnic groups. Many Anglo-Celtic parishes are only growing older. We believe the present leadership of the Uniting Church is not taking the business of evangelism seriously, in seeking new members or in establishing ways members can be encouraged to grow in personal holiness. They are too busy in the 'maintenance ministry', just keeping things going.

Some are so busy defending the behaviour of minorities they have forgotten Jesus told us to win the world. Some clergy have been inadequately trained in the skills of evangelism, or in the principles that grow a church. The constant complaint against ministers is that they have forgotten how to visit members or to practise pastoral care. Yet the Uniting Church is the denomination best positioned to win Australians to Jesus Christ.

However, our denomination is not known for its commitment to basic Biblical attitudes but of commitment to Christ as Saviour, of upholding the Scriptures as the basis of faith, of personal holiness in the life-styles of its leaders, in openness to the movements of the Holy Spirit and in obedience to the Word of God. The Uniting Church In Australia is in deep trouble. If it is to be an authentic Australian church then it must come to grips with these basic Biblical attitudes. But these are the issues no member of the public attribute to the UCA.

The Presbyterian Church in Scotland faced these same issues in the 16th and 17th centuries. Godly men led church members to bind themselves in a covenant to their faith. For two centuries 'The Covenanters' bound themselves by commitment to God to renewing their church and their personal spiritual lives.

The Methodist Church always used the last night of the year or other anniversary to express their gratitude by renewing their covenant of faithfulness to God. The idea of a covenant is central to all of scripture. John Wesley wanted his people to remember that Covenant with God at every communion and at the beginning of every New Year. On December 25th 1747, John Wesley first urged his Methodists to renew their Covenant with God. From 1755 an annual Covenant Service was held at the end of each year and the option has been brought over into the Uniting Church in Australia.

The Covenant Service has been held since 1812 in Australia. I wrote to all churches and ministers concerned with the restoration of The Uniting Church to its Biblical basis in 1997 suggesting the renewing of personal commitment to Christ, the reaffirmation of the Biblical standards of holiness in living in obedience to the Scriptures, to appropriate forms of service within the community, in using the Uniting Church's Covenant Service annually when most appropriate in their churches and to encourage members to sign in a meaningful fashion 'The Covenant Card'. I drew up the Covenant Card to reflect these concerns.

Those who joined 'The Covenanters', I wrote to with suggestions for prayer. It was my hope that from the grass-roots membership of The Uniting Church we would enrol committed Christians, praying and working for the evangelical cause within their church in Australia. This has worked well. Subsequently a movement called 'The Reforming Alliance' has been established and joined by hundreds of congregations and thousands of members. But the UCA bureaucracy ignores them.

The recent conflicts in the Anglican Communion, first in England and then in the United States, over the question of ordaining 'gay' bishops have revealed a deep fault line in Christianity. This is not in the first instance a debate about sexuality or even disagreements about the contents of scripture. The fault line goes deeper and can be summed up as a fundamental difference in vision in terms of the relationship between Christianity and culture.

Martin Robinson of the UK Bible Society, says, 'Put very simply, one group believes that the Christian faith has to adapt to its cultural setting and the second group believes that on occasion culture has to be resisted. Another way of expressing the same issue would be to ask, 'Who sets the agenda?' Is the agenda of the Church set by the world or should the agenda of the Church flow from the Bible? Most of the time this difference of emphasis is not noticed because, fortunately, these agendas often coincide. The needs of the world and the concerns of the Bible on many matters - compassion for the poor, the hungry, the oppressed - are identical. On other occasions they do not coincide, they collide.'

This fault line is so deep that now it has emerged it could mean a rather titanic fight of significant proportions - not exactly a fight to the death, but there will not be an agreement to differ, to continue to live celebrating our diversity! The fault line is no longer confined to camps in the Western world but has exposed fissures around the globe, with the great growing churches of Asia and Africa taking a Biblical, conservative view.

The 'liberal' view speaks of the inevitability of progress. They argue that one day Christians realised that slavery was unacceptable and that it was no good arguing from scripture that it is approved by God - slavery had to go. One day, the same thing happened concerning the ministry of women - scripture was reinterpreted in the light of growing knowledge and enlightenment. The liberals in the Church say: 'Today it is the turn of the homosexual community to be liberated. Any one who speaks against the ordination of homosexuals, same-sex marriage and their life style as being anything except normal is homophobic and a dinosaur.' This is a slur on the conservative viewpoint.

There is however one rather glaring flaw in that argument. The pro-slavery position was taken by those who wanted to accommodate Christianity to the 'realities' of the day. It was in fact those awkward evangelicals, who argued that the world had to adapt to the standards of the gospel, who championed the cause of the abolition of slavery. To pretend that it was the evangelicals who championed the cause of slavery is not only to turn history on its head, it is also to expose a fundamental weakness in the position of those who always want the agenda to be set by the world. It was the evangelicals and their insistence on Biblical truth that brought about the change in attitude to slavery.

It was the same with the emancipation and suffrage of women. It was the evangelicals who founded the Women's Christian Temperance Union that became the first women's organisation in the world to fight for women's right to vote, to own property and to work for equal pay. Those with liberal theological disposition were fighting their own wars at that time, especially adapting to the world on the creation issue. The liberals came to the women's issue half a century after the evangelicals and then started to re-write history in their own reflection.

The result of all of this? We accept the fault line theory. The implications are clear. I have called upon UCA Evangelicals to establish an Evangelical Assembly, a new national body to which evangelical or covenanting congregations could belong. This Assembly would be a national body rather than a state synod. This Evangelical Assembly would remain within the Uniting Church in Australia, be loyal to the Basis of Union and fulfil the emphases of the supporting documents and confessional statements honoured in the founding of the Uniting Church. It is possible that 500 congregations could join with us? The nation-wide Presbytery for Korean Churches would be a precedent.

Further, UCA members should support evangelical care agencies and re-direct all moneys to them. We do not have to support those organisations within the church that spend moneys given by faithful members of congregations in purposes and in support of those activities evangelicals find against their conscience.

We need to stand in solidarity with each other. There are tactics being used against individual evangelicals that include harassment by telephone calls, e-mails and the threats of withdrawing ministerial status. Some UCA ministers, for example, have been treated in the most disgraceful manner, threatened by telephone calls from both Presbytery and the Moderators. Personal visits are a minimum to express concerns, but to be stood aside from life-long ministry by telephone raises all sorts of legal issues. How are ministers to know the calls were genuine? How do ministers know e-mails are valid and authentic without proper verification? Would these methods be substantiated by a legal case against unfair dismissal? In such events, we must stand together. Sack one of us and you have to sack 300 of us! The use of fear to enforce allegiance to the opinions of the bureaucracy is an absolute disgrace.

We need to support evangelical, ministerial, theological education. Ministerial education is the key to change and the UCA is in some turmoil on the quality of ministerial graduates. There is dissatisfaction among parishes with the quality of the people being ordained. There is also the cost of turning out each ordained minister.

It is very difficult to reform existing educational ghettoes. Rev. Allan Thompson in Victoria, chair of the Task Group on Theological Education for the 2003 Assembly, recommends greater flexibility in education, but UTC and other Synod funded theological colleges fight for their rights to be the only training and recognising agencies in each UCA Synod.

The Wesley Institute For Ministry and the Arts is on a par with the United Theological College, via their membership and accreditation in the Sydney College of Divinity. The Wesley Institute each year trains more students in a wider variety of courses, both community, arts and ministry streams by a larger faculty and staff than The United Theological College and we do it without any financial support from any Synod whatsoever. At mid 2005, the Wesley Institute of Ministry and Arts has 430 full-time students, over 100 faculty and administrative staff and in the past twelve months has had over 4000 part-time, short term courses by students in vocational and community education causes.

Today in the USA, the evangelical seminaries have larger student populations than the denominational ones. We look forward to this day and urge evangelical churches to support evangelical Australian colleges for ministerial training. I predict that shortly the United Theological College will be closed because of its cost and the standard of its graduates.

One example of the culture clash centred on the issue of some UCA bureaucrats living in homosexual relationships. Hundreds of faxes, e-mails and letters were received from parishes, presbyteries and individuals to support the stand taken by about 80 of our Elders under the Chairmanship of Dr Tony Chi (a former UCA Moderator) to redirect funds from the Uniting Church Assembly to areas of Uniting Church Mission. Our Elders did not believe in paying the salaries of persons living openly in immoral relationships outside of marriage while holding positions of church leadership. The issue is not just several church leaders practising homosexuality; but does the Uniting Church in Australia place itself under the authority and standards of the scriptures?

The Gay and Lesbian Lobby and their supporters in NSW Synod and Assembly offices decided not to address the issues but to turn the focus on Wesley Mission and myself. A group of lesbians and others held a sit-in in Wesley Church. They then initiated a move to end my ministry.

Early in November 1997 I became aware that some person unknown to me had made a formal complaint against me claiming that I had violated the vows made at my ordination, engaged in grave conduct unworthy of a minister, failed to comply with provisions of the constitution of the Uniting Church and failed to comply with a resolution of a body of the church. This is a serious matter. If true, this complaint should end my ministry! I understood that there were about 20 pages of evidence and attachments.

I soon found out that my doctrine and personal morality was not questioned but my use of some words in some twenty sentences taken from some 300,000 sentences available publicly on the Internet. Together they made a couple of paragraphs, but the substantiation of the charges took up the rest of the pages. I eventually discovered, although not told by either the Standing Committee nor the Pastoral Relations Committee, who the Complainant was. She was a former Moderator and a former General Secretary of a Synod Board. I had spoken to her in Presbytery meetings without her revealing she was the complainant. The Complaint came before the Presbytery Standing Committee and the Pastoral Relations Committee. I was interviewed at length about the complaint. The PRC and PSC decided to pass the matter unresolved to the Synod Counselling Committee.

I met twice with members of this Committee. This Committee read but decided not to raise most matters with me in the first two-hour meeting. But in the second two and a half hour meeting with the complainant present they did raise these matters of substance. It is important that the reader know the substance of these serious charges. I took a short hand reporter with me who took down all comments.

The example first mentioned was from my sermon on John the Baptist standing up against the authorities on a matter of conscience. I indicated we had seen few national prophets in our time but mentioned Rev. Sir Alan Walker who, as a prophet like John the Baptist, spoke against authority, 'a lone voice...' The complainant stated the word 'lone' was a slur upon the memory of other voices at the time, specifically her husband in Perth. I was stunned. Of course other people had protested against the Vietnam War, including me, but the difference between us was that Alan Walker had national stature. People also spoke in every village against Herod, but John the Baptist was a national figure. If I had said Walker was 'a' prophet that would have been acceptable. The Committee decided I must write to the complainant and apologise on behalf of her late husband.

The next complaint involved one of our church services which was interrupted by a group I described in 'Mission Talk' as being 'lesbians and others', who staged an attempt to occupy the pulpit and sit in Wesley Church overnight at a time when I was conducting a worship service and later, a prayer meeting. I had previously spoken against a lesbian Uniting Church minister who was living immorally and in disregard of the standards in scripture continuing to occupy a senior position in the Uniting Church Assembly. That spurred the protest.

In the report on the interruption to our worship in our church paper, I mentioned that the leader of the protest was a minister whom I named. He had issued the press release and had given radio interviews thereby attracting a number of others to join in the protest. This included a group of women wearing badges and identifying themselves with the lesbian movement. By using the word 'lesbians' first I gave the impression that he was the leader of the lesbian group. I have never considered this minister as anything but a man. The Committee decided I must write and apologise to him. There was no apology for interrupting divine worship in Wesley Church. 400 worshippers who had gathered to worship and witness six adult baptisms were disgusted with the protest meeting in a worship service. The media attended in large numbers with TV cameras looking for a major story, but on realising there wasn't one, soon went away.

Another example concerned a sentence in a sermon when I said, 'We can uphold the scriptures as the word of God.' This statement was declared to be offensive. The complainant declared that in doing so I violated the vows made at my ordination because I agreed to uphold the Basis of Union, but 'The Basis of Union does not speak of the Bible as the word of God.' The Committee were obviously ill at ease in discussing this. I affirmed my belief in Jesus Christ, the incarnate word, the regnant word, the living word and who is only known from the written word of God. The issue remains. The Counselling Committee did not want to adjudicate on this!

Yet another example concerned my use of the word 'bureaucrat' to describe a person who worked in the church bureaucracy. The Committee, after the strongest urging by the complainant, agreed I must not use that word. Despite the fact the official organisation of the Synod and the Assembly operates with all the traditional methodology and nuances of a typical bureaucracy, I was directed never to use that 'b' word again. Are all clergy under the same prohibition? What happens if in a rush of blood, perhaps after a Coca-Cola, the dreaded 'b' word slips out? Does the Counselling Committee reconvene to consider ecclesiastical discipline? Am I then directed to appear before a higher court of the church? For how long is the prohibition on the use of the 'b' word? Do I get a remission of time off for good behaviour? This kind of decision fails the tests of consistency and logical extension. Yet I remain under the discipline of the church and I hope the 'b' word never passes my lips again. This was pure nonsense.

And so on the discussion went. At no point was my exegesis of the scriptures questioned. I always spoke vigorously but truthfully out of my deep concern for the Church and its direction. I have never rejected the councils of the Church nor their authority. Yet this was the fifth time I had had to meet with a committee or group or write and explain these same words of which the complaint was made.

The process was secretive. I am prohibited from mentioning the names of committee members nor attributing any quotes. The complainant was anonymous for some considerable time until I discovered her identity. The process was delayed, taking eight months. Justice delayed is justice denied. There is in the process an accusatory assumption of guilt. There is no process to determine the accuracy of charge, which in my case contained untruth and inaccuracies. The whole process fails the principles of natural justice.

The Counselling Committee was courteous, patient and thorough, however I was not allowed to raise issues of inaccuracies and errors in the complaint itself. I prevailed on the point of denial of justice and gained an apology from the complainant for her errors of fact. My speeches have been censored and my vocabulary restricted.

Is this all a good result? Apologies were made in writing as outlined above. Reconciliation? I did not have a problem with the complainant in the first place. My letter and invitation to meet her went unanswered. My previous image of her was as a Moderator of the church. I now have an image of a former leader of the church spending hours pouring over thousands of my sermons in print and on the Internet, church paper articles and magazines circling words. Has the process exacerbated the problem? Was the whole exercise a good use of time and effort in the work of Christ? Consider the time and effort of more than a score of people involved in the Pastoral Relations Committee, Presbytery Standing committee, Presbytery Secretary, Chairpersons, members of the Synod Counselling Committee and so on. The Committee encouraged me in future to speak more carefully. My flippant offer to be uniformly dull seemed to meet with approval.

What of the hurt and stress placed on me by the complaint process? Not a word. Is this process designed to intimidate ministers and stop them from speaking boldly or raising issues in sermons? Do ministers have rights against vexatious complaints? Is the Church becoming a place where anonymous thought-police check your words for political correctness?

It is happening. This was revealed when our computer system check on who accesses our internet material (designed to reveal the numbers and origins of people interested but now not used) revealed from December to February '98 the most frequent access came from computers who included in their registration 'nsw.uca' (synod computers). As the offices of Wesley Mission and the NSW Synod are adjacent, this does seem comical. On one Tuesday morning there were five accesses from the Synod office computers to my sermons in five minutes. Who is watching whom?

I reminded the complainant that Jesus says (Matthew 18:15-17), 'If your brother sins against you, go and show him his fault, just between the two of you. If he listens to you, you have won your brother over. But if he will not listen, take one or two others along, so that 'every matter may be established by the testimony of two or three witnesses.' If he refuses to listen to them, tell it to the church; and if he refuses to listen even to the church, treat him as you would a pagan or a tax collector.' I asked, 'Why did you not ring me and suggest we talk if these issues troubled you?' I was told, 'That is not the Uniting Church way.'

I am sure God will not bless these 'dirty tricks' campaigns. One journalist contacted me and said he'd have no part of this attempt to damage our work, despite being sent leaked information.

The Ordination Controversy

The great aim of all student ministers is to graduate and be ordained. It took a total of six years full-time study for me to complete both my theological studies and university degree. To graduate from both was a time of great excitement. It had been a long haul with much sacrifice by myself and my girlfriend who later became my fiancée and eventually my wife. Beverley had worked for three years in the latter stages of my study, enabling me to spend my efforts on my studies full-time. At the same time, I was working the best of 60 hours a week in the growing slum church.

In between our social protest and social welfare work, the grind of studying philosophy, logic, biology, genetics, mediaeval philosophy and the like continued. Occasionally the exam results turned up honours and one dreadful year the biology paper failed and required a supplementary exam in the middle of the January holidays before a successful pass was achieved.

At the end of my theological course, the studies of Old and New Testament, New Testament and Classical Greek, Church History and Apologetics were completed. All that remained now was for graduation and ordination in November 1959. The fifteen or so students who were graduating with me were all looking forward to marriage. In most cases we had been engaged three, four or five years. We were not allowed to get married during our course and as soon as the graduation was completed there was a stampede for hometowns around Australia. The following two or three Saturdays saw the long anticipated marriages of almost all of those students.

The joy of marriage was only tinged with the sadness of leaving each other. When a group of 60 men plus a few women live together in a college for three, four, five or more years, a very close bond develops. The extended family is very real and to leave that family after all of those years was a traumatic experience. Fifty years after I first entered college I still feel the closest bond of friendship with those other young men who started studying with me.

The highlight of the whole course lay at the moment of ordination. The ordination was prepared for by spiritual devotion over the previous week. We fasted for the couple of days prior to the ordination in order that we might be in the right frame of spiritual dedication. We had studied the biblical passages on the laying of hands and devotion and fulfilled all of the spiritual requirements. Then a selection of ministers, church leaders and representative ministers and Elders of the Federal Conference of Churches of Christ in Australia, representing several states where the denomination had students in the college, came forward to where the ordinands knelt before them on the platform. In an atmosphere of devotion we answered the questions about our faithfulness to Jesus Christ, our belief in the trinity, the inspired word of the scriptures and our obedience to serve in the proclamation of the word of God. Then, as we knelt, the representative church ministers and Elders of the Federal Conference of Churches of Christ, gathered around us laying hands on our head and in prayer and dedication we were ordained into the ministry of the word and sacrament.

After all of those years I was now really a minister.

Of special meaning to me was the choice of one of the men of the Federal Conference of Churches of Christ, a former president, who joined with those who laid hands on my head. It was the same Dr W.A. Kemp who had presided over my earliest growth in my mother's womb as our local family doctor, who had been there at the time of my birth, who had delivered and hung me up by the heels, spanking me on the buttocks to produce the first cry of life. It was he who, as a surgeon, had removed my appendix and my tonsils and cared for me in all troublesome childhood illnesses. It was he who, as the president of our school council, as Mayor of our City, as Magistrate in the Childrens Court, as Elder within the local church and as family doctor, had guided me in my earliest days of boyhood need and questioning. It was also he with whom I had discussed entering the ministry, as he was also Chairman of the Board of the Federal College of The Bible of Churches of Christ in Australia.

It was only natural that he who had held me up in the air by the heels and spanked me on the buttocks at my birth, who had placed his arm around my shoulders at the time of my father's death in companionship and encouragement and who had shaken my hand when I left the Church to enter the College for training, should also lay hands upon my head in blessing at the moment of ordination. I went out into the world of the Parish of Ascot Vale and Newmarket now as a newly ordained minister.

There was an interesting twist to all of this.

Twenty-one years later Wesley Central Mission Sydney invited me to come to be its Superintendent in succession to Rev. Dr Sir Alan Walker. I had accepted that invitation in November 1977 and began ministry at the end of January 1979. A few weeks before my installation as Superintendent of Wesley Central Mission and welcome as a minister of The Uniting Church in Australia, a question was raised with the President of the Uniting Church in Australia, Rev. Dr Davis McCaughey, about whether my ordination as a minister of Churches of Christ was accepted as valid by the Uniting Church. The Uniting Church had previously declared that any minister ordained by a denomination and represented within the Australian Council of Churches was acceptable within The Uniting Church as a valid ordination. But the Presidential ruling which surprised all of us was that the ordination twenty-one years previously was not valid or acceptable to the Uniting Church. A fresh ordination was ordered.

There were many surprised leaders within the Uniting Church who received this news. But I must say I found the whole experience of my re-ordination a time of remarkable spiritual blessing. I found it strange that a church that did not believe in re-baptism should practise re-ordination. But because it was the ruling of the President of the church I accepted it as a discipline and in humility.

This time 1,300 people packed the Lyceum Theatre in Pitt Street to witness my second ordination. Scores of members of the Sydney Presbytery gathered round and letters were received from large numbers of people assuring me of their prayers and best wishes as I commenced a new ministry. This time I knelt in prayer and submission after answering the very same questions and re-submitted myself to the ministry of God.

No green student minister in the slums this time, but a minister of some twenty-one years standing. But I can assure you the same thrill of ordination was present as the leading church dignitaries of the Uniting Church in Australia gathered around my kneeling person and laid hands on my head.

In my speech afterwards I indicated that I believed the President was wrong and that my first ordination was a valid ordination but that I could never despise the prayers and best wishes of such a huge gathering of people and if it were in the mind of the Uniting Church to re-ordain me as an annual affair, I would certainly be willing to comply. Subsequently the presidential ruling requiring my re-ordination was revoked - but after the event! That graduation, ordination and re-ordination remain as three of the highlights in my spiritual pilgrimage.

In the 20 years after my first ordination I completed further studies at Melbourne University and London University; studies in counselling, chaplaincy, Christian education, business management, psychology and graduate theology at the Melbourne College of Divinity in the United Theological College, the college that trained ministers for the Uniting Church.

The direction to be re-ordained was highly improper and was theologically wrong. The Uniting Church did not believe in re-baptism and it certainly did not believe in re-ordination. No one wrote to me and told me that this was going to be a new requirement. I was just told by a phone message, shortly before the induction, that it would need to be a re-ordination on the basis that my first ordination was somehow or other not legitimate.

The Chairman of the Sydney Presbytery Dr Jim Udy and the President of the Assembly of the Uniting Church Rev. Dr Davis McCaughey, had decided quite wrongly that I should be re-ordained. It was like saying my marriage to Beverley had not been legal and that I should be remarried.

The problem was that this was not discussed either with me or with anybody else, so when 1,300 people gathered in the Lyceum Theatre to witness my induction as Superintendent of Wesley Mission they were surprised to see on the order of service which had been hastily rearranged and reprinted that I would be re-ordained. Many of the guests including Bishop Jack Dain of the Anglican Diocese of Sydney were outraged.

The interesting thing was that this decision was neither explained to me before hand nor were there any apologies afterwards. Some like Bishop Dain of the Anglican Church wrote at length saying how theologically wrong the action was and went on to say, 'I greatly admired your fearless statements made so graciously in your reply and I think that as far as it was humanly possible you yourself have put the record straight. It was not until I was in enjoying that delightful cup of tea that I realised from others who spoke to me that the issue was quite a thorny one in the Uniting Church.' Thorny one indeed. The Uniting Church paper was full of letters from Ministers who were outraged that a colleague minister with 20 years of experience and mature ministry, who had conducted classes for other Uniting Church ministers in how to evangelise and to grow their local church, should be forced to be re-ordained. It was regarded as an act that was injurious both to my standing as a minister and to that of Churches of Christ in general.

The Churches of Christ Federal Conference Executive (who had previously written to the Uniting church affirming the fact that I was an ordained minister in good standing with their denomination) and the Department of Christian Union sent letters to the President and to the Assembly of the Uniting Church.

I found it strange that the Secretary of the Assembly of the Uniting Church, should send me drafts of what he proposed to say in reply of these letters for my comment. He was a diplomat par excellence in the Uniting Church and he realised that in this matter the Uniting Church President had goofed. However, this didn't mean that anyone should apologise. Rather his letter said, 'It is unfortunate that in dealing with the case of Mr Moyes there was again some confusion on our part. In the procedures for the ordering of the life of the Uniting Church there are three levels of responsibility in this matter:

The Assembly, our national body, is responsible for determining the criteria to be applied and the principles that should operate in the acceptance of ministers from other traditions.

The Synod, or State Body, is responsible for determining whether or not a particular applicant complies with those standards and in Mr Moyes' case this was quite obviously so. Subject to the approval of the Synod it is our Presbytery or Regional Council, which is responsible for the actual reception and recognition and induction of any such minister into an appropriate settlement. It appears that some of those responsible for the exercise of responsibility of the various levels were not completely clear as to where their responsibility began and finished. In the event time over took us and these matters were not properly and thoroughly resolved before the occasion for the reception of Mr Moyes arose.'

In other words the Church had made a mistake. I have discovered that it is not the role of church bureaucrats to apologise for errors. The church bureaucrats are no more willing to say 'sorry' than some politicians. What they try to do is get out of it without people realising there is egg on their faces. I never received an apology from the President of the Assembly even though a later body reviewing his decision overturned it and indicated that his decision was wrong.

The Uniting Church set up a body from its assembly to closely examine all the issues concerning ordination and to make some additional regulations so that this mistake would not happen again. Consequently I was not only the first minister of another tradition to be inducted into the Uniting Church ministry upon its commencement as a new denomination in Australia, but I was the first and last to be re-ordained. Apart from indicating that the presidential ruling was wrong, I never went into debate on the issue.

The issue raged as a debate in a number of church papers and many other denominations wrote about the issue indicating the sense of superiority that the Uniting Church had if it were to require ministers from other recognised denominations to be re-ordained. I chose not to become involved in the debate and there were few people apart from the President and the Chair of Presbytery who tried to defend their actions.

The thing I learnt out of this, was that human regulations can become complicated and are frequently in error. When they are in error it is the responsibility of the minister to humbly submit to the discipline and direction of the Church even when that discipline and direction is wrong. We are to believe that eventually truth will come out and wrong directions will be corrected.

I have seen enough of church life over the years to know that this situation re-occurs from time to time. However we have to be big enough as individuals to accept the discipline and direction of the Church and bureaucrats within the Church need to recognise that they can be wrong and learn when to say 'sorry'.

From my point of view it would not be the last time I would need to correct a President or Moderator when they were plainly wrong in the eyes of Scripture and of God. I also learnt not to hold my breath while waiting for an apology.

It was the regulations of the new Uniting Church that was the problem. The Uniting Church in Australia has more regulations that there are words in the Gospels. What Jesus made simple, we continued to complicate. As the same Dr Davis McCaughey said, 'The Uniting Church has too many regulations. We do well with tearing the book of regulations in half and throwing away half. As far as I am concerned, it does not matter which half!'

Within the UCA the evangelicals are frequently defeated by the political skills of the bureaucrats. But they will win! The members of EMU (Evangelical Members of the Uniting Churches) and other evangelical organisations, have been too submissive, have lacked the political nous for using the regulations to our advantage and are too committed to working in the congregations where the only growth in this church occurs to spend time fighting within the bureaucracy. But one of the Sydney Archbishops said to me recently that evangelicals had to at least tithe their time, so that at least one tenth of our endeavours should be directed into bringing the bureaucracy into line with evangelical truth.

The real issue is: is the Uniting Church still under the authority of the Bible and does it accept the Bible's clear commands as relevant for today? Those who change moral standards, do so because they do not accept the scriptures as authoritative and relevant.

The high water mark of the liberal position has already been reached. The decisive factor in the emergence of a different kind of debate is the role of Christianity in the southern hemisphere. Thinkers from the growing churches of those lands have refused to accept the line of such as John Shelby Spong, whom they see as saying something like, 'Let us go forward to the nineteenth century.' The liberal theological position that flows from nineteenth century thought still sounds modern and progressive but it is fast losing its allure. For this reason alone, the Evangelicals will win the spiritual warfare in which we are engaged.

As Martin Robinson of the UK has written, 'The future of the faith is now in the hands of Lima and Lagos, not Canterbury and Chicago.' In other words, the old liberal denominations with their immoral proposals are moving far from the faith of our fathers. Evangelicals hold to the truths set forth in the Scriptures, the Basis of Union and the confessional statements referred to therein. Those who hold to an evangelical and spirit-filled faith will enter the future.

But that will not come automatically. It will require the prayer life of The Covenanters, the political boldness of the Reformers and the commitment of the Evangelicals. The political skills in using the regulations and out manoeuvring the evangelicals were learned in the old school of left wing politics, where some of the church bureaucrats trained and served in local political branches. The Uniting Church Assembly, which consisted of some 280 people mostly employed by the church in bureaucratic roles, has been soundly rebuffed by their membership.

The Melbourne Assembly resolution has been used to give Presbyteries the additional right to approve ministers for ordination in spite of homosexual behaviour. Congregations across Australia were shocked and dismayed at this decision. Thousands have subsequently met in hastily organised protest meetings. A petition demanding the rescinding of the Assembly motion was presented to the Assembly Standing Committee meeting to consider the events of the Assembly.

24,000 Uniting Church members from over 500 congregations signed a petition, which was delivered in 16 volumes. Thousands of letters and notes expressed the deep spiritual and emotional dismay and concern of Uniting Church members and adherents following the Assembly's decision. They did not believe that the concept of, 'It is O.K if you happen to live in right relationships instead of being celibate if you are single and faithful if you are married' was acceptable Christian practise in the light of clear Biblical teaching.

The grass roots members believe that the Assembly of the Uniting Church have placed themselves outside the One Holy Catholic and Apostolic Church, in contravention of paragraph 2 of their Basis of Union. They also are appalled that the proposal was not referred back to other Councils of the Church as the Assembly is obliged to do where a matter is 'of vital importance to the life of the Church.' The President, Dr Dean Drayton, was clearly in error in making a ruling that the matter was not of vital importance to the Church. This ruling must be overturned.

The hierarchy have been rejected by their members. Some members of the hierarchy have expressed their total shock at the strength of the resistance from congregations. The celebration by the politically astute gay and lesbian lobby within the Assembly was short-lived. No church can proceed as a true Church of Jesus Christ by cutting and pasting bits of the Bible they find politically incorrect. The Church must live according to the precepts and commands of the New Testament.

Even the public at large acknowledge this. All of the opinion polls taken by newspapers and televisions stations concerning the ordination of homosexuals living in a relationship have strongly affirmed the Christian position that church leaders should obey the scriptural injunction about holiness of living and freedom from all sexual relationship except for marriage.

There is a concern worldwide for the future of main-line denominations like the Uniting Church in Australia. Main-line denominations are in decline everywhere. Church membership has been eroding for the better part of the twentieth century. Some observers have predicted their demise. Prof. Thomas C Reeves, Professor of History at the University of Wisconsin, in his well researched book *The Empty Church: The Suicide of Liberal Christianity* asks: 'Why are (mainstream) churches failing to teach right from wrong? Why are young people abandoning them? Why are church leaders so quiet in the face of growing moral anarchy? And why do they spend much if not most of their time promoting counterproductive social and political causes?'

The American mainline churches have been in a serious and unprecedented numerical decline, losing between a fifth and a third of their membership. The US Methodist Church has lost 1,000 members every week for the last 30 years! Theologically liberal churches are rapidly greying due to aging membership. Methodist Professor Stanley Hauer was of Duke Divinity School said recently 'God is killing mainline Protestantism in America and we goddam well deserve it.' The Anglican Church in Canada is being bankrupted by claims from sex abuse victims. The Roman Catholic Church in America, although powerful and wealthy is facing the greatest crisis in its history. How do theologically liberal clergy, out of touch with the members in the pews, gain control of mainline church structures? Why are views expressed by the hierarchy so often out of tune with their members?

Dr Jim Heidinger of the United Methodist Church claims the hierarchy 'often have difficulties in the parish because of their views and then they begin searching for power. There is little else for them to do. Conservative evangelicals, on the other hand, tend to stay out of the political side of church life and concentrate on spreading the gospel. The result is a liberal takeover of church authority.' That is true of the Uniting Church in Australia. Consequently, mainline denominations have fallen for current fads, political correctness and cultural captivity. Liberal Christianity is indistinguishable from a dozen humanitarian causes. It may cease to be really Christian.

The result is terminal. Secular humanism has triumphed over the faith of our fathers. The social, political and sexual agenda of church officials find little support in the pews. Members of the Church are discouraged about the direction and future of the Church we love.

The Uniting Church has undergone an intensive debate over sexual standards among church leaders and the acceptance of homosexual activity as a Christian standard of behaviour, yet two city churches appointed prominent lesbian ministers and their livein lovers. These appointments are made in great secrecy without proper debate even though they affect the standards and public image of all of the churches. In the Uniting Church the weapons in such a debate are not Biblical arguments but slur words. Members who seek to uphold Biblical truth are called fundamentalist, reactionary, sexist and homophobic, while critics describe themselves as inclusive, modern, liberated, victims. The debate has degenerated into slurs and derogatory terms.

Rev. Craig Bailey says, 'Our denomination and its structures have been hijacked by those who reject an informed, Biblical position on matters of life and faith. They have rejected it in favour of a liberal ideology that relentlessly extols universalism at the expense of truth; experience at the expense of revelation; and humanism and subjectivism at the expense of Biblical standards.' Many members feel they are suffering more from the Church than they have ever been called upon to suffer for the Church. Can people who believe Biblical standards are the norm, accept what is not true to their convictions? Thousands of members have moved from mainline denominations into Baptist, Charismatic and Pentecostal churches. Others remain 'believers' but cease to be 'belongers'.

The National Church Life Survey says The Uniting Church has become a church of older women. Close to two thirds of UCA members are women over 60 years, one third being over 70 years of age. Our numbers have declined. Twenty-five years ago we were double the number of Baptists, today we have equal numbers. The Australian Christian Church, a network of Pentecostal, Apostolic and independent churches, has replaced the UCA as Australia's third largest denomination. It has 1,000 churches and 180,000 members. In Sunday attendance it ranks as number two denomination in Australia. The inaugural President, Pastor Brian Houston said: 'The ACC has drawn together a huge network of churches. Together they represent a vibrant, united and thriving church with answers to the challenges of modern day life. This means a focus on social justice, supporting people in need through our welfare organisations and providing contemporary worship relevant to every sphere of Australian society.' That was the kind of statement said a hundred times, thirty years ago when the Uniting Church came into being. Wesley Mission's International Congregation is the only very large evangelical charismatic congregation remaining in the Uniting Church. All the others have left.

Unfortunately, the democratic spirit is being eroded by a move towards centralised authority, financial recording and approvals. A Cardinal in the Australian Roman Catholic Church tells me he does not have the authority unchecked that one NSW UCA bureaucrat has!

There is a spirit in the UCA of mateship abroad. We have domesticated leadership passing it round among a bunch of mates. We must renew our church in several ways:

CHURCH LEADER

1. Uniting Church members must put their faith in Christ not in structures. Professor Herbert Butterfield said: 'Hold onto Christ and for the rest be totally uncommitted.' At the heart is our commitment to Christ as the incarnate Son of God, Saviour from sin, risen, reigning and soon returning Lord. We evangelicals have that commitment to Christ, so we weather aberration within or attack from without. Denominational structures are very human institutions, full of man-made regulations and less than Christian politics. Our faith is not in the structures of men but in the Lord of glory! The temple of God is holy, but that doesn't mean it is perfect. With Christ in our hearts, we can live in an imperfect structure. The problem is that structures move money from mission to bureaucracy. More structures, more Synod staff, more regulations, more duplication of oversight and over lapping committees and more meetings - but no increase in membership except for membership levies to fund the structures. Wesley Mission Sydney pays over $800,000 in bureaucracy fees and levies annually - $18,000 a week to belong! How that could be used to evangelise!

2. Uniting Church members must hold to the scriptures. Church leaders do not decide church doctrine. We hold to the living Word as revealed through the written Word. The battle is: does the Bible have authority and significance today? Evangelicals present the intellectual and faith responses to the nature and place of the Scriptures in the Church and our lives. We do not propose interpretations of the scriptures (liberationist, feminist, post-modernist or any other), which are available only to the select few, with particular training. We simply state in advance: we commit ourselves to obey what the Bible says as can be understood by committed Christians. We believe, not what is new, but what is true.

3. Uniting Church members must commit themselves to personal holiness and morality. High personal moral standards set Christians apart, help them witness to their faith and uphold Christian values. Dean Kelley states, 'No strong religious movement ever got far on a diffident, believe-and-let-believe approach.' There is no future for any denomination in which anything goes and nobody cares. Any move from Christian moral standards is to a moral vacuum. We are committed to moral standards and that includes what we do in secret and in our bedrooms. Holiness and morality are expected of all Christians, especially those ordained.

4. Uniting Church members must obey the Great Commission to evangelise. We call the world to Christ, not the Church to be conformed to the world. Without a commitment to bringing people outside of God to faith in God, from sin to righteousness, from death to life, the Church is already dead. The only way a church with membership decline, growing older and failing to retain its youth, is to survive is to practise aggressive, intelligent and effective evangelism. Young adults respond to that enthusiastically.

5. Uniting Church members must come to grips with multi-culturalism. The Uniting Church has the highest proportion of people born in Australia of any

denomination with more than 90% being English speaking only. But evangelical congregations have started more than 100 ethnic congregations throughout Australia with Korean, Chinese and Pacific Islanders predominating. But most of these are mono-cultural, not multi-cultural. It was the people from non-English speaking backgrounds and the Aboriginal and Torres Strait Islander Congress that supported our views in the sexuality debate. They hold Christian values that should be in every church.

6. Uniting Church Members must serve the community. Many liberals talk about justice, but it is the Evangelicals that do the work and give the money. Visit any of our caring centres for the aged, the sick, the mentally ill, the disabled, the disturbed, the homeless, the drug addicted and so on and you will find Evangelicals who express their faith in caring service. There is great community service being done in the Uniting Church and the people who are active in personal service are the Evangelicals, not humanists.

In the Uniting Church of Australia there is spiritual warfare (Eph. 6). The battle is with spiritual and dark forces in high places. It is a battle primarily for the Bible's place in the life of a believer and its authority within the Church. Although the issue has been fought over whether clergy living in homosexual relationships outside of marriage could be ordained as clergy within the Uniting Church, the bigger issue is what role has the Bible in the Uniting Church today and what is its authority? It is a battle the Evangelicals with their high view of scripture must win - but it is a battle that they will win. You might well ask why will they win? Here are ten reasons why the Evangelicals will win:

1. Evangelicals are better equipped for spiritual warfare. They may be naïve politically and have been out manoeuvred by the tactical nous of the Church's multitudinous regulations constantly used against them, but the battle essentially is a spiritual one and that is where the Evangelicals are better equipped because they possess the whole armour of God. They know how to use the sword, which is the word of God both in attack and defence. Although reluctant to get into the nitty gritty of spiritual warfare, the evangelicals have realised that they are equipped for such warfare.

2. The Evangelical giant has been aroused. The decision made by the 2003 Assembly of the Uniting Church in Melbourne to approve the ordination of practising homosexuals has shocked the grass roots membership of the Church. Thousands of ordinary members have now joined at crowded protest rallies held all across Australia. Evangelicals had to lose the vote at the Assembly in order to awake the slumbering giant within the pews of the churches. It is the same in the United States where the evangelical and conservative membership has turned the tide, which for twenty-five years has been successful in winning every liberal change brought about in the main line churches.

3. Old-fashioned liberalism in Australia is already a spent force. There is a lack

of leadership within the Uniting Church in Australia. We are all mates together and every now and then we get someone whom we elect as first mate. The Uniting Church is like a cruise ship that keeps going round and round in circles. The small gay lobby ingratiated themselves into the Church's bureaucracy. Even the President admitted that he was 'greatly surprised' with the reaction of the grass roots membership. People who worked in the paid bureaucracy of the Church are often greatly surprised by the grass roots majority. It is the sign of just how out of touch they are in spite of holding high office.

4. Para-church ministries have taken the interest, the time and the money of evangelicals but now they are helping their evangelical colleagues by encouraging those within the Uniting church to stay there and fight for their rights as Christians whose time, interest and prayer has made the Uniting Church what it is today.

5. Evangelicals are younger, richer and more energetic. If you look at the old time liberal clergy in the Uniting Church you will discover that most of them were trained in the 1950's and 60's. None of them can stand up and point to any significant growth in any congregation which they have led as old time liberals. The clergy suit an aging and dying membership. But among the evangelicals and charismatic Christians within the Uniting Church, it is the young adults who are making the pace. All of the growing churches in Australia are evangelical. The largest congregations are evangelical. While the average age of all the people that attend Uniting Churches is 66 years, the average age of the thousands of people who attend services at Wesley Mission Sydney is 31 years. The evangelicals across Australia are younger with more disposable income and are willing to put their money where their mouths are. They do not want their church hijacked by minority lobby groups.

6. There is a new ecumenical coalition coming into being. There is a commonality of doctrine and viewpoint on many of the great issues facing the Church today, found among Roman Catholics, Anglicans, Orthodox, Protestant and Pentecostal Christians. They have great concerns for the issues of quality of life, of faithfulness in marriage and celibacy in singleness, in being opposed to liberal, abortionist and euthanasia advocates. Those Christians across all the denominations are networking and they stand united and strong against the advance of homosexual clergy.

7. The Bible is never outdated. There are people who always want to talk about their interpretation of the Bible and who are willing to treat the Bible as a book of interesting characters and information with as much authority and inspiration as a telephone directory. But Evangelicals know something that has been forgotten: *'you have been born again, not of perishable seed, but of imperishable, through the living and enduring Word of God. For, 'all men are like grass and all their glory is like the flowers of the field; the grass withers and the flowers fall but the Word of the Lord stands forever.' And this was the word that was preached to you.'* (1 Peter 1:23-25). Dean Paul

Zahl of the Cathedral Church of the Advent in Birmingham, Alabama, USA, recognises that the recent election of the Episcopal church's first openly homosexual bishop has profound theological implications. He says the action 'demolishes the Good News of salvation.... It demolishes salvation because it asserts that what Scripture calls sin is not sin. When there is no sin, there is no judgement. Without judgement, there can be no repentance. Without repentance, there is no forgiveness. The decision fashions a God who is oblivious to sin. It thus denies the redemption of the world to a whole category of persons.'

8. You cannot fool all of the people all of the time. The history of fifteen years of dialogue and discussion over the homosexual issues within the Church reveals a litany of church cover-ups, lies and secret meetings. But the grass roots membership of the Uniting Church has woken up. They are aware of immorality in high places, of lesbian sex, heterosexual adultery, homosexual partnering among church leaders and they have had enough of it. They are no longer fooled by church, bureaucratic cover-ups and secret meetings. To our shame, clergy, living immorally, have even been recommended to more significant positions. Evangelicals have now drawn the line in the sand.

9. The fear tactic is losing its power. For many years ministers have been fearful about future placements, about their housing and superannuation but there is now a new sense of freedom. Ministers are standing up in public protest meetings saying 'For years I have been fearful of my job because I know that if I speak out on these issues the Church bureaucracy will fail to appoint me to any new church. I was fearful of my career. But not anymore! I realise I cannot be silent but I must speak out for the faith once and for all delivered to the saints.'

In the same way churches were fearful of standing up against the trends of bureaucrats, however they are no longer frightened of the threatening talk that they would lose their property and that the Church bureaucracy holds the titles. Many congregations have walked away from their properties and those who haven't are determined to stay in and fight for their rights as people who have both paid for and prayed for their church facilities. Evangelicals are no longer afraid of taking legal action to preserve their rights. Legal opinion at the highest level is being engaged. Class action suits are possible.

10. Evangelicals are learning to play the liberal game. For a long time the liberals counted on the Evangelicals remaining silent or leaving the Church in disgust. Evangelicals are not known for their political cunning nor for their willingness to engage in long debate and bitter dispute. Now they are no longer leaving and remaining silent. They are prepared to speak up and fight for the truth. But they do so clad in the whole armour of God, 'each piece put on with prayer.' That prayer power cannot be underestimated.

The battle will be fought in all of the mainline denominations. In the United States and in the United Kingdom the great mainline churches, that have been losing membership and significance in society for decades, have found revival and renewal through the younger more committed Evangelicals. The same will happen in Australia.

In mid 2005, I began to receive requests to consider nomination as the President Elect of the Assembly of The Uniting Church in Australia. These requests seemed to be totally unconnected with each other. They came from responsible members in most parts of Australia. But I cannot discount the thought that some hopeful person was e-mailing people of like mind across the nation. They all said basically the same thing - that they believed that God was leading them to ask me to consider his will for me and to be prepared for election as the next President of the Assembly of the Uniting Church. God may have been speaking to them, but he was not speaking to me! I replied saying I was deeply honoured but declined. Our church does need leadership to take the bureaucrats back to Biblical lifestyles and beliefs, to where the grass-roots membership believed they should be. That would be a painful five years for a President, moving against an entrenched group of bureaucrats determined to hold their positions. For these people are basically unacceptable to congregations in any other position.

I declined, not because I was afraid of standing for election, because after all, in 2003 I had stood with 292 other candidates before 4.6 million voters, with my photograph on posters outside every polling booth in the state and on two million 'How to Vote' cards. I did not mind going before the public for election. And I did win, being elected by sufficient No 1 ballots so that preferences were not required.

That is the primary reason why I was not willing to stand for election as leader of the Assembly of The Uniting Church in Australia for the following five years. I had already been elected for the following eight years as a state senator to the Legislative Council of NSW. Now I was serving in the oldest parliament in the land, not only as a member, but also as the elected Chair of many important Government committees and inquiries. I was writing reports to the Parliament and making recommendations that would impact on the lives of all citizens. In many of these recommendations, I was recommending a more Christian treatment of people and society. This was a new ministry. My speeches were unfettered and I was able to make every comment I desired on Christian matters, delivering them into Hansard and the official history of our land.

After retirement from 27 years at Wesley Mission, I will spend most Sundays preaching in scores of churches across the land who have invited me as a special visiting preacher. But I will also attend one local church as a worshipper. There are a number of good churches near our home, including two very large Community Evangelical Churches, each with hundreds of members. The Uniting Churches near our home we have visited regularly on our holidays. They exhibit the same divisive tendencies and spirit of despair as do the rest of the Uniting Church. When we visited one of the Community Evangelical Churches, we found not only large, young vibrant congregations, but several Uniting Church ministers, who, having left the Uniting Church ministry, have made this church their home.

There is deep concern among grass roots members that the Uniting Church in Australia is dying. The statistics undergird this concern. One hundred and fifty former Uniting Church members are welcomed every week of the year, into membership in Baptist, Pentecostal, Evangelical and other denominational churches. The Winter 2005 edition of 'The Travelling Emu' states in an article on the splitting of the Uniting Church that, 'a lay and ministerial network of contacts throughout the Uniting Church in Australia (UCA) provided information on losses from the UCA over the issue of homosexuals in leadership in the Church. About one quarter of the losses occurred after the Eighth Assembly in 1997 and three quarters after passage of Resolution 84 by the Tenth Assembly in 2003.

More than 6500 attendees have left the UCA, many of whom were leaders in their own congregations. There have been splits in 109 congregations (with an average loss of 50 persons per congregation) and 41 new congregations have been formed outside the UCA.

43 ministers have resigned or retired over the homosexuality in leadership issue, 14 uniting churches have closed and one presbytery is dysfunctional. The UCA is in denial over the losses and it was reported on ABC Radio National's Religion Report that the figures are 'exaggerated'. They are in fact less than the true total. Unless the UCA accepts the reality of the situation and rescinds Resolution 84 and reforms the Church, a widening of the current schism is inevitable.'

Many laypeople who have prayed and sacrificed for their church and are dismayed at the serious likelihood of their church splitting before it reaches its thirtieth anniversary.

The same article continues: 'During the 60's and 70's there was much enthusiasm for the union of the Congregational, Methodist and Presbyterian Churches in Australia. This was achieved in 1977 after the Methodists voted state by state in favour of union, but the Congregational and Presbyterian churches voted church by church, with the result that about one third of Presbyterian and some Congregational churches did not join. Unfortunately, the formation of the UCA, which many hoped would promote church unity and witness, did not decrease the number of denominations.

In 1977 homosexual acts between men were illegal in Australia. Appropriate Christian sexual behaviour was paraphrased as 'celibacy in singleness and faithfulness in marriage', but the UCA Assembly in the 1980's declined to affirm this principle for its ordained ministry. The trend in society towards acceptance of gays and lesbians was mirrored in the UCA by liberals and a gay lobby group.

The Assembly Standing Committee (ASC) appointed a 'committee not representative of the whole church' which produced in 1996 an Interim Report on Sexuality. The church was asked to respond to the report and there were more than 8000 responses. Overall 82% of the reports from synods, presbyteries, parishes, councils of elders, congregations and individuals were opposed to homosexuality in leadership. In the analysis commissioned by the ASC, it was estimated that 30,000 people had responded. Faced with this overwhelmingly negative response, the ASC did not accept that this represented the authentic voice of the Church and the committee produced a final report, which was presented at the Eighth Assembly in 1997. This caused deep divisions within the UCA and losses of members, which were glossed over.

At the Tenth Assembly in July 2003 the issue of practising homosexuals in leadership within the UCA was debated and what became known as Resolution 84 passed after a strong appeal for 'unity in diversity'. This caused severe destabilisation of the Church. EMU (Evangelical Members within the Uniting church) arranged a petition protesting against Resolution 84, which was signed by over 22,000 people. The petition was presented to the ASC who chose to ignore it. In September 2003, EMU organised a Summit Meeting at which the Reforming Alliance (RA) within the UCA was formed. The RA organised a National Survey with three simple questions on the issue of homosexuality in leadership that was opposed by Synod General Secretaries and by liberal church councils and ministers. Despite this opposition, completed questionnaires were received from 27,014 members and adherents in 1459 congregations of which 88% were opposed to Resolution 84. This overwhelmingly negative response is similar to the 1996 negative response of 82% and shows that UCA members have not changed their opinion.' (Dr Howard Bradbury, Canberra, May 20, 2005)

The intransigence of the gay and liberal lobby in disregarding the viewpoint of its membership makes the splitting of the Church certain. Already much of the strength of the Uniting Church has already dissipated. The Uniting Church is not a democratic institution, but a rule by those who believe themselves fundamentally superior to ordinary believers, whose opinions do not count.

Loyal grassroots members should remember that the Uniting Church was essentially a piece of ecclesiastical carpentry, tacking one part of one denomination onto another. If it falls apart the whole church of Jesus Christ is not diminished. Faithful members will simply move to their neighbouring church where Jesus Christ is honoured and the Bible is upheld as a source of authority for Christians.

This does leave the property assets, hospitals and aged care facilities in the control of the liberal lobby, which is what they want. Some of these will be sold to generate funds for their own salaries, as has already happened in some Synods. But the rest will gradually continue as secular institutions, funded by the governments as has already happened with some church schools. The Uniting Church will continue as a rump, until it peters out, as has happened with other branches of the Christian church over the ages. At the moment, the only uncertainty is who will eventually turn the lights out.

BUILDER

Chapter Five

For the last fifty years of my life I have been building. Although trained and called to be a preacher of the Gospel, I have constantly spent time planning, designing, building and altering houses, hospitals, churches, nursing homes, retirement villages and so on. I have had some part to play in the building, occupying or developing of over 400 buildings, together worth several hundred million dollars.

Architects, developers, builders, concreters, town planners and the like have trooped in and out of my offices and battles have been waged with councils, environment authorities, banks and the like with most battles usually won. No wonder the Housing Industry of Australia declared at the opening of some award winning houses that one of Australia's leading builders was in fact a preacher!

In the slum areas of Melbourne we realised the buildings needed immediate repair. We jumped into the task. I remember Beverley, heavily pregnant, up a twenty eight foot ladder painting big walls with me close to midnight. We built additions to the church, a carport for the Manse, new fences and the like.

At Ararat, even in a brief ministry, I drew up plans for the total development of the site with new toilets, church and manse. We built the hall, kitchen and toilet block, concreted the paths, painted the walls and started on plans for a new manse. The manse was eventually built and forty years later I was invited back to open the new church renovations.

Up to now the buildings I was designing and working on had mostly volunteer builders and very small budgets. When I came to Cheltenham the scope was widened – now we were working with professionals and a multi-million dollar budget. Later this was to become teams of professionals and budgets of hundreds of millions of dollars.

Within the family, building was always in vogue. With the help of eager children, I built a cubby house 2 storeys high with an outlook over the rooves of houses to the Bay, with hammocks, blinds, ladder, slippery pole, sandbox and a whole lot of features to make the kids happy. Then we purchased in 1971 our own home at Dromana. That was going to be a big challenge.

Australians know much about moving mountains. We have shifted Mount Tom Price, Iron Knob, Mount Hammersley Mount Isa and Broken Hill. We can shift mountains by using heavy machinery. But how can you shift mountains by faith? With faith you require only two things: work and persistence!

I decided to turn the Dromana house into a two-storey house. As I could not lift it up, I decided to go down. The house was 45 feet long and 25 feet wide. We had to go down about four feet. There was not enough room under the house for a machine; it had to be done with a shovel. I said to the mountain of earth, 'Be moved!' And the Lord said to me, 'Get a wheelbarrow!'

I got under the house and started digging. I filled up a wheelbarrow and wheeled it round to the front. We had half an acre of land on a gentle hill, so I started building up the bottom of the hill. Then, another barrow and another, then fifty. Every Monday with a pick and shovel and a barrow and I said to the Lord, 'Move this mountain,' and the Lord said, 'Wheel the barrow!'

Gradually, I began to see a hole. It was then I discovered a great truth about dirt. More comes out of a hole than was in there originally. A hundred barrow loads of earth levelled the front lawn. Two hundred barrows of earth meant that the block beside us was now level. In went the first rumpus room and then the laundry.

Meanwhile, we had to bring in barrow loads of concrete, new house stumps, windows and dividing walls. But the earth was moving and the house began to increase in size. After another two years I had shifted enough earth for me to add a garage and workshop. I said to the Lord, 'Move this hill,' but the Lord said, 'Keep wheeling. You and I are in this together.' I said, 'Yes, Lord, but I'm the one who is getting hot!'

Gradually the lawn area became smooth. Then came more concrete and, finally, the big, double rumpus room. Seven years after I began digging, the hill was removed. We finished the walls. I did all the plumbing, electrical, concreting and building myself, up to the standard expected by the council building inspectors. We then moved in the fittings and put up the table-tennis table. The windows worked and the lights were fixed. Everything was beautiful. The furniture was in and the carpet was down and we now had a house double its original size. Then Wesley Central Mission said, 'Come to Sydney!'

When we put our Victorian home on the market, an interested purchaser said, 'What a lovely smooth lawn you have.' He did not know that faith, plus work, plus persistence had doubled the size of a house and turned a hill into a smooth lawn! The improved value of that first house in Dromana enabled us to purchase an investment property also in Dromana to improve in value while we shifted to Sydney.

The value increased but it was a long way away for us to keep an eye on it. Beverley's sister Gwen and her husband Jim did, but they then unexpectedly died within a year of each other. So we sold that house and purchased a new brick home on the side of a hill, overlooking the ocean at Terrigal. This Wamberal home was three storeys and enough room for us underneath to dig out the dirt, level the back yard and build a large rumpus room for the kids. That project was Dromana all over again. They loved it and we enjoyed the view. But going up and down three flights of stairs lost its attraction, so we sold it and looked for a larger area of land and with flat terrain. We found it on an acreage complete with dam and small orchard of fruit trees at Tumbi Umbi (Aboriginal for 'tall trees'). We had a very large number of tall trees (most over 80 feet high). Soon we had our livestock in. Peter and Trina brought their goat, dogs, sheep, fowls and ducks while they lived there while building their own home on an acreage not far away. Tumbi Umbi was to become our home for retirement.

To make it how we wanted it, some more digging, another concrete slab and a magnificent study, the size of two rooms. Then a veranda built by Peter around two sides of the house - 66 metres long and 4 metres wide - the equivalent of about 8 additional rooms. Then, based on the lovely Dutch roof barns I saw in America, I designed and Peter built a 2 storey barn for all our garden implements. Then a tractor and woodshed and a new hen house. By the dam we built a duck house and soon the place was filled with life. This is the home to which Beverley and I have retired to and from where I do my writing for Parliament and the media.

At the same time, we were living in Wesley Mission's manse at Roseville. That was inadequate in many ways until I got the idea to build an internal staircase, remove the roof and build as a second storey a magnificent study, covering an area of four large rooms, with plenty of shelves for books and windows looking out in every direction over the rooftops and the National Park lands. Building the house while you were living in it was not an unusual experience for us!

The first really big building for which I had responsibility was the Christian Retirement Centre at Cheltenham. The first idea for the CRC Cheltenham grew from an approach by Bernard Belgrove, on behalf of Rollands Hance and Co following an explosive Australia Day Dinner in the Moorabbin Town Hall which I addressed raising important questions about Australia's future. This was just weeks after the sacking of Gough Whitlam and political feeling ran high. But out of it came a meeting with Robert Hance, Michael Tinsley, David de Garis and John Bailey.

In August 1975, the church voted to build the first Christian Retirement Centre and shortly after a second, Greenways Retirement Village. The church started fundraising for facilities and the community centre. The Mayor organised a fundraising concert. I spoke at more than a hundred meetings raising money and we purchased a piano, billiard table, bowls mats, large TV, nurse unit furniture, sick bay facilities, library books and much more. The first residents moved into our second retirement village, 'Greenways' in August 76 and into the CRC in November '76. Beverley and I helped many residents shift personally and each one became a close friend. We helped our first thirty residents pack, shift and unpack. On many a night I was pushing someone's refrigerator into place or connecting up a washing machine.

The members of the Cheltenham Church of Christ were strong in their support of the development of both villages. Of the paid staff great help was received from minister colleagues Geoff Benson, Stanton Wilson, Malcolm Humphries and Maurie Conrey, Social Worker Joy Rainey and office secretary Joy Kavanagh. Our nurses Julie Acquroff, Helen Hall, Jan Robins, Marion Todd and Jean Freeland gave wonderful service. Steve Waixel and a great group of volunteers planted the lawns and gardens.

Outstanding service was given in administration by Col Junor, John Flavin, Malcolm Humphries and Graham Hall. The Board of Management all served voluntarily and physically did much work on the site. I remember with appreciation the service given by the Management Chairman Wal Steart, Church Board Chairman Don Stokie, Church Secretary Graham Hilbig and Treasurers Charles Ferris and Ern Henderson.

Many women helped greatly in settling residents, setting up the community lounges and providing visitation. I remember the work of Pat Hilbig, Muriel Stafford and Fay Ferris particularly. Seven men joined with me in being trained by Graham Mortimer to gain our special bus drivers' licence and in our 18 seat Toyota, drove residents to free picnics at Sovereign Hill, Coal Creek, Swan Hill Pioneer settlement and other places. I only did the training program for the special bus drivers' licence to encourage the other men. In the end I received an articulated truck drivers licence. A minister of religion was then and has ever since been licensed to drive a heavy truck or semi-trailer.

Over 1000 people attended the opening of CRC by the Governor of Victoria, Sir Henry Winneke. Fay Ferris conducted our four choirs and musical ensemble and brass in a wonderful musical presentation. We announced that day the commencement of Stage 2 of CRC, together with the building of ' Pine Lodge' and the building of stage 2 Greenways. 1977 and 1978 saw all these major additions completed. We had gradually acquired the additional houses and land for these buildings. Church Secretary Graham Hilbig did a great deal of work to make this possible.

In those thirteen years of ministry the real mark lay in the number of buildings that were built around the Cheltenham Church of Christ. A new manse was constructed; a new office for the church, as well as the twenty-three unit Christian Retirement Centre. Greenways Village, which went on to have ninety seven units and a nursing home and then the Christian Retirement Centre stage 2 of thirty six new units plus two new tennis courts, then Pine Lodge with sixteen more retirement units, three houses to be demolished for car parking and another to be built as a centre for administration.

The church was developing and growing, adding to its properties and staff numbers and going out in faith for multi-million dollar developments. When the time came to announce my resignation, I indicated that I wanted to stay for one more year - our thirteenth - so that in that year we could completely clear any debts on the entire property, leaving the multi-million dollar campus in pristine order with new buildings, a regular maintenance program and no debts at all. We finally purchased land for a new Church and I made some sketch plans. The new Church was constructed on the site, roughly conforming to the sketch plans, a few years later.

My wife and I have found that our prayers have been answered by God, sometimes in ways unexpected and sometimes through people who did not even notice that they were the instruments of God. God's promise is assured and our prayers are answered. That is why we live with confidence. We know that he hears our prayers and answers our needs.

One day in 1977, we were at our church at Cheltenham, Victoria. There had been a lot of property expansion in our church and our frontage had grown from 60 feet to 100 feet. As the congregation increased, we decided that we needed even more property. The only way we could achieve this in that intensely built up area was to buy houses. We bought one five houses away, then four away, then one away, then two away. But No.11 would not sell. We bought No.14, then Nos.13 and 9. Gradually we gained more area for development and our frontage went from 120 to 200, to 400, to 600 to 1400 feet! New buildings went up.

We spent several millions of dollars and we owned all the properties in the street, except No.1 in Pine Street! We needed it. Two lovely, elderly ladies lived there and I got to know them. I said, 'Some day, when you are ready to sell, we would like to buy because we need the property to complete our development plans.' They promised that they would sell to us.

When our expansion programme was at its height and we had no money, the old ladies chose that time to sell and shift! We had no money! I thought, ' How can I get that property and fulfil the need we have?' I walked along the street, looking at the house and land and I said, 'I believe, God, that You want us to have this property so that we can minister to the needs of the people in this area.'

As I stood there, I said, 'Lord, I believe that You want your church to have this opportunity for growth and in the name of Jesus Christ I claim the house and land for the church.' I had never done that before and as I prayed, standing in the middle of the road I felt a real goose.

A nephew of the two ladies was a member of our church. I said to him, ' George, would you talk with your old aunts and tell them we will negotiate a price.' He agreed. A week went by. He came back and said, 'We are getting closer to the right price, now.' I replied, 'Well, George, make sure it is the right price for us. Just do it quickly, because we haven't any money.' George said, 'Don't worry. I'll be back.' He returned to tell me he had placed a small deposit on the property. We were greatly relieved. My task then was to find a way of raising the money.

Next thing, there was a ring on our doorbell! A wealthy builder, who lived in the next street, was standing there. I said, 'Come in Bill.' He walked in and said, 'I thought I'd better tell you that I have bought No. 1 at the end of Pine Street.' I said, 'I don't believe it.' He said, 'I have.'
My response was, 'Listen, I have prayed about that property. You know that we have wanted to buy it. We have asked our church to pray about it. We intend to raise the money as soon as we know the price.' He replied, 'I knew that you were after it and that I had to act quickly. I went round last night and paid a deposit. I have bought it!' As his was a proper deposit, I guessed he had rights under Law over our minimum holding deposit paid by George.

I said, 'Bill, you will regret this. Why did you do it?' He said, 'My daughter is getting married and we thought it would be good if she lived near us, just over the back fence.' 'Yes,' I said, 'I know about the wedding, I am conducting it. But I think you will regret what you have done.' Bill left and the property, which I felt God had promised to us, for which I had asked in prayer, in his name and for the needs of his people, had gone to someone else.

It was a lovely wedding and the bride and her husband made a fine couple. They were going to be very happy, but they made a firm decision. They said to their parents, 'We don't want to live next door to you. We think it is important to move away and live in our own house someplace else.'

Bill, then, had to get tenants. The first lot used to drive their motorbike up and down the hallway. The second lot had a barbecue in the middle of the lounge room. The third tenant hammered pictures anywhere and everywhere around the walls. The fourth had regular barbecues and the smoke and rubbish went over the fence into Bill's place. Broken beer bottles were thrown into his swimming pool. He came to me, complaining about the tenants and all the trouble he was having. I said, ' Bill, I told you.'

After the fifth collection of terrible tenants, Bill came round and said, 'Listen, do you want to buy that property?' I replied, 'No, not now. We haven't any money.' He said, 'I'll do a deal with you. If you give me the contract to put up the new building, I will give you a fair price that is competitive. I need work for my tradesmen right now. I'll build whatever you want and when the building is finished I will give you, free, the titles to the property.' So it was. Seven months afterwards, 'Pine Lodge' was built on the very land we had prayed for and we never paid a cent for it!

The Apostle John once wrote: 'He hears us whenever we ask Him; and since we know this is true, we know also that He gives us what we ask Him; and since we know this is true, we know also that He gives us what we ask from Him.' (1 John 5:15).

The church at Cheltenham had now completed a tremendous program of building developments purchasing old properties, demolishing them and building a new manse and offices, five retirement villages catering for more than 300 people, a nursing home, tennis courts, extensive car parks and gardens and in the process the largest campus of probably any Protestant church in the nation. This meant as a minister I was used to dealing with finance, legal agreements, building contracts worth many millions of dollars and companies. This was all in preparation for the shift to Sydney.

After my appointment in 1977, I spent all of 1978 in preparation before shifting to Sydney. In this time I wrote a 150,000 word thesis describing what I intended to accomplish in this ministry, 'TRANSFORMING THE CITY CHURCH'. [Moyes, G.K. Transforming the City Church. (Unpublished) U.T.C. Library.] I was very proud to have inherited Wesley Lyceum Theatre, given to the Mission in 1905 and the relatively new Wesley Centre. Wesley Centre, built in 1966, had become the hub of the Mission's growing pastoral and head office activities. But by 1979 I was seeing it in a new light: a wonderful facility that still had over a million dollars of debt owing on it, was facing large maintenance costs and was a facility standing in the way of a more efficient use of the land.

From the height of the new Sydney Tower at Centrepoint in 1980, I looked down on the property of Wesley Mission and the newly formed Synod of the Uniting Church in New South Wales and realised that what was needed was the complete removal of The Mission Settlement Building, the removal of Wesley Chapel, the removal of Wesley Arcade of shops and Christian enterprises and the removal of the recently rebuilt Lyceum Theatre and Wesley Centre, at that time the finest church complex in the Southern Hemisphere. It would also require a total rebuilding of the whole site with expanded facilities! This was a daring insight. We would need to excavate two acres of Central Business District land to a depth of eight storeys then from ground level go forty storeys up.

This meant a project that would alter the skyline of the city of Sydney. It would mean the construction of a massive complex using the air space above the total site (51,000 square feet) in such proportions (12:1 Floor Space Ratio) that the new development would be large enough (686,000 square feet), when leased, to provide the total cost of the Mission's portion of the construction. It was a grand vision. During its construction it would be the largest building enterprise in the city (Hely & Horne, Stuart and Perry: 'Piccadilly Plaza' Design Concept, August 1983). This projected development brought Wesley Mission a great deal of commendable publicity.

The initial projection of the cost was one hundred million dollars, an astronomical sum, but before the decade was over this sum would have risen four times. What would be accomplished on that site would not be at the expense of other developments, for Wesley Mission was to simultaneously embark on the most ambitious building program ever to be undertaken by any church in the world. Another one hundred million dollars of land acquisition, of buildings and the construction of new facilities would be undertaken in a huge expansion and renovation program in other areas of the church's ministry.

I had seen the retirement villages we had built serving a real purpose in the lives of people who could take a whole of life tenancy and whose families would receive 90% of their up front payment back when they vacated and another tenant moved in. As property values escalated, we were able to return 100% of all ingoings. I discussed the developments with the Mission Board one night in our lounge room. They decided to go ahead with three villages I had sketched out. 'What one shall we do first?' asked someone. 'Let's do all three simultaneously' I replied. So we started on the $100 million project. Those four projects alone were costing four hundred million dollars and we opened each one debt free. Starting with a million dollars of debt we now had four hundred million dollars of assets with no debt at all.

New initiatives in evangelism would be undertaken across the nation by television and radio, new missionary support in USSR, India, Bangladesh, new programs of support for village life in the Philippines and India would be undertaken and more than two hundred new services for the poor and needy would be established. All of these would require additional property, the appointment of new staff and a sustained fundraising program beyond what had ever been attempted by a church before. My life suddenly became a constant round of meetings with architects, planners, financiers and bankers, builders and others in the industry.

Today Wesley Mission gives thanks to God for the successful completion of all these major works, without any residual debt and at the height of its power looks forward to serving the needs of the community and witnessing to Jesus Christ.

The ministry of this single church is so widespread that few people ever get to see it. In one hundred suburbs, in dozens of rural and inter-state areas and in a number of countries overseas, this church conducts a wide- spread ministry. Yet everything it does is according to careful strategy and Biblical precedent as it seeks to minister in both Word and deed. Its philosophy of care is continually spelled out to staff and members to remind people of the basis of its work. Its development has been due to the applications of Church Growth principles.

Over a period of seven years, the design concepts of our new CBD complex were developed, changed and eventually approved. Approvals were given at all levels for the redevelopment. We were building in conjunction with the Synod UCA, a four level shopping plaza, double the community service area we previously held - nearly 3 acres - including restaurant, youth facilities, auditoriums, rooms and halls, a 500 seat Wesley Church, a 250 seat Lyceum and a state-of-the-art 990 seat Theatre and a 31 storey office tower that would have 4 floors used by Wesley Mission with the rest leased out to help pay for the building costs. Underneath it all would be a five level car park with parking for 400 vehicles.

There would be direct access into the main David Jones buildings and an air-bridge over Pitt Street to the Monorail and the Hilton Hotel and to the new building on Market Street and Pitt and from there to Grace Bros making an above ground shopping loop. Another above ground air-bridge was to be built over Castlereagh St to take people directly into our building from the Sheraton Hotel and St James Railway Station. We would also liquidate the $750,000 debt left over from the building 22 years ago in Alan Walker's time, which we had been reducing but upon which we are still paying heavy interest after all of those years.

To allow the new building to commence required us to shift into the Plaza Theatre, George Street and into a series of multi-storey buildings adjacent to the Theatre in Wilmot Street, alongside the biggest theatre complex in Sydney. This was the area where the people were walking every night and all the weekend. We would be directly on the bus route, two blocks down from Town Hall station and along the brightest lit street in Sydney. We believed this to be an excellent ministry area while the new complex would be built.

Companies often shift head office, but for Wesley Mission it was a more complex move. We would shift our corporate headquarters; shift our church, its worship services and group activities; shift our School for Seniors; shift our 24-hour a day telephone counselling centre, Lifeline; shift our welfare and personal counselling centre; shift our media division. This was to be a major relocation involving hundreds of staff and thousands of people.

To this end, all of my preaching at the time was on the Urban Ministries of Jesus, looking at the principles in city ministry so that our people were being prepared to shift.

We used the shift as an opportunity for a new thrust in public awareness and outreach. The church is often like a snail that only advances by putting its neck out, but then, after looking around, decides to pull its head in and retreat into its shell. We are made of sterner stuff. For 175 years we had been on the streets of Sydney doing a job of caring for it. We know our job and we do it well. We would not retreat. We faced the future with confidence and commenced new youth ministries and outreach programs to street kids.

Although the decision to demolish and rebuild a bigger and better Wesley Mission caused a lot of trauma, it proved to be the easiest part.

We faced one hurdle after another. As fast as they solved one problem another-cropped up council permits, site inspections, water-board inspections, electricity-board approval, sewerage, town- planning, D A (Development application) B A (Building application) and a host of other requirements too numerous to list. We had not only to design and build the Pitt Street complex but also the George and Wilmot Street complex, which in itself was a multi-million dollar reconstruction of existing adjacent buildings.

In carrying forward the tremendous undertaking Richard Menteith and his associates needed the patience of Job and the Wisdom of Solomon. Thanks are due to our Task Force: Chair Ed Walker; Secretary Robyn Dyer; Colin Gillmore (Director), Stan Manning, Andy Pettigrew, Peter Tebbutt and Malcolm Burrells with Richard Menteith and myself being in the driving seat. Despite the setbacks, the proposals and counter-proposals, the worries and headaches, God answered our prayers for help and eventually all the preliminary requirements were sorted out by July 1988.

The biggest headache was trying to find temporary accommodation for the business offices and staff. We rented three different buildings-there wasn't a hope of getting them all together-and they all had to be remodelled to suit our needs and linked by new stairways, fly overs and corridors. The temporary premises were not time-efficient, work-efficient or money saving, but we had little choice. Even the temporary four storey mid city premises was a bigger building proposal than ever previously undertaken by any church in the nation. During these years Stan Manning, Richard Menteith, John Bush and their staff provided valuable help. It would never have happened without them and a remarkable team of helpers and volunteers who did what ever was asked of them.

Long before the Mission's temporary location was ready the demolition squad moved in, working around the staff in the old Wesley Centre. Board meetings convened with members shouting to be heard above the din of battering jackhammers and the crash of falling timbers. Telephonists, with a telephone to one ear and a hand pressed tightly over the other, endeavoured to carry on conversations to the noisy accompaniment of heavy boots tramping by doorways minus doors. Catering staff, office girls, pastors and teachers all battled along trying to concentrate on their tasks, while brawny fellows with tattooed arms worked around them tearing out windows and removing fixtures, scattering dust, debris and bent nails in their wake. Nobody actually said so, but it seemed that while the demolition company worked with great gusto at the Pitt Street premises, the renovator-builders at George Street properties seemed to be purposely dragging their feet.

A crisis appeared inevitable. It came late one Friday afternoon when word spread that workmen on the George Street renovations had found a 50 cm by 37 cm piece of asbestos behind an electric power board. Instantly the relevant unions called all workmen off the site. Work stopped at the Wilmot and Central Street sites also, although no asbestos had been found on them. Nothing could be done during the weekend but as soon as I reached my office on Monday morning an official connected with one of the unions came to see me.

'It's going to take months for that place in George Street to be thoroughly examined and cleared of any suggestion of asbestos,' he announced. 'The law says that my workers must not be in the building until it has been checked for contamination.' He then demanded every workman on site be sent by taxi to have chest X-rays, everyone to be given a new set of work clothes and boots and several health checks.

Work on the renovations was so far behind schedule now that I could not entertain the thought of it being held up for months longer. The man's cocksure manner had already aroused my suspicions.

'Is there anything that we can do to help speed up the process?' I asked. 'There is,' the official replied with what could have been a trace of triumph in his voice, 'but it will cost you money.' I made no comment and the official continued, 'If I had $40,000 to share between the workmen they would do the search themselves and once they were satisfied that the site was safe, they'd pretty quickly get on with the job.'

I said nothing and taking my silence for consent the union official hurried on. 'If you want that to happen, bring me the money in a brown paper bag to the bar of the hotel on the corner of Pitt and Wilmot Streets tomorrow at 1 p m. Don't bring anyone else with you.'

I took a deep breath. Was this really happening? Was I hearing correctly? Surely such blatant bribery only took place on TV, not in real life. I replied firmly, 'Wesley Mission is a Christian charitable organisation and we will not pay bribes to have the building site cleared. We will use every other lawful method to get the work done. Good morning to you, Sir.'

Next day I by-passed the unions and went straight to the building contractor in charge of the George Street alterations. Without using threats or coercion I pointed out the illegality of the unions' demand. After letting that sink in for a moment, I quietly let the contractor know about the many influential people in the building industry and town-planning office who were not only my personal friends but were sympathetic toward the Wesley Mission. The builder would not want his company to be black-banned for demanding bribes, would he?

The building contractor hastily denied any knowledge of the affair and to prove his honesty, in the weeks ahead he worked hard to have the site checked and declared clear, so that the men could get back to finish the renovations.

Even so there was a three-week gap between demolition and renovation when our staff had to occupy temporary quarters in the Teachers' Federation auditorium in Sussex Street. I declared these three weeks as a time of spiritual renewal for the Mission staff and delivered a series of powerful addresses on 'Living in the Wilderness.'

September 25 1988 was moving day. At the appointed hour a crowd of more than a thousand people accompanied by bands and banners, marched down Pitt Street to the George Street theatre. This building, with the others at Wilmot and Central Streets, became the Wesley Mission's headquarters for the next three years until the new Wesley Centre was finished.

However, the Unions had the last laugh. When the crowds surged into the building they found that the lift drivers were on strike and would not allow the lifts to be used to shift furniture up to any of the offices. As well as that, the $1 million renovations were far from complete. Much of the building was still scarcely usable. There were hard days ahead for mission staff and worshippers alike.

In the long run it probably cost Wesley Mission far more than $40,000 to maintain its integrity, but no one complained. Our church stood by its principles.

Spring Fair was scheduled for two days after the move to these temporary quarters and Beverley and her helpers faced almost overwhelming difficulties. In among the jumble of furniture stacked outside unfinished offices they had to find places to erect and decorate their stalls; some vital areas lacked electricity and could not be utilised; masses of delicate handwork and perishable stock had to be brought in and set out on their respective tables while all around them workmen sawed and hammered and filled the air with noise and sawdust.

Despite all these drawbacks, at the appointed hour the premier's wife graciously declared the Fair open and thousands of buyers crowded inside. Two days later the annual Spring Fair had raised $217,000, the second highest amount in its history – a fitting tribute to Beverley as Spring Fair President and her hard working team of volunteers.

So on with our rebuilding of the new Wesley Centre. Our plans from the earliest days were lodged with a quarter of a million dollars payment as our levy to the City Council under the Lord Mayor Doug Sutherland, for off-street parking. Later all underground parking was banned by the City Council who rejected our plans for an underground parking station for our office workers and congregations. We protested strongly that we had approval and the City Council had received our quarter of a million dollars and had already spent it. Then the State Government stepped in and sacked the Council and some staff for corruption. Three administrators were then appointed - all three members of my Rotary club of Sydney! I felt I now had a fair chance of getting our point of view across. The Administrators willingly listened to me.

A search was found in the City's records and there were our plans and receipts. So while no other central business district Sydney development has since been allowed to have car-parking underground, we have ours simply because the records were found by some efficient filing clerk to prove our rights! When God is in the development and wants his building built, no official opposition can halt it. Their own forgotten records allowed it! They happened to be found by a young girl assistant in the Housing department, who also happened to be a member of our church! God had surely placed her there.

A little prior to this I had an unusual confirmation of my ideas. One very dark night, I was being flown in a small, single engine aeroplane from Bendigo, where I had been speaking at the University, to Tullamarine, Victoria, where I was to catch the last flight back to Sydney. My pilot was Russell G. Withers, Managing Director of Pacific- Seven Pty. Ltd., the owner of hundreds of 7/11 stores.

Russell knew we were in the planning stages of building a new Wesley Centre. I was troubled because it involved demolishing the very fine Wesley Centre built only fourteen years previously under the leadership of Sir Alan Walker and on which we still owed over a million dollars. Furthermore, Sir Alan had given me ten very strong reasons, which I still kept by my desk, why we should not redevelop our total site with a huge building many times the size of the existing collection of buildings including Wesley Centre. The new young minister was threatening total destruction of all he had builtand he was not pleased.

The decrepit buildings on Castlereagh Street and in Wesley Arcade concerned us. I was troubled about the need to refurbish the Lyceum Theatre and Wesley Centre, which had been rebuilt only fourteen years previously, but whose low cost fabric was now showing wear and tear and high maintenance costs. I was dismayed at the small, dark and mouldy Wesley Chapel, even though I knew it held a place of endearment in the hearts of Sydney Methodists. They had argued at the Annual Conference of the Methodist Church for a century about the necessity of having a fine, proper church in which to worship in the centre of the city. It seemed to me that total re-development was the only answer.

I shared my concerns with Russell Withers and in the dark cockpit of the small plane, he told me about the U.S.A. supermarket chain, A & P, the biggest chain in the world. They had slipped from being the greatest supermarket chain and had to close a thousand stores because they had not kept their stores up to date and looking good. He commented, 'The successful store operator in my game refurbishes his store every three or four years top to bottom. So have a look at your own site. You can't help an old location but you sure can help an old store.'

'You can't help an old location but you sure can help an old store.' That was true. Our historic location in the very heart of the Central Business District was superb. The land value was perhaps as high as $100 million - and we had it covered in the most part by low-level buildings more than a century old!

We could not help our old location but we sure could help our old property! So I wrote to The Board of Finance and Property of the Uniting Church and suggested that together we redevelop the whole site in what would be one of Sydney's great building projects. They agreed. Committees were established and over several years approvals were gained, plans were drawn and re-drawn, a developer, Capital Land Corporation, a financier, Australian Guarantee Corporation and a builder, Multiplex, were locked into one of the most complex series of leases you could ever imagine. I appointed our own independent architects to check every detail and watch over our interests.

There are still many more building programs to come. Recently in 2005 we 'turned the sod' on two massive new developments for housing the frail and the aged. These have a combined budget in excess of $80 million for the 2005/6 year. What has been the combined value of all the buildings I have overseen being constructed? Somewhere around $500 million.

Then there is a new hospital on the drawing board and thirteen other projects all at some stage of being built. One panel of the dodecahedron is rightfully called 'Builder'. Another example of building started in the mid – 1990's in what we called 'Homes For Hope'.

I had the privilege of joining Craig Knowles, the Minister for Housing in NSW and Phil Haig, CEO of HomeWorld, in laying the first bricks on the HomeWorld 'Homes For Hope'. This has been an initiative of two staff members, Dian Ball and Paula Duncan. Wesley Mission gained over half a million dollars through the sale of the first house. This was followed by more than twenty, high cost houses that would be auctioned with the total proceeds coming into Wesley's accounts to be used in social welfare.

HomeWorld at Kellyville was the world's largest display village with more than 100 premier homes built by 40 of the nation's top builders competing against each other for public approval. Allam Homes built our homes; Aussie Home Loans provided a $100,000 interest free loan to the purchaser; BBC Hardware provided over $100,000 of materials; Harvey Norman provided over $100,000 of furnishings; Boral provided over $100,000 of building materials; 2UE provided over $100,000 of advertising; The Sun Herald donated $100,000 of advertising and TCN 9 made a special Current Affair program on the development; Daewoo gave us their most expensive car for the garage. The pool was donated by Blue Haven pools; Lego conducted a national Lego Competition for kids with Air New Zealand took the four people to Disneyland as the prizewinners. 200 people paid $200 each to go on a Captain Cook evening dinner cruise featuring an auction by Alan Jones with all proceeds coming to us. We had brought together all of these people to facilitate house building.

The next year we built four other Homes For Hope, including one on the Gold Coast and three in the Hunter. All work was donated and total proceeds went to help Wesley Mission's full range of ministries to the homeless children, youth and adults cared for by the Mission. This building initiative has brought us in over $5 million in cash in the first few years and a total of about twenty million when all are sold. But our homes have won national awards for design and construction and our fundraising concept won us national fundraising awards. Awards were one thing, but strategic planning must come first.

In July 1985, our church members studied the theological requirements of a city church. When we had our theology right, we then drew the specifications from itand the architects made the theological requirements and the specifications possible. We start building with our theological insights not with designs and pictures of our architect. Those nine theological requirements will explain what it is that we wanted to build. Our theological understanding determined our building complex. In 1978 I wrote:

'The future of Christianity lies in its ability to effectively reach the people of our cities. The City Churches are on the frontline of the work of God in the centre of the greatest groupings of people in history. Yet the existing City Churches, while they continue their present patterns of ministry, are doomed to failure! The great empty Churches and Cathedrals of the major cities of the Western world bear mute testimony to this grim prophecy. Only new City Churches can fulfil the mission of God.

Contrary to our Akubra bush hats and four-wheel drives, mankind is not by nature a rural creature. People by nature are city creatures. Adam was a rural creature, but his son Cain lived in a city. Mankind has long left behind the concept of a rural Eden and has headed for the city where he finds the fulfilment of his desires. Every achievement of humanity in art, culture, government, religion, politics, scientific and technological achievement has been born and developed in cities.

If Christianity is to impact upon mankind, it must do so in the cities of the world. Only a new City Church is viable.'

These nine theological understandings must transform our ministry:

1. Sacrament: The City Church has a sacramental ministry. For the Church is a

symbol of God's presence within the city. The Church reminds the world that God is at work in that city and that he can take ordinary lives and transform them by his power.

When the Church administers the Sacraments in worship, it is participating in one of the most important things that ever happen within the life of the Church. When a person comes either to receive the Sacraments of Holy Communion or of Baptism, there is an affirmation about God being present in the life of that person. That person has been claimed by God and is loved by God. God loves these people in a special way and offers them his power for living within this City. So when the young child is faced with the pressure of a peer group to experiment with drugs, or to become involved in juvenile crime, or when the older member is tempted to be dishonest through his business, or to commit adultery, that person knows God already has a place within his life. Consequently their behaviour may change.

Through the Sacraments people recognise that they are loved and accepted, that the Church loves and accepts them. It further says that the Church believes in possibilities in people and that by God's power lives can be transformed and renewed. When God has been present within the Church and his people renewal takes place.

Hence, the City Church must be built possessing the signs of the faith - a Cross symbolising the Name of the One in whom we meet, a font for infant baptisms and a baptistery for adult and believers baptisms, a free- standing communion table, a pulpit that is open on all sides and movable, together with open space for alternative forms of worship including drama, music groups, mime and dance. The symbols of the sacrament must be on view every minute the front doors are open and brightly illuminated to capture attention.

2. Salvation: The presence of the City Church is a reminder to the whole world of the forgiveness, healing and hope that God offers those who accept his salvation. That message of salvation must be passed on to others. Emil Brunner says, 'One who received this Word and by it salvation, received along with it the duty of passing this Word on. Where there is no mission, there is no Church and where there is neither Church nor mission, there is no faith.' (*The Word and The World*, p.108) The new city church must continue to point to salvation in Jesus Christ. Hence evangelism is primary in all we do.

Human nature has not changed since Jesus walked beside Galilee. In spite of all our technological and scientific ability we still have the same problems. Ours is 'the age of anxiety'. Something is still radically wrong within the heart. Neither education, technology, psychology, nor scientific progress answers personal need. The Bible indicates that apart from God we are sinners needing salvation. The new City Church must proclaim salvation that God has provided through Christ. Only Christ saves from sin.

But sin must not be conceived of only in terms of personal, transcendent and vertical relationships with God, but also in horizontal and structured relationship with other people. Many city people are living in bondage, needing liberation in both the horizontal and vertical aspects. These people suffer under economic exploitation, social, political or cultural oppression and spiritual deprivation and bondage. The Church must proclaim the good news of what God has done through Jesus Christ. The City Church offers in partnership with God the possibility of a new creation, of liberation and of an eternal future. Hence we must proclaim the Gospel. We must publicly proclaim the Gospel and privately counsel the salvation to be found in Jesus Christ. Salvation is the reason for our presence among the people of the city.

3. Sanctuary: There exists in human hearts a need to find a transcendence in city living. City dwellers need the elevating experience of worship. Where concrete replaces lawns and trees, where factories shut off the sunset and where the noise of traffic substitutes for the song of birds and wind in the trees -the human spirit is dulled. There should be 'inspiration in a sanctuary so arranged and furnished as to be satisfying to the eye and quieting to the mind. Here in the worship service they can be lifted out of their cluttered, man-made environment, into the presence of the God who set the stars in their courses and laid the foundations of the world. Through participation in that worship members of the congregation may find meaning in life, strength and courage for ethical living and Christian peace in the midst of a troubled society.' (Murray H. Leiffer, *The Effective City Church*, p181). Hence a new church should be a place of quiet refuge - carpeted fully with soft drapes, wall hangings, soft natural lighting, stained glass from our heritage and the atmosphere during non-service times encouraging prayer and meditation. The city church must be a sanctuary in the concrete city, pointing beyond itself to a deep and satisfying relationship each can have with our Creator.

4. Security: People in the city always feel insecure. But the Church can provide a sense of security in the midst of rapid social change. It can provide an eternal stability, a point of reference when all about is in a state of flux. Through counselling and preaching the city church emphasises spiritual security for people who are transient on earth, yet who through reconciliation with God, possess an eternal destiny.

So many city folk face loneliness, feel fragmented, alienated, depersonalised and powerless. Personal wholeness and healthy interpersonal relationships are difficult. Their devotion to the things of this world seems to shut out ultimate concerns. The Church is given by God a ministry of reconciliation; bringing the warring and the divided self together under the Lordship of Christ; helping the defeated to find dignity, courage and power; and, first in importance if not in sequence, reconciling them to God even if now they are unaware of him and uncommitted to him.

Hence the city church must have areas where people can be at home, feel welcome and find friendship. An original font, display of historical memorabilia and old stained glass remind people that Jesus Christ is the same yesterday, today and forever. They feel secure when they see our Christian heritage that reminds them of childhood, mother, Sunday School.

5. Seminary: The City Church must equip Christians for their personal ministry. This involves all aspects of Christian education and of developing those gifts that lie dormant within each individual. Wesley Mission has thousands each week in small groups and classes, so adequate meeting rooms are required, together with all the electronic and static requirements for good teaching: mid-week, at night classes and on weekends. From the time we opened Wesley Centre we have developed our education programs. By 2005 we had 425 full-time students and 4000 doing part-time courses, in our Wesley Institute, 1750 in our two Schools for Seniors and over 1000 in our Church have groups each week.

6. Servant: It is the will of Christ that his body, the Church, will be his servant people in the world. Our Mission depends upon the willingness of his servants to see the need of mankind and give themselves into the service of the gospel. The ministry of the Church, rightly understood, is the ministry of the whole people of Christ helping meet the whole range of needs of people.

This service will take many forms. It will take immediate form in providing the care, support and provision needed to give social relief and welfare to those who are hurt by society. It also involves long-term care and prophetic leadership to correct social injustice. The Church must involve itself in the fulfilment of its mission of caring for the poor and the powerless. The followers of Jesus must have a special concern for the poor and powerless. Hence we can provide instantly food and clothing, rent relief, a place to shower and the basin and towel of humble service beside the bread and wine.

7. Society: When flying over a city, you can see the structures of the city carved into the landscape. But a city is more than its limits and layout. The substance of cities lies not in their buildings, their freeways and overpasses, but in its social organism, the way people live together. The roads and streets are a network of communication, the houses and buildings are shells in which we sleep and work, but the life of the city is in the relationships that exist between people.

At the heart of every city is personal participation. Those churches around the world which make a contribution to the life of the city do so by bringing together the people of the city into participation one with the other. Against the impersonality, loneliness and lack of communication between people who live in a major city lies the Church with its sense of participation, communication and friendship.

That communication takes place over a table in the restaurant, in the lounges, in the church library, or in the social activities churches are able to create. Through dialogue and contact, a sense of participation and co-operation breaks down the barriers of isolation and loneliness. The city church must be putting some heart into a society, some content into our communication and some fellowship into our acquaintanceship. Hence, space and facilities for informal and formal groups, eating areas and a cafeteria are essential, comfortable lounge chairs scattered throughout the building, newspapers and magazines, fresh arrangements of flowers and hundreds of ferns and real plants - no plastic here! This is to remind us of the beauty of creation. (However I note Wesley Church has now added beautiful silk flowers!)

8. Space: Churches must provide space within the city. City streets are lined with building crammed against building, fighting each other as they reach for the sky. Small streets and laneways are overcrowded, as buildings seem to touch each other at the top. There always seems an overbearing pressure of buildings within the city and many people feel entombed within those city streets.

But the church breathes space. High roofs and quiet atmosphere give a feeling of space to the spirit. I am sure this is the reason why many people come in off the street to the quiet and peace of an open church during the middle of a busy day and sit for a moment of quietness, prayer and meditation. As their eyes are lifted to the stained glass windows, or to the high ceiling, they have a feeling of expansiveness within their soul. The Church breathes a spirit of calm and peace in overcrowded lives. The City Church can be the lungs of the city. We have built a magnificent Dunbar Library with 10,000 books available for borrowing. We also have a free video, CD, DVD and tape library available for those who cannot afford to buy or rent entertainment and education.

9. Spirit: The city church is the only provider of the essential human spirit. Every city dweller ingests some of the pressures, some of the tensions and some of the attitudes of the city. People who live their lives within an oppressive and hard environment cannot help but be infected by the spirit of their community. But the city church can give people a new spirit. Here is the promise of a new creation, of a citizenship that goes beyond this earth to heaven and a promise of a heavenly city, not made with hands but eternal in the heavens. This spirit transcends and overcomes the attitudes and the pressures from the outside street.

The hope of the Resurrection and the joy of Christian fellowship add a dimension to the inner urban dweller's life. This extra dimension, which comes through encounter with the living God, puts life into the existence of city people. Every city dweller needs a sense of transcendence, of hope and of spiritual experience which takes them beyond their immediate environment. Mankind as a whole needs a hope that will hold their lives fast and give them something beyond what they have already and can ever achieve.

The church's ministry provides a sense of meaning, hope and transcendence that adds a fundamental dimension to living. City churches have an enormous task to transform lives to become the agents of God's compassion and his ministry to the people of the city. This aspect of transmission and communication can be aided by good use of the media. A theatre capable of video presentation, TV transmission and radio broadcasting can help fulfil the function of establishing and transmitting the spirit of the people. Production facilities, a broadcast studio and a film-editing suite were included from the start.

When a city church has the rare opportunity of re-establishing itself and of building to the next century, the architect has the privilege of drawing the lines round theology and of making the Church real in the centre of the streets. 'You can't help an old location but you sure can help an old store.' That was the challenge we faced more than a decade ago. God has been faithful to our efforts to fulfil that challenge of making a new beginning for his glory and for the service of our city. This building is the facility to enable us to become his church to this city. No other church is so strategically situated in the Central Business District nor so finely equipped.

The ministry areas alone cost some $40 million and were opened free of debt! There were thirty-two opening celebrations attended by 35,000 people.

When they enter our front doors for the first time, many people have declared they thought they were entering the lobby of one of the two international five star hotels adjacent the church. Others have compared it to the great shopping emporium next door 'David Jones', authoritatively described as ' the most beautiful store in the world.'

In the foyer and reception area, we have a bookshop, one of the few Christian Bookshops in the CBD. To your right is Wesley Restaurant which hosts hundreds of city business people each day for breakfast, lunch and dinner or for morning and afternoon teas. Wesley Centre provides catering facilities for office functions and executive conferences through the restaurant and offers an up-market package for special meetings, celebrations and conferences. Our restaurant was judged and awarded gold star rating for a medium to low price facility.

As you go further into the Centre you approach Wesley Church. This seats 500 and is the worshipping home of some of our Sunday and weekday congregations. Wesley Church is fitted with a new pipe organ and a baptistery. It has retained the original stained glass windows, which beautified the old Wesley Chapel previously on this site. A second public area opens off the same lounge area and is known as the Lyceum. This too is used for our youth and Rotuman worship services. Both the church and the Lyceum have multi-lingual translation facilities.

One level below are function and activity rooms, some large enough to contain several hundred people while others are designed for smaller groups and adult study classes. These activity rooms are used seven days a week by our parish,

Sunday School, mid-week groups, School for Seniors and other forms of training and education. A large kitchen can cater for over 800 people.

The third floor houses all of the offices of the Pastoral Division. Here people come for counselling from the large pastoral staff, or for membership classes. Here are also the offices of Sydney's School For Seniors with its fourteen hundred students. Some classes are taken in this complex which also houses music rehearsal rooms and areas for drama and dance. The large Dunbar Library of 10, 000 volumes offer reading and study facilities for church members in English and Chineseand for School For Seniors.

A major attraction of Wesley Centre is the 1,000 seat Wesley Theatre. This theatre is the home to Wesley Mission's larger congregations each Sunday for many mid-week activities as a performing arts centre. Wesley Theatre has a large stage and music podium suitable for orchestras and drama and dance, a baptistery built into a side wall, multiple-translation equipment, a wide screen for film, slide and video presentation and a state of the art, electronic computerised system for sound and lighting.

The unique Christie Theatre Organ is built high into another wall of Wesley Theatre. This theatre organ dating from the 1930's is renowned across the nation. From the opposite glass wall, parents with small children can feel part of all services without the children disturbing the rest of the congregation. All the items of furniture for Sunday worship have been specially designed and constructed to fit the decor of the theatre. Every single item has been donated by church members and friends. Outside the theatre doors, are 374 car parking spaces for worshippers, underground in the same area of land!

Just outside the main lobby of the theatre is a well-stocked kiosk with refreshments and the John Lees Chapel for prayer and meditation. This whole area is fully equipped for thousands of visitors. Within two areas a score of telephone lines enable personal counselling following our national telecasts each week and for special financial appeals through the media.

All these facilities and meeting areas are accompanied by open and spacious lounge areas in which visitors can relax. The whole Wesley Centre is easily accessible by the disabled through lifts, escalators and gentle ramps.

Above these levels is the massive office tower. One level is set aside for the senior staff of the church as they provide management and expertise to our 450 other sites across the state. Here is our art department, media department, legal department, human resources, information technology, fundraising and senior executives plus conference and Boardrooms. Between 1985 and 2005, we provided accommodation for an additional 2000 people who now live in one of our properties and office facilities for the extra 2500 staff we added.

LEAVING A LEGACY

Apart from the major redevelopment of its mid-city church and office complex, another one hundred million dollars was raised for land acquisition, buildings and the construction of new facilities for further community service. New initiatives in evangelism would be undertaken across the nation by television and radio, new programs of support and more than one hundred and fifty new services for the poor would be established. All of these would require the purchase of additional property and the appointment of new staff and a sustained fund-raising program beyond what had ever been attempted by a church before.

Worship is central to all we do. We were born in praise to God and today we find resources and strength for our total ministry through the worship experience of our people. If our people did not gather for worship, to hear the Word of God and to proclaim the Gospel, all point and purpose to all the good deeds of service we undertake would be lost. That is why every person employed by Wesley Mission should be a committed Christian and a member of a worshipping congregation.

In the centre of Sydney's central business district, the central experience of the thousands of people touched through the life and work of Wesley Mission is the worshipping community. It is precisely at this point where Wesley Mission is different from the other great social welfare agencies operated by denominational boards of churches, government welfare services, or those other agencies for the community's good, which, while born in a Christian environment, have now lost their Christian witness. Wesley Mission is unique in that it holds worship and service together. We proclaim on our worship bulletins every week, 'The end of worship is the beginning of service'.

Service and worship are inextricably bound together. Over the century we have maintained an increasing involvement in the worship of God by the people who serve in his name. Every Sunday this church has been the centre of the worship of God for people who live in the inner city, for those who come and uphold this centre of worship for the benefit of others, for tourists and visitors, for folk down in the city from their normal country home and for international visitors who find in a strange land a place where they can worship God and feel at home.

But services are also held in Wesley Church every day of the week except Saturday, not just on Sundays, for the benefit of those who work and live in the city. Each of those daily services provides a different emphasis and attracts a different congregation. One service, Sing and Praise, celebrates the goodness of God in music and song. The Healing Service is a service of witness in word and laying on of hands with prayer for those who are ill. Lunchtime Inspiration is a service to lift the spirit in worship and praise to God. Chapel-in-the-City is a service of preaching the positive power of God to lift a person's life. Mid-city Communion is a quiet and reflective communion service aimed at encouraging our personal devotion. Here communion is shared, baptisms are held, weddings are celebrated, funerals are conducted and special services designed to minister to the office worker and shop attendant.

Wesley Theatre is the scene of the main worship services of Wesley Mission. It is strange to many that we did not build one large, beautiful church to seat everybody at one sitting. Our understanding goes against that common trend. We have multiple facilities for worship and over 55 services each week, each with a differing ethos and feel about them. Many have different theological emphasis and other differing styles of worship. We offer a smorgasbord of worship experiences. Here, there is a service and a congregation to suit everyone's personal desires.

For 90 years Wesley Mission has used a theatre to proclaim the gospel of Jesus Christ every Sunday night through wars, depressions and times of affluence. Its congregations have been varied. Hundreds of people from the widest variety of social, economic, educational, ethnic and vocational backgrounds joined together in one purpose to worship God and to proclaim the gospel of grace. Over the years the `Church-in-a-Theatre' has been the centre of prophetic preaching, of frequent controversy and of faithful proclamation. With one of the finest theatre organs in the country, a magnificent screen and all the facilities for first-class cinema operation, the Church-in-a-Theatre operated according to its name. It was a church worshipping in a theatre and therefore used lighting, sound and the screen every week to effect.

During the preaching and the reading of the Scriptures the verses are shown on the screen for people to follow. The success of this theatre as a centre of worship and evangelism was seen in the multiplying of crowded services throughout Sunday. When the decision was made to demolish the downtown properties, it was a unanimous decision of the membership to build a new theatre, a centre for the performing arts and a Convention Centre with state-of-the-art facilities which would house the church's major worship services, not a traditional cathedral style church.

Wesley Theatre congregations are probably the most egalitarian church worship service in the world. Here you will find literally professors and physicians, prostitutes and alcoholics, teachers and computer programmers, skid-row drunks and homeless teenagers, sitting side by side and hearing the proclamation of the gospel.

Stalwart Christians, who could have been much more comfortable in their own environment in their local suburban church, have committed themselves to this service week by week to uphold the preaching of the gospel and to enable the message to reach those in the community who desperately need the power of God to renew them. It is a fact that causes rejoicing, that on every Sunday for the past century lives have been changed, challenged and converted through the power of the gospel. One exciting development in the last two decades has been the development of ethnic congregations. From an early beginning of a handful of Pacific Island people, services have been conducted weekly in four languages Fijian, Rotuman, Samoan and Tongan and from that handful of people twelve vibrant congregations of Pacific Islanders meet weekly for worship, communion, cultural experiences and fellowship around the meal table.

In 1979 I commenced a service for Asian people and that International Service has grown from strength to strength. Today every Sunday morning a congregation numbering one thousand from a variety of countries of origin meets in Wesley Theatre to praise God. That is followed by a Chinese service to cater for hundreds of Chinese speaking people. A Spanish Congregation was established and now thrives as a separate congregation of several hundred. An Indonesian congregation has also recently developed, as has an enthusiastic Japanese service. Massive celebrations, our largest services, combining all our congregations for a special occasion, are held in the largest facility in the nation, or outdoors, such as when over 50,000 attend our Christmas service and pageant.

Wesley Mission believes that in every large city there is a significant number of people who are either resident within the central city area or its immediate environs, who live at their places of work, as nurses in hospitals, students in dormitories, or caretakers in large city buildings, who together with visitors to the city, international travellers, tourists in motels, businessmen in hotels, seamen on board ships at the docks and ordinary people who week by week are not attached to a local suburban church, need to find a place to worship.

Today through Wesley Mission thousands of people each week worship God. The church is the only centre in society that brings people together for worship, to encourage them to capture the feeling of transcendence in life and to help them find resources to equip them for living.

One further aspect of building was the facilities for Wesley Institute.

Wesley Institute For Ministry and the Arts is a university level Christian college in the arts and Christian leadership. Over four hundred full-time and over 4000 part-time students and a very strong faculty make up the college body. It has schools in dance, drama, music, counselling, theology, missions and visual arts. Vocational and community education students are trained by professionals in their special field, but all do core subjects from a Christian perspective. We purchased a very large government secondary college and rebuilt much of it to suit the Institute.

This College is the first of its type to be fully accredited by both federal and state educational bodies. The potential of this college is enormous, especially as increasing numbers of students from the Third World and USA discover its standing and capabilities. Christian ministry is much wider than the pulpit ministry and these Christians are trained to minister through the arts.

The new Wesley Centre was designed to enable performing artists to have the finest facilities in making their presentations to the city.

BUILDER

The Apostle Paul saw the cities as the decision-making centres and their life the civilising force for the rest of the empire. His strategy was to win the empire by winning the cities. Over the centuries the Church built great cathedrals dominating city squares and church bells peeled across the city streets. In another era, the preaching from the pulpit of city churches had tremendous influence over the attitudes of people in the cities.

Today, the Church does not have any protected place in the life of the city. But it still has its charge to win men and women to Jesus Christ and in a country like Australia where 86% of our people live in seven cities, to be effective in our evangelism of this country. To be nationally effective requires us to be effective in our evangelism of her cities, particularly Sydney. Greater Sydney, between Newcastle and Wollongong houses one out of every three persons in Australia. The Lord Jesus Christ has given us the Church to proclaim his gospel to people in this community. Wesley Mission has been faithful to its ministry of evangelism.

There have been some Christian missions, both in Australia and overseas, that have changed from evangelism to welfare and then from the provision of welfare to the seeking of justice. We are not critical of their evolution of concepts, but we believe that evangelism is still primary in our tasksand that all other emphases are in association with it. Consequently, Wesley Mission has lived by evangelism. We believe the Church is only the Church when it is the Church in mission.

Behind all the ministry lies the adequate building program that has given us the tools to do the job.

MEDIA PRESENTER

Chapter Six

I was always interested in communicating the good news of the Gospel through the media. If people came to church then I wanted to show them in the best way possible the good news and this would involve music, drama, film and audio-visual. If people didn't come to church then I wanted to find ways of getting out to those people where they were and show them in pictures or in word-pictures what it was they were missing. In any event the main aim was to communicate through the media the good news of Jesus.

When I was a Pastor to the slums in Ascot Vale and Newmarket we did our presentations as colourfully as possible, except in those days of the 1950's and 60's we used slides, lots of thirty-five millimetre slides, using the new colour film that had just been produced by Kodak. We even got quite professional at writing scripts, filming actors in a drama and synchronising the slides to a taped script. We also used some young actors with eight-millimetre movie film.

Some of these were done in black and white so we had the Charlie Chaplin style and effect. And others were done in colour with all the panache of a young film producer and director. Inside the church above the porch we put up a spotlight so that it could be used in evening services to highlight some dramatic presentation and the curtain that covered the double doors could be drawn up and opened like a professional theatre, revealing a rear projection screen upon which suitable pieces of film or slides could be projected to create the right atmosphere, or very simply to be used as a teaching aid with maps and points presented.

When I became a country parson in Ararat in the 1960's once more a great deal of energy went into the production of drama, a play for Easter and Christmas, the presentation of good music with spotlights and again the use of movie film. But now technology was marching on and we were able to produce some colour eight-millimetre film.

How people loved to come to see themselves on the screen in the church, having been featured in some church picnic or youth activity. It was in those middle nineteen sixties that I first was introduced to the mass media.

I was invited to do a number of interviews on television at BTV Channel 6. They were broadcasting at the time in black and white but nevertheless it was television. Radio was in its heyday and I broadcast interview spots and Christian commentary on a whole host of country radio stations, travelling from country town to country town to record material, going to 3BA in Ballarat, then on to 3BO Bendigo, then on to 3CV Central Victoria at Shepparton, down to 3CO Colac and back via 3HA Hamilton.

I never did all of the stations at any one time but over a couple of years made programmes on them all.

Then an Executive Producer of BTV Channel 6 rang me in Ararat and asked if I would do a series of late night epilogues. In those days not even the television station had a video recorder and even the epilogues had to be done live. I would drive, usually accompanied by my wife, baby daughter Jenny and new-born son Peter down to Ballarat arriving just before midnight in order to get made up and ready for the close of transmission.

BTV 6 was running at night with only one staff member present. He would set me up on a chair in front of a set and get the right turret on the four turret black and white camera focused on me and then rush upstairs until the film had finished. As soon as the film was finished and he had discharged the final two or three ads, it was simply a matter of the red light being switched on and suddenly there was I in living black and white at 12.30 am and speaking to all the countryside that could receive BTV Channel 6.

At the end of five minutes the light went off, the station played the National Anthem and both of us went home. Meanwhile my wife sat in the car waiting, having settled down our little daughter Jenny asleep in the back seat and then as we drove back home the hour-long journey to Ararat she would heat the baby's bottle by putting it on the car heater. Most cold, wintry nights we would have the heater on full blast, holding Peter's bottle up to the outlet so he could have warm milk.

I discovered then in the country town of Ararat that people everywhere in vast numbers watched television, even to the close of transmission.

Many of my colleagues in the ministry would say, 'You're mad. Fancy travelling all that way to Ballarat in the middle of the night just to be on TV!' I wouldn't argue with them. But the fact was I was speaking every night in those five minutes to more people than they had ever preached to in all of their lives with every Sunday put together.

When I became a suburban Minister in the Cheltenham Church of Christ a couple of years later, we continued to present the good news of Jesus, using the media in church services. Only now, we used colour eight millimetre film complete with sound stripe. Don Stokie, the young pharmacist, had set up state-of-the-art equipment and he managed to attach living sound with recorded music and spoken documentary to the eight millimetre films we made of all of the activities in the church. All of our church activities were filmed and we would put on evenings when everyone turned up to see themselves.

Then when I went as a preaching evangelist to New Zealand or the United States of America, or somewhere else, I usually took loads of colour film that later on we edited, spliced together and turned into one-hour specials on two reels. Then we invited people to come to our home, on one night all those whose surnames began A to D, the next night E to H, the next night I to M and so on until hundreds of people would have attended the supper and film nights in the manse. They felt they were part of these successful programs.

These were great ways of getting to know your people and building fellowship with them.

As usual we produced plenty of drama in them, skits and action, again using light and sound to the best of our ability on a limited budget.

It was then that I discovered the State Film Centre and the Canadian Film Library with their magnificent libraries of sixteen millimetre films. Frequently on a Sunday night we would use in the middle of a service a situation out of some film, perhaps only three or four minutes long, just simply to set up a situation against which I would then preach the good news. Every Thursday we would load up the film projector with some film to take off to Cheltenham High School, then on Friday to the Mentone Girls' High School where we used films to tell the message of the good news and to provide Christian teaching.

On balmy summer nights after Church we had open-air summer film festivals and sometimes over in the church lounge films on particular issues that were topical to that day.

But it was while I was a suburban minister that the work that was done earlier on country radio stations and with the black and white four turret camera at BTV Channel 6 in Ballarat started to take hold.

Melbourne's leading station, GTV Channel 9, was moving into colour. They needed a new image and a new way of presenting their epilogues at night. In those days ministers used to record the epilogues for showing at midnight or half past twelve in the morning.

Because GTV Channel 9 had video recorders, unlike BTV 6 in Ballarat, I was able to record six at a time with five minutes available every night for an epilogue and ten minutes available on Sunday. Most viewers who religiously watched the epilogue didn't realise the amount of effort that was required in scripting a five-minute programme every night on television. But in a way I became well-known to those who regularly stayed to watch the last of the night's programming.

In those days GTV 9 used to claim they had a quarter of a million viewers watching. I always reckoned that a quarter of a million viewers were far more people that I could reach with the good news of Jesus than I ever would by just staying in my church waiting for them to come to me.

One day the Executive Producer of Programming at Channel 9 rang and asked, ' Would you care to come in for a test? We're looking for a regular Epilogue personality and we'd like to have a look at you on our new colour cameras.' I remember quite vividly in the waiting room of GTV Channel 9 meeting with the other person who had been called in for the screen test. I was overawed when I first met him. He was Rev. Tom Thomas. He was almost bald; he wrote regularly in the Saturday papers and was Dean of St Paul's Anglican Cathedral, Melbourne. He was a great preacher, a warm friendly person with a smiling rotund face. And there he stood thrusting his hand out to greet me in friendship, wearing a black suit, black socks, black shoes and a simple white collar around his neck. I felt rather awkward.

I, as a young suburban minister, knowing that I would be on colour television wore my latest outfit. I blush when I think of it now, but I was wearing a powder blue suit with wide lapels and wide flared trousers, white shoes, a red shirt and a wide white tie. It sounds ghastly now, but it was the fashion of the mid-sixties. My hair was long and curly. Both of us were made up and then the Executive Producer came down to meet with us.

I'll never forget his opening comment. He looked me up and down, then looked the Anglican Dean up and down and then turning to the Dean, a man who had so much wisdom and theological knowledge and an eminent position within the Church and said to him quite bluntly, 'We have just spent $6 million on colour cameras and you come in here in black and white! Thank you for coming. We'll call you if we need you.'

And so it was that I became the regular Epilogue man on Melbourne television. I wrote scores of scripts that today fill some filing cabinets. It was much easier to make six Epilogues and one Sunday night ten minute special in one afternoon in the television station and I really enjoyed the work, particularly the art of working without a script and being able to stare right down the camera so that I would look straight into the eyes of those who were watching.

Those newsreaders who read from the television prompters always gave away the fact that they were reading, not by the tone of voice but by the movement of the pupils of their eyes. I was determined to avoid that. I don't know how many

Epilogues I made in those years as a suburban minister, but I know they stood me in good stead. I would also have something in my hands to introduce the subject, such as a New Guinea drum with python skin top, if I were to speak on the Mission of the Church or a crusty loaf of bread if I were to talk on Jesus the Bread of Life. In the late seventies when we moved to Sydney I commenced a half hour television program on Channel 9, a half hour program that still runs twenty-seven years later all around Australia, on the Channel 9 network. The man who asked me to come onto the Nine network offered me studio and transmission costs valued at $500,000 per annum to go on his network at a time when religious programs from USA paid for the airtime, as they still do.

Today over seventy channels present Turn 'Round Australia twice every week to the largest audience of all religious television programs and five times a week on the pay television channels. This is the only program to be on free to air and pay channels.

Through the ministry of television week by week we have been able to speak to millions of people across this nation and beyond and we have followed up with specials produced every year from the Opera House and our Darling Harbour Christmas, the most watched Christmas programme in the nation. Wesley Mission, in association with Mary Lopez Productions presented An Australian Christmas at Darling Harbour for 15 years from Tumbalong Park. Darling Harbour came alive with the true story of Christmas. With some well-known female personality I would tell the Biblical story. The pageant was one of the most popular family events at Darling Harbour and was one of Sydney's premier community events.

And radio.... we mustn't forget those early days of starting on 3BA and 3BO and 3CV and the like. When I came to Sydney in 1979 the General Manager of 2CH rang me up and asked if I could do four spots a day on 2CH. The General Manager of 2CH was Mr Chris Brammall. He was a large genial man who said to me with a warm smile of greeting when I arrived to do my first recordings of daily spots, 'I hope you do well. Most ministers don't last on this kind of programme. They run out of material after three months.' I looked Chris in the eye and said, 'I won't.' He looked back at me and with equal firmness said, 'What makes you so sure?' I replied 'I have already four thousand scripts at home of illustrations and quotations suitable for radio spots and they are typed up and ready to go.' For fifteen years I had been writing suitable material and having it typed up by volunteers because I knew that one day I would use them.

Through Wesley Mission's purchase of 2GB many years later I became Chairman of Harbour Radio Ltd and in 1990 I invited Chris Brammall to join us at 2GB where he became the very popular General Manager. When I was broadcasting on this station, he was the boss. And he still had me doing four one-minute spots a day.

MEDIA PRESENTER

When I had first arrived as Superintendent in the late 1970's I announced on my first Sunday that I would develop a national Christian television program, which would be telecast weekly. This would be the first Christian television program conducted by any one church with one presenter in Australia's television history.

Because I would be there every week it would be the first time that we would have one presenter on a regular basis 52 weeks a year. I believed continuity was absolutely essential if we were to get the message across. Not only that, for the first time in television history we would develop a television program that would be so good for the station that they would be prepared to pay for it. This was totally new thinking.

Turn 'Round Australia began a weekly half hour program, which is seen on more television stations in the nation than any other and has now been running consistently for the last 27 years. By 1983 I felt what we had been doing was ready for development in a totally new way.

On the 5th April 1983 I wrote to Martin Johnson, whom I had just appointed as our new Director of Media, Stan Manning, our General Manager of the Mission, a confidential note in which I said, 'I want to share with you what I think will be the most significant development we have undertaken in our media work. I think the time has come for us to develop Turn 'Round Australia into a new direction by producing a special series of programs, which will be used in a wider purpose and then being remade for our existing TRA format. My plan would be to conduct a special series, each running for 12 weeks for each of the next 3 years. During this period of twelve weeks we would have these special programmes around a unified theme with music inserts and an increased number of visuals. These would be suitable for personal and group studies in churches and I would produce a study book to go with the texts plus Bible passages and key questions that could be used by individuals as well as groups. We would then market the series of twelve videotapes together with the booklet on the texts. The theme for the special series of twelve would be 'The Life and Significance of Jesus', followed by, in 1984, a series on the Apostle Paul and then 'The Early Church', covering the rest of the New Testament.'

I then outlined how I would see the first 12 programmes developing, asked the people to meet with me and discuss this development and then in a single sentence say, 'We could use films from Israel or else go to the Holy Land and film them on site.' Martin Johnson replied, 'the idea for the proposed new TRA series sounds exciting and challenging. I appreciate there are still many decisions to be made regarding the series, however if we are planning to put them to air in the first half of 1984 we need right now to do some work on the contents of each of the 12 episodes.'

Martin then went on to show how he had developed the skills to produce such an historical series while he was on a year long Rotary scholarship at the San Diego State University in California, USA.

The idea of going to Israel and producing a series of 12 films on the life of Christ began to catch on. The big problem was money. We didn't have enough money to pay for the cost particularly if we were going to go on and make a total of 36 half hour programmes to be filmed on more than 150 locations in Israel throughout the Mediterranean Islands, Greece, Italy, Lebanon and Syria. I recognised that such a program would cost more than a million dollars and there was no way Wesley Mission could afford this. We had only just reached the situation where we had been covering the past debts that had accumulated for years.

The catalyst was to come quickly in the form of John Gormley, the Managing Director of Perpetual Equity Limited who said quite simply, 'Why don't you establish a film production company and raise capital from investors?' The idea was an appealing one but how could we go about developing a film company and raising such money? This was beyond the experience and expertise of us all. However we went ahead and established Wesley Film Productions Limited a company that achieved its approval from the Australian Government as a film production company able to raise investment capital and provide taxation and profit benefits. The board of the new company was made up of senior staff from Wesley Central Mission and Jim Mein of the Uniting Church of NSW, who took the role of an independent investor's representative.

We eventually gained approval from the taxation office, the Australian Film Commission, The Australian Home Office, Corporate Affairs and a whole bunch of other Authorities. I then called together a group of people who might share the vision. Some of them were personal friends, some were members of my Sydney Rotary Club and some were donors to Wesley Mission. One night in Wesley Centre I showed a sample videotape Martin and I had prepared showing how I had the vision of taking the gospel message to Australians through film, the sale of videos, the making of CD's and cassettes and the production of 36 half hour television programs. And to do this we would need to cover for the first series, $265,000.

In order to give people an idea of what it would be like we used a television technique called Chroma-Key. I stood in the studio while behind me photographs from books on the Holy Land were 'keyed' into the background. I walked around waving my hands and described the situation and told the story of Jesus meeting the woman at the well at Sycar.

It was very amateurish but after I had finished every one understood exactly what was intended. I asked people if they would fill in an investment sheet and on that first night $186 000 had been promised by people as investors. I was staggered! Shortly there after we had reached a total of $265 000 which was enough to cover the budget for the first series which I was now calling 'Discovering Jesus'.

To prove our own commitment to it, my wife and I had invested all of our savings as well so if this thing was going to fail, Beverley and I would go down with it. One of the things that our investors really appreciated was that the Australian Government, in order to encourage an Australian Film Industry, was providing 133% taxation deductibility for the total investment in the film. That certainly encouraged our investors. I have now before me a list of 25 investors who put up the $265 000. I only found out later on that many of the investors said to each other, 'Well I don't expect to get anything back out of this, but it's a good thing to get behind a person who has got a vision as big as this.' The investment of our savings did well as every other investment and from the first cheque we purchased a new family car, a gold Ford Fairlaine that served us until 2005.

It was one thing to raise the money by investment but now came the difficult task: I had to write the book and then write 12 scripts. Martin Johnson was an invaluable aid as he had studied script writing during his time at San Diego State University. He took my text and turned it into 12 documentary screenplays. We needed to get our proper 124ZAB certificate to make such a film internationally and Richard Baker came to our aid to help it through the minefields of government bureaucracy.

Martin Johnson brought together an interesting team of people. I was the executive producer and Stan Manning and Richard Baker were the Associate Producers. Martin would be the Producer and Director and I would be the writer, the presenter and the host. From New York, Martin had called cinematographer Robert Draper. Rob was a brilliant cinematographer and was going to go on to make his mark as director of photography on a number of very large, big budget films in the United States. Our assistant cameraman was Theo Cremona, who was then working in Europe. Our sound recordist was Bronwyn Murphy who had worked on some major Australian productions as had the production coordinator Alison Chambers. Production assistant was Sue Draper and editor was Greg Punch.

Telecine was the responsibility of Chris Hewat and Brian Himsley and Vicki Haynes were the on-line editors at Channel Nine. The graphics were done by Cathy Gribble, a member of staff at Wesley Mission. Our production accountant was Dick Menteith who had an enormous job over the next 15 years although he didn't realise it at that time. My old colleague John Graham would come with us as our stills photographer and our foreign liaison officer based in Israel was Shmuel Moyal. Our solicitor Bryce Bridges headed up several legal people who were responsible for all the investment documents and all of the relationships with countries overseas.

As soon as I had finished writing the manuscript for the book and the outline of each of the first twelve films, we sent off a crew of four people. The Cinematographer, the Production Manager, Photographer and Team Coordinator to do a location survey in Israel. They went to all of the major sites that I had mentioned and looked for about 150 location sites where we would actually do the filming. They tested the levels of light, the areas where we would stand and the areas from which we would shoot the films. The survey team finished their work and returned to Australia with hundreds of still photographs. These photographs were then assembled into order according to my scripts, which would enable us to visualise what we would later film.

We brought the team together and flew out of Australia while other team members came from across Europe, America and Great Britain to join us in Israel. The team worked from January to April 1984 and produced not only all the footage for the films but material for the 12 television programs as well.
The result was 25 hours of Kodak 16 mm film that had to be made into 12 televi sion programmes and 12 films. Greg Punch spent countless hours editing the 25 hours of film. We produced both Betamax and VHS copies in order to provide the various markets. By this time I had the idea that these would sell internationally. The brilliant music of Robert Coleman sung in Israel and orchestrated in Nashville Tennessee was made into an LP record and cassette, which sold widely.

The television series was stunning and was shown at peak viewing times all over Australia. The videos went on sale and immediately were snapped up. We were selling videos at the rate of $10 000 worth per month and within a few months the 1000th video set was purchased by a Mr Hardman of North Sydney.

In between filming I had finished off the book manuscript for *Discovering Jesus*. However I had set myself a very difficult task because I was writing four books at the one time: *Confidence in Time of Trouble*, which was to be published by Vital Publications, *Discovering Jesus* which was to be published by Albatross, *Twelve Steps to Serenity* which was being published in Australia and England by Hodder and Stoughton and Mission On, which was to be published by Vision Press. All books were going to have good sales.

In fact Discovering Jesus was a highlight in the publishing career of the Australian publisher John Waterhouse. He made arrangements to publish 10,000 copies on the first edition and 5,000 copies on an American Edition. Later this book was to go through several other editions. In the April 1984 issue of *Australian Bookseller and Publisher*, the book *Discovering Jesus* was written up as Australia's best selling religious book. It was beautifully photographed and illustrated by John Graham. We had hired a helicopter to get unusual angles in a country of a million photographs but few had been taken from a low flying helicopter. Later I was to sell all of the still photographs, for which we had no use, to Lion Publishers in the UK for a large amount of money. They were more than recouping our costs. I still see them illustrating books today.

John Waterhouse said, 'We set out to produce a book that commends the Christian Gospel to people outside of the Church. While it is still early days it is our hope that many of these encouraging sales have gone to this intended audience.' John also encouraged me with the writing of two other books, *Discovering Paul* and *Discovering the Young Church. Discovering Jesus* was used in colleges and secondary schools throughout the United States but our biggest delight was to come 15 years later when it was published in main land China in Chinese when each of the three books of the series was to be printed in numbers exceeding 500, 000 copies each. A former Chinese student of mine, Miss Lolita Chan, oversaw the production, distribution and sales of these books.

Richard Baker and Martin Johnson had attended the National Religious Broadcasters Media Expo in Washington DC. He wrote back excitedly, 'The response for *Discovering Jesus* was nothing short of amazing. The series certainly far outshone anything I have experienced in several years of marketing secular documentary films overseas. Literally hundreds of inquiries were received for the video pack and book and many more for television broadcast rights on stations all the way from Florida to Alaska. Several major distributors of Christian films and television programmes want the US distribution rights to the series. I am also able to confirm that the technical standard of Discovering Jesus is equal to the very best ever produced in the United States of America. It soon became clear that the series has a tremendous potential both for broadcast nationally and for home, church and school use in the USA.

The time had come for me now to write the next two books in the series *Discovering Paul* and *Discovering the Young Church*. I also had to write 24 scripts. Martin Johnson was again an invaluable help in these scripts. We also needed to get a new round of approvals from the Australian Government and Film Corporation for this next series. We also had to raise another $700 000, although that soon stretched as I developed new ideas.

I wrote to the Department of Foreign Affairs in Canberra pointing out that this next series of films would be made in some of the most difficult countries of the world. Rome, Greece, Turkey, Malta, Cypress and Israel were OK but we also wanted to go to some of the warring Middle Eastern Countries. I thought we had better acquaint the Department of Foreign Affairs in case they had to pull a jailed film crew out of some difficult country. I gave them the schedule of the countries to which we were going and the list of crew members. I insured every person for a million dollars each. On this trip I took my 21-year-old son Peter. Our previous visit had involved an immense amount of heavy carrying and I was utterly exhausted. He took care of all of that work as well as good times talking together when I was not the boss or the executive producer, but 'Dad'.

I had never been so tired in all of my life. In order to get what we called the 'National Geographic Colour' in our film shots, we got up at 4:30 am, travelled to the film site and with the first light, placing beautiful blues and violets in the sky we would film free from any tourists troubling us. In fact people later would constantly say they couldn't understand how we would be in some of the best known tourist spots in the world without a tourist in sight.

The reason was quite simple. We set up dolly tracks for the cameras, concealed lighting and we filmed just around dawn for a couple of hours. At the end of that time we would all go off and have breakfast together, reassemble on board a big bus capable of taking forty people that we had sent down from Germany and head for the next site. We slept on the bus and then got ready for all of our sunset filming. Again, against the beautiful sunsets we filmed other sequences. Our 'auto bus' was equipped with toilet, kitchenette and so on, so we could sleep, travel, eat, sit round a table to work on scripts or whatever.

We filmed our sequences on more than 180 different locations, which involved many changes of clothes for me and we would repeat each sequence several times so that those who would edit the films would have many options from which to choose. Every article of clothing was numbered and every sequence would have the wardrobe numbers in succession.

For *Discovering Paul* and *Discovering the Young Church* we had hired Simon Walker who had composed the musical scores for 40 films. His budget was high but it involved the use of some of Australia's best musicians, studio time and tape stock for magnificent music backgrounds. Like everything else this was done at a first rate level. Our team was out in the field for more than three months filming and I joined them during September 1985 through to November 1985.

Looking back I am thankful to God that we now had a good product that I was able to show to a new group of investors and upon seeing it more than $750,000 was invested. In the middle of October I wrote a letter to all of our investors from Ephesus in Turkey. At that occasion we had been shooting for thirty days without a break.

I wrote to them, 'Each day we are up and on the go by 4am and we start shooting about 5am. Our shooting finishes at sunset at about 6pm. The bus then takes the whole team back to where we are staying, where we shower and have a team meeting to discuss the next day's schedule, have an evening meal, wash clothes and fall into bed. Many people wonder how we have such wonderful light in 'Discovering Jesus' and no tourists ever in a shot. The secret is we do all of our important shots before crowds are out and about.'

In the same letter I reported that we had shot in Malta, Italy, Greece, Macedonia and Turkey and had filmed more than 450 sequences so far. Every place mentioned in the New Testament has had something filmed on that location. I added a simple Post Script, 'P.S. While I have been away I have also made 12 radio programmes for 2GB, each an hour long and I have planned a series of four new books. The whole crew appreciate your interest and prayers and your support for our loved ones back at home. We have 14 days of filming to go in Turkey and Israel. God's blessing be with you.'

By the time the series was cut and edited and produced we had two other successful series ready. World wide, Richard Baker had signed agreements with the production of the series into German for distribution throughout Germany, Austria and German-speaking Switzerland, in French not only for use in France but also through out Africa where French was spoken, in Italian by San Paolo Films with lip synchronisation for use throughout Italy, in English for distribution on the major television networks in the United Kingdom, had made a significant sale to public television in Botswana and in the USA. Our man on the scene, Al Nader in Chicago, had arranged for our entire series to be repeated on the public broadcasting system right across the United States. But even more amazing was the Spanish-speaking edition, which was screened over and over again throughout South America, in Santa Clara, Argentina, Paraguay, Uruguay and other Spanish speaking countries. Further editions were sold to Canada and many other places.

The story of these three films didn't end there. We had lots of 'off cuts', which were not used in the three series so a couple of years later we put all the off cuts together in a fourth called 'Discovering Israel'. Our investors were happy. Many of them received back more than three times the amount of money that they had invested, with the earlier investors doing best. After 12 years we closed down Wesley Film Productions Limited as having completed its task.

The Sydney Morning Herald finance pages wrote an article under the heading: 'Cecil B. de Moyes' saying, 'If you are asked for the names of the most commercially successful film makers in Australia, top of the list might not be the Rev. Dr Gordon Moyes who is heard regularly on 2GB and the channel 9 network, but he also runs Wesley Film Productions, which not long ago completed and got wide sales for a 12 program documentary on the life of Jesus. The 12 half hour episodes of Discovering Jesus have already been seen by about 4 million people on 37 stations around Australia and the next two series are expected to get bigger audiences. All of the extras you normally connect with commercial promotion such as video release, translation rights and worldwide distributions are already tied up including translations in French, Italian, Japanese and Spanish. The remarkable fact is the first series has already returned 23% of its sponsor's money, quite apart from having earned them a full 133% tax deduction. Moyes said most of the investors were Christian businessmen who liked the project and appreciated the tax break, but who had no serious hopes of getting their money back'

I will always be appreciative of those people who trusted us and who received a benefit.

We have now reinvented the series, adding to my original commentary on site dramatic representation of the events as I describe them and this has seen new releases: The Man Who Changed the World, The Apostle Who Changed the World and The Church that Changed the World. Then a new series on The Birth of Jesus, The Parables of Jesus, Teachings of Jesus and The Disciples of Jesus.

Now they have been re-produced on DVD and this opened another million dollar market.

Who would ever have dreamed that multiple millions of people in many languages and in scores of countries would have heard the Gospel because we had faith to put it together in an Australian company that became the most successful of its kind, simply called Wesley Film Productions. Wesley Film Productions Ltd was then to produce other films in widely separate parts of the world.

The anniversary of the landing of Australian and New Zealand soldiers at Gallipoli every year challenges us all. The stories of that event, together with the various myths and legends that grew up in the youth of nationhood have meant that Australians have a special place in their hearts for that Turkish Peninsula. Like many others of a later generation, I wondered what it was all about and studied the history, read the diaries... I was watching the film, Gallipoli on an aircraft when I realised that the Australian soldiers were being shot on wide sweeping sand beaches. I kept thinking, why are they not scraping some sand barricade, some trenches?

But Gallipoli is not like that. I knew that from geography lessons. Its beaches are rocky, even flinty, solid stone. It took a lot of effort to dig rock trenches to give them shelter. Every fresh brigade on landing, were mown down by the machine guns up on the cliffs. You could tell, looking at a pile of freshly uncovered skulls, which belonged to the allied forces – they all had bullet holes in the tops of their head from the guns firing down upon them. The Turks were fighting to defend their homeland and families from invaders.

So bad was that film, in mis-representing the hardships our troops faced, I decided to take our film crew to Gallipoli and film from inside the trenches. This was the first time since 1923 when the burial party arrived that a film was made on the actual site. I researched the history, wrote the scripts, raised the money and set off to Gallipoli. I took the same 40 member crew with me to Gallipoli I made my own pilgrimage to Anzac Cove. As I walked the beaches, climbed into the trenches, read the tombstones and thought of piles of contorted flesh of young Australian manhood, I realised that here, in a foreign country, will always be a part of Australia.

Col. Mustafa Kemal, who led the Turkish resistance so brilliantly in defending his own country, later became Attaturk, President of Turkey and the man who brought Turkey into the twentieth century. In 1934, Kemal Attaturk spoke of the Australian war dead some of the most moving words I have read:

'You heroes that shed your blood and lost your lives,
you are now lying in the soil of a friendly country.
Therefore you rest in peace. There is no difference
Between the Johnnies and the Mahomets to us

where they lie side by side in this country of ours.
You the mothers, who sent your sons from far away countries,
wipe your tears. Your sons are now lying in our bosom,
and they are in peace. After having lost their lives
on this land, they have become our sons as well.'

As I stood in tears reading those words and reading the names of the young men fallen, who lie buried in the cemetery known forever as 'Lone Pine', I realised that on the west coast of Turkey part of the heart of Australia lies buried. Far greater numbers of Australians would be killed and wounded in later wars and other war cemeteries would be built in Europe, The Middle East, South East Asia, the Pacific Islands, Papua New Guinea, Malaysia, Korea and Vietnam - but Gallipoli holds part of the heart of Australia.

Long before it was popular, I made the film, *Our Magnificent Defeat.* For about 15 years it was screened every Anzac Day across Australia. It played some part in the renewal of interest in people going there. That was to lead us to making the other documentary films including youth specials on drugs, sport and sex, using a whole series of celebrities popular with teenagers.

One of the films Martin Johnson, Beverley and a small team made that thrills me was *Inside The Great Wall,* a film that examines the Church in China under persecution. I have long been a 'China Watcher' and a chance to see my three books translated and spread throughout China and the opportunity to speak to Chinese pastors from the Underground Church who had been persecuted in jail for so many years, touched me deeply.

There are thousands of unmarked graves in China of faithful missionaries who died taking the faith to the Chinese. Most missionary gravestones were destroyed during the Cultural Revolution, which burned churches, books, libraries and institutions of learning and any sign of Western influence. One newly erected gravestone marks the grave of the Olympic Gold Medallist and China missionary Eric Liddell who was the subject of the great film *Chariots of Fire.*

But there is one grave in Hueili in the Western province of Sichuan that I wanted to see. My desire goes back to when I was a teenager attending youth camps in the old Waterman Camp buildings at Monbulk, Victoria. I remember the sonorous tones of our leader, Laurie Trizise, telling of the origin of the name. Will Waterman was a young missionary in Hueilichou during the 1920's and 1930's. His young fiancée Grace travelled out to be married to him there, trekking 15 days through the mountains of the upper Yangtze River. The Watermans and the Andersons were married in a double ceremony by Dr Kilmier. Joan and Win Waterman were subsequently born there. It was there that Will Waterman, the clever linguist, died at age 35 of peritonitis and was buried in the Mission compound. The deep tones of our Camp Leader told us on a still summer night under the stars, around a camp fire, that an Australian heart still lies in the heart of China.

I was determined to make a pilgrimage and try to see if anything of the church in Hueili remained. Nothing had been heard of it since the evacuation of Australian missionaries after the Communist take-over in 1949. Then in July 1996, as I was making my plans, I heard that my friend, Jeff Weston, with his deep missionary interest had just made the pilgrimage. I was thrilled at the news. The church remains. The old buildings built by Australian Churches of Christ during World War 2 still house the only Protestant congregation in the area.

Each Sunday over 400 Chinese people meet in worship, filling the building. Many have been imprisoned and beaten for their faith. The church has endured fifty years of persecution. Pastor Wang has led the work since the Communist Government came to power. He was imprisoned for 14 years for his faith. He died in 1993, but his widow continues as Pastor assisted by three elders. The work of pioneer Australian missionaries remains.

In 1925 Will Waterman wrote, 'Our territory supports unnumbered multitudes. There are half a dozen distinct people and languages. Everyone here is to be won for Christ - with your help.' His wife Grace in later years prepared my college meals during my years of study. She often talked at night with me telling me much of China. I remembered the Watermans, Kilmiers Andersons, Clarks and Rosa Tomkin and others who achieved much in China. One impression the visitor gets from the Christians in China is that their faith is thriving. There are few examples of churches seen on major streets and few in public places. But I did see a number of clearly identified churches in rural areas from the train as we travelled the length of China. Contact with government Religious Affairs Bureau officials enabled a visit to a registered church that is usually packed with people. Within the towering housings apartments, small squalid street level houses and on rural farms, unknown numbers of home churches (as they prefer to be called) meet, but there is no directory of these except by word of mouth from careful members.

The registered churches are growing. Since 1979, over 12,000 church properties have been handed back to the local church councils for use in worship. Sunday schools are not permitted, youth activities for people under 18 years are banned, evangelistic outreaches are not allowed, but worship is. In most major cities the Council of Churches (government registered) is listed in the telephone book and will give you worship times. One of the Three Self Patriotic Movement Churches in Beijing, a government registered church, was built as a Methodist Church in 1840. It has been burnt down three times, wrecked by the Boxers in the Rebellion of 1900, damaged by the Japanese occupation from 1937 to 1944 then closed down by the Red Guards in 1966 during the Cultural Revolution.

But in February 1998 while I was there, it was packed with 2000 crammed into the church and annexe, with another 1000 packed into the basement watching by closed circuit TV! Bibles were sold in their bookshop from the Amity Press with a long queue of purchasers. I saw one elderly man purchase about twenty Bibles, pack them on the back of his bicycle and ride off without attending the service, probably to go to some unregistered church.

The Amity Printing Foundation, with paper and support from the United Bible Societies, has printed 16 million Bibles, Testaments and hymn books since 1988 and up to 3 million portions will be published this year. Almost all of these are sold by registered churches in major cities. Roman Catholic and Protestant members of the registered churches number about 3 million. There are several registered seminaries with about 300 students and Walter Birklin Ministries has received permission to conduct about a score of pastoral training schools in major cities with Western lecturers since 1991.

The unregistered underground churches, however, have seen greater growth. It is estimated that 85% of the Christians in China belong to unregistered churches meeting in homes. Government estimates acknowledge now up to 30 million home church believers. Underground leaders told me they estimate 50 million members. China watchers talk about 70 million Christians in total in China. I have been told by leaders of the unregistered churches that there are about 50,000 groups currently in China. For China, every statistic is an approximation. One home church where I spoke was held in a university dormitory block. It was filled with students and lecturers. They were thrilled with the dozens of Chinese Bibles Beverley and I gave them, which we had got past customs illegally. The location of their underground church is constantly being revealed by other people who hear the singing. Yet they manage to move before the police arrive each time and still keep their members all informed of where they'll meet.

I met with many leaders, including several that were imprisoned for their faith for many years. One fine man had been beaten constantly to force him to deny his faith. The beatings which he described graphically for me, continued in prison for 23 years. Another lady doctor still works as an evangelist at age 93! She was forced to sweep the streets during the tyranny of 'The Gang of Four'. Their location is highly secret and involved back street travelling, many phone calls and several encounters with members of the government Bureau of Religious Affairs and the police.

Several of the team I was with were stopped, searched, interrogated, had Bibles confiscated and all details entered upon government computers against any further entry into the country.

One underground leader I met does not keep his location secret. Pastor Samuel Lamb of Guangzhou, refuses to move and has lived on and off in the same three storey narrow house belonging to his grandfather and father for 68 years. I say 'on and off' because he had to flee the Japanese in the 1940's. He started a house church at Easter 1950, just after the Communists came to power. The Public Security Bureau has outlawed this church in his house. In 1955 he was imprisoned for one and a half years. In May 1978 he was imprisoned for brainwashing for five years where he counteracted communist teachings with memorised portions of the Bible. He was sent from that five years confinement to 15 years slave labour in the Shanxi Talyuan Xiyu Coal Mine. It was here he composed many hymns, which are sung in the underground churches today. After 20 years imprisonment he was released in 1978 and returned to the little house and started services again. Then 300 people attended crammed together in the tiny rooms on three levels. By 1986 over 1000 people were attending three services.

In 1988 the Government tried six times to close him down. He started over again. On Thursday February 22nd 1990, at midnight, over 50 police smashed their way into his narrow house and confiscated all the Bibles, hymnbooks, recorders, close circuit TV, organ, tracts, pens and pencils and Pastor Samuel Lamb was interrogated for 25 hours. That Sunday Pastor Samuel Lamb started all over again as more than one thousand people stood in tears in a totally empty house. The same thing has happened in 1991, 1992, 1993, 1994 and 1995. Nothing happened in 1996.

In 1997, Pastor Lamb was again interrogated over Hong Kong's return to China from Britain. The next year the church held more services, conducted 351 baptisms and averaged over 2,000 people attending weekly. Today, over 2000 a week are attending the five services (each of 2 hours duration) with about 80% (my estimate) being young people. The authorities again tried to close his house church down and this time he was forced to re-locate.

I was with him when Government officials said that if the church stays open beyond a certain date, Pastor Lamb will be fined $50,000 and in default, an extended period of imprisonment. He does not have the money. He is 78 years of age and in poor health, suffering from degeneration of the spinal discs and cerebral arteriosclerosis. But whatever happens now, I am sure Pastor Lamb will start again. These Chinese Christians need our prayers.

Since October 1996, Government restrictions and human rights violations have dramatically increased. I met with a colleague of Pastor Peter Xu who on September 25th 1996 was sentenced to ten years imprisonment for 'disturbing the public order.' Another pastor told me of his colleague who was arrested and kicked to death in prison, leaving a widow and three little children that the churches are supporting. The Roman Catholic Bishop Su Zhimin of Baoding has been imprisoned, for the sixth occasion, having spent over twenty years in prison. Several hundred Roman Catholic school children have been forced to renounce their faith or else join an official church in order to attend school this year. House church pastors told me that when their members become known to the Religious Affairs Bureau, their electricity is cut off, their education is ended and their employment is terminated. Several told of houses where home groups meet having been bulldozed to the ground.

The US State Department declares that human rights violations have dramatically increased, including torture, forced confessions and arbitrary detentions. The faith is being tested. The 140 years of Protestant Missions up until the Liberation of 1949 has borne great fruit in the lives of faithful Chinese believers. But the situation at this moment is the worst since the Cultural Revolution (1966-1976). One bright spot is that in taking over Hong Kong (July 1st, 1997), China took over 13 seminaries producing evangelical graduate students for ministry who are keen to serve anywhere in China. The Red Dragon is breathing fire and smoke, but the Christians are thriving and are faithful even unto death.

The film we made, *Inside the Great Wall,* captures all the sights and sounds and interviews in the churches, with their great leaders under persecution. It was shown nationally on television and thousands of copies purchased. Once more I wrote the scripts and hosted the program, Martin Johnson produced and directed, but this time Beverley was an associate producer. We used this video to promote the work of the Bible League as they printed, smuggled into China and distributed hundreds of thousands of Bibles.

****

When I first started appearing regularly on Television in 1964 I discovered that people either hated you or supported you. So the letters started to come: 'I can't stand your fat smiling face, I watch you every week. You scumbag supporting the corrupt and illegal government run by…' and so on. Then there were those that said, 'I know you never ask, but please find $2 to support your work.'

I decided I would reply to every letter, including the hate mail. I also decided I would be different from the American Christian preachers on TV who were always appealing for money. They sometimes took up a large part of the program, urging believers to send money to buy more time to have more outlets where they could urge more people to send money to buy more time so they could urge more people to send…. I predicted our Australian people would get sick of that kind of religion.

I was right. Over the next twenty years almost all of those religious beggars went off Australian television. Unfortunately a new group of Pentecostal ministers using the same old begging routine, are currently buying Australian TV time. Not wanting to be treated like them, I decided I would never accept any payment for speaking the gospel on television and would never accept any personal gifts. I would appeal for support for Christian missions, but only for those I did not operate personally so my appeal would be at arms length from those using the gift.

I would also receipt every one of those gifts to others and send every person who contacted me an annual report with our audited financial statements. After forty years on television every week, I believe I am the only Christian presenter to operate like this.

Today after thousands of hours of telecasting and hundreds of thousands of pieces of mail, I receive virtually no hate mail and no criticisms of our financial approach. I have never been paid for any of my television work. This has involved setting up a large staff to help me with the answers to people's letters, telephone counsellors to answer calls for spiritual help and a production team to produce the program. But I did break one of these rules - once.

A lady from Sydney's north shore, a Mrs Cruikshank, rang me at my home one Saturday afternoon. 'Are you the Dr Moyes who speaks on television?', she asked. I replied that I was. She said, 'I have your address from the telephone book. I would like to come around this afternoon because I have a gift for you.'
I replied, 'Thank you Mrs Cruikshank, but I have a policy of never accepting any gifts from viewers. If you want to show your appreciation for our TV ministry, then send a gift to one of the Christian ministries I promote on the program.'
'No. I have a gift for you personally. I want you to have it. You don't live far from me, so I will come down now.'
'I am sorry Mrs Cruikshank but I do not accept any gifts personally. That has been my policy now for many years.'
'Well, I must give this to you, because I have been keeping this for more than fifty years to give to you.'
That got me in! I replied rather patiently, 'Thank you Mrs Cruikshank but you couldn't have been keeping this gift for me for more than fifty years, because I wasn't born fifty years ago!'
Mrs Cruikshank was not to be put off. 'I want to give you a gift that once belonged to my father who died a long time ago. It is a pair of gold cuff links he used to wear and I want to give them to you, because I notice you always wear cufflinks.'
'That is right Mrs Cruikshank. I do. But I still do not accept personal presents or gifts.', I replied.
'Well these ones were meant for you and only for you. I have been keeping them all these years. I remember you speaking one day about the significance of names of people in the Bible and how parents give children names that have significance for them. And you have special names.'
I replied, 'Well, the only way my names are special, is that my mother gave me the four surnames of my four grandparents. Gordon was my maternal grandfather's surname; Keith was my maternal grandmother's surname; Mackenzie was my paternal grandmother's surname and Moyes was my paternal grandfather's surname. It's a bit of a mouthful, but I guess my mother couldn't leave out one grandparent.'
'Of course not,' replied Mrs Cruikshank. 'My late father was named after his four Irish grandparents in the same way. His name was Grantley Kieran Mackearney Marsh. He died over fifty years ago.'
'Well that is a bit of a mouthful, like my name,' I told her.
'Yes, But you haven't grasped the significance. When he died I kept his cufflinks to give to the man who had the same initials as my father had engraved upon his cufflinks. You are the only man I have found in more than fifty years that have

the initials, G.K.M.M. I want you to have the cufflinks I have been keeping for you for more than fifty years.'

I treasured them.

Our venture into radio brought the most violent reaction from some within the Uniting Church. A 1979 Quadrant survey of 2000 citizens didn't even list Wesley Central Mission among the first 25 charities. I knew we would have to do something to increase public awareness of our work if we were to compete for the public's limited charity dollar. I knew radio exposure would do that best.

A similar survey a decade later showed that Wesley Central Mission had crept up to tenth place and by 1995 another Quadrant report revealed Wesley Mission ranked as third best-known charity. With that in mind in 1980 my plans emphasised radio programmes and spots over 2CH and 'Sunday Celebrations', which took the form of a half hour of sacred music and exposition tied into the College for Christians. Then 2CH changed its policy and the worship service from the Lyceum Theatre was broadcast live on 2KY and a two-hour program, 'Country Gospel', became my weekly talk programme. This continued until 1983 when 2GB invited me to commence a talkback programme. When the opportunity presented Wesley Mission secured some 87.7% shares in Radio 2GB, worth $3,087,000. The WM Board were greatly excited over this deal; they considered that it had enormous potential for spreading Christian ethics and the gospel message of God's wonderful love for 'every nation, kindred, tongue and people.' (Rev. 14:6)

Unfortunately an influential segment of the Uniting Church did not share this view. They contended that it was unethical for a religious body to virtually own a secular radio station. They totally ignored the benefits, concentrating instead on a prolonged attack against the Wesley Mission leaders. Publicly, privately and in the press they criticised the 2GB personnel, the programmes and the presenters. For more than half a decade they kept up their concerted censure. Led by Rev. Harry Herbert the press were presented with a mixture of lies and distorted facts.

I think they were still rankling over my appointment as WCM superintendent. Not once did they even grudgingly admit that Wesley Mission showed foresight in acquiring the radio station. The ownership of that 2GB occasioned me more worry and attracted more criticism than any other of our moves. Before our time as owners, investors lost millions of dollars due to well-meaning but incompetent management. Ratings fluctuated, personnel came and went. We were able to buy the station shares cheaply because of these problems. Then we set about improving the situation.

Wesley Mission had a policy of not censuring trained journalists, a policy others in the church bureaucracy could not accept. I was often rung in the middle of the night to be told by some listener some nighttime broadcaster had sworn or expressed an un-Christian viewpoint.

Station personnel came and went. We lost John Laws to rival 2UE. Michael Carlton left in a childish huff because I showed him he was not attracting advertisers to make the extra salary increase he was demanding viable. Derryn Hinch came and declared that he would be No. 1 in Australia by the end of the year beating John Laws and that he would 'see Rev. Gordon Moyes out the front door by Christmas'. He never became No. 1. He never beat John Laws and at Christmas I held the front door open as he left.

Clive Robertson joined us and was immediately liked by all. When I offered him a salary package, I included a new car. He replied, 'I don't need a new car, I am happy with my old one!' This was the only time a new employee has ever said that to me.

Although the all-important ratings climbed steadily they were slow and for several years the overall condition of 2GB remained far from the ratings top. However we were turning the station around without wasting any money.

The new management also succeeded in reducing expenditure by $5 million per annum but still it could not keep pace with costs, which remained around $1 million above income. Some Synod leaders wrongly said we were paying this from offerings or fundraising. That was a childish understanding. Buying rating success was the way to go bankrupt. Careful expenditure control would produce only medium level ratings, but that approach was beginning to return all costs and make small profits.

In mid 1995 the vociferous minority in the UCA synod made threats against Wesley Mission for our share holdings in 2GB. Each monthly Board meeting at 2GB records the better management and slow climb to profitably. In March '93 I wrote, '2GB is increasing revenue but still not quite covering costs. Ratings are slowly moving up. An additional $1 million a year would see it going well. We need to reduce staff but the very overstaffed newsroom is heavily unionised and any retrenchments will see a flurry of adverse articles in the major newspapers. We need to come up with some bright ideas.' At that stage 2GB had no debts to anybody except a past debt prior to Wesley's time, of $1.2 million to the Federal Government for licence fees. We were being charged 18% on this old debt. My frequent trips to Canberra to resolve this were to no avail.

In June '93 I wrote, 'We are still struggling at 2GB to get programming as we want it, to get rid of some of our difficult investors from years ago, to reduce costs which are still about $1 million pa above revenue, to increase revenue which is currently $6.2 million per year (up from last year by $1 million). But we have lowered costs since we became involved by $5 million per year. Our plan was to offer to buy out existing shareholders at ½ cent per share to get rid of the negative and divided Board. The Federal Government and the banks were standing strongly behind our business plan. They provided two advisors and were affirming of our goals and administration. We now owned 86.7% of the company. Our ratings were at 5.5 percent. If we could rate at 6% we would be profitable'.

In April '94, I wrote, '2GB finances are improving according to plan. In the last 9 months our revenue has grown by $900,000. The next three months will see us in profit.' There was the problem of the residual debt from before we came onto the Board. It was $14.2 million two years earlier and we had reduced it to $5.5 million. That was a marvellous achievement. I now offered to buy that debt from the State Bank for $3 million cash. They agreed. We then negotiated with the National Australian Bank for a $3 million loan to 2GB (not to Wesley Mission) at extremely low interest rate. Hence in 2 years the residual debt had been lowered from $14.2 million to $3 million on interest, long-term repayment basis. February '95 saw '2GB ratings increase to 5.9 % with a 27% increase in listeners. We have almost made it.'

Just when it seemed we were on top of the 2GB situation Rev. David Milikan, formerly of the ABC, published a defamatory article on Wesley Mission, 2GB and myself. It was full of factual errors. Our solicitors from both Wesley Mission and 2GB declared it clearly defamatory. I decided not to respond with litigation. Over the years I have rarely responded to people who have criticised us. Usually they are non-achievers who are racked with envy. But this gave the Synod opposition some ammunition for their attack on us for allowing some of our broadcasters the right to state their opinions on issues that were not politically correct. I wrote at the time, April 95, 'I have insisted that we will support freedom of speech on 2GB so long as it is not defamatory, illegal or immoral. But the Synod wants 2GB to be a 'politically correct' station. (representing the left wing views of some of the bureaucrats).'

In September '95, I wrote, 'Met with the Uniting Church's Board of Finance and Property with General Secretary Jim Mien over our ownership of 2GB. They are sympathetic and appreciate our financial results but they are paranoid about Rev. Harry Herbert's mounting an attack on us at the next Synod.' At the '95 Synod, I recorded, 'The attack on 2GB was vicious, led by Harry Herbert. Their methods of debate and innuendos on our financial handling of the matter were disgraceful. Synod voted for a long list of unethical issues (comments by our Broadcasters) to be declared unable to be discussed'. I then announced a bombshell. 'Recognising that Synod was moving to a position where any investment in the media above 7% of shareholding was to be declared unethical, I announced I was in negotiations to sell our shares at a good profit, retain a 15% shareholding to give us continuing Christian influence on the Board, legally tie the purchaser into giving us continued air time of four hours per week, hold all the benefits of ownership without being responsible for the repayment of the one loan to NAB nor any future debts nor for everything said on air.'

There was stunned silence. The Synod officials were dumbfounded. I had approached John Singleton, the owner of 2CH to buy our shares and form a joint company that would cut our overheads by $2 million per year, which would drop straight to the bottom line. I had cordial discussion with John Singleton and he agreed to buy the shares we had purchased two years earlier for half a cent each for 33 cents each plus whatever we had put into the company. We would retain 15% of the merged company, retain all our on-air time, be paid $6.5 million cash and Richard Menteith would remain on the Board and I would remain as Chairman of the Board.

This valued our shareholding at $10.6 million which was far in excess of our total purchase cost, any loans made to the company, plus 12% interest on our investment, remove any threat of a future need of cash investment or future liability for any debts that may be incurred. It would also give us air-time access on 2CH to Wesley Mission. No one on the council of Synod seemed to have the capacity to realise what a good deal this was. That is a church problem – the people who go to such meetings are laymen, usually retired or women not at work, or clergy who live in a Synod owned house, drive a Synod-owned car, have never had any business or company experience and whose greatest expense is at the Supermarket check-out. This description also includes most of the Synod officials who are not able to comprehend business matters.

The two moderators at this time were Rev. Ken Cornwell (a minister at Wesley Mission who in the previous three years of service at above the recommended salary had increased his congregation from 63 to 69) and Rev. Dean Drayton who had been on our Board for several years. Both had access monthly to all our financial statements, monthly reports from the 2GB Board, took part in Wesley Mission Council and Board decisions approving all of our activities with 2GB, yet in the Synod meetings, revealed none of this but voted with the Synod bureaucracy. Their silence spoke eloquently to us of them.

The next few years were interesting on the Board of 2GB. Alan Jones and a group of other people joined the station and John Singleton did what we could not do because of the adverse articles that would have been written against us – he sacked 70 journalists and other workers. No articles were even published of criticism of this; no editor would do that against the owner of an advertising agency that purchased square meters of advertising space every week! There were two ironies about this – this allowed 2GB to employ the right wing broadcasters who spoke against all the left wing political activists in the Synod. Our ownership had not satisfied these political activists in the Synod but we had kept a balanced approach, even if the extremes were sometimes 'politically incorrect'.

The second was the resistance to our 15% shareholding continued and we were not allowed to contribute any extra shareholder funds at a time when a new share issue of millions of shares were made in equity for a debt deal. This meant that in 2005 when the company's value reached $108 million and all shareholders value were extremely high, Alan Jones was suddenly $14 million richer (on paper) but the Uniting Church missed out on at least $15 million if we were to hold onto those shares.

The newspapers had a field day. One reported this and another reported that. Some portrayed me as the villain, others as the hero. The public did not know what to believe. As the documents were signed, God's seal came in an unexpected way. One of 2GB's elderly listeners, Jack Richardson, who had no connection with any church, visited me to discuss his vision of helping others. Supported by his accountants and legal advisers, he met with me and handed over $11.7 million--the largest donation ever given to me. My insistence that radio would pay off better than they could ever believe was justified. Over the next few years our original investment of $3 million had returned us in cash over $33 million, not counting this donation of $11.7 million. It had been a tremendous financial success.

With the Jack Richardson proposal gift of $12 million lost by Rev. Harry Herbert's actions and the 2GB missed revenue, the Church has paid dearly for continuing the employment of some of its officials and for not having in office people with business and management qualification or as Moderators people who have foresight and courage.

At the 1995 Synod I stated: 'No money invested or loaned by Wesley Mission into Harbour Radio Ltd has ever been lost, ever. All loans given to the company have attracted back to Wesley Mission a 12% interest rate, which is almost double what we were receiving from the Uniting Church Trust. There are no future loans or guarantees required and we will have made a significant financial return on our capital. In the meanwhile, our fund-raising from the general public has increased by more than $1 million p.a., a listener who has never been inside a Uniting Church arranged for Wesley Mission to receive $3 million from his estate, special radio appeals have raised $250,000 for Uniting Church activities and our public awareness has now taken Wesley Mission to being second only to the Salvation Army as the largest welfare work in NSW.'

'The Church has always wanted access to the media. Wesley Mission for the first time gave the Uniting Church what the Roman Catholic Church and the Methodist Church in other states had - a commercial radio licence. Now we shall have paramount influence in two commercial radio stations with more than 750,000 different listeners each week. We will have 10 hours weekly of Christian broadcasting and profitability upon the merger.

'Moderator, when you broadcast next Sunday night over 2GB, your sermon will be heard by more people than attended all the Uniting Churches in Australia next Sunday. And our counselling lines will be busy with people professing conversion to Jesus Christ - an event not found frequently in the Uniting Church, but which now occurs every week over radio.' Unfortunately the political activists

in the Uniting Church show no interest in evangelism.
Always beware of those who would take us out of the public arena to the comfort zone of talking to only ourselves.

The next few years were plain sailing on both 2GB and 2CH but the time came when Dick Menteith and I were satisfied that all conditions of the sale were finalised and our last portion of the sale price was paid. That was the time for us to resign from the Board and myself as Chairman. I was replaced by Sam Chisholm, one of the top media managers in the world. He was the man who did the deal with me twenty-five years earlier while he was General Manager of the Channel Nine Network and we commenced our national television program, Turn 'Round Australia.

Wesley Mission is grateful to God for seventeen years broadcasting on 2GB and The Macquarie Network, through a series of ownerships. Under the new management 2GB and 2CH again rose in the ratings stakes but the recent hiring for broadcasters that led to the station's improved public response came at great cost. I then recommenced on Radio 2 with our normal broadcasting.

There is a down side about being seen on television across the nation every couple of days and being heard constantly on radio and being read about in magazines and newspapers and that is being recognised. I love people to come up to me and make some comment, but every day, on public transport, walking the city streets, in restaurants and shops people just stare. They recognise but do not smile or speak, just stare. That is a little unnerving. I often smile at them and speak and that unnerves them!

But that is a minor matter – staring is one thing but being innocently blamed and therefore threatened is another. My life has been under serious threat many times. Even in church. Once after speaking out about the inappropriateness of a lesbian minister living in a relationship with another woman, continuing as the Uniting Church's head of 'Mission', a group of lesbians plus some male friends decided to invade my church and physically assault me. Before that service I advised two friends and members who had been remarkably converted, a man who was a Kung Fu expert who had been converted from an abusive sexual relationship and a woman, who had been a lesbian who had a black belt in Karate, who had also been remarkably converted. After church, as I farewelled people, these two stood either side of me in a protective manner. The threatening abusers melted away!

One night, a credible witness told me I was to be stabbed by a man I had never seen or met. He wanted to do it during a televised service. That night 2 men, wearing overcoats sat in the front row immediately in front of the pulpit where I was to preach. Our large security man came and sat beside them. During the sermon no one moved and nothing happened. At the door later, the security man showed me a razor sharp carving knife he had taken from underneath one

Clockwise from top left: Gordon (far right) with his sisters, Lorna and Nola, his mother and brother Robert, 1954; Gordon with his first book 'How to Grow an Australian Church', 1974; Gordon and Beverley on their wedding day 12th December 1959; Gordon with Robert Schuller sharing a cup of tea on the film set of TRA (1979).

Clockwise from top left: Jenny, Peter, David and Andrew, 1979; Gordon at Vision Valley, 1979; Jenny and Ron's wedding, 1983; Gordon with Billy Graham at his 1982 USA crusade

Clockwise from top left: Father of the Year, 1986, (from left) David, Andrew, Beverley, Gordon, Trina, Peter, Jenny and Ron; Gov. General Bill Hayden receiving copies of 'Discovering Jesus' (1987); Chairman of the Radio 2GB Board, Broadcaster 4 hours each week, 1986; Moving to George Street for rebuilding of Wesley Centre, 1987

Clockwise from top left: Gordon on the Sea of Galilee - the making of 'Discovering Jesus', 1984; Gordon marrying Peter and Trina, 1988; Gordon marrying Andrew and Rebecca, 1992; Gordon and David a David's graduation at Sydney University (B. Th), 1989

Clockwise from top left: Gordon marrying David and Leisl, 1989; Gordon President of the Rotary Club of Sydney 1993-94; Gordon on 2GB 'Sunday Night Live with Gordon Moyes', 1998; Gordon, Beverley and son Andrew at Government House Sydney for Beverley's investiture as a Member of the Order of Australia, 1989

Clockwise from top left: Gordon and former NSW Premier, Bob Carr, at the launch of Goldie Downs biography of Gordon's Life, 2000; Gordon with Fergie, Duchess of York, Visit to Lottie Stewart Hospital Dundas, 1994; Gordon moving from George Street Sydney to new Wesley Centre, 1987; Gordon with Jack Richardson, benefactor, being given a cheque for $11.4 million for the Aged Persons Welfare Foundation, 1996

Clockwise from top left: Gordon and Beverley at Government House - Investiture of AC, 2002;Gordon at Parliament House, 2003; Swearing into the Legislative Council, NSW Parliament, 2003; Roseville Manse Rotuman Congregation annual visit, 1995

Clockwise from top left: Gordon with Prime Minister John Howard and Superintendant's Award winner the Rev. Robert Smith at Spirit of Mission, 2005; Gordon preaching, 2005; Gordon, Beverley, Jenny, Peter, David and Andrew with the Gov. Gen. Peter Hollingsworth at Government House, Canberra for Gordon's Investiture of AC, 2002; Gordon and Professor Touyz admire the new Peter Beumont Centre for Eating Disorders on 2nd August 2005

of the overcoats. He had also organised the video cameras to record the people and the discovery of the knife. One man was identified from the videotape by police, who later arrested him and charged him. Unfortunately the security man is now always present. The days of innocence have gone.
But it was twenty years of speaking with people about their needs and cares that put me in the most danger. Not always do I agree with a person who rings talk back radio. And some times, usually with people who make racist or terrorist-like remarks, my disagreement with them leads to threats of violence against me or even death. Because of the time delay button, I do not allow these comments to be broadcast.

After a series of these, the radio station had to change its procedures to prevent access to radio studios. Once a man threatened to kill me with a shotgun because I supported a certain court decision by a judge. Later that night, as I was preparing to go home just after midnight, my wife rang to tell me to stay in the studio. She had seen an armed man walk up our front path and sit on our front steps waiting for me with his shotgun. She was brave and calm. She turned off the lights and rang for a police patrol. They arrived but he ran off into gardens of our neighbours and escaped. When I eventually came home that night we had no idea or not if he would come out of hiding to shoot me, or just wait until the police had gone and appear at the windows. After that I always came home with a taxi-driver named John Aquilina in his taxi. He waited until I was safely in the house. Another time, I talked a deeply disturbed man into surrendering his rifle to me. He did that, took me into his house and gave me another ten guns. I put them up in my roof until there was an amnesty and he agreed to them being sold to the police and he received the cash for them.

But another case stays in my mind. In July 1984 the front door bell on a house a few streets away from mine rang. The house was the home of a Family Court Judge, Mr Justice Ray Watson, a strong supporter of Wesley Mission. His wife, Pearl Watson, answered the door. A huge bomb exploded, killing her and demolishing the front of their house. At that time there was much controversy over the decisions of the Family Court, on Justice Lionel Murphy's alleged interference in the NSW court system, Premier Neville Wran's legalisation of homosexuality between consenting males, an alarming Royal Commission into organised crime and a big push by drug trafficers. Members of the community were angry on many fronts.

One radio caller seemed to me to know details of the attempted assassination of Mr Justice Ray Watson that were unknown to the general public. He rang again and again. I notified the police investigation unit who encouraged me to keep talking to the man. Gradually I learnt he was the father of an only child ordered by Mr Justice Watson to remain with his mother. My caller rang me at home every morning (my home phone number has always been in the telephone book). Then he rang me at work several times a day.
With the knowledge of the police I invited him to come and visit me. He was a

desperate father, but was he desperate enough to plant a bomb? Gradually the police gathered the evidence. There was not enough to convict him, although a senior policeman told me he was the main suspect. He felt safe revealing information to me. He confessed to a terrible crime. His only son was being sexually abused by his mother who was living in a lesbian community. The details were revolting. So one night he had called on his wife, threw a bucket of petrol over her and lit it. She was horrifically burned. He was charged and imprisoned. I saw his wife's scarred body and face in hospital. Now the boy had neither mother or father to care for him. The father was absolutely paranoid with lesbian employees of the Department of Community Services who may be involved in caring for his son. I appealed to the court to release the boy into my custody and I would arrange for some of my Wesley Dalmar Staff to care for him in a safe house at a secret location.

When the father was released from prison, he demanded I reveal the location of his son. At the direction of the Department of Community Services I refused. He then turned his wrath against me. The next day he visited some of my childcare staff demanding details. They were traumatised. They felt intimidated and at risk and subsequently walked off the job. The police then told me that while he was the prime suspect in the bombing case, they were taking it no further. The man kept ringing and coming to see me. I always managed to calm him down and walk him out of our premises. I let his threats against me go un-argued. Nothing further happened. No one has been charged with the murder of Mrs Pearl Watson to this day. The impact on Mr Justice Watson was devastating. I kept a watchful eye on any potentially risky situations that may have endangered my life. The presence of a man with a loaded shotgun on my doorstep at midnight waiting for me to return was never far from the front of my mind. Then in 2004, early one morning, I answered the phone and it was him - the prime suspect in the Watson bombing. I remained respectful, informed the police and did what they suggested, which was to avoid personal meetings. Being well-known through the media involves risk, even if you have done nothing to exacerbate the problem.

I decided in 2003 to use the media in a set of lectures on Australian history. Australia's Christian foundations have been hidden by secular historians, educators and journalists. But Australia was founded by committed Christians in many fields. We never were a pagan secular community. Some of our greatest nation builders were men and women of faith.

I researched carefully and from our great libraries I obtained their letters, diaries and artifacts and prepared a series of lectures to be given in the Wesley Theatre. About 300 people attended each one and the screen was filled with historical quotes, pictures, maps and their achievements. The response of the public was overwhelming. The lectures on the sea explorers, the land explorers, the first women, the convicts, the governors, the missionaries, the educators, the pioneers were all recorded on film and audiocassette and released as a series. Libraries in schools, churches and communities purchased sets and many were donated by television viewers. I repeated the series on radio and television and it is my intention to repeat them as a lunchtime series in the NSW Parliament Theatre. There have been many remarkable stories come out of my years doing four hours every Sunday night on the No 1 radio station in Australia. One concerns a call to me one night just before midnight. At about five minutes to midnight in 1988, I received a call from a young woman who was sobbing. Her name was Melody. Later Melody wrote her account of what happened:

'It was the winter of 1988. It was cold and pouring with rain. It was after 11:30pm and I was driving back to Sydney having spent the weekend in Canberra saying goodbye to my friends. I had decided that the only way out of my problems was to kill myself. I had no self-esteem, believing that the abuse I suffered as a child and a young teenager was all my fault. As the trucks came thundering towards me out of the dark, I thought how easy it would be to steer my car underneath the front of one of them. It would be a quick and easy death. As I drove I usually listened to cassettes, but on this particular night I turned on the radio to see if I could find a friendly voice. As I listened I heard the announcer say that if anyone wanted him to pray for them, then to give him a call. It was Gordon Moyes on 2GB and immediately I knew I had to call. 'I have to stop and phone. This is my only chance!

'I was just leaving Goulburn and as I looked to the side of the road, there was a phone booth. I wondered if it would work and if I had any change. It did and I was put straight through to Gordon on the air. I was pretty upset and it took a while for me to tell Gordon why I had called. But I remember he just kept on talking to me. He didn't even say the prayer that he normally says when he closes the program. After the program finished, he kept on talking to me off the air. That telephone and that link with another human being became my only hold on life. When we eventually stopped talking, I had calmed down a little and begun to see that maybe there was some way out of the deep depression I had sunk into. Gordon had made me promise to call him as soon as I got home. I remember the relief in his voice when I called him at 2:30am in the morning to say that I had arrived home safely. When we were talking on the air, he had asked people to pray for me. Those prayers were the only thing that carried me through that night and beyond.

'During my teenage years I had always blamed myself for everything that had ever gone wrong. I felt utterly worthless. My life had no purpose and all I could see was that I had caused problems for everyone. In my depression I decided that the best thing I could do was to kill myself so I wouldn't be a burden anymore. That late night call to Gordon on 2GB changed my life. My life turned around a complete about-face! I began to see that what had happened to me was not my fault. I was not responsible for what others had done to me!

'After I understood that and I put the blame squarely on those who had done wrong, I was able to take the next step in the process of healing to forgive those who had hurt me. I had also made a decision to take God at his word and believe that what the Bible said was absolutely true. God said He loved me in his word therefore it was true God loved me! I read the story of the unforgiving servant in Matthew. (Matt 18:23-35) God had forgiven me many things yet he still loved me. I also started to see that God loved those who had hurt me too and had sent Jesus to die for them as well. Slowly it sank into my heart that if God could love and forgive them and then who was I to hold something against them. My only option was to forgive them and trust God with their lives. That step brought such freedom into my heart and for the first time I really saw what Jesus meant when He said, 'I came that you might have life and have it abundantly.' (John 10:10)

'Since that time my life has been filled with God's love and the joy of sharing his love and his gospel of redemption, grace and wholeness with others. The change in me wasn't something that happened instantly; it was a process that had to be diligently worked through and couldn't have been done without the love and support of friends who let me cry and who prayed for me. Because of all that God had done in my life, I wanted to work full-time for Him and the opportunity arose for me to go to Africa at the beginning of 1990. It was a fantastic time of seeing God's faithfulness over and over again as he supplied my every need and as he taught me constantly from his word. My own spiritual life grew amazingly and it was such a joy to see peoples' lives change radically upon hearing of the grace of God and the salvation He has made ours in Jesus. I spent seven months in South Africa, a month in Zimbabwe and England and three months in Canada. Each place was different and in each place God had different things he wanted to emphasise, but in them all God's word was, 'I love you'. This is what has given me the strength to go on when my life seemed worthless, not just overseas, but here as well.

'Now I'm back in Australia and grateful for the opportunity to say thank you to anyone who heard that first call to 2GB and who prayed for me. And to those of you who have friends who are struggling with thoughts of suicide and worthlessness, don't give up helping. In Jeremiah 29:11 God declares, 'I know the plans I have for you, plans for your welfare and not for calamity, to give you a future and a hope.''

There are a couple of points that Melody didn't know at that time. When she rang me at five minutes to midnight in tears and in the pouring rain from the phone box outside of Goulburn where she had been waiting to kill herself by driving her little car in front of an oncoming transport truck, I said to my listeners, 'Now I always close with my prayer. But tonight I do not want to have this prayer because I want to keep talking to Melody. Those of you who are Christian, would you please pray for me and Melody while we have this discussion and I'm quite sure your prayers will help us resolve this problem.'

So the program ended without the prayer as usual. But out among my listeners, many people earnestly prayed for Melody and my discussions. Over the next half hour or so, I talked to her on the telephone. I suggested that she come on towards Sydney and I would drive to Liverpool and meet her. However, she said she felt quite confident that she could drive home to Lane Cove and ring me from there, which she did. I made arrangements to meet her the next day and over the next few weeks we met several times and one of my staff provided Melody with a great deal of encouragement and help.

Her life was put back into order and her visit to Africa, which she mentioned, was an absolute triumph for her as she went to help some of the most underprivileged and poor people in the world. From time to time I still talk with Melody and I am just grateful to God for those who prayed throughout our discussions.

Some time later, an elderly lady wrote to me and told me that when she heard the suicide call from Melody and when she heard me say that I was going to keep talking to her and I asked for listeners to pray, this elderly lady wrote, 'I got out of bed and knelt beside my bed and prayed for Melody as if she were my own grand daughter. I prayed over and over again, in fact, it was daylight before I got up from my knees.' God heard her prayers and enabled us to resolve the problems and as a result, Melody today is living a fruitful and effective life. Who knows just what is the outcome of our sincere and effective prayer?

The influence of the media in changing lives is beyond imagination. It can start in the most ordinary of ways.

There is a photograph of me on a stand outside our church advertising our services to people passing by in the street. I have just heard that photo saved a woman's life. She lives in the western suburbs but every day travelled to down-town where she worked in a nearby bank as a Customer Services Officer, what we used to call a bank teller. Each day she went a few doors along the city street to a club that provided cheap meals. Her life was empty, despite a good marriage, a nice home and three children. After lunch, seeking a thrill, she played the poker machines sparkling along the walls. As time went by she skipped eating to spend more time on the machines.

When her money was gone, she borrowed from the bank's cash drawer, planning to replace it with winnings. For some reason, no one noticed at the bank she frequently transferred money to make up for deficiencies in her cash drawer. Then she developed a means of covering her transactions. When the bank finally uncovered the paper trail, as banks always do, she had embezzled over $800,000.

In the Dowling Street Court, she was sentenced to a custodial period in the Emu Plains Women's Prison for 11 months. Her family and her life fell apart. While in prison, like hundreds of prisoners across the nation, she watched my television program every week. She heard the testimonies of former prisoners who found that Jesus Christ filled their emptiness. She longed for that inner filling and vowed upon release, she would seek guidance about Jesus. Upon her release, the old emptiness was still there. Almost automatically, she caught the train into the city and started to walk back to the club and the poker machines. At the last minute, thirty metres from the club's doors, she saw the sign with my photograph.

She stopped. She remembered the television programs and her questions about Jesus. This was a moment of decision. Which way? She decided to walk into Wesley Centre and come and see me. She did not make it to my office. Instead, she turned into our restaurant and had a long cup of coffee while she reviewed her life. Without anyone speaking to her, she prayed for Jesus to enter her life, to take away her compulsion to gamble and make her a better wife and mother. He did and he did! Filled with joy, she walked out of Wesley Centre and continued down the street with purpose and assurance, right past the enticing doors into the club and past her old bank. She has continued to walk tall since. Jesus now fills her every need. There is no need for the gambling thrill. The media is powerful in allowing God to meet peoples' needs.

ENTREPRENEUR

Chapter Seven

Wesley Centre

While our new Wesley Centre was being built, we met in temporary premises in the area of the city where lots of teenagers hung out. We developed two programs:

Cityrock captured the interest of young people. For many years I have wanted to see a citywide youth rally on a Saturday night providing good Christian entertainment for young people and a strong outreach to street kids. Both purposes were served with strong attendances from Christian youth and up to 100 street kids being invited into the presentation each time to hear the gospel message. A number were converted.

The aim of having a program packed with youth from churches all around the suburbs has still not been realised, although gradually the message is being spread and more are attending and enjoying the programs.

The name Cityrock was carefully chosen. City because this is an urban ministry to kids in the suburbs and in the streets of the city; Rock because that is the genre of the music and the basis of our theological understanding. We want young people to find security, a solid foundation for their future, a rock upon which their lives can be built.

Too many young people have no sure foundation for the building of their lives. They have no solid basis of morality by which they can judge their actions and no sure example from their homes on which they can model their behaviour. They are building lives on other kids' ideas and behaviour patterns and modelling futures on television and music stars lives. They are building on sand.
It is never too soon to start young people in the right direction. To wait as many parents do until their children are teenagers is to ignore the most powerful years of childhood development. Once, when I was talking to parents whose teenage son was placed by a court on probation under my oversight because of his behaviour, they said to me:

'We have always believed in letting our child grow up without moral instruction so that when he is older he can make all the right decisions for himself without our influence. When do you think is the right time for us to start raising all these issues?' I replied, 'You had better get started now. You have already wasted the most valuable fourteen years!'

During the late 1970's while I was still in Melbourne anticipating coming to Sydney to become the Superintendent of Wesley Mission, I was thinking of the special social needs the people of Sydney were facing which would become problems in the community during the forthcoming 1980's. It was at this time that un-requested, a bank sent to me one of their new bankcards that was just being issued. I did not want it and had not asked for it, but it just arrived in my letterbox.

I suddenly realised that in a city like Sydney with millions of people receiving bankcards that they had not requested, that hundreds of thousands of people would go on spending sprees and very shortly personal debt would become a major problem. We had a whole generation of people that were not trained in using credit cards and the temptation to buy on credit would be too much for them. I realised that vast numbers of people would not be able to control their spending, going into debt even for groceries and household needs.

I was convinced that large numbers of people would, in the decade of the 70's, end up in debt and financial strife and much of it would be caused by new credit cards.

I decided that Wesley Mission would need to be in the forefront of helping people with their debts. I had enough experience to know that one of the major causes of suicide was the inability to pay financial debt and the worry that that caused. I also knew that many marriages broke up, foundering on the rock of financial debt. I conceived the idea in late 1977 of running a service at Wesley Mission that would be called 'Debtline' to balance off our counselling service called 'Lifeline'.

In September 1978, I sent a folder to Sydney ahead of me to Stan Manning our then general manager, Arthur Oakley, the remaining minister in the pastoral department, Dr Jim Pendlebury and Keith Walkerden our honorary secretary. It contained 160 new ideas that I wanted to develop in Sydney when I arrived to keep Wesley Mission growing and serving the community.

This included resident funded units in retirement villages like I had developed in Melbourne, which have since made such a big impact on the life of the Mission. Another of my ideas was 'the institute for World Evangelism to train ministers from South East Asia and the Pacific Region specifically in the areas of church growth and evangelism.' This idea of mine was actually taken up and developed by Sir Alan Walker following his retirement many years later and is now known as the Alan Walker College in North Parramatta.

Item #152 on this 1978 paper read: Plan through Lifeline, to develop a credit-control counselling centre when we move Lifeline into Wesley Centre. Seek government assistance to employ a person to give counselling to people who have debt problems and who have an inability to control their credit especially on the new credit cards.

The Mission was accepting of these new ideas and I very quickly began the work after my induction and re-ordination as the Superintendent at Wesley Mission. I appointed a young research officer, Clare Hogan, to do a research report on personal debt in Australia in June 1979. Her report, received a few months later, made very clear that we were going to have a massive problem in the Australian community over people's problems in handling debt.

In November 1979 I announced that Wesley Mission would establish 'Debtline'. We started with a number of trained volunteer counsellors from 'Lifeline' and gave them special financial counselling to help people control their debts, repay them and learn how to handle credit. We started with two volunteer counsellors and opened the offices at night for families who worked during the day. In the first month we had 288 people come for counselling. There was no other financial counselling service available in Australia at that stage. I commenced a series of training courses for other Lifeline counsellors who could help specialise in financial counselling using bank officers, accountants and other people with specialist financial skills. I had specialists come in to lecture in consumer law, budgeting, consumer protection and financial counselling. Our volunteer counsellors however, were being overwhelmed and we needed full-time staff. I advertised during June 1980 for a suitable leader of the work and on the 9th July 1980 I announced that Mrs. Betty Weule had been appointed. Betty had completed some training at Wagga TAFE and had good experience in counselling people. Unfortunately Betty had been in hospital for surgery and it took a little time for her to get underway.

By September 1980 I was able to report that the two experienced volunteer counsellors had been persuaded to leave their jobs and to work full-time with us in face-to-face counselling. Betty was at the helm and was starting off in fine fashion. In my first interview with her she persuaded me to change the name from 'Debtline', which she believed had a very negative connotation, to 'Creditline'. That was a good move. Betty worked with us for the next twenty years.

In the next few months Creditline received tremendous support from the Public Solicitor's office, the Housing Commission, the Inner City Legal Service, Westmead Hospital, the Child Abuse and Prevention Service and many other organisations.

We approached the National Bank and they agreed to set up consolidation loans to help clients. The Commonwealth Bank also provided joint name savings accounts with the Mission as a joint signatory and people who were hopelessly in debt began to put part of their wages each week into these bank accounts but could only withdraw the money when we were joint signatories. We went to their credit providers and to the people to whom they owed large debts and indicated that we would handle their accounts and that the debts would ultimately be paid but we needed time and cooperation from the providers. In most cases we received that co-operation instantly. What I didn't realise was that in years to come there would be people whose debts would run into hundreds of thousands of dollars and many well over the million-dollar mark and who would never be able to repay. We had to develop for these people a new service to help them realise the significance and seriousness of bankruptcy.

In those days credit counselling was in its infancy and Betty Weule and I were interviewed on a score of television and radio programs. One of our young staff, Ian Garvin, made his first Supreme Court appearance for a bankruptcy case to explain to the court exactly how we could help them get on their feet again.

By November 1980 the courts were beginning to ask Creditline to do a report on all cases going before them and the official receiver was holding over some bankruptcy actions to enable Creditline to work out an alternative solution. Mr George Cady the official receiver has worked with us consistently in helping people find their way out of debt.

We were convinced that we had to help educate people in using credit cards, although this really should have been the responsibility of the credit providers, the banks and the lending companies. So we started lectures on consumer education in schools. We lectured social workers in how to help people and with the cooperation of the Housing Commission and the Prison Authorities have lectured to people in Housing Commission areas and to prisoners in jails.

We also decided to take head on some companies that were creating big debt problems for people. I went on radio and television over Easter 1981 and announced that over 950 of the 1000 clients who had come to us with impossible debt, had credit hassles with Walton Stores. In those days Waltons had a business buying bad debts from other companies. They would raise the interest charge and through door-to-door salesmen would encourage people to purchase more goods, far beyond their capacity to repay. Having brought this to the attention of the public through radio and television, the Waltons company threatened me with a $250, 000 defamation writ. There was a jail sentence also hanging over my head if I didn't recant and take back the accusation and apologise. However I refused to do that because the facts were right. Betty Weule came with me and we confronted the Waltons company in their store, meeting with the managing director of Waltons and the chairman of the board with our evidence. John Walton chaired the meeting. When we presented our evidence Waltons stores backed down, apologised, withdrew the threatened writ and agreed to six areas which we had drawn up in order to help their customers.

This made good newspaper and television copy at the time and Creditline was on its way. It also led to thousands of people coming to Creditline for counselling. Wesley Mission had a tiger by the tail!

We rapidly increased the staff at Creditline and the number of professionally trained and competent advisers. People by the tens of thousands each year received credit counselling and were helped with their debt problems.

The support we have had since from the finance industry, from the courts and banks and from governments has been outstanding. We started to open other offices at Westmead, Macarthur, Bathurst, Castle Hill and then in an amazing flurry all over Australia, including places as remote as Alice Springs and in the middle of the Simpson Desert.

You might wonder why we would have a Creditline counsellor in the middle of the Simpson Desert? Well, one of our guys drives a four-wheel drive through the most remote areas of Australia to tribes of Aborigines. You wonder why they have debt problems? Here is an example:

Not long ago he was involved with our Wesley Legal Service, which has four professional solicitors working full-time taking companies to court over gambling and debt problems and in taking three companies to court for their actions of selling products to Indigenous people in the Simpson Desert.

These three South Australian Companies had sent sales people into the remote camps of Aborigines in the Simpson Desert to sell them products. One was our largest seller of Encyclopaedia. Apparently since moving on to CD Rom there were large numbers of Encyclopaedia Britannica sets available for sale and a salesman had travelled through the Aboriginal communities selling sets of encyclopaedia on low deposit but long term repayments for very high prices. Another company had sent a salesman selling second hand Holden cars to Aboriginal people in the camps on low deposits and very high interest charges. Another company had sent vacuum cleaner salesmen to sell vacuum cleaners valued at more than $2000 each to people who had neither carpets nor electricity. Our legal service set up to tackle such companies and take them to court. In each case we won and in all cases had the unfair contracts cancelled.

Since I started Creditline with Betty Weule as our first full-time staff person there has been a change in Bankruptcies in Australia. For many years most bankruptcies were big named, highflying businessmen like George Herscu, Laurie Connell and Christopher Skase- high flying multimillionaire corporate losers. Most people in those days going into bankruptcy were corporates who had debt beyond their capacity to repay. However in the 1980's we detected a new trend: most bankruptcies were not as a result of a business but were personal bankruptcies. And that's when Creditline arrived. When I commenced Creditline the 1978/79 financial year showed that 52% of bankruptcies were personal but by

1988, 70% of bankruptcies were personal. Bankruptcy was becoming common among those who had no property and now among homeowners bankruptcy is increasing even though under bankruptcy laws any saleable asset, including the family home, is liable to be sold to pay creditors.

I began to see also that there was a problem compounding these bankruptcies because most of them were not matters of personal extravagance in living, but were due to an increase in gambling. That is why in 1984 I started a gambling counselling program and trained people who specialised in gambling counselling. How that developed is another story of incredible timing! We were the first professional gambling counselling service in Australia and the first person I appointed, Mitchell Brown, headed up Wesley Gambling Counselling Service for many years. It has grown to become the largest gambling counselling service in Australia. It trains gambling counsellors for scores of services throughout Australia and provides information, support and back-up for every gambling counsellor in the nation. In the same way Creditline has trained financial counsellors and we find them in centres all over Australia. We run a '1800' number and counsellors anywhere in the nation can ring for help and guidance from our expert counsellors.

Unfortunately the problem of debt through credit cards expenditure and debt through uncontrolled gambling is continuing to increase. Both of our services are the largest of their kind in the nation.

I soon realised that we had to do something on behalf of some of these clients, to save them from unscrupulous operators, like the big licensed club near us in Pitt Street where a grandmother in her 80's had stupidly spent all of her money on the poker machines. The first time a member of her family knew about it was when she discovered that mother was unable to leave them anything in her will. The manager of the club had provided credit facilities for the grandmother to continue playing the poker machines. He had then introduced her to a bank manager in North Sydney who took out a mortgage on her home to give her more money to gamble. We took both the bank and the licensed club to court and won. The lady's debts were cancelled and the two managers were sacked. This led us to help the government write new legislation and Betty Weule has been a wonderful asset to governments, as they have written more restrictive legislation to help control companies to provide a duty of care to compulsive gamblers. Many companies throughout NSW have now been taken to court by Wesley Legal Service and in every case that I can remember we have won. Wesley Mission's Creditline and Gambling counselling service have been the lead organisations in sticking up for the battler and for those who through their own stupidity have over-spent and over-gambled.

We discovered that we should also support the families and children of such people and so many programs have been developed to help people going through such trauma. I remember for example, one young family with 5 children, including a baby with a hole in the heart, who came to us for financial counselling. The Father had been sick for three months. They had a finance company loan of $3000 but with the sickness were unable to repay that $3,000. They took out a consolidating loan which increased the debt to $11,000 but this did not give them one cent more but only covered interest and repayment charges. They then took out a George Adams loan at 140% per annum to pay the finance company. They then took out a Walter Pugh loan at 162.4% per annum interest to pay the George Adams loan. Bankruptcy seemed to be the only alternative. Yet for ten years this family had stayed home. They had no car and enjoyed no outings. It was ten years since the parents had had a night out alone. Creditline re-established them until they had a small balance in a credit union bank account we opened for Christmas. We sent the family on a holiday without cost to Vision Valley. The children were excited, the parents were tearful. The children's reaction as they were being driven to the valley was hard to believe: 'Look at the horses', 'There's a cow'.

On Sunday afternoon we collected the family from Vision Valley to drive them back to their own home and four young cannonballs threw themselves at us, 'We rode the horses. We were in the canoes. We didn't find the cave. We had scones and cream and chicken for dinner.' The parents looked dazed but ever so relaxed and happy. The mother said, 'I haven't cooked a meal for days. I just can't believe it's happening.' To help people re-establish themselves, to educate people in handling their income, to renew their lives, that was our aim. If as Christians we would have them live according to the teachings of Jesus they would never get into such financial or gambling difficulty.

It has become popular among some trendy people to sneer at the protestant work ethic, but those who follow the teachings of Jesus Christ are saved from the traumas of financial disaster. He starts not with our consumer greed but with our commitment to himself. He calls us to a complete re-ordering of our priorities, including our finances.

In 1988 I was troubled by the numbers of young teenagers on the inner city streets all night. A number of them assaulted and robbed late night revellers, women on their own and those who appeared drunk. I appointed a couple of tough street workers to start work each night at midnight. With the approval of the Company, we set up office and counselling in an all night McDonald's store. This helped us to make contact with these nocturnal ferrals and the presence of our staff kept the store safe. Soon it was seen a more permanent place was needed on the streets.

Bill Locke, incoming President of the Rotary Club of Sydney 1989-90, asked if we could do more if we had more money. He inspired the Rotarians to raise $170, 000 for a program I devised. We leased a three storey building in the CBD, paid a bunch of graffiti artists to decorate it inside and out and opened 24 hours a day. Free food and dry clothing was provided by the firms of Rotarians. Kids were encouraged to watch videos and talk with our staff. When a sense of trust was established they were invited to go to the second floor. There was gym equipment, snooker and other games – and another counsellor. As trust was established then we invited them to discuss their alcohol or drug dependence, why they had left home and how they could develop a plan for their future.

Many of them were helped to return to school or into employment. 7,000 street kids in crisis were helped in the first year. More than 1,000 completed intensive counselling. Hundreds were re-united with their families. Then we purchased 8 specialised 'Street Smart' vans, equipped with hot drinks and food and trained 400 counsellors to work on rosters to every night reach those on the streets. Fifteen years later the program is still running well. The Rotary Club of Sydney won an International Achievement Award for this Street Smart Project.

In the video of 'StreetSmart', played in Rotary television programs all over the world, was a very developed young fifteen year old, Amanda. She had the body of a woman and the mind of a child. She had been a ward of the State but had run away from foster homes and youth centres. The State did not know where she was. She had been abused constantly by every adult she had met. She would not let us help her. She mistrusted all adults!

While I was speaking with her, on the film, she was lying on a beanbag. Her very ample bosom heaved, an effect I did not have on young women those days. And to my surprise from between her breasts a pet rat crawled out over the top of her tee shirt. The rat crawled up through her hair and sat on the top of her head. This was her pet rat she nursed in her bosom.

Not long after that film was made, I told her story on radio and six weeks later received a call to say police had just removed the body of a 16 year old girl from Croydon Road, Hurstville. She was lying on the footpath and the police had found a rat inside her tee shirt. Was this the girl I had known? Could I identify her? She was buried with only half a dozen present. When I was talking with Amanda I realised that all the adults who figured in Amanda's life, from the time she was first raped as a seven year old to the time she died on the streets at sixteen, were rats and the only one who demanded nothing from her was a rat. We realised we need a good accommodation centre for youth like Amanda.

In 1988, at a dinner of businessmen, Max Connery, a Sydney attorney, approached me to give me a cheque as a donation to that work. I said, 'I do not accept cheques from lawyers.' That stunned him. 'But I want to give you some money', he said. I told him I wanted three infinitely more valuable gifts: prayer for our work because Christians are able to sustain the pace only through the support of praying friends; his continuing interest for at least three years and his influence to gather ten more solicitors to hear about how they could help homeless youth. He volunteered all three and gathered together 14 lawyers to hear our story.

With that group I again said, 'Put away your cheque books. I need three infinitely more valuable gifts: prayer for our work, your continuing interest that goes beyond just a cheque and your influence to each gather ten more lawyers to hear about how they could help homeless youth.' So I then addressed 140 solicitors and judges. I told them about the homeless and asked them, 'I want you to pray for our workers, to continue your interest for at least three years and I want you to take out your chequebooks now and fund a new home for street-kids!' They gave me that night $200,000, a large property called 'Stepping Stone' and have raised $500,000 since!

We can understand human motivation from the Hierarchy of Human Motivation described by American Psychiatrist Abraham Maslow. Maslow describes seven basic human needs that motivate people into certain behaviour patterns:

1. Physiological needs - nutrition, elimination, sex, sleep
2. Safety needs- security, stability and freedom from fear
3. Love and belongingness needs
4. Esteem needs- self-esteem and esteem from others
5. Need for self-actualisation- to know self
6. Desire to know and understand
7. Aesthetic needs- beauty, music, religious experience

Maslow states that all seven of these needs are intrinsic to human personality - but not all of them are centre stage, in the forefront of consciousness or currently motivating a person's life. The need that is in the forefront of consciousness and that is currently motivating the individual will be the lowest need that is basically unfulfilled.

For instance, the basic, rock bottom human needs are physiological - nutrition, elimination, sex, sleep. If these needs are not met, a person spends most of his time in an attempt to fulfil them. Until these physiological needs are met, he ignores his other needs that are present in the background of his personality. For street kids at Streetsmart who are starving and homeless, they do not expend much energy asking philosophical questions or painting landscapes.

However, if a person's basic physiological needs are met, but his safety needs are not - they become the theatre of his conscious and motivated life. People desire safety, stability, freedom from fear, anxiety and chaos. They prefer the familiar; they want predicability and order in their lives. They want to know that the rug is not going to be pulled out from under them. If they are insecure, they will work to achieve security. Even having their own bag of possessions becomes vital. Try to take away that bag and a person might kill you: it's their security. If they feel safe, then their motivated activity shifts 'upward' to satisfy their needs for love and belongingness.

At this level, they desire love and affection in meaningful relationships and they seek a peer group with which to identify and in which they belong. They join a gang. That is why StreetSmart is painted with graffiti designs, because the kids are safe in that atmosphere, for it is theirs. That is why that girl constantly had her pet rat round her neck, because it was the only genuine creature who responded to her with warmth, without demanding sex from her. Her only friend was a rat, because all other acquaintances were rats.

When a person's needs for love and belongingness are essentially satisfied, then the need for esteem takes centre stage. At this level, people seem to crave esteem from others. They desire reputation, prestige, status, or at least attention, recognition, or appreciation. At this level, people are also searching for self-affirmation from what they believe to be significant achievement, accomplishment and competence.
Only now with physical and emotional needs met, with a sense of security, can a person take an interest in appearance, hair care and dress sense. Appearance means nothing to a person who is hungry, homeless, insecure and friendless. It takes self-esteem and esteem from others before a person takes pride in their appearance. To say, 'Why don't they dress nicer?' is to reveal you do not know what it means to be physically empty and totally insecure and without love.

When a person's need for esteem from himself and others is basically met, then his motivated behaviour becomes 'self-actualising'. At this ' highest' level on the hierarchy, people work to realise their inner potential. They act to fulfil their destiny, to realise the purpose for their birth and to express their individuality. It is only at this level that a person fully comes to appreciate beauty, truth, creation, music and God.

We must meet people at three basic levels that everyone needs to withstand life's storms: levels of existence, relationships and growth- ERG. It is only when these needs are met within, that a person can fully understand true security which is in building your life upon a true foundation in hearing and doing God's word. They must be free from pressing need to fully understand that true security comes alone from God.

Wesley Mission responded to the needs of people on the street, not just with band-aids: the emergency relief, food, clothing and accommodation that is a basic right for people, but with programs aimed at bringing people to confront themselves, making for personal self-awareness, causing people to consider their future, encouraging self-help, providing employment training and placement programs of people into jobs and better accommodation. Then when the person is ready, they can see we act out of an even higher motivation and desire them also to know true inner security that holds them fast in any storm.

What we are doing is not a piecemeal approach to an institutionalised social problem, but a careful strategy where each piece fits in with the other.

Streetsmart is a street level contact point, as is City Rock. Basic medium accommodation needs are met in Stepping Stone and Cottee Lodge while longer accommodation and personal development and employment skills are provided at Forrest Farm, Desert Park and the Bernard Smith teenage independence program. They are encouraged to develop outward looking skills in our trekking and wilderness programs and Vision Valley. Counselling is provided at Youth Line from our specialist Drug and Alcohol Counsellors. Work and employment skills are provided by our Wesley Uniting Employment programs. The Job Club helps them gain employment and fellowship and a sense of belonging may be found in our Youth Groups. The task becomes fruitful when people respond in commitment to God and service to others.

Youth Networks is an integrated approach to the primary physical needs of food and clothing, accommodation and work, then the deeper level self-awareness and self-motivation, then the deeper levels again of self- esteem and self-awareness, for it is only when a person has developed a true sense of his own self, is he in a position of being able to appreciate God and the world about him and come to true security.

The motivation to start a new life and find self-esteem is an important starting point for a person to come to faith and to find the true security that comes only from a life that has its foundation in God. Then they can withstand any of life's storms.

A similar approach was used when I conceived the idea of a family makeover centre to change the lives of all family members at the same time. We brought together a wide variety of our resources to create a multiple resource, cohesive program to work with dysfunctional families whose multiple problems require a total response. Intensive commitment with families are needed if a real difference is to be made. One organisation announced it would spend up to 20 hours with selected families.

Wesley Mission spends 168 hours every week for nine months with families in what is the most intensive and extensive intervention, according to family need, ever in Australia's history. The families live in two and three bedroom apartments in Cartwright, Sydney, New South Wales, in the Noreen Towers Community, a large-scale community consisting of extensive lawns and gardens, with three two- storey blocks of accommodation each with eight 2 & 3 bedroom units.

There is also a Family Makeover Centre, which consists of a new hall, stage and kitchen, which will become the focal point for many of the group activities and training programs. Small rooms are also available for private consultation.

The aim of the Family Makeover Centre is to take in damaged, at risk, homeless, single parent families and help them to discover skills for independent living in the community. Multiple resources are available to cover each area of disadvantage. There is a maximum accommodation capacity of up to 60 persons in this community. Our aim is to work with 9 families at a time and to also house on-site staff. The families, most of whom are headed by a single parent, stay for up to 9 months, paying New South Wales Department of Housing rates to rent the 2 & 3 bedroom properties. These rates are a fixed percentage of the income of the families and generally speaking we care for severely disadvantaged people, so their rents are extremely low. The types of families housed on this site vary according to their homelessness, risk factors, alcohol and drug dependence, gambling problems and the like. We house families with multiple disadvantages and disabilities.

The management of the Wesley Mission Family Makeover Centre is by Wesley Mission Community Services, using resources from our Wesley Uniting Employment & Wesley Homeless Persons Services, with other resource personnel being used in specialist activities. Each person lives in a family unit, which we furnish, if required. Each family is supplied with a gift of a computer with Internet access, because the teaching of family members to become computer literate is part of the total program. Wesley Mission uses its benevolent and charitable organisations to provide whatever welfare needs the family might have and specialist teams from our medical and psychiatric, counselling and family support services as required. In the Makeover Centre there are continuous programs conducted over the nine-month period. They include the establishment of Alcoholics Anonymous groups for those people for whom this is appropriate. There are quite a number of people in the local surrounding community who also come in for this program. Groups of gamblers also meet weekly.

There are a series of other programs run by other competent trained personnel over the nine months including programs developing self esteem, credit and financial counselling, strong programs of mental health services, including professional psychological interventions using Cognitive Behaviour Therapy and Dialectical Behaviour Therapy, as required.

The staff conducting these networks work in association with the Psychology Departments of Sydney University and Macquarie University and the National Depression Initiative.

There are other programs concerning Gambling Counselling, training in Child Protection issues, Family Values and Parenting Models, using the resources of Wesley Counselling Services and Wesley Child and Family Services.

One difficulty often found is finding a way to motivate family members to gain such help. We thought of that. These families are encouraged to attend whatever program has been worked out with this by our case-managers. Both children and parents can earn credit points by attendance, which are then redeemed towards significant family holidays. I approach travel firms for some holiday sponsorships. That solves the motivation issues.

Each family has two mentors to help in educational support doing such things as homework help for school and TAFE students and lifestyle help for mothers, including cooking and family management.

This program is dependent upon corporate and community support. I sought support from significant corporations to not only provide financial support for one family, but to provide two members of their staff to act as mentors with that one family covering both the educational and lifestyle mentoring. Some staff are interested in helping as well as in the company's financial support. The Prime Minister commended this program with a gift of $250, 000.

We also provide scholarships for children, allowing each child to receive a scholarship enabling them to join a local sporting team including the purchase of sports gear, or a culture program including music lessons. The Youth Performers Academy of the Wesley Institute provide lessons throughout the nine months of the family stay at the Makeover Centre in whatever field of music young people and children may desire.

It is an important part of our total program that every family upon leaving the program has an appropriate family member employed. To this end Wesley Uniting Employment provides the skills training to enable them to get suitable jobs. Better housing is essential so Wesley Mission Homeless Persons staff helps each family into their own independent housing.

This program is designed to enable dysfunctional families to live effectively and independently. It brings the widest range of skills ever assembled in Australia to help families cope with multiple disadvantages. When we support the family we support the whole nation. We reduce the cost of dysfunctional people in society, reduce the cost of the welfare system and reduce the costs of running hospitals, jails and charities. When we have better families, we not only have a better nation, but we are making a contribution to a better world.

Another example of entrepreneurial programming lay in our development of Habitat for Humanity. 'A score of homeless families this year will enter their own homes by giving 500 hours of sweat labour instead of large deposits,' I said in a New Year's Day message in 1988.

'Their standard brick, three bedroom houses will be sold for only $25, 000 because they are being built on land donated by municipal councils who want to help poor families, erected by tradesmen who are donating their labour without charge, by builders not charging any profit on the new homes and by the financiers not charging interest on their mortgages for fifteen years.'

'At long last the community understands the tragedy of the homeless in Australia. We have a national economic disaster which has left people homeless in larger numbers than any bushfire, cyclone or earthquake we have ever experienced.

Decent one-income families can no longer qualify for housing loans because of the high repayments. 76,000 people are on public housing waiting lists. They will inhabit heaven before a unit owned by the NSW Government! 60,000 are living in rental property in danger of eviction. 40,000 are living in substandard properties. Over 20,000 live permanently in caravans; home is wherever there is a community laundry and public toilet.'

We had just established 'Habitat for Humanity', an inter-church housing building organisation established in all the Eastern States which organises teams of volunteer tradesmen and builders to build houses on land donated by municipalities. 'In 1988 we still needed land inside Sydney, but 31 municipalities outside of Sydney have offered land and to them we will bring 300 volunteer tradesmen to build houses for the poor making them available for $1000 deposit plus 500 hours of sweat labour, at a total cost of $25,000 repayable over 15 years without any profit or interest being charged.'

Finance was raised by churches and voluntary organisations such as the Rotary Club of Sydney for the house-building project.

'With all the talk by politicians and commentators, no-one has yet come up with a more imaginative plan to the current malaise, nor organised so much grass-root support. The first houses will be opened before the end of June this year and local committees will select local families solely according to their need.' That was our vision and gradually it took shape.

Habitat for Humanity is the largest home building organisation in the world. Some 100,000 Habitat houses have been built in the past 20 years. Wesley Mission brought the founder, Millard Fuller, to Australia to set up the organisation and started recruiting volunteers, gaining land at low cost or no cost, talking building supply companies into donating materials and raising funds to build the houses.

The family chosen to own the home has to save $1000 deposit, (i.e. training them in savings), 500 hours of personal sweat effort (i.e. to show their commitment) and with the volunteers building and master builders overseeing the houses are built with donated money, materials and labour. The family are then charged the actual cost, which they pay back over 15 years without any interest being charged at all. Repaid money is used to build more houses. This voluntary effort, which inspires so much local community contribution, is now a national organisation building in all states, including New Zealand and Papua New Guinea. For many years I served as National President.

One particular group of Australians who have the worst housing are Aboriginal families. Survival for Aborigines in the harsh Australian environment has always been intimately linked to their families and kinship groups. European settlement had a devastating impact on Aboriginal families. Only the resilience and strength of Aboriginal families enabled the survival of Aboriginal culture.

A chronic lack of community services has resulted in Third World standards of living among many Aboriginal groups. Despite decades of promises, little has changed to improve the basics of life for Australian Aborigines. In 1971, a survey at Royal Darwin Hospital showed that one in five Top End Aboriginal children suffered malnutrition before their second birthday. A study in 1993 found no change; ten years later there was still no change. In some Aboriginal communities, half of the children suffer malnutrition. Dr Alan Ruben, who made the study, says the rate is worse than that in Kurdish or Somali refugee camps. Unless the 'circle of paternalism, dependence and pauperism' is broken, it would be much more difficult, if not impossible, to solve.

Today may indeed be too late to do more than continue to 'soothe the dying pillow'. Aborigines do have to change - many illnesses are related to poor hygiene, bad diet, lack of exercise, smoking, alcohol and failure to follow medical advice. But there is increasing evidence that water, working toilets, proper housing and good medical care have to be provided first. If amenities such as toilets and water supply are provided and are properly built and maintained - which can be done at a surprisingly low cost - Aborigines, contrary to stereotypes, use them enthusiastically and do not vandalise property. Under these conditions there can be 50% reduction in infectious diseases in one year.

While President of the Rotary Club of Sydney, I challenged my members to get their hands dirty with me every Saturday. Each Saturday, some of our volunteers from the Rotary Club of Sydney and Wesley Mission work to rebuild houses in Eveleigh Street, Redfern. This is Australia's worst slum. Some of these urban Aborigines are generations into poverty, illness, unemployment and despair. Bad accommodation makes worse their plight. This was the site of several racist riots. We cleared and shovelled garbage because the City Council garbage collectors refused to go into the area because of attacks against the white workmen. We went and shovelled the garbage to clean the streets so we could start building. Chief executives, general managers, lawyers and doctors, led by a clergyman, shovelled two years of putrid garbage.

Then, the Governor of NSW, Rear Admiral Peter Sinclair and Mrs Sinclair, called in to see the progress of the Habitat for Humanity affiliate we established there. I feel we are seeing the truth of the old prophesy from Isaiah 58:11-12 'The LORD will guide you always; he will satisfy your needs in a sun-scorched land and will strengthen your frame. You will be like a well-watered garden, like a spring whose waters never fail. Your people will rebuild the ancient ruins and will raise up the age- old foundations; you will be called Repairer of Broken Walls, Restorer of Streets with Dwellings.' It was becoming true in the slums of Sydney.

As Millard Fuller, the International President of Habitat For Humanity described this work: 'Habitat For Humanity works in partnership with God and people everywhere from all walks of life, to develop communities with God's people in need by building and renovating houses so that there are decent houses in decent communities in which people and live and grow into all that God intended.' When we started building again the burnt out ruins, it was a tough job. But that year not only built a building but also built great Rotarians.

One Thursday night in the early 1990's I attended a Christmas party in the three storey Federation hostel we run in Erskineville. Knowing that I am a non-drinker who fights the extension of the liquor trade, some might be surprised that I had bought a pub on behalf of Wesley Mission. But we bought the great old pub in 1991, de-licensed it and turned it into home for ten previously homeless people. Among ourselves it was called 'the pub with no beer'. Ten formerly homeless people now have their own fine home. The former bar is now a spacious lounge and dining room. All the upstairs rooms are now theirs.

The newspapers had a field day reporting every aspect of the move and stressing the fact that the hotel-residence would be a 'Pub with no Beer.' I just kept my fingers crossed that the media did not find out that while the renovations were in progress the hotel was still fully licensed. I shuddered to think of the headlines if that became public: 'TEMPERANCE ADVOCATE HOLDS HOTEL BEER LICENCE'. Fortunately the newshounds did not sniff out that information.

At that party every one of our residents said to me how much their home meant to them. Once pubs had ruined their lives by helping them become alcoholics and eventually all of them had lost families and homes to drink, but now a pub was serving them, not with beer, but accommodation and without a drop in sight.

Olga, one of the residents, said to me, 'You ought to buy more pubs, close them down and make their rooms into bedrooms for more homeless. There are more homeless on the streets growing older these days and some of them are pretty crook.'

Her words reminded me of one of our staff of years ago, Charlie Woodward. Charlie was known as 'the converted burglar'. Charlie Woodward began a men's meeting at the then Central Methodist Mission (the former name of Wesley Mission Sydney) in 1905. He was added to the full-time staff in 1917. Charlie Woodward had spent many years in the gutter. As a boy he was handed to the police by his headmaster for stealing toys from his playmates, he descended through a long list of drunk and disorderly and housebreaking charges, mainly due to his uncontrolled drinking and gambling.

On 5 January 1905 he entered a mission hall to plan the theft of the organ. Charlie said in his own words, 'A companion said to me one day as we stood in front of a mission-hall in Redfern, 'I want you to give me a hand to steal the organ out of that place.' I consented that I would help him.

'At that mission-hall every Thursday night a men's gospel-meeting was held with coffee and biscuits. I made up my mind that I would go down on the following Thursday night and have a look round as to which would be the easiest way to get the organ out.

'When the night came there were over a hundred men present and amongst them were burglars, pickpockets, jockeys and thieves. The earnestness of the young preacher, Mr Yarrington, touched my hard heart and, glory be to God, instead of removing the organ, before the meeting closed I had my sins removed.

'I went into that mission-hall a gambler, drunkard, thief, burglar and about one of the greatest scoundrels that could be found in Sydney. I thank God I came out a changed and a saved man. The night I got converted we had three robberies planned out for the following week. I was truly born again. Old things had passed away and all things had become new, and now I can sing with a rejoicing heart, 'Happy day, when Jesus washed my sins away.'

Charlie Woodward remained a consistent Christian worker thereafter, never again being involved with drink, gambling, or the police until he died during World War II. Charlie regularly visited railway workshops for lunch-hour meetings. He visited the cells at the magistrates courts at Redfern and Newtown to work among drunks and petty criminals. When men were freed from prison he met them, helped them with money or to find a job and invited them to the Lyceum Theatre to hear the gospel. Results were limited but worthwhile.

He also visited the Chinese quarter of Sydney with New Testaments and tracts. The special interest in this work was to win back young women who had joined the opium dens in Chinatown before they became hopelessly addicted to opium.

Today we still work among thieves and criminals, drunkards and young women who are in danger of becoming addicted, seeking to convert people to God.

Olga's comment stuck in my mind after I left the 'pub with no beer'. I had told them about Charlie, who used to hold lunch time meetings among the railway workers, just behind their 'pub with no beer.' Olga's words reminded me there were many homeless on the streets who were now growing older and some of them were 'pretty crook', in very bad state of health.

I called some of my staff together and we discussed Olga's idea. The trouble was that pubs for sale were rare. We would probably have to start from scratch, raising money, getting plans and approvals, funding for staff and then building. But that is what we are good at. So we got to work. Just before the next Christmas, our first twenty residents moved into a magnificent state-of-the-art community hostel at Smithfield for frail, aged homeless people.
They had been living on the streets and parks of Sydney. Now that they have a

new home everyone has their own individual space. Everyone has large private bedrooms and marvellous facilities. Our caring staff live in the community with them. These frail, homeless men and women are the kind of people that newspapers describe in their stories after every cold snap. 'A man died of hyperthermia last night in a Surry Hills park.'

Now they have a home of their own. I welcomed them in and we held a Christmas party. One man, who had only one leg due to liver, kidney and artery disease resulting from alcoholism said to me, 'This place is too good for us.' But it is not. Here is a man who has been lost in sin, for whom Christ came and whom in Christ's name we have rescued. This is part of the reason for the season. I told them at the party we would call our new cluster of homes, 'Charlie Woodward Lodge' after our converted criminal who gave 35 years to caring for the homeless of Sydney through Wesley Mission.

However, we felt providing houses needed something more for the people of the city, so Wesley Mission went a step further in developing its leisure ministry in the development of Desert Park. This is a 500-hectare property in the `Ninety Mile Desert' area of South Australia. Settled just after World War II, the area was made suitable for farming, with the addition of super- phosphate and other fertilisers. Joe and Joyce George, a Christian couple, owned the property and as they approached retirement they decided to make Desert Downs available to Wesley Mission for $600,000, plus another small property and house where they could live.

Desert Park was being developed as a youth rehabilitation centre and church camping site. We added accommodation for 150 people, a swimming pool and other facilities. As we come into contact with young people through our Street-Smart and Youth Networks programs, we have the option of sending them to Desert Park to work on the property and receive counselling at the same time. The Manager and his wife, were experienced farmers as well as very capable counsellors.

Getting young people away from the influences of the city and then giving them something physical to do is a most effective way of helping them overcome their problems. However the concept is to send only three or four young people at a time so they can receive individual attention and supervision. However to fund this work we developed 'farm-stay' holidays for Japanese school children. About 1,500 a year have travelled to Pendleton Farm Retreat winning for us a national tourism award.

Without local support, Desert Park would be just another sheep and cattle property, but with community support through working bees, the property promises to make a real difference in the lives of Sydney's homeless teenagers. As well as growing sheep and cattle, Pendleton Farm Retreat also grows people. Every overseas student receives a bible in their own language and witnesses a series of

Australian fauna up close as well as sheep shearing, cattle mustering and our on site kangaroos, emus and koalas.

Another such development is Mangrove Mountain Retreat. They were given about 100 acres of Crown Land at Mangrove Mountain to run a medium term training program for teenagers. There was land but no residential buildings. The program has centred on skills acquisition and self-esteem raising so that the participants have the opportunity to become contributing members of society. Over 5000 young people stayed with us each year. But in the early days we had neither the accommodation nor the money to build. The answer came in a most unexpected way.

I approached Work Skill Australia, who ran the Work Skill Olympics. Every year building apprentices compete in the Olympics by being given a specific project, such as wiring a switchboard or building a house frame, to complete within an allotted time. In previous years the objects built by the apprentices have been taken apart and destroyed after the judging, but one year I suggested building apprentices prefabricate three accommodation units for re- erection at Mangrove Mountain.

At the same time, the bricks, wiring and other materials used to judge the skills of the bricklayers and electricians be re-used at Mangrove Mountain. After the frames and roof trusses for the three accommodation blocks were completed in a mid-city exhibition where the building trades section of the Skill Olympics are held, they were dis-assembled and transported to the Mangrove Mountain site. I puzzled how to get them transported, so I called in the Australian Army engineers and within hours the low loading trucks were on their way. Then teams of building apprentices from Sydney's trade Colleges (Technical and Further Education) spent two days each on site, re-erecting the units. Horticulture students installed the gardens. Today, accommodation, dining facilities, swimming pool and a high ropes course cater for thousands every year.

Vision Valley

The conference centre is used primarily for Operation Hope programs and Wesley Mission's camping programs for disadvantaged children. School groups, churches and community groups also use the facilities.

Vision Valley, located at Arcadia and less than one hour from the heart of Sydney, is set in 35 hectares of native bushland.

This 224-bed retreat centre employs 103 staff and was assisted last year by 176 dynamic and committed volunteers. It is one of Sydney's busiest conference centres and outdoor adventure activities are always a highlight of the camp, with horse riding, abseiling and rock climbing the most popular activities. Vision Valley includes the 72-bed Stringybark Lodge.

Mangrove Mountain Retreat
Mangrove Mountain Retreat is located at Mangrove Mountain on the scenic Central Coast hinterland and is set on 45 hectares of native bushland, adjoining the 1000ha McPherson State Forest, 80 minutes from Sydney.

This 100-bed retreat employs 17 staff and is assisted by 65 magnificent volunteers. It is one of the Central Coast's busiest retreat centres and attracted nearly 7,000 people over the past year. The most popular adventures include the giant swing and the 180-metre flying fox.

Operation Hope
Operation Hope is a unique and exciting camping program that gives children from disadvantaged backgrounds a chance to grow, achieve and develop in a challenging, caring environment located in two beautiful bushland settings. Unfortunately many young people and children carry a deep sense of hopelessness and poor self worth generated by years of neglect, abuse or violence. However, a week at either of Operation Hope's two campsites - Vision Valley or Mangrove Mountain - can be a life changing experience. At the end of an Operation Hope camp, children know they have been listened to, believed in, cared for and trusted. Moreover, their self esteem and self worth have been restored, secure in the knowledge that others care for them and that they have a contribution to make. The camping program is run as an early intervention program for children 9 to 14 years of age. Most of the children are wards of the state and come from a range of welfare agencies including Wesley Dalmar, Burnside, NSW Department of Community Services, Mercy Centre, The Smith Family, Barnardos and Anglicare.

The food is great and the activities are challenging: abseiling, horse riding, swimming, canoeing, archery and rock climbing, among many others. Each activity builds confidence and esteem; each child is supported and encouraged as they take the next step and grow in confidence. Operation Hope has sponsored more than 5,000 underprivileged children to attend camps at the Vision Valley campsite since 1992. Many have returned as counsellors keen to share the care and wisdom given to them as campers in years previous. Donations from Rotary District 9680 - the local Rotary club, trusts and individual givers enabled hundreds of young people and children from disadvantaged backgrounds to attend Operation Hope programs.

Here is an example of one of the children who attended:

Tina, 13, had suffered physical abuse from her stepfather and sexual abuse from her stepbrother and was living on the streets as a prostitute. The Department Of Community Services referred Tina to Vision Valley through their Emergency Protective Foster Care program. Carlingford Rotary supplied the funds for her to attend the Operation Hope camp. Tina arrived at the camp shy & very nervous, but during the program she began to grow in confidence. 'This shy and withdrawn girl slowly became a new person by becoming wholeheartedly involved in every activity,' said John from Operation Hope. During the daily half hour discussion and reflection times, Tina began asking deep and searching questions. 'Tina shared how she had never felt as loved as she had at Vision Valley and how for the first time in a long time she felt like she was a somebody,' John continued. He saw the incredible change in Tina's demeanour. 'Tina is a living example of the difference Operation Hope can make in a young persons life,' he said. Operation Hope camps seek to convey the statements, 'I believe in you'; 'I trust in you'; 'I know you can handle it'; 'you are listened to'; 'you are cared for' and 'you are important to me'.

Serenity Farm and Lodge

Drug addiction is one of the most depressing new facts of life in any city. Many churches over the years have provided care for people in need, but have done very little to help in total rehabilitation. Wesley Mission has sought to come to grips with this problem by providing staff and centres dealing specially with drug rehabilitation.

Several psychologists who specialise in drug and alcohol counselling spend their days involved with people affected by drugs of varying kinds. Wise counsel and practical guidance is the first step to help people overcome their addiction.

Total rehabilitation is a long and often heart-breaking process involving a network of supportive agencies from other areas of Wesley Mission. Some are helped by Methadone treatment, others by 'cold turkey' withdrawal and others by long sessions of psychiatric counselling and psychological and financial counselling. Our Christian psychologists decide upon the appropriate method. Alcoholism is the result of the most common form of drug abuse. Wesley Mission established an alcoholic rehabilitation centre at Horsley Park. Three Serenity Farms were established in January 1982 as quiet retreats where homeless men and women could recover from the damaging effects of alcohol and discover a new lifestyle. The farms provided an ideal opportunity for men and women to escape from the skid-row scene and develop a new lifestyle.

The work at Serenity Farm would not be possible without the dedication and the commitment of caring and supportive staff that minister in the name of Christ, led by Nerida Dunkerley. A wonderful band of volunteer men and women support the residents during their journey to sobriety and new life. The whole aim of a ministry to those who are addicted to drugs, alcohol, gambling and other substances, is to help them develop as whole people so they live lives of freedom and independence. Our site was re-established by the Government after compulsory acquisition by the Sydney 2000 Olympics of our three farms for the new Olympic Equestrian Centre. On the new site, the work continues as before.

Wesley Mission helps thousands of homeless each year. Most are children, accommodated through our Wesley Dalmar Child and Family Care program. Edward Eagar Lodge, our entry point for homeless adults provides crisis and medium-term hostel accommodation for 63 men and 13 women. We have a church for homeless people, a day centre, welfare assistance, meals, shower and laundry facilities, recreational activities, liaison with statutory bodies and referrals to and from other agencies. At our Serenity House we provided supported accommodation for 42 homeless men this year. This work is currently being re-organised. Our Wesley Rehabilitation Services helped homeless men and women who were recovering from addictions. Grace Manor accommodated 12 women and Turnaround accommodated 25 men. In the first seven months of operation, 27 men left the Turnaround Program, 21 of whom moved into independent living. Two women moved into independent living from Grace Manor and now have regular access to their children.

Wesley Community Housing provides supported accommodation for 239 persons in 21 locations across Sydney. 32 clients attended training courses and 56 obtained full-time and part-time employment. We also support the Sudanese Settlement Services with short-term accommodation, as we do with the St George Community Housing and Ryde/Hunters Hill Community Housing. Many of our homeless people are members of our own Church of the Homeless, while others have joined the Bardwell Park Uniting Church, Newtown Mission and our six Community Housing Bible Study groups. Some have become members of the Campbelltown Church of Christ, two of our clients have become commissioned members of the Salvation Army and one former client is now a deacon at the Yagoona Baptist Church. It is a very positive picture of service amongst the homeless.

Overseas Council

When Jesus gave us the Great Commission to go into all the world and preach the gospel he gave us a command that has never been repealed. Every Christian in every church has to be interested in taking the message of the gospel to people who have not heard it. Wesley Mission has always been committed to the support of first the Methodist Church and then of the Uniting Church of its ministry to people in other countries. Every week, a portion of the total offerings given in all congregations are sent to the Synod in order to help in the ministry of reaching overseas people with the gospel. The Uniting Churches overseas ministries cover about thirty different countries of the world. Funds are sent to help local congregations and skilled people are sent to help not only in the proclamation but also in the work of education, agriculture, village development, teaching, orphan support and many other programmes. At Wesley Mission we have also adopted a number of programmes to help people in other countries by additional giving by the congregation.

When I came to the Mission in the late 1970's the Mission had the International Leadership Training College. This was an initiative set up by Sir Alan Walker to bring an outstanding leader from each of a dozen countries each year to give them an internship at Wesley Mission. After a year of training with Wesley Mission they were to return to their countries and provide some local leadership. Each year the Mission paid for about a dozen students from countries like Korea, Hong Kong, Papua New Guinea, Fiji, Tonga, Samoa, India and other parts of the world to train as interns.

In 1980 I realised we had a problem with this programme. A number of the students didn't want to go back home and one Korean lady, while she was about to board an aircraft at Sydney Airport had gone into the female toilets and literally just disappeared. Incidentally, three years later we found her married to a Korean in Sydney and by then she was an Australian citizen. What disturbed us was that those who were trained and competent, when they returned to their own countries, inevitably applied for scholarships to go to other countries, particularly the United States of America, so our whole plan of training good quality leaders to serve the Church in their own countries was being undermined by the natural tendency to go to the other paddock where the grass was greener.

About this time I discovered an organisation that was intent on training Christian leaders in their own country. We would provide funds to train the students to provide libraries within their theological seminaries, to provide funds for professor support and to encourage local theological seminaries to become accredited with proper degrees with world accreditation. This meant the student was kept in their own country, they were trained in their own language, they did not have visa and immigration problems, they did not need to return to their homeland for leave every couple of years and they were trained for life in their own environment. This was a much better way of doing mission.

The organisation that I discovered was The Overseas Council for Theological Education and Mission. It was a long-term missionary, Mr John Alison, a friend from Queensland who informed me about this work and indicated that the founder from the United States was visiting Australia. That is how I came to meet Dr Charles Spicer and his wife Phyllis. They were delightful people who had established this Overseas Council for Theological Education to do the very thing that we felt was necessary. That is to train leaders in third world countries by building up their theological education, by providing professor support, accommodation, individual student support and library support to help them establish their facilities. The thing that impressed me about Dr Spicer was the story of what had happened at the Seoul Theological Seminary. Seoul Theological Seminary had started after the Korean War and had attracted a significant number of the best of Asian theological brains. Very quickly the number of students grew from 200 to 1000 and then to 2000. With the help of the Overseas Council for Theological Education, the Seoul Theological Seminary grew with new student accommodation being built, new classrooms and facilities. With the booming Korean economy and the commitment of Korean Christians to theological seminary development, the seminary began to grow very rapidly indeed.

For many years we supported from Australia, America, Canada, New Zealand

and Great Britain students in the Seoul Theological College. After a while it was quite obvious that oversees help was no longer necessary and that the Koreans could develop that ministry themselves. I am pleased to say that 20 years after I first started supporting a Korean student, that Seoul Theological Seminary today is the Seoul Christian University with over 30 000 students and a world-wide reputation for high academic qualifications.

John Alison, Charles Spicer and myself agreed that we should establish the Oversees Council for Theological Education in Australia. So in those early years after coming to Wesley Mission we established an Australian Board which included John Alison and myself as Chairmen, Robert Coles, a friend from Victoria and the heir to the GJ Coles fortune, Kimberley Smith, an accountant in Victoria and Robert Kerr a distinguished and benevolent Christian businessman. Over the years other people were added to the board.

The major role of the Overseas Council in Australia was to raise funds to support students in third world countries. One of the first countries we began to support was Croatia. Little did we know how much the Baulkans were going to appear in world history during the 1990's. The Evangelical Theological Seminary of Croatia was founded by a man who became a close friend Dr Peter Kuzmic. Peter had an excellent PHD, was a very committed evangelical and I first met him in 1983 at a world conference which I attended in the United States. From that moment on we began to provide funds for students at the Evangelical Theological Seminary in Croatia. Since the conflict developed in the 1990's with Kosovo, Macedonia, Serbia, Croatia and Albanian residents in these countries, the Evangelical Theological Seminary has been bombed, blasted by tanks and suffered destruction, rebuilding and destruction again of all of its facilities, yet Dr Kuzmic continued his lecturing, building up of staff and gathering theological works for the training of young ministers.

Right throughout the Kosovo/Croatian/Serbian conflict the Evangelical Theological Seminary kept training ministers for their own people and in a world where thousands of people perished the presence of their own ministers, was of great blessing and comfort to the people. Today there are more than 300 students in the Evangelical Theological Seminary of Croatia and Dr Kuzmic is still continuing to train students to minister among people in all of that devastated area. Whatever money we raised in Australia and provided for student support and in particular for the rebuilding of their library and replacement of theological works has been abundantly blessed. Two of our good Sydney supporters joined the board of the Oversees Council: Mr Phillip Goh of our International Congregation and Mr John Dingle and a Senior Manager of the AMP society and formerly State Manager of Queensland, South Australia and New Zealand. John eventually followed Rob Kerr as Chairman of the Board. After 10 years or so, I stepped down from both the Chairmanship of the Board and then gradually from fundraising.

Frequently we had visitors from overseas theological colleges visit Australia and we would organise dinners of supporters to support the ministry in those countries. The Overseas Council for Theological Education had provided support for buildings, professors, accommodation and individual students.

One of the theological seminaries that Australians have supported particularly has been the Nusantara Bible Seminary in Indonesia. For more than 20 years we have provided funds for this seminary and today they have about 400 students training for ministry. Their graduate ministers are now ministering right throughout Indonesia.

There are a number of seminaries in India that have been supported in training large numbers of Indian ministers in places such as the Allahabad Bible Seminary. They have had more than 900 ministers graduate with bachelors and masters degrees, of whom over 98% are still in full-time ministry.

Today the Overseas Council for Theological Education are supporting 4,500 students in more than 100 different evangelical theological colleges in 63 countries of the world. Apart from that the council has provided 68 campuses with new buildings, lecture rooms, accommodation blocks and libraries and have been responsible for providing the facilities in educational centres for more than 30 000 Christian students currently studying for the ministry.

When Jesus gave us the commission to go into all the world, he gave us a command that every Christian should respond to and support. Throughout the last twenty years of my life one of the real pleasures has been to see the results of the support we have given to theological education in third world countries.

Live N' Learn Centre

The Minister of Housing, Dr Andrew Refshauge and myself, declared open a new centre in Miller called the 'Live N' Learn Centre' during 2002. There are 29 units each with bedroom, kitchen, laundry, bathroom and study provided for twenty-nine young people between the years of 16 and 25, who are in danger of homelessness and dropping out of education. These people have a desire to go on with their education but cannot live with their parents. Living on the campus are Wesley Mission tutors and counsellors who teach living skills. Here is a partnership with a local 'Live N' Learn' community board, with the Department of Housing providing the building and the Premier's Department making a major grant. The CFME Union provides our staff costs. Wesley Mission runs and manages the staff. Local businesses have provided furniture, white goods and computers. The Commonwealth Government provides financial help for the students and Work for the Dole teams who maintain the gardens. It is a whole of community project. We expect to re-duplicate that program across the whole state, then the nation. Those 29 young people will graduate and cease to be dependent upon welfare, being independent and capable of facing life's stresses.

The whole community is engaged in helping deserving young people to continue with their education and not fall into homelessness and illiteracy. It is prevention at its best. The campus itself is a huge, multi-million dollar property with 32 complete units. The Department of Housing has spent $800,000 on renovations and it is in first class condition, with only the last units to be finished. Living on the campus are Wesley Mission tutors and counsellors who teach living skills and provide motivation and management.

Mount Druitt Integrated Youth Service
Also a day in April 2002 was an exciting and rewarding day for the team at the new Mt Druitt Integrated Youth Service and the staff of Wesley Dalmar.

The Mt Druitt Integrated Youth Service, partners and resources existing services in the Mt Druitt area. All of these developments came about as innovative and entrepreneurial programs, usually involving many services, support groups and hundreds of people of good will, which we brought together in a co-coordinated way to solve a serious community problem. I guess a seal of approval came in 2003 when at a dinner for 500 or more businessmen and women, I was proclaimed NSW Entrepreneur of the Year.

PASTOR
Chapter Eight

Tears On Paper

I write a lot of hand-written letters. Whenever I have a moment to spare, I reach for my pen and paper and dash off a letter to someone. Every person I know on the annual Australia Day and Queen's Birthday Honours list receives a letter. About a hundred people each month are listed by their date of birth to remind me to send them a letter just before their birthday. Everyone having a baby, or graduating, or getting a new job, or facing surgery, or grieving - as far as possible - receives a letter.

Being in Parliament helps of course. I receive hundreds of messages each month requiring advice or action, but there is a great deal of time one has to sit in Parliament for procedural motions or debates that are of little personal consequence. So I asked the President if the Parliament would build me a small writing table so I could write my letters during those times when I had to sit there and when I was not making a speech. Thus a lovely polished letter-writing table was built for me.

On my study table at home is a nineteenth century, folding writing box, beautifully polished with leather top, complete with pens, paper, ink and envelopes so that at any moment I can write to some friend.

You might think I could use some competent secretaries. I do. At my work at Wesley Mission, I have four competent people to help me with my mail-opening up to a thousand letters each week, sorting them, then typing, helping me answer them and finally posting them. In my Parliamentary Office I have other staff doing the same thing.

But there is something special about the hand-written reply. For one thing, people tell me that in the stack of mail they may receive in one day, they will always open the hand-written envelope first. And they will inevitably keep the hand-written note when the computer-generated mail is thrown out.

But many letters are paper spotted with tears. This week a woman unknown to me wrote following a sermon I delivered on the radio:

'I would like to thank you for last week's sermon. It touched my soul. My belief has been strong all my short life of 35 years. But I am drowning for the past three years. I wish I could leave my life behind, but I do not want to sin or hurt people. I really struggle. Even now my marriage feels too much pressure. People are using me. Why do I have to help people? When will I have my own life? Am I being selfish or self-centred not having the desire or motivation all the time to want to help or serve people as God wants me to, or to serve my husband as he would like? I may not have a fulfilled life on earth now but when I go to God it may be better. I would like it to be better here though....'

I wrote back immediately, mentioning that according to God's Word, in spite of all her difficulties, it can be better here. She did not need to go to God now to find inner peace. Power was available to enable her to cope and find fulfilment in this life. Perhaps a suicide was prevented.

Another letter mentioned in passing the coffee shop where the woman worked. Her situation was desperate. I called in unexpectedly. The waitress put a cup of coffee beside me and I noticed how weary she looked. At the end table of the small shop were her five children. They were aged from twelve years down to one. The older girls were looking after the baby. They cared for each other. Mother and children were poorly dressed.

I mentioned who I was and thanked her for her letter. I asked her, 'Where does your husband work?' The reply came from the oldest child, 'I'd need x-ray vision to see where he was!' I gathered it was a long time since they had heard from him. My heart went out to a woman who was struggling with keeping her family together and trying to get enough money to feed, clothe and house them. We would need to help them.

Every week I receive letters from farmers unable to cope with the drought. I have sent cheques of $1000 each to more than one hundred and fifty such farmers, each with the hand-written letter. I have had a team of generous donors who have entrusted me with that money they have given. One letter to me this week reads:

'Due to the ongoing drought conditions I apply for any assistance that may be available. I wouldn't normally ask but I am hand feeding my cows hay. To get the cows to eat this dry feed, you have to give them a supplement (mixture of molasses, urea and water) to stimulate their appetite. This supplement costs $450 (highly inflated price in these drought times) I had obtained a recipe off another lady that saved me $350 but as soon as the cows started eating the home made supplement they started dying. We tried to save as many as we could by sticking a hose down their throats but to no avail. We lost a total of 31 cows, which is about 1/3 of our core breeding stock. These were some of our fattest and

healthiest cows as these would push in first to get fed. We were devastated at our loss.

It is hard to fully understand how we worked just to keep them alive. They are on agistment. Michael drives one hour each way, every second day to feed and water them. We pay $770 per month for the agistment as all the stock routes have been closed. Our overdraft is now $60,000, our credit card is $16,000 overdrawn and climbing, plus there is another loan of $15,000 that was used to purchase 2 row-weeders in 2001. Any assistance that you can offer will be gratefully received.'

The letters show the tears from toil. They show hearts bleeding in people who cannot cope.

The next letter came from a wife; whose husband and she have been long term unemployed. Her letter said:

'Gordon, I am so ashamed to have to ask for help again. I feel desperate and depressed, in fact, we both are suffering from depression and been on medication for years and tried to overcome it but it is making it almost impossible to get and keep a job in the present climate. I am so scared that we are facing eviction. I don't know what to do. Have borrowed money from our relatives and can't ask again. We just need help and advice. Please telephone me.'

Through people who trust me with their gifts, I was able to send a hand-written letter, telling them I had sent $1000 to pay off all that was owing to the estate agent and so stave off eviction. That has solved their immediate problem, but their car is unregistered, their telephone is about to be cut off, their credit rating is zero, their accommodation is sub-standard and their children are living with others. We will have to help them.

I recently published some figures from last month's breakdown of contacts: 524 contacts from depressed people; 500 contacts from anxious people; 420 contacts from people with nowhere else to turn; 203 contacts about broken marriage; 142 contacts concerning sexual abuse; 124 contacts where gambling is out of control; 120 contacts from parents with teenagers off the track; 107 contacts from people who did not want to go on living; 103 contacts from people who were alcoholic; 71 contacts from people with drug related problems; 52 people who wanted to kill themselves. And so on. Every one of these people need resources other than their own. The testimony of many people is that they could not have coped if it had not been for the fact that whenever they reached a crisis in their life, they turned to God's helpers.

Naturally, Wesley Mission has developed systems where people ring and talk immediately with those so deeply troubled. We have people who ring every week - those who are lonely and at risk. We have understanding secretaries who know how to sift the letters, start answering some immediately and give me ones that need the personal touch.

I am amazed at how hand-written letters are saved. I was asked to conduct the funeral of a man with whom I had corresponded. Before the funeral I visited the family. I asked if I could read a passage of Scripture before I left and would they like me to read from their father's Bible. Someone fetched it and as I opened it, here was a letter I had written him more than ten years earlier. He had read and re-read that letter.

A homeless man was kicked to death in an inner city street one night. The police asked if I could identify him. How did they know to contact me? The police found in the homeless man's pocket a hand-written letter I had given him once. It had been folded and unfolded a thousand times and was now almost a scrap, but he, who possessed nothing, cherished it.

When the floods recently devastated many farmers, I searched through thousands of addresses to find those who had written to me over the past twenty years who lived in the flooded areas. I found 288 families and wrote personally to each one, telling them we loved them, were praying for them and wanted to help. We could send manpower to help with the cleaning up, clothing, financial counsellors and money to help. What I did not realise was how much we encouraged each of them.

One farmer wrote to me recently. Here is the message:

'Dear Gordon, your letter to me last year meant so much as you reassured me of God's love. I had thought we had been forgotten. Our local community forgot and not one person in the area came to see how I was managing. The local church forgot, because while they prayed for the flood victims no one came out to give me a hand. I kept your letter on my bedside table and read it night after night, often in tears. It helped keep me going. I did not ask you to help me, but just your loving concern was enough. For eight months after the floods I have had to move my cows every day round the stock routes to get enough pasture to keep them going. Then I have to milk them twice a day and what with bringing up the children and keeping the farm going, life has been very hard, especially when you are a woman on your own. No one else seemed to care, but the love of God and your church people expressed in your letter have kept me going. Please find a cheque for $50 to help someone else in need.'

That letter broke me up.

The pen is mightier than the sword! The nib can go where nothing else makes a difference. I do not mind sitting at my computer typing this for you, provided you pick up your pen and write to someone now.

One of the greatest agonies - and one of the greatest delights - in commencing as Superintendent of Wesley Mission in 1979 was the fact that I also had oversight of the Dalmar Children's Homes, where 134 children resided. There was an awesome responsibility of having the legal oversight and responsibility of 134 children, but the work of the children's homes was bedevilled by debt, housed in old and inadequate buildings and was plagued by staff problems. The work needed immediate attention.

The main centre was at our Dalmar Children's Homes at Carlingford. It had been built as a large orphanage, capable of caring for more than 100 children in the 1920's. There were a number of cottages scattered around the grounds and a pre-school which had opened first in 1918 which was run in a very fine manner by Mrs. Yvonne Petereit for many years. The buildings were spacious and the grounds were extensive.

There was another big building in Pymble, which was like a mini orphanage, where 30 children lived and that had been for sometime, until recently, under the leadership of a fine Matron, Enid Kerr. This home came as a result of the generosity of a Sydney solicitor, Mr Ken Bernard-Smith, who gave money for the acquisition of the property in Pymble in 1960. The old mansion was big enough for 30 children plus staff and the grounds were attractive and gave the children plenty of space.

A smaller building had been bought in Burwood and was known as Wesley James after a generous man who had left a legacy to the Mission. This had been purchased in 1972 under the leadership of Rev. Alan Walker but was now giving us great concern, particularly from inadequate staffing. One of my first jobs was to appoint Doug and Marina Greenslade, a delightful married couple who became 'Cottage Parents' and provided great stability for a number of years. The children they cared for were the same age as my children and a close bond developed between them, so they visited our home and we visited their home.

The fourth Centre was Gateway at Lewisham, which had also been opened in 1964 by Rev. Alan Walker. Children arrived at this centre in a terrible condition, often in the middle of the night being brought by police following family disputes, arguments and even murders. Staffing this centre was an absolute headache. Not long after Gateway opened, we opened Lifeline and Lifeline counsellors now had a resource to which they could send families in crisis.

There was one bright light on the horizon and that was the leaders of the work, Terry and Diane Freeman, a very fine, dedicated Christian couple who did their best to support the staff to consolidate the work and to inspire people to help. They presided like a mother and father over this huge family of about 134 children and staff.

The great Dalmar Fete and Country Fair, which were held annually in November, raised $20,000 a year, which was much needed in those days. The Country Fair brought the children's homes and the children into the centre of concern for people who lived in the community.

I realised within weeks of becoming Superintendent that something urgent had to be done with the whole concept of childcare. The first thing was to stop the compulsory attendance of the children and staff at the 7pm Lyceum Theatre Church Service. The adults loved seeing a hundred or more children present but the kids hated this compulsory attendance. Instead I encouraged the children to become involved in a dozen local churches in small groups where they could become integrated into the community.

The Dalmar Children's Homes had started with the Central Methodist Mission building a 'home for neglected children' in Woolloomooloo in 1884. The Mission paid for the care of some 20 neglected children who came to us from the area around Woolloomooloo and the Rocks. Strangely, the Methodist Conference refused to financially support the care of children, a position the denomination has continued to this day.

In 1900 the Central Methodist Mission obtained a fine country property at Croydon and was able to expand the work to house 32 children. This Centre was built by Parramatta Road, but the complaint was that Croydon was too far from the city for people and parents to visit the children.

In 1922 the Central Methodist Mission moved again, this time right out into the country, to Carlingford and built there children's homes able to take 130 neglected and abused children. If Croydon was too far from the city, Carlingford was an impossible place. No one but farmers lived there. There was no electricity, no water and no made roads.

The Methodist Church must have looked at envy up Pennant Hills Road where Colonel Burns had provided property and endowed Burnside for the Presbyterian Church. The Presbyterian denomination rallied behind Colonel Burns (famous for the publicly listed Burns Philip Company) and strong endowments and shares meant that that work was comparatively affluent compared to the Methodist effort, which struggled every year to pay its way. Only the untiring efforts of the ladies auxiliary enabled it to continue. The Methodist Conference gave no financial support whatever.

The Methodist Conference had a curious relationship with the Dalmar Children's Homes. The Conference decided not to financially support the work in any way! However, individual Methodist Churches (depending upon the whim of the present Minister), Sunday-School children and Women's Auxiliaries rallied behind the Central Methodist Mission in providing care for the children.

For the last 110 years the Methodist Church and Uniting Church have consistently failed to support the amazing work of caring for children in their name. I had inherited an important work, which every week went further into debt with an antagonist Synod Board that was totally opposed to us raising funds in Uniting Churches. The Uniting Church Board of Social responsibility was keen to force out of Office the Burnside Children's Home Board, take control of all its assets and use the Uniting Church investments to fund their operations under Rev. Harry Herbert. The Board members who were forced out were ropable; the Uniting Church lost scores of good volunteers. Rev. Herbert could not overthrow Dalmar and Wesley Mission, so decided to limit our access for funds, until he found another means to access Dalmar's funds and assets.

Many individual Methodist families, however, provided support from the time we shifted to Carlingford. The Cowlishaw, Newman, Norman, Cull, Vickery, Waterhouse and Stewart families gave significant donations to build cottages for children. About 12 children would live in each cottage, usually with one or two single young women as the 'Cottage Parents'. During the day they had the support of a domestic to do the washing and ironing and volunteer ladies who did darning, knitting and sewing. These women in charge saved us from most of the serious allegations raised later of child and sexual abuse.

Carlingford was so far out in the country in those days that there was no electricity to the children's homes until 1929. All the children helped in growing vegetables in the large vegetable gardens or in chopping the wood or in bringing the cows in for milking in the milking shed. This was no different to life on any family farm. The staff throughout the 30's, 40's and 50's were led by Matron Dorothy Barnett, who gave 35 years of amazingly competent and dedicated Christian care. She surrounded herself with a very dedicated staff of practical country girls who loved and cared for the kids. For them, it was an escape from their own farms and many met and married young men from the Central Methodist Mission.

After the war Mr Donald Stewart was appointed the first Superintendent. The Mission at that time needed a male Superintendent by government legislation so that orphaned British children from the war could be brought to Australia. He set a high standard of care but died unexpectedly in 1961.

The Dalmar Children's Homes were led by three extremely competent Superintendents' in my time: Terry Freeman, Terry Mudie, our first fully trained psychologist to take the position and Kerry Brownsey. Over most of the 80 years prior to this we have been served by a very large number of these fine, dedicated Christian women from country churches and who worked with 12 to 16 children as well as undertaking very heavy domestic duties. Many of these staff that served for long periods of time were greatly loved by the children and even now in retirement keep an active contact with the Old Boys and Old Girls Association of the Dalmar Children's Home.

So when I came to Wesley Mission we had these four properties, some huge debts, no support, the bureaucracy of the Church, a changing social attitude as to how children should be raised and a continuous problem of having to fund the operational costs with little support coming from the Government or from the Church as a whole.

So in 1979 I took the decision to completely examine all of the work that we were doing, our staff structures, our properties and the like and do a complete review of our assets and liabilities, including the land we owned and our staff training procedures and the like. We called in an expert Psychologist, Geoffrey Fox, and commissioned a top to bottom report. Our friend Sheila Walkerden, a trained social worker, had recently shifted to the United Kingdom and we commissioned from her a report into trends in childcare in Great Britain. My General Manager at the time, Stan Manning, took a keen personal interest in the review and our desire for change.

For 80 years prior to this, while the Dalmar Children's Homes never received any money from the Methodist Conference, it was enthusiastically supported where Ministers of local Methodist churches approved Sunday School scholars and Women's Auxiliaries supporting us. Unfortunately, by 1977 when the Uniting Church came into being much of the denominational pride of the former Methodist churches in supporting their own Methodist Children's Homes disappeared. At the same time Australia was rapidly moving into an era when there was decline in Sunday School attendance and an increase in the number of women in the Australian workforce, which meant a dramatic decline in the number of women able to attend auxiliaries to help raise money for such matters as child care. These three declines I realised would end up with the children's homes going out of business within 10 years.

With the review on our philosophy of child care and our resources underway, I realised I had to develop better means of fundraising to keep the work going in the meantime and to expand it in the new desired directions. For one thing this would mean greater support from the Government. The Government's support for childcare was deplorable. The Victorian government supported care for children at a rate of 80 cents out of every dollar spent on their care. The Queensland Government provided 100 cents in every dollar spent in caring for children and as well as provided capital grants for new buildings. The New South Wales Government was only providing 18 cents in each dollar spent and no finances for capital development. I realised that a campaign was needed to help the Government change its thoughts and policies. I immediately launched stinging attacks on the Government through newspapers, radio and television and through direct confrontation with some of the politicians concerned. I remember in particular a bruising meeting with Rex Jackson the Minister responsible for the Department of Community Services. Rex was a tough labour politician who had come up under very difficult circumstances, being cared for in a children's home himself. He was a hard man and had to exercise government policy. My meetings with Neville Wran were also difficult and on one occasion ended with the Premier calling me a 'damned nuisance' and it was made very clear to me that government policy was appropriate and unlikely to be changed.

We kept the pressure up and it was not long afterwards that there was an amazing change, with Neville Wran announcing that children would now be subsidised to the extent of 66 cents in the dollar. It was still far below Victoria and Queensland but nevertheless it was great improvement from the old situation. However, even this increase from government support was not going to save our situation.

The answer came from an unexpected quarter. Mr Harold W. Cottee, who with his wife Lois had been a tremendous support to the Methodist Overseas Mission Department and the Central Methodist Mission, had died. Mr Cottee had given his names to drinks and jams that had successfully been sold across the nation and part of most Australians daily food intake. He left in his Will an orchard at Paringa in South Australia consisting of 500 acres and 80,000 trees. The orchard was plagued with problems including water, poor management, root rot and leaf curl. But his highly competent and experienced son, Harold S. Cottee, indicated that if Wesley Mission were prepared to own the orchard and operate it with the funds going to the Dalmar Children's Home he would give continuing oversight and care to the running of the orchard.

Harold S. Cottee's willingness to do this in memory of his father was the most God-sent blessing in the history of Dalmar Children's Homes. It meant that the orchard, now helped by an infusion of funds from Wesley Mission to pay $120,000 of debt, would be run competently and would sell citrus fruit, with all the profits going to aid needy Sydney children. That work continues to this day. Millions of dollars came to us as God continued not to change muddy river water into wine, but into sparkling orange juice.

But that was not the end of the Cottee family's generosity. Although we were caring for 134 children at that stage, I was greatly disturbed by the fact that we were not doing enough to help young teenagers, either when they came out of our care or when they left their own homes and came into the streets of Sydney. There was almost weekly increase in the number of street kids in the heart of Sydney.

This demanded two approaches. One was the development of a street ministry which did not get underway for the next few years but which eventually became StreetSmart, a place where street kids could stay. It was the most effective street ministry in Sydney and now replicated in major cities all over Australia. Someone brought to my attention the sale of a small convent in Ashfield. It had been established by a group of German nuns to provide residential care for girls on the streets of Sydney. The sisters had worked valiantly for years in providing such accommodation for young street girls.

Unfortunately the same financial woes that were besetting the Dalmar Children's Home also beset them. Without the support of congregations and donors nearby, they were unable to continue. I went and visited the sisters and I was greeted as if I was the answer to their prayers. For months they had been praying for a Christian organisation that would provide help for young people living on the streets and if such a Christian organisation were found they would sell their convent at a very reasonable price. I indicated that we had intentions of providing care for both young males as well as females and the sisters readily accepted that. After a time of praise and singing we agreed on a price of $132,000 - a very reasonable price for a building in good repair that had 18 bedrooms in it! The sisters did not want to make a profit. They wanted to cover their losses and return to Germany knowing that all they had worked for would continue in good hands. I agreed to buy the property even though at that stage I had no money whatever.

The Mission did not have that kind of money and I didn't know where I could borrow it. It was then that a kindly word from Harold S. Cottee indicated that his mother Lois might be able to help. With some fear and trepidation I went to Mrs. Lois Cottee with the request - would she give us $100,000 towards the purchase of an 18-bedroom house to care for street kids? Mrs. Cottee was overjoyed to be asked. She had no hesitation whatever in helping us with this new development, which would be named Cottee Lodge in honour of her husband.

As I left with my heart beating and walking six feet above the ground carrying boxes of goods that Lois had gathered for our next Spring Fair, she called out to me as I went down the stairs: '$100,000? Is that all? How much is it going to cost you?' I answered her from the bottom of the stairs, 'Well it is going to cost $132,000, but I felt I could only ask you for $100,000.' 'What a silly thing to do,' she said. 'If you need $132,000 then ask me for $132,000. Come back up here.' I walked up stairs, put down the cardboard boxes of goods for the Spring Fair and Lois wrote out a second cheque, this time for $32,000. The two cheques together totalled $132,000 and paid the entire cost of Cottee Lodge. For more than 20 years now Cottee Lodge has continued to meet the needs of homeless young people in the Ashfield area.

That wasn't the end of my problems however, because it was going to cost another $40,000 per annum to run it. The Government was not inclined to help because they believed that street accommodation for young people was required in Kings Cross, not in Ashfield. My argument with the Government department was that every accommodation service that had been supplied in the Kings Cross area only provided an overnight stopping point for kids, who the next morning went out on to the street to commit crimes, to abuse drugs and to engage in prostitution. Accommodation services in the heart of Kings Cross only aided in their illegal activities. We needed to get people out of Kings Cross, if ever we were going to rehabilitate them. The beautiful Cottee Lodge has proved that over and over again.

By the time the Fox Report and the Report from Sheila Walkerden from the United Kingdom had arrived, we knew that we had to move right away from the large institutions at Carlingford and Pymble and move to smaller houses. Here children in groups of 3 or 4 could be cared for. We would also develop large scale fostering programs where foster parents would concentrate on caring for one or two children at the most. This concentrated care would bring better results then what we had been achieving try to care for too many in one place.

In 1983 I opened our first house at Mount Druitt and then another one at Whalan and very quickly houses at Blaxland, Penrith, Quakers Hill, Castle Hill, Riverstone, Grantham Heights, Blacktown, Lindfield, Killara, Dulwich Hill, Tuggerah, Rouse Hill, Lakemba and many other places. As our fundraising improved we got more family group homes.

Besides this we recruited hundreds of families, many of whom had already grown children and who now still wanted to provide a second chance for children where their own families could not care for them. This foster work is now the backbone of all that we do.

In 1993 we engaged Professor Don Wright to write a history of Dalmar's Centenary of Care. He contacted hundreds of old boys and girls and former staff and other residents and wrote an excellent history. He also discovered that over a hundred years of caring, there were very few examples of any forms of abuse. I put this down to the fact that most of our staff were committed Christian girls who came from good country homes.

In the first 90 years of the Dalmar Children's Home, including 10 years of my oversight, we had cared for 10,000 children. In the next 10 years, following the opening of all of these family group homes, we also cared for 10,000 children. Today every three years we care for 10,000 children.

The need for good quality family care and childcare is dramatically increasing. We have developed dozens of preventative programs in helping men be better fathers, parents be supported by volunteers who come in as extra hands, programs that teach parents how to drug proof their kids and a whole range of specialised programs to improve family life. These preventative programs are having good impact but the need for care for those who do not undertake the programs is still a continuing one.

Thanks to individuals, donors and generous benefactors who have left property, or parts of their estate in their Will, Wesley Mission has expanded greatly the care for children. Over the last 20 years more than 80 other childcare organisations have closed down or gone out of business and the individual demand on us is a continuing one.

From the day I arrived and discovered I was responsible for 134 children, the care of children has continued to be a priority in my role as a pastor.

A role of a pastor is not only focused on the people of the worshipping congregations of your church. In a real sense, any minister relating to the community becomes the pastor to the community. The Pastor is called upon constantly to conduct weddings and funerals. Sometimes these are important state occasions for leading citizens and sometimes for unknown homeless people. I treat all alike and in the days of burying people from the Mental Asylum who had no known relatives at all, I always gave them a full funeral.

The pastor becomes a leader in community groups, school parent councils, service organisations, sporting teams and the like, often as chairman or President. I found these community expectations very demanding and difficult to combine with my core business in the Church.

One such organisation in which I have enjoyed office and leadership for over thirty years has been Rotary International. One of the first things I did when I came to Sydney was find where the Rotary Club of Sydney met. In those days it used to meet in the old Tattersalls club in Elisabeth Street. It had about 350 members and was regarded as one of the finest clubs in the nation. I duly went along as a visiting Rotarian and attended a luncheon and then a second and a third. A couple of members asked if I would like to become a member of the Rotary Club of Sydney and of course I indicated that that was my desire. My wife was in full agreement. She felt my membership in the Rotary club of Cheltenham over the years had been one of the most significant experiences of my life and believed that meeting with a large group of men from various business, professional, political and religious affiliations would be good for me as Superintendent of Wesley Mission.

I indicated to the friendly Rotarians, International Vice President Doug Stewart and Fellow Howell Swanton, that I would be pleased to be welcomed into membership. Rotarians cannot transfer from one club to another. The process of membership has to be undertaken the same as if the Rotarian who was presenting for membership was just another person in the street. Even though I had been a club president and was a Paul Harris fellow that didn't mean a thing. I soon discovered how true that was. Six months went by and in spite of regularly attending the Rotary club of Sydney weekly meetings; no one approached me to say that the process of becoming a member was in hand. I paid my fees at Cheltenham where I continued to be a member, even though I now lived in Sydney and attended each week doing a 'make-up' as a member of the Rotary Club of Cheltenham. Eventually after nine months had passed the process of being welcomed into the Rotary Club of Sydney was completed.

Rotary has always believed in doing things by the book. My first lesson about not trying to take any short cuts with Rotary occurred when the best part of ten years earlier I had decided to start myself the Rotary Club of Cheltenham.

At the Cheltenham High School, a school of some 900 teenagers, the Principal was Mr Bill Fowler. Bill Fowler was a dedicated educationalist. He was also a fine Christian and member of the local Presbyterian Church. But the thing that came home to me as I worked closely with him over the years was his enthusiasm as a member of the Rotary Club of Moorabbin.

Bill always spoke warmly of his Rotary Club and had invited me to be guest speaker on one occasion. As I looked at the eighty or more members of that Rotary Club I realised what a great asset to the community of Cheltenham it would be if we had a Rotary Club.

I had always wanted to be a Rotarian ever since I started addressing community service clubs at Ararat in 1963 and 1964. The Rotary Club of Ararat was certainly the hub of the whole community. Here were all the key men - the businessmen, commercial and professional men. Here was the money and the political clout of the community. When I spoke at the Rotary Club of Moorabbin I realised it was the same there. What Cheltenham needed was a Rotary Club.

I had gained by now the idea that unlike other clubs who enlisted good hearted and willing people to serve the community, the Rotary Club was distinctive. The distinction which made Rotary different was called 'The Classification Principle'. It meant there was one person only from each classification. For example, there was one doctor, one dentist, one lawyer, one builder, one undertaker, one school principal, one grocer and so on. I found out, however, that if there were two papers in the community there could be an editor from each paper and as for clergymen there could be one from each major denomination.

The point about the Classification Principle was that it was not just one person from each classification. It was the one person who was generally regarded as the outstanding practitioner in his particular field. For example the one lawyer would be the person who was best regarded by his peers in the community. The one doctor was the one generally regarded as the outstanding physician in the community. The one surgeon would be regarded as the outstanding surgeon, and so on.

As a result Rotary brought together an incredible cross section of men who were dedicated to community service. And they were the most influential people in the community. Not knowing anything at all about how a Rotary Club commenced, I decided the best thing to do was to learn by trying. I thought I would start the Rotary Club of Cheltenham.

I didn't know then that there were very strict laws about how a Rotary Club could grow in an area. For example, the nearest club to the area would have to cede the territory over to the new club and define the limits of it, because members of that new Rotary Club would either have to live or work within that area or territory. Then the District Governor, who was responsible for the activities of fifty or more clubs round about the area would have to decide if the time was right to develop a new club. He would then approach one of the neighbouring clubs and ask them to undertake the program of extension that would lead to a new club being formed. There would be two or three District Governor's special representatives appointed who would have a task over a period of twelve months of getting to know the community well and getting to know the potential new Rotarians would be, and then approach them.

Rotary does not accept as members people who just offer themselves. They have to belong to a classification for which there is no other present member in the Club. Then all members are entitled to nominate the person who would then suit that classification. Then a check is made on the person to see if he is of the ethical standard required of a Rotarian before the person was approached and asked.

I did not know any of this at all. But over a period of several weeks, whenever the moment grabbed me, I thought of significant people in the community who would make good Rotarians and wrote their names under their classification. Gradually the list that I kept in the bottom draw of my desk grew longer as I considered the outstanding men in the community of Cheltenham.

One day Bill Fowler rang me and asked if he could come and see me about a Rotary matter and introduce me to a couple of the fellow Rotarians from Moorabbin. It sounded as though I was about to be sounded out for membership in the Rotary Club of Moorabbin. That would have been a great honour but I felt it was more important that we have a Rotary Club for Cheltenham itself.

Bill rang at the door of my study and as I welcomed him into the study he introduced to me John Dack and Compton Hocking of the Rotary Club of Moorabbin. After some pleasantries and chitchat we came to the point of their visit. John Dack started, 'We're planning to commence from the Rotary Club of Moorabbin a new Rotary Club here in Cheltenham. We have come to you because you have visited the Rotary Club of Moorabbin and been our guest speaker and we had in mind that you would understand what a Rotary Club is all about. We had in mind we should invite you to become a Charter Member and wondered if you could recommend any suitable men in the community for us to visit about the idea of commencing a Rotary Club.'

Compton Hocking then joined the conversation and indicated to me that the task of starting a Rotary Club was a very serious one and involved a long procedure, but the way to start was with a list of suitable potential members, none of whom could be spoken to or approached until the District Governor officially launched the club. Then, as his special representatives, they would interview each man and ascertain whether they would be suitable for the new club. Compton Hocking continued, 'So we've come to you to ask if you know one or two men whom you would consider would make good Rotarians in the proposed Rotary Club of Cheltenham'.

I paused for a moment and wondered whether I should reveal what I had been doing. I decided I should put all the cards on the table. Reaching down to the bottom drawer of my desk I pulled out a typewritten sheet. 'I've put down on this typewritten sheet the twenty five outstanding men in the community of Cheltenham, together with their current occupations and their telephone numbers and addresses. You will see that I have marked Geoff Chambers, a solicitor from Charman Road, as the best candidate for President. I've further marked Don Campbell, the Manager of the Commercial Banking Company of Sydney on the corner of the highway, as the best of the bank managers in the community and one who would make an ideal Treasurer. Brother Theophane Quinnell belongs to the Order of St. John of God and I believe he would make an excellent Rotarian. As a matter of fact each of those men there are really outstanding in our community. There is Harry Ramler of Ramler Furniture. He is a Jewish man and a fine character. And Daryl Davis - he is the Pharmacist up in the shopping centre and one I believe would be excellent in committing himself to acts of community service. You will notice that Arthur Rose the undertaker is mentioned there. I included him because his brother Lawrence is a member of your Club at Moorabbin.'

The three men looked at each other and nearly fell off their seats. Bill Fowler merely turned to the other two and said, 'What did I tell you?' John Dack took the lead, 'And you? Young man, what do you propose to do in the Club?' I replied, 'I will organise them. Probably Club Secretary would be best.' The rest of the meeting dissolved into laughter as the men told me I had just broken every rule written about the establishment of a Rotary Club but they accepted my judgement and they would go about the business of visiting the people on the list.

That's how the Rotary Club of Cheltenham began back in 1972. It was put together in record time and the District Governor was duly notified that suitable Charter Members were available. The District Governor's special representative said it was the easiest Chartering of a new Club that they had ever been involved in.

Of the twenty-five people on my list, twenty-one became Charter Members. The District Governor for that year, Jock Andrews, was very proud of the new Club and in fact still keeps in contact with me. Today Jock lives in Sydney.

A few years ago I returned to Cheltenham as guest speaker for their twenty-fifth anniversary of the Chartering. It was great to see a strong and virile Club still continuing with many of the same people I had originally recommended. Recently at a Melbourne District Conference where fourteen hundred Rotarians were attending I met some of the members of the same Club. I have enjoyed every moment of my thirty years as a Rotarian.

But if you are a Rotarian you have to expect that you will be busy. Over those years I have been a Club Director several times, Secretary, Vice President, President twice, Past President, Director of Club Service, Director of International Service, Director of Vocational Service, Director of Community Service (twice), bulletin editor and printer, Chairperson of Classifications, Chairperson of Fundraising, District Director, District Community Service Director, District Governor's Advisory Board, Member of the Nominating Committee, Fellowship Committee, Public Relations Committee, Club and District Conference Organiser, Developer of the Rotary District Retirement Village, Awarded a Paul Harris Fellowship, been the recipient of the prestigious Rotary Club of Sydney Vocational Service Award, recipient of the Rotary International's Distinguished Service Award and speaker at several hundred meetings of Rotary Clubs, as well as conferences, assemblies and conventions at district, regional and international levels. Being keynote speaker and addressing 25,000 Rotarians at an International Convention would be a lifetime highlight.

Looking back upon this list of activities I suddenly realise that my fellows have never invited me to be Treasurer! I wonder what stopped them? Every one of these activities has brought me satisfaction. Working together with teams of Rotarians, either as a team member or a team leader, has provided the means of acquaintance and an opportunity for service. I have been wonderfully blessed by the friendship of other fellows and spouses whom I would not have known but for working alongside each other. That involvement was a long-term preparation for being President of a significant club such as the Rotary Club of Sydney, where I had been a member for fifteen years. Twenty years after I was the President of the Rotary Club of Cheltenham, I was elected President of the Rotary Club of Sydney.

To be elected as the president of the Rotary Club of Sydney was one of the proudest but most humbling experiences of my life. It was exactly twenty years to the day that I became a president for the second time. The year between the 1st July 1993 and the 30th June 1994 was one of the busiest of my whole life. It brought Beverley and I a great deal of personal satisfaction. I brought together a wonderful team of Rotarians in Sydney who would work with me in making it an outstanding year. I told my colleagues on my first day as president that I had four aims.

Firstly, I wanted to confirm the Rotary Club of Sydney as Australia's principle forum for public leadership. In order to achieve that I had already chosen 45 outstanding speakers from across the nation to address the club, including the Prime Minister, the previous Prime Minister and other outstanding people. Every one of the 45 speakers was well-known in public life and leaders in their field. Furthermore I decided that we would aggressively develop our number of women members. Rotary had just agreed to have women members and many of our older members at the Rotary Club of Sydney were very opposed to that move. Three ballots about whether we would approve women as members had been lost. I received a letter signed by a number of men who indicated that if we were to push ahead with female members then they would leave. In my opening address I indicated that we would be very pro-active in seeking women members and if any member decided that they would leave because of that, then we would greatly miss them. As far as I was concerned there was no argument. We would rapidly increase the number of women members. None of the objecting men left after I started inducting women members.

The second goal was to confirm that Rotary is on the cutting edge of social issues. That meant we had become a much more multi cultural and heterogeneous community reflecting our nation's diversity. In order to do this I would develop a whole range of programmes to help our membership understand what was happening in society and that we would initiate a whole programme of hands on activities to involve our members with the homeless, with building houses for people whose homes had been destroyed by a hurricane in Fiji and in helping street kids in the heart of Sydney. The issue that I proposed that created the most publicity and indeed controversy was to bring work parties every Saturday into Everleigh Street, Redfern, and work with the Aboriginals in the community in rebuilding their homes and cleaning up Australia's 'Street of Shame'. The garbage men of South Sydney had refused to collect the garbage from Everleigh Street for some time because of the tax on their garbage trucks. But it was my plan to lead a team of professionals like lawyers, doctors, dentists and CEO's of large companies into Everleigh Street to shovel garbage, to clean up the community, to clean bricks and to rebuild a house gutted by fire during one of the riots in that area.

That was going to be one of the most gut wrenching and exhilarating experiences of my life. Many members in the Rotary Club of Sydney look back on those Saturday mornings as life changing experiences for them. Incidentally our club and my key man in this project, Past President John Randall, received a world commendation for this as our outstanding Rotary project.

The third goal I had was to confirm that the Rotary Club of Sydney was the outstanding Rotary Club in the Southern Hemisphere. To do that would involve training Rotarians in leadership, involving members in our total programme and becoming involved in a number of high initiative programmes. One of those received front-page attention in the papers when Premier John Fahey announced it on my behalf. He announced that during the contest to win the right to stage Olympics 2000 in seven years time that the Rotary club of Sydney had put forward a proposal to provide home hosting with free bed and lodging for the parents of every athlete who desired to come to the Games. John Fahey said that that proposal was the one that tipped the balance in favour of Sydney being the host city in the year 2000. The Rotary Home Hosting Programme was one of the most significant voluntary projects during the Sydney 2000 Games. My experience as the first Australian Olympic Chaplain convinced me that 97% of athletes won nothing and their very young average age meant they needed their parents – and most parents couldn't afford to stay in hotels.
Our fourth goal was to confirm the fact that our Rotary club of Sydney had a

sense of freshness about it. We would have new members, younger members, more female members and more members from a multicultural background. To help me in this I had two outstanding Vice Presidents, Steve Koroknay and David Greatorex. Both served with distinction. My friendship with Dr Greatorex grew and a short time later he became a member on the Board of Wesley Mission. When Professor Alf Pollard died in December 2000, Dr David Greatorex became the honorary Secretary of Wesley Mission and we worked in an even closer partnership.

There was one thing that I did not promote. I had indicated that in spite of the fact that the Rotary Club of Sydney had raised usually about $200,000 a year to help others in need that fundraising would not be my primary role, that we would have no special presidential projects and that the pressure to raise money that we had endured for several years would not be made during my year of office.

Not that I was shy on raising money because I had raised several hundred million dollars from Church members, the public and the community at large for some of Australia's major charity projects but I felt that this was not the time for a major thrust in fundraising.

However, one year later the club was to prove me wrong. For within that year, without making fundraising a major emphasis in the life of The Rotary Club of Sydney, those members had raised more than $700,000 for the needy of our community. We had raised more than $500, 000 toward training unemployed youth through a programme with the YWCA. We gave money to Rotary health research, thousands to library development, to the Fred Hollows foundation, youth research, heart research and bush fire relief. As well we were notified we would receive more than half a million dollars through people deciding to write to the Rotary Club of Sydney into their wills. This was by far the most money ever raised by the Rotary Club of Sydney before or since.

There was one other final point. I was asked to go to Sri Lanka on behalf of Rotary in Sri Lanka and the Sri Lankan Government to develop in that country the guidelines for a programme of helping street kids and young addicts as we had done in Sydney. That programme also received several hundred thousand US dollars to help it get on its way, mainly through my visits and special pleading to the consulates in Columbo. It had been the most successful year financially in the history of any Rotary Club in Australia.

That is it for me. I am a non-destiny person in Rotary, believing the greatest privilege is being an ordinary member involved in serving the community and the highest Rotary honour in Australia, is to be the President of the Rotary Club of Sydney. Outside of the Church the greatest pleasure I have found has been within a fine team of community leaders who have been members of the Rotary Club of Cheltenham and of the Rotary Club of Sydney.

During 2005 a new history was published which to my surprise carried an assessment of my leadership in the Rotary Club. 'The Rotary Club of Sydney 1921-2005 Achieving for Others' was written as a scholarly work by Professor Brian H. Fletcher, one of Australia's outstanding academic historians. He wrote:

'In 1986 the Reverend Dr Gordon Moyes, Director of the Wesley Central Mission, had started Habitat for Humanity in Australia, an international organisation of which he was National President. Its aim was to provide houses for needy people with accommodation problems. In 1988-89 the Sydney Club made available volunteers and material to help construct a house at Plumpton for a single mother and four children who had lived in a caravan for six years. That children were involved strengthened the Club's desire to help and pointed to another area of concern.

In 1987 a document had been produced raising the question of what might be done for the growing number of young people living in Sydney under conditions that placed them at risk. Investigations were carried out and in February 1989 the incoming Board decided in the forthcoming year to look for ways of providing housing and rehabilitation for 'at risk' children in the inner city. This was welcomed by Gordon Moyes, who was involved with a similar project that had government support.

He looked to the club for cooperation and suggested that if a building was found it should be named Rotary Lodge. Subsequently, the Board decided that it could not proceed with the idea of a Rotary Lodge but it did respond favourably when the Wesley Mission opened a centre known as StreetSmart at 169 Liverpool Street. This provided a haven where young people could seek counselling and help in achieving reconciliation with families. They could also be referred to agencies that could help with accommodation, drug rehabilitation and employment. President Bill Locke threw his weight and skills behind what became known as the Kids in Crisis project. Together with others he had been deeply moved by the Burdekin Report and an ABC television documentary series entitled 'Nobody's Children'. The club succeeded in raising $100,000, which was placed in a Trust Fund designed to underwrite the cost of a youth worker at the Wesley Centre for three years.'

One of the other positive consequences of the admission of women was the fact that it reduced the average age of members. This was something to which Gordon Moyes drew attention in his inaugural address as President in July 1993. He observed that, when he had joined the club in 1979, 16% of the membership had been less than 50 years old. Now the figure had risen to 25%, an increase he considered, 'mainly due to women members'. Significantly, it became his goal and that of subsequent Presidents and Boards to infuse young blood into the club. In March 1994 the Membership Development Committee took steps to bring together members under the age of 40, partly to make them feel more at-home and encouraging others to join, partly because it was felt that with proper encouragement they would do much for the club.

On 28 June 1993 the energetic Reverend Dr Gordon Moyes AM, became only the second clergyman to be made President. He brought to the club the unbounded enthusiasm that influenced every aspect of a life inspired by a desire to help the needy. This had become evident while he was serving as a Minister in Melbourne, where he became President of the Rotary Club of Cheltenham and was awarded a Paul Harris Fellowship.

Appointment as Superintendent of the Wesley Central Mission in Sydney in 1979 gave him further opportunity for service and this he seized with relish. His achievements were recognised by the Sydney Club, which gave him the prestigious Vocational Service Award in 1991.

In a stirring luncheon address delivered on 29 June 1993, he outlined his plans for the next 12 months. These comprised a comprehensive range of initiatives, amongst them a decision to establish the Rotary Club of Sydney Policy Committee, which was to formulate a 'Rolling Strategic Plan' and provide oversight of 'many of our projects'. Chaired by the new President it also contained Past-Presidents Ray Hodgkinson and John Wallace, together with President elect Denis Cortese. Much was accomplished and the Annual Report prepared at the close of Gordon Moyes' period in office was one of the most extensive and far-reaching ever issued. Covering 56 pages and copiously illustrated with photographs, it depicted the club as 'the outstanding Rotary Club in the Southern Hemisphere, possessed of a 'sense of freshness' that placed it at the cutting edge of public issues.'

One of the areas I looked forward to working in when I came to Wesley Mission was with some disabled people. I had started in a small way during my suburban minister days in Cheltenham, setting up a special class within the Sunday School for children who suffered severe physical and mental deficiencies. One of our boys, David, was in a wheelchair. He could neither speak nor see properly and he had no limbs that would function.

However, I arranged with my Rotary Club the purchase of a then revolutionary Golf Ball typewriter for him. In his Sunday School class we attached a long wooden peg to a band that fitted on his head and by using his head he would hit the pointer onto the letter and spell out on the typewriter his answers to questions. That very preliminary work with David, which led us to putting in ramps to the church and places for his wheelchair with plenty of room for his grandmother to sit beside him, started me on an intense programme of caring for the disabled.

When we came to Wesley Mission we operated a centre called 'Pinaroo'. It was a large hostel for about 45 severely disabled people. The trouble with this hostel was its very strength. Its strength lay in caring staff who made beds, cleaned floors, cooked meals and took disabled people out and helped them have an enjoyable life to the full. But I soon saw that in caring for people in a lodge like this and by doing so much for them, we were further disabling them. What we really needed to do was help enable them to do whatever they could do for themselves.

I remember in 1980 and 1981 having meetings with their parents explaining that we wanted to deinstitutionalise these severely disabled young people and have them live in house groups of four to a house with one carer. Instead of us doing their banking and money for them we would teach them to handle their own money. Instead of taking them for rides in our disabled persons bus, we would go with them until they learnt to travel by bus and train and to be independent. Instead of spending all the time in the presence of carers we would encourage them to go to sheltered workshops and earn some money of their own.

Noble though these ideas were we were met with total resistance from parents. Parents had gone through the big break of having their child leave home now to live in someone else's care and they didn't want us to make them independent. Many of the parents were quite elderly and they wanted to spend the rest of their lives knowing that their disabled adult children were in total care. They would never have to worry about them ever being out in the community, travelling by train, or going into a supermarket to buy food. The parents, without realising it, wanted their disabled adult child to be so cocooned with safety that they would never develop what capacities they had. They were disabling even their capacities.

Our view was just the opposite. I wanted to make those people as independent as possible and to help them develop whatever skills they had to their maximum use. I wanted them to undertake courses in cooking, to go to a TAFE course to learn how to handle money on their own and how to cook and buy food for their own kitchen. It was inevitable that we would have conflict with some of those parents and I was always glad of the support of my colleague Rev. Colin Wood, who helped me negotiate very prickly meetings with very tense parents.

We succeeded, eventually, with opening about 25 houses into which we placed a staff person plus three or four disabled people. The story of that enterprise throughout the 1980's and 90's was one of great success. Almost every one developed within their capabilities. Some became so independent that they took courses at TAFE, learned to cook, learned to travel on public transport and got jobs away from sheltered employment. A number of them eventually became the leaseholder on their own house property. Many of them learned to travel independently and to save their money, to travel overseas and go to Disneyland or wherever their chosen destination was. Several got married and we still have today a close contact with a number of those people who have been married and have set up their own homes.

We are extraordinarily proud of how those disabled people developed their skills and abilities. That first step was followed by many other initiatives to help the disabled. Wesley Mission is today the largest provider of services to disabled people within NSW. We have many different types of services and we look after hundreds of disabled babies, children, young adults and aged disabled people.

Many of those disabled have become firm friends. I was very moved a few years ago on Mother's Day when Robert Bates a 55-year-old, profoundly disabled man who helped us every Sunday night by handing out Hymn sheets to everybody who comes to worship, purchased a Mother's Day card and a gift to give my wife. He regarded Beverley as his mother.

I have often had people who come to church of a night wonder what kind of church this is when they see a profoundly disabled man sitting at the front doors of Wesley Theatre wearing a solid helmet on his head to save his very tender bones when he falls accidentally handing out the hymn sheets. Many people find it difficult to confront a disabled person but allowing Robert to share in the taking up of the offering and in the handing out of the hymn sheets that all of God's children are welcome and everyone of them has a place where they can exercise their gifts of service.

Sometimes our friendship with disabled people has brought us great sorrow and great rejoicing. I can never think about the sorrow that has been brought upon us by some serious disabled person without thinking of Trevor Young or Steven Seymor. Trevor Young was only in his early twenties. He used to sleep rough in the back alleys around the streets of the Central Business District. I found him huddled in a doorway one night in an alley that ran between a café and picture theatre in Pitt Street. I asked him where he was sleeping and in halting speech was told that he just slept up the alley. I told him that we had beds where he could sleep and showers and breakfast in the morning, a hot breakfast which would help set him up for the day and that what he needed to do was to go to our Edward Eager Lodge.

It was a damp night and rain was beginning to fall. In those days, without a mobile telephone, I went back to my office, telephoned Edward Eager Lodge and told them I'd sent the young man up to the Lodge to get a bed for the night. The night manager told me they were already full but he would do what he could to find him a comfortable and a dry place.

The next morning I heard a dreadful story about Trevor as soon as I arrived at work. The Lodge was overcrowded with people and we have a strict rule that we will not allow mattresses on the floor in fire escapes in case of an emergency evacuation. The night was raining and there were many people - more than 500 who were sleeping out in the parks and in the alleyways and backdoor ways of the city. Trevor told the night manager not to worry, that he would come back in the morning and then book in for a bed the next night. I don't know what happened then but apparently Trevor went round the back of Edward Eager

Lodge. The rain started to come down very heavily and looking for a dry spot this young, mentally disabled man lifted the lid on one of our large dump bins. He recognised it was out of the rain and he would be warm there. He crawled in among the garbage and made himself comfortable. Apparently he fell into a deep sleep. He awoke the next morning to violent movement. In the early hours of the morning the garbage truck came and picked up the big metal garbage container and lifted it over the cabin where the driver sat and emptied the contents, including Trevor, into the back of the garbage truck. Without realising what he was doing the garbage man replaced the big steel bin and pressed the level which compacted the garbage in the back of his truck and Trevor was compressed to death. No disabled young person should be homeless on their own sleeping in the trash bins.

I am sad every time I think of Trevor and I think of him every time I see a trash dump bin being emptied into a garbage truck.

Or when I think of Steven Seymour. Tears well up in my eyes as I think of Steven. Every morning from 1987 for the next 7 years, Steven met with me for a cup of coffee or tea. In 1987 when our head office was in temporary accommodation in George Street while we were building our large new Wesley Centre in Pitt Street, Steven Seymour would appear at the door of Wesley Centre waiting for me to arrive. In those days he used to come in and have an early cup of tea with the Lifeline counsellors who had been on duty all night. Then he learnt that he could come in to Wesley Centre and meet with the early arriving members of our restaurant staff. Every day they would give him a free breakfast and a cup of coffee.

By the time I had arrived he was full of good food and tea and coffee. He would wait just where I parked my car and then accompany me to my office. Steven would spend the entire day with us and would find out where I might be going during the day. Steven was of medium height with dark hair and a scraggily beard. He always carried over one shoulder, a bag containing all of his possessions. He had several teeth missing and the rest were a mixture of green, black and white. He had lived for 16 years in the Gladesville Psychiatric Hospital and then in a lodge at Leichardt.

Steven was addicted to the streets. No one could get him away from the streets and whenever we found him a better place of accommodation he would only stay a night or two before he would come back to sleep somewhere around the streets.

Steven was a gentle man. He was very clean in his personal habits but very timid and fearful that people would bash him at night. He had the conflict of being afraid of being on the streets at night and desiring to sleep out under what he called the 'Starlight Hotel' rather than indoors. Several times while he has been sleeping on the street or in a back alley or in a doorway he was robbed of his few possessions. Many times he was bashed up by young hoodlums who found him a very easy target because he could not strike back.

In the seven years that I knew him Steven never drank alcohol, never smoked and never took any illegal drugs. He was just a gentle child of a man. When he was born, he was born with an intellectual disability and he was born into a dysfunctional family. I found out that his sister had left home at 15. A brother had left home in his early teenage years and the life between his mother and father was one of alcohol abuse and physical violence. Steven somewhere slipped through the cracks and as a boy ended up in the Gladesville Psychiatric Hospital. Upon de-institutionalisation, which occurred in the mid 1980's, Steven was one of those people sent out into the community into a house where he would be looked after. The fact was, the boarding house proprietor took the money but did not look after Steven. After a while Steven was on the street and I suspect the boarding house proprietor was still receiving money to care for him. When we moved into our new building in Pitt Street, Steven moved with us.

Every morning, early while it was still dark, Steven would be waiting for the first person to arrive, which was usually one of our cooks or chefs from Wesley Restaurant to open the doors. Our staff would let him in because he was no trouble and because they liked to give him a cup of tea and some breakfast. On Tuesdays, Steven knew I would go to Rotary and he would be there waiting for me to come down in the lift from my office and there he would be waiting with his bag with all his possessions hooked over one shoulder and he would walk with me down to the Rotary Club of Sydney meeting in the Hotel Windsor. He would lope along beside me, skipping from foot to foot and saying over and over again, 'You're my friend aren't you Gordon? You're my friend.' I kept reassuring Steven I was his friend.

When I got to the Hotel Menzies I would say that I had to go to my meeting and Steven would quite naturally peel off and lope over to Wynyard Park where he would sit in the sun. An hour and a quarter later he would be waiting at the front doors of the Hotel Menzies for me to exit. Then he would lope along beside me and we would talk all the way with Stephen saying over and over again, 'You're my friend Gordon aren't you? You're my friend.' I always assured Steven that I was his friend. We always made sure he had a few dollars in his pocket and that he was able to get some lunch. One time in 1994 Steven's Birthday came around and the staff at Wesley Centre gave him a birthday party complete with cake and candles and gave him the gift of a wristwatch. It was not a fine delicate gold watch, that wasn't Steven; it was a large ostentatious brightly coloured plastic watch with a battery and hands. He was so proud of his big watch and wore it constantly; the watch had cost us less than $20.

No one ever accepted responsibility for Steven but in 1992 through the miracle of the radio station when I told something of Steven's life, his sister, who had long lost contact with him, recognised I was talking about her brother and she made contact with me. I reunited brother and sister after twenty years. That's when Steven found out that both his mother and father had died some years earlier. I would love to tell you that his sister took extra responsibility for Steven, but the fact was that having made contact with him she no longer wished to be in contact.

In 1994 I was rung early one Saturday morning. The constable from the Surry Hills police station told me that Steven had been attacked in the early hours of the morning and had been robbed of his watch. He had run away from his assailant who was seen to chase him, eventually catch him and then savagely kick him to death. They told me it was hard to recognise his face. The only way the police were able to find someone to identify him was that when they went through his bag of possessions they found several photographs of me cut from our Wesley Mission magazine. The police rang and asked if I could come and identify him. Beverley and I quickly dressed and went to where the body of Steven was. It was hard to recognise him owing to the swollen and beaten nature of his face. There was no doubt about it, it was Steven and he had been robbed and kicked to death for the sake of a watch worth less than $20.

Over the road several stories up two cleaners were completing their tasks when they saw the assault. They came down and gave a very good description to the police of the assailant. I met with the police on a continuous basis over a period of several months but no one has ever been arrested and charged with his murder.

I told Steven's story the following Sunday night on the radio and indicated I wanted to hold a service in Wesley Church in his memory and I wanted people to say to the community that we cared for a disabled homeless man like Steven. I was overwhelmed. Flowers arrived from all over the state and more than 300 people attended an incredible service of tribute and praise to one of God's very special, frail children.

But there are other very disabled people whose stories mean a great deal to us and who bring us joy. At the same time as I first got to know Robert Bates, I also got to know Angie. Angie was a well know female who moved from bar to bar in the Kings Cross area. She had been a prostitute for many years in earlier life but when I came to know her she was just an older woman who was dirty, diseased and very alcoholic. She couldn't exist without cheap wine. Her clothing was dirty, her body was smelly and her blood shot eyes and raucous voice put fear into any one. She used to go from hotel to hotel and would frequently slump on the floor at the bar and beg men to buy her drinks.

Years of smoking had scarified her throat and her loud raucous harsh voice made her the most unladylike women you could ever find. I didn't know much about her in those days but some time in 1980 she arrived at a service at Wesley Mission's Edward Eager Lodge. In those days there were very few homeless women on the streets but Angie was one of them. After taking a Sunday morning church service I had a cup of tea with her and while we were drinking the tea asked her why she had come to Edward Eager Lodge.

She told me she had resisted the thought of going to any of the homeless person centres run by the Welfare agencies. She laughed with a harsh crackling voice, 'You'd never catch me in one of those places.' I said to her, 'Well, why have you ended up here?' and she replied quite simply, 'One night, two men rolled me in a lane behind a pub. They pushed me on the ground and went through my clothes looking for money. They wouldn't touch me 'cause they thought they'd get the scab. They took what money I had, but I didn't have much, maybe 15 cents. One of the men stood over me, undid his fly and p...ed all over me.' She let the enormity of that sink on me. Then she continued, 'While I was laying in the lane and he was p....ing on my face I thought, 'I'm gonna go up the Lodge and see Noreen.''

So that was how Angie came to Edward Eager Lodge and to Rev. Noreen Towers, who has worked among Sydney's homeless in such a wonderful way for so many years. As we finished our cup of tea I said to her, 'Do you like it here Angie?' She replied, 'It's beautiful and I never want to leave.' I replied to her, 'Well, I hope you do leave but not to go back to the streets. I want you to leave here and come into a new place we're just starting. It's out at Horsley Park and it's called Serenity Farm. It's a lovely place set in farm lands with cows and chooks and a couple of dogs and a cat and a few other people we're helping get their lives straight. Would you like to go out to the farm Angie?'

Angie said, 'Not on your life. I've never been out of the city and I'm not going to any farm.'

I got to know Angie well as she lived in Edward Eager Lodge over the next couple of years. We saw some improvement in her lifestyle. She was cleaner, she became more docile and she began to get her drinking under some sort of control, but still she wasn't willing to make any effort to really overcome her alcoholism.

One day Rev. Noreen Towers said to me, 'When you go out to the farm, you're going to get a surprise. I've got someone out there who will be the last person you expect to see.'

Just as Noreen had predicted, when I arrived at Serenity Farm at Horsley Park those three houses we had on about 14 acres of rolling green hills, there in the centre house was one woman, the first woman to come into our alcohol recovery programme, it was Angie Brut. When I walked into the kitchen there she was, with her hands in washing up water looking out over the café style curtains at the animals grazing on the paddock behind the house. I gave her a big hug and welcomed her. Sitting in the lounge were four men who were her housemates during their recovery from alcoholism. I decided I should have a talk with them. I said 'Fellas, this is a bit of a risk for us. This is the first time we've ever had a woman living in one of our houses with men. I want you men to treat her like a lady because if you treat Angie like a lady then she will grow to become one. I want you to open the door and let her go first. I want you to help her with the jobs around the place and when she comes into the room get out of the chair and allow her to sit down. And I want you to listen to this very clearly - I don't want one of you men ever trying to get into her bedroom at night!' From behind the kitchen door came a raucous voice 'They'd better not try to get into my bedroom or they'll loose what they've always been proud of!'

Nothing more needed to be said. Angie stayed with us in the alcoholic recovery programme. She was now dry, sober and her general health improved immensely. After about two years I was told there was a lady waiting to see me outside my office. I asked my secretary to bring her in. Standing before me was a lady who bore some resemblance to someone I had once met but that was all until she burst out laughing and the harsh crackly voice came through. 'Angie, what have you done?' I said to her. 'I didn't recognise you!' Angie laughed again, 'You blokes get fooled because a girl changes her hair colour. And I've got a new set of choppers; it makes all the difference to your face if you've got a mouth full of choppers. I haven't had teeth for years.' Angie got down to the business of telling me why she had come. She was well dressed, well presented with a blue rinse and new teeth. Now she said to me, 'Mr Moyes, I've cleaned my life up and I wanna get a job. I'm wondering if I can work in your restaurant.'

In our restaurant? I was trying to present people with an image of a reasonably priced high quality service restaurant. It didn't seem as if Angie would fit there at all. But I knew if I said no it would probably dispirit her greatly. I told her I'd take her on for a trial for a month. Angie that day donned an apron and started to clear away dirty dishes from a table of people who came into Wesley Restaurant. At the end of the month she'd been earning her wages, was reliable and apart from a few occasions when we had to teach her how to keep her thumb out of the soup and not to laugh so loudly she was a perfect waitress. Angie Brut fell in love with one of our recovered alcoholics, Charlie, and my colleague Rev. Peter Davis married them. A short while afterwards they shifted from their rented premises to a home they purchased interstate. They became associated with a local church and became regular attenders in a home Bible Study group. They corresponded with me regularly until Angie died a few years ago after nearly twenty years of sober, happily married life.

When you're working with the disabled and the homeless there are treasures, treasures you will never forget, like Robert Bates and Trevor and Steven and Angie and Charlie.

As a pastor I was vitally interested in the work of young people. Beverley and I ran dozens of youth camps; attended hundreds of boys and girls club meetings, teenage club evenings and young adult club activities and camps. For some years Beverley was the leader of the girl's Good Companions Club and I was leader of the boy's Explorer Club. Both had large attendances of girls and boys.

Then I was asked to bring my experience to bear on the State Boys Brigade movement as State President. The International Boys' Brigade was begun in 1883 by William Alexander Smith, secretary of the Sunday School of the Free College Church in Glasgow. The Boys' Brigade pre-dates Lord Baden Powell's Boy Scout movement by twenty- five years.

Beginning with thirty boys the movement quickly spread worldwide and in a few years had grown to 250,000. The Boys' Brigade trains boys aged 11 to 18 in spiritual, physical and social activities, with the ultimate aim being to develop well-balanced young men who are ready to take their place in society.

Though not as well-known as the Boy Scout Movement, their system of earning badges for various activities camps and other programmes was almost identical. I spent a lot of time providing State Leadership, attending camps and taking the salute on our large marches through city streets on 'Founder's Day' and in speaking at special church services and parades. This also involved raising money for the Boys' Brigade and ultimately led to me to being elected as the New South Wales president from 1988 to 1994.

I also supplied the Brigade with numbers of sermons, articles and speeches on themes relevant to the boys. The Governor of New South Wales was patron of the Boys' Brigade and every year I was invited to Government House on the occasion of the presentation of the Queen's Badge, the movement's highest award to successful young men. I was then elected national President of the Boys Brigade and followed similar activities throughout each of the states. I visited the Governor General and was a speaker at the International Boys Brigade Conference in Singapore. Two heart attacks followed by heart surgery forced me reluctantly to step down from these positions but I have continued to value the ministry to boys and to the work of the Boys Brigade in particular.

These activities did bring us into constant contact with the Governors and the Governor General, but these formal occasions brought us into an even closer personal relationship with these dignitaries. I was appointed by Executive Ministries as Chaplain to Government House Canberra and to the Office of the Prime Minister. This resulted in our names appearing on many invitation lists to VIP functions, including Royal tours. At these important dinners I was invited to say grace before the meal began. Similarly, at the Australia Club I was invited to preside over various functions, make speeches and say grace.

One such important occasion was the visit of Prince Philip from the United Kingdom. In this position I also formed a particular friendship with Bill Hayden and his wife Dallas while he was Governor General and discussed Christianity with them. This led me to present the Haydens with our video series on Discovering Jesus at the request of the Governor General.

Holy Communion

One of the highest privileges a pastor can have is to lead in the celebration of Holy Communion. For fifty years, every week I have celebrated Holy Communion. I have used a variety of liturgies, written hundreds of modern liturgies and conducted hundreds of home communions for aged, frail and shut in Christians. I regularly carried a small communion set and while visiting the aged and shut in or in aged care institutions, set up a small table and celebrated the sacrament.

It is easy to become over familiar when handling 'holy things' but I have always regarded this as a great privilege. Weekly communion over fifty years, is a source of spiritual strength upholding my spiritual life.

A Country Parson

After my seven years in the inner slums of Melbourne, I spent time in Ararat doing the work of a country parson.

In all the fast track learning on how to become a country parson, I guess I have not told you about the ordinary things we did day by day that made a country minister's life a busy one. Everybody recognises that the leadership of worship is important and I was pleased to see within the first year the worship attendances doubled for each morning and the evening services had an increase of 150%. But there were many other things a country parson did week by week. In my first three weeks, in order to re-establish a Sunday School and attract children from the area to come into Sunday School, I ran a week long programme of 'Happy Hours', where vigorous and happy activities for children were conducted every afternoon. Soon more than 250 children from the community were coming in to the Happy Hour programme and, four weeks after we arrived, we opened a new Sunday School, with 94 children. In the first year we averaged 109 children plus 19 trained teachers. All of those had to be obtained, trained and established within the first weeks of ministry.

We had a shortage of ministers willing to teach Religious Instruction in the High School, so I undertook to teach 700 children in large classes every week. We started a Boys Club with a strong programme of gymnastics and team games and soon 32 boys plus 13 young leaders were working with me in physical jerks and team competitions. We started a Christian Youth Fellowship with more than 30 teenagers regularly meeting each week. Fourteen young adults came to the first weekly meeting of the Young Adult Fellowship, a Mens Monthly Breakfast attracted 42 men, 22 girls started attending a mid-week Girls Club, three table tennis teams were started and a girls netball competition established and a young men's table tennis competition started. All the organisation and leadership came to rest in my lap.

During the week we started with a bible study, which soon grew into a series of house church study groups, each studying the same bible passage, which I would prepare early in the week for lay leaders to use and then to develop with the adult study groups. We also discovered that people enjoyed praying so we set up house prayer groups, with morning, afternoon and night meetings on several days a week where groups of people would come together to pray for all of our work and undergird it with their personal commitment. We discovered that people of every denomination would join together in order to pray for our community.

On Tuesday nights I trained a group of men to visit the homes of non-church members and explain the significance of faith in Christ and membership in the church. The men came visiting with me and over the next month 35 adults made commitments to Christ and were baptised. On Thursday mornings I would appear in court as the only Probation Officer in the area to take responsibility for young men who had been violating the law. Pastoral visitation occupied three afternoons a week. I was not only visiting the aged, the sick and the infirm, but also every man connected with the church at his place of work.

There was an afternoon a week spent in chaplaincy up in the J Ward, where Victoria's worst criminally insane were housed. I went from cell to cell being carefully locked in for a fixed period of time with each prisoner and then spent time at Aradale in the mental hospital, where I ran an Alcoholics Anonymous programme. There were working bees on Saturday mornings and any spare night was usually spent talking to a community club. I addressed more than 100 different community organisations in two years. We trained people as counsellors to guide young people in the problems they were facing and 84 adults attended a six-week course. More than 40 people attended a four weeks course in training for church membership. The work of a pastor in a rural area was rich and varied.

But I guess the most lasting impact I had in those early days as a country parson was to start broadcasting on 3BA Ballarat and 3CS Colac in brief presentations of Christian messages, which, 25 years down the track would lead to speaking to the largest radio audience for a Christian programme anywhere in the nation. It was while I was in the country that I appeared in my first regular television programmes, speaking after midnight in five minute epilogues broadcast from BTV-6 Ballarat and BCV-8 Maryborough. Since that time I have been involved in more than three thousand telecasts and many films and countless videos. Newspaper articles and features became a regular part of life and I learnt the art of writing for publication.
I visited the people on the farms and found they appreciated me spending a few hours with them. A pastoral visit to a farm was different to a pastoral visit in the slums. In the slums I would call at a person's house, have a cup of tea in the kitchen, discuss their family and personal problems, read some Scripture and have a prayer for each person in the household.

But on the farms I worked alongside the farmer for perhaps the rest of the day until he finished and went up to the house for tea at sunset. Working alongside some of the farmers built incredibly good relationships. Country people judge a minister by his willingness to do some hard work. So I helped in digging a well, sinking a bore, rounding up sheep, crutching sheep, dipping, drenching, lambing and shearing sheep, spreading hay, stacking hay bales, harvesting wheat, loading bags of oats onto a truck, tipping grain at the silo, plucking chooks, milking cows, eradicating rabbits, shooting foxes, erecting fences, felling trees, shifting water tanks, driving a tractor, making a dam, repairing farm gates and doing a hundred and one other odd jobs around the property. A good visit, some hard work, a cup of billy tea out in the paddock and then a couple of hours later going up to the farmhouse for another cup of tea, a round of Scripture and prayer with the family and finally heading off home with a bottle of clotted cream or a cabbage from the garden. Country people loved it when the parson stripped off and worked alongside the men. I carried a change of clothes in the boot of the car and some hand cream to help my soft hands recover from the blisters. The country is a wonderful place for people to develop their skills and their interests.

We had launched within the church what we called 'A Plan For Progress' which ended with the new hall being built, the running of a community-based youth evangelistic mission and various forms of ministry within the community.

We were strong on our care for the poor. For some reason that I have now forgotten, we collected nylons, the laddered stockings of ladies in the community - for use by poor refugees in Korea following the Korean War. One thousand, five hundred pairs of nylons were shipped off to Korea.

We gathered together food parcels for poor families, organised youth working bees to do the gardens, mow the lawns and clean the houses of the aged and frail in the community. The young people met together for working bees, where we mass-produced wooden toys which were assembled, sanded and painted for distribution to the Royal Childrens Hospital.

Probably the most difficult task we ever undertook was to convince about thirty women in the Christian Womens Fellowship, mainly elderly and conservative country women, to regularly attend a ballroom dancing session in a locked ward of fifty men in the Aradale Mental Hospital. Most of these unshaven, rambling and disorientated men had told me that what they missed more than anything else was the opportunity to dance with a woman. I tell you, I led some trembling and very frightened women into afternoon ballroom dancing in the Mental Hospital, to the accompaniment of 78 records on a wind up gramophone. But the church was committed to the community and proclaiming the Word of Jesus Christ and doing deeds of helpfulness to people.

We loved the work. We worked hard every day. Living next door to the church, the church became an extension of our family life. There was no such thing as working hours. The day started when Selly the chook man would arrive in our house at six in the morning, walking in the back door calling out that it was time we got him a cup of tea and that he had been up for hours before delivering his day old chickens to the railway over the road from the manse - and it continued non-stop until the last teenager had been dropped off at home following a youth club at night, or we had gotten home from speaking at the Rotary Club or Lions or women's Penguin Group. There were no weekends off and in fact, no day off at all. We worked seven days a week for sixteen or more hours a day. There were no union regulations or rules and we put in a hundred hours a week every week.

Looking back, it all seems rather exhausting, especially as I read an article in the press entitled 'The Human Dynamo', which outlined my activities. It was exhausting but with great highlights and much enjoyment. For almost fifty years I worked one hundred hours a week and my wife made it possible by joining in what I was doing on top of caring for our home and children.

As a young country parson I had met a host of characters around the gateway to the Wimmera. They were interesting characters who were going to stay as part of my life. I would never forget the stories concerning these people and I wrote them in my diaries. There was Ballarat Bertie, the drunken steam train driver and Keith the fireman who played a dreadful prank upon him the night he went to sleep when he was bringing the steam train into Ararat. There was Tom Varney, the criminally insane prisoner in J Ward, who today is a businessman of some standing on the Gold Coast and Lyall and Ross Knudson, the bachelor brothers who had fought for forty years and who each ran one half of the Ararat General Providore. There was Hans Joseph Schmidt, who used to collect all the waste from behind the hotels and restaurants and boil it up to make Smitty's Soup for Geoff Judd's pigs. Rabbito Bill, who used to eradicate the rabbits on the farms for a living but always made sure he left the young ones in the warren to ensure he had a good crop next year. There was Chook Head Clarrie, who chopped the huge tree down that had grown too close to his house, only to see it fall the wrong way and totally demolish his house. There was Big Mumma Bertha, who came into town with some good time girls for the truck drivers, but who was run out of town by Eugene Horton and the Ararat Players who were rehearsing 'Annie Get Your Gun'.

I have retained a lifelong friendship over those years with the Methodist Minister Rev. Geoffrey Stanton Crouch, who once went to revive faith in a lapsed Methodist family only to get bogged on their farm, have his car ruined and then discover that the family had been visited by me the week earlier and had been baptised and come into membership of the Church of Christ. There was Captain David A.J. Wilson, the Salvation Army officer with whom I preached in the open air and who received a surprise Christmas gift, which was eventually discovered as the stolen Christmas lunch from the Anglican vicar. There was also Chris Fisher, the journalist who helped me immensely by writing hundreds of articles about our ministry and outreach.

I'll never forget 'Old Dr Gwen', who wore a man's army overcoat and boots as she made her rounds among the farms and cared for the poor people in the community and the Wheatons, who ran the Miram Country Store. Or Frank Gason, who rode into Ararat on a pushbike and who became Australia's largest tractor cabin manufacturer and who was to become Australia's sixth largest car manufacturer.

A host of people in that country town played a part in our lives. Young people like Marilyn Duffy, who ran off to Adelaide with the travelling salesman and poor 'Plain Jane' who had a difficult task living with a fashion plate mother. There was Harry Riley, the insurance man who taught me more lessons about successful pastoral care than anybody. But above all, there were friendships that made a difference to our lives. There was Ron Johnson, the train controller who became a dear friend, Loy Fleming, the cow cocky who taught me to divine water and a hundred other lessons that every young minister should know, and dear Geoff Judd, whose farm became our second home and whose death upon his tractor robbed me of the closest male friend I ever had in adult life.

One of the greatest joys of being a country parson was to spend time with Ken Sellwood, as he discussed with me the call to ministry and then, a year later, to send him off to Theological College duly candidated for training for the ministry. Our joy was to turn to sadness one year later when, as a young student minister returning from a Sunday congregation, Ken's motorbike skidded in the rain and he was killed. The church was packed once more, this time in sadness, as we laid his young body to rest in the Ararat Cemetery.

Another joyful memory was sitting down with John and Margaret Boatman, young farmers with a young family of Methodist background, to discuss with them the implications of training for the ministry and turning their back upon the country family property. I encouraged them to enter Queens College and train for the Methodist ministry, and John Boatman became a highly regarded Uniting Church minister.

A Suburban Minister

I was 25 years of age when the time came for me to leave that ministry in the country. We had set our sights on America but the arrival of first born son, Peter, and the gradual involvement in the community of pastoral care dimmed the vision of further graduate study and at a time when the vision was most vulnerable, the Conference of Churches of Christ in Victoria and Tasmania decided that rather than risk a promising young minister by allowing him to go overseas, they would organise a significant call to ministry that was bound to keep him in this country.

And so I received an enquiry to see if I would become senior minister at the Cheltenham Church of Christ, one of the largest congregations of the denomination in Australia. The church was already 110 years old and had fine property and large congregations. The heavy word was placed upon me that I should not reject this call.

However, the desire for further graduate study was still strong and so I rejected the call, planning instead to leave the following January for America. A second time a letter of request came and this time with a greater note of urgency, indicating that the strategic significance of placing a young man into such a large and significant pulpit.

Beverley and I decided we should at least listen to what they had to say. We agreed to meet half way between Ararat and Cheltenham, Victoria and meet with the Parish Secretary, Treasurer and Chairman. They had done their homework well. We met at a motel and they had a book of clippings from newspapers with headings like 'Dynamic Young Minister To Leave Ararat' and 'Youth Loses A Great Friend'. Another full page article was headed, 'A Man Who Made News Everywhere' and other newspaper and magazine cuttings were headed 'Moyes Regrets His Ministry Here Was Only Temporary', and 'Church Of Christ Led To Grow As Never Before'.

They had more statistics and background information on me than I ever imagined. My new friends shared in convivial conversation as we ate together in a fine restaurant and then sat down around a table to listen to what they had to say about the call to a new ministry. Everything they had to say about the church and the challenge that was there before us excited us. It seemed that God was opening up for us a new direction - not in Indianapolis but in Cheltenham, Victoria.

As we left the congregation's three representatives holding their formal invitation in our hands we started on the road back to Ararat to think over this new change in our direction and challenge to continued ministry in this country. But, had we known what would happen next we may have had different thoughts. For during the two weeks I indicated I would like to think and pray with my wife about this new call, I visited Melbourne and took the opportunity to call in on the present minister, who was in his sixteenth year of service. He was a man I had admired greatly from a distance, a former missionary and a man of great statesmanship. He had been President of the denomination and was regarded as one of the finest preachers in the country. He was now in his early sixties and at the height of his powers.

I called upon him, paid my respects and asked if him if I could find out some details about the church and especially, when he expected to be vacating the parsonage. 'Leave the manse?' He looked at me through his rimless spectacles, 'I didn't know I was leaving either the manse or this church!' I suddenly realised that while we had been talking to the Chairman, the Secretary and the Treasurer of the Church Board they had not spoken to their existing minister. An awful wave of regret and dismay swept over me. I immediately left the situation with our questions unasked and wrote a letter declining the offer and breaking off all negotiations. As it happened, some weeks later the incumbent minister decided to resign and left the church without ministry and now, for the third time, came an invitation from this church.

To go or not to go, that was the question. It was the question that Beverley and I and our two young children pondered as we drove back towards Ararat. It would be a turning point in our ministry and a move from being a country parson to a suburban minister.

Funerals

A minister has stories to tell about conducting funerals. I have conducted funerals for more than a thousand diseased persons, visiting the homes of the grieving families. Consider the problem that ministers and undertakers have when, in the middle of the flood area, they have a burial in a cemetery. The Ararat cemetery was built down by the Ararat creek.

When the Ararat creek flooded most of the cemetery went under water. One morning I was burying a former patient from the Aradale Mental Hospital. These were government funerals known as 'pauper' funerals. The deceased had no known relatives and consequently the funeral was put on early in the morning so as not to interfere with more important funerals that would be conducted later in the day. Only the undertaker, his driver, the gravedigger and the minister would be present. On such occasions the minister and the gravedigger would lend a hand in carrying the simple pine box in which the poor deceased's body lay.

Even though there was no one present I always gave that funeral the same service as I would for anyone else, except when it came to the eulogy there was usually no information known about the person other than what I could find upon the card of admittance. As many of the people I buried had been in the Aradale Mental Hospital for 30 or 40 years and as the details of their admissions during the 1930's were very sketchy, there was virtually nothing I could say. However, I always gave the deceased a full Christian burial, talking about the Christian hope of resurrection for those who had faith and of emphasising the inherent dignity and worth of each human being in the eyes of God, even though this person had been mentally defective and probably did not even known their own name. The undertaker got very impatient with my full service. He wanted a quick job.

One such morning, early, Mr Dunne and his driver were carrying the pine casket towards the place of the burial. When we stopped Mr Dunne said irreverently, 'Oh God, look at that grave. It is full of ruddy water.' Since the gravedigger had finished his job last night, the water had seeped through the sodden earth and filled the grave to the top. Mr Dunne, with the coffin perched on one shoulder, looked at me. 'If you don't mind, Rev.,' he said, 'I want to get this box in as soon as possible. Otherwise we are going to have problems.' I did not mind so we had the committal first and then I conducted the service.

As soon as he and the driver put the coffin into the water-filled grave I understood his problem: it floated! As it is very hard to bury a floating coffin, Mr Dunne and the gravedigger standing by, Old Busby, a grizzly alcoholic looking fellow with a big bushy beard and the most incredible amount of dirt always on his person and clothes, started shovelling wet clay on top of the coffin. When enough clay was piled on top of the coffin, it very slowly slid down into the water. Satisfied, Mr Dunne and Old Busby stood back and I went on with the service.

I said some prayers and quoted the great verses about Christ being the resurrection and the life. I read the 23rd Psalm and then some passages from the 19th Psalm, which seemed appropriate to this poor person. I had just reached the point of our Lord talking in John 14, when I read the words: 'Let not your heart be troubled. You believe in God believe also in me. In my Father's house are many mansions; if it were not so, I would have told you. For I go to prepare a place for you.' Immediately as I said the words 'Prepare a place for you' from the water beneath my feet, deep from the bottom of the grave, came the unmistakable sound of 'blurple' and a large bubble came to the surface. It was then followed with another 'blurple' and 'blurple'. Then a whole stream of bubbles came up to the top of the water.

Suddenly I had a picture of poor old John in the coffin below affirming his faith in the words I had just said. Old Busby started to laugh but I was determined to keep my dignity and give the poor deceased a proper burial. Mr Dunne the undertaker was standing in his best black clothes trying to keep a straight face but every time I finished a sentence another three or four large bubbles would reach the top of the surface and break. I could see I wasn't going to win. I've got an idea that Old Busby and Mr Dunne the undertaker had deliberately planned to get that coffin in first so that my sermon and service would be cut short on that cold winters morning by the bubbles which came to the surface. It certainly worked. I could not cope with the noise of the bubbles and finished up the service and left old Busby the job of filling in the flooded grave.

Water in the country is essential to everything that happens. Some of the time there is just not enough of it and some of the time there is far too much of it. There certainly was that first day when I took a winter's funeral in the Ararat cemetery.

Sex Offenders

Probably the least liked of all people to come before a pastor are the community sex offenders. They are at the bottom of the social ladder - especially those who offend against children. No one else in the community will talk to them. Yet like most sinners, they need to be counselled, helped and guided.

Whenever there is an offence against children by an adult, society closes ranks against that person. Sexual abuse against a child is unforgivable by those who have been hurt. Often the abuse upon a child is so traumatic not only for the child at that time who is robbed of his or her innocence and normal childhood growth, but it may also be long term and have a profound impact upon that persons ability to enter into a marriage or into a trusting relationship with another adult. All of us know the horrendous consequences of child abuse.

One of the things that came right into my face in the first months of being at Wesley Mission was the fact that when child abusers have finished their term in prison they discover themselves total rejects in society. They usually cannot go back to the place where they lived because the local population is very much up in arms against them. Slogans are spray painted on the front of their house, rocks are thrown through their windows and the people want the dirty pervert moved out.

Neither do former friends or business acquaintances want to have anything to do with the offender. So what does the offender do? Where do you go when there is absolutely nowhere to go to? I have known over the years a number of sex offenders against children to have committed suicide, finding that death was preferable to living with guilt.

And some come to Wesley Mission. The first of many I met was in 1981 when a man, new to me, started attending our church services. Not only did he attend our church services but he also attended some of our volunteer functions. In the middle of Sunday afternoons he would always come and help some of our volunteers set up tables for the Lifeline tea for the homeless we conduct every Sunday evening. It was obvious from just a simple conversation with him that he was a single and rather inadequate man. When I asked him about his work he told me that he was a manager of a video games centre, which was attended by crowds of children, but he refused to open it on a Sunday afternoon. I was rather cynical of this explanation. He believed that the work he was doing as a volunteer at Wesley Mission was far more important than making profits on a Sunday afternoon. After a couple of weeks he hinted to me that he would be happy at any time to be a helper at a youth camp that was coming up and also if we needed help in our Sunday School.

Red lights began to flash in my mind. I never allow men whom I do not know thoroughly to become involved in either youth camps or Sunday School teaching. I asked him to come and have a cup of coffee with me and we would talk about it.

I explained to him why I would not allow him to become involved in these two ways he had suggested. He looked at me with big open eyes, 'But I thought you knew me.... You're a friendly person and I thought you would have recognised me. The fact that you spoke to me told me that you did know me and you were going out of your way to talk to me.'

I instantly knew there was a story attached to what he had to say and encouraged him to talk on. He was open and frank. 'I'm Hedley Smythe of Baulkham Hills. You know, the Scout leader. In 1976, I was in all the newspapers. Don't you remember it? I was one of the worst they ever caught. 87 counts against Scouts at camps. But I'm completely reformed now, I will never do it again. Can I stay and work here? I am a very experienced youth leader.'

I looked at him squarely. 'No I did not recognise you. I was only appointed to this position in 1977 and I guess that by then the scandal of your paedophile activities had been put behind by the community. And no, I will not allow you to work with any of our youth camps nor children nor Sunday School.'

He looked absolutely crest fallen. 'Can I stay in the Mission?' I thought for a moment and then replied 'You can stay coming to the Mission to the adult activities on these conditions; that I tell at least a dozen of our elders and leaders who you are and what your story is so that they can be on the lookout at all times. This is to protect our children and youth but it is also to protect yourself from getting into any compromising situations. And further, I want you to come and see me at least once a month just to have a chat and you can raise with me then any problems that may be coming up. If you do find that you're being overwhelmed by the old temptations I want you to ring me day or night. I will always spend time talking with you and together we will work them out. But I want you to understand this very clearly, for the sake of the children who are here and our young people and their parents, if I ever catch you talking to any child or young person then you will be barred from the Mission. There is no second chance. Do you understand?'

Hedley nodded, he promised me most sincerely that he would never again re-offend. He had learnt his lesson and his time in gaol had been so brutal and the beltings he had received from other prisoners had so penetrated his mind that he would never ever offend again. We watched Hedley like hawks. It was quite sad really because apart from one or two of us who went out of our way to speak to him he developed no friends. In fact he found it very hard to relate with adults and we wouldn't allow him to relate with any children or young people.

As the years went by I gradually dropped off the appointments. Hedley came in and out of a service, shook hands with us, drew his heavy overcoat around him and walked out into Pitt Street. Over the years of talking with us, ours was the only place he could come and get a cup of tea and speak to at least two or three people.

I was wondering what we should do with Hedley some years ago when he took a stroke and he was placed in a nursing home. I still see him every now and again, as Beverley and I attend the nursing home and take a service among all of the residents. Adults who abuse children inflict terrible abuse upon their victims. The victim's whole life can be ruined by the physical and sexual abuse of some adult who had the child in their power. Those adults usually manipulate the minds of children so the child feels that if they are to say anything then they will be punished. Hedley has received severe punishment both from the community and from his own mind as well as what he suffered at the hands of other prisoners. But it is nothing compared to the suffering of the children he abused.

A few years ago another sex offender against a small girl came to my attention. When I first met him he was an unemployed homeless young fellow of about thirty years of age. Rufus was his name. He had been sleeping round the streets of Sydney for some time before he came into one of our centres. We found out over a period of time that Rufus had no family, at least no family that cared. We tried to trace down any known relatives but again we were unsuccessful. I always regarded him as a very sad and sorrowful looking person. He somehow didn't belong to the homeless persons scene. He, like many of the homeless, was intellectually impaired and was quite slow. I always felt that if there was a mother or even some woman who cared for him then he would be a totally different person. But finding willing mothers to care for intellectually disabled homeless and unemployed people is very difficult. Rufus drifted in and out of our care over a period of years.

One day I was in one of our homeless persons centres I was having a cup of tea with a group of our clients. I noticed Rufus standing at the back of the group. He was handing out some sticky buns to people who had already got a cup of tea and I could tell within that fleeting moment that he was quite a different person. Leaving the people with whom I had been speaking, I caught up with Rufus as he did his rounds with the tray of sticky buns and started to ask him how he was getting on. He was almost totally different in his outlook. And that was because of a volunteer and his wife who came to our homeless persons centre. This couple were very fine Christian people who were wanting to help other people less fortunate than themselves in the heart of the city. They gave themselves to regular visitation of the homeless. Frequently they brought their three young children with them. The oldest was about 14. Wanting to do something more for one of these people the couple invited Rufus to go on a holiday with them down to the South Coast. They had hired a holiday house by the beach. And so Rufus joined the three kids and the volunteer couple in what must have been a wonderful holiday...until it happened.

I heard the story from several sources and I don't know all the details. But apparently the adults asked the kids if they would be all right playing while they went up the street to do some shopping. The three kids were all busily occupied and Rufus stayed with them.

Their youngest child, a little girl went into the house. According to one of my sources, Rufus later said: 'We were playing hide and seek and she went and hid. I put my hand under the bed to see if she was there and I touched her down here'. He pointed to his crotch. When the parents returned their daughter was very distressed. The oldest boy was having a great deal to say about Rufus. My understanding was that there was an indecent assault with Rufus touching the girl's panties but there was no penetration of the girl and no violence. Never the less the parents did what was right and reported the offence to the police thinking that the young man would be severely reprimanded, would be frightened by being detained in the police cell and that would be a good lesson for him.

Everything went wrong from that point on. The police charged him and received permission from a magistrate to detain him in the cell as he was a homeless person with no fixed address and it was feared that he would not return to the court. Someone contacted me and I sent one member of our staff down to visit him in the cell and another member of staff to go to the family and provide them with comfort and whatever support they needed. The parents recognised the risk involved in volunteering and blamed themselves for leaving their children. The little girl, fortunately, showed no signs of continuing trauma.

My staff person was a well-experienced colleague and he, like myself, believed that Rufus would be brought before a magistrate, given a stiff lecture and then released into the care of Wesley Mission. We would have the job of oversighting him for probably six or twelve months. I will never forget the time when my staff member came back from the day in court. 'I can't believe it. The magistrate has sent him to gaol for fifteen months!' I couldn't believe it either. I had been to court hundreds of times during my early life as a parole and probation officer and I had never heard of a first offender being sent to jail for fifteen months on the matter of indecent assault. But the fact was Rufus was homeless. The magistrate apparently thought that a stiff prison sentence might bring him to his senses and stop him re-offending. There was no question that Rufus was guilty. The only question was what was the best punishment to fit that crime.

In this case I am glad to say that the little girl apparently suffered no ongoing trauma, although I am always very slow to make that observation because sometimes the trauma does not come out until years later.

When Rufus went to gaol there commenced a series of unbelievable events. Often prisoners assault those whom they call 'rock spiders', who sexually abuse or assault little children. Sometimes the assaults are grievous.

Over the next few months as my colleague went and visited Rufus in a Wollongong Prison, I heard terrible stories of the assaults upon him. Rufus was an easy target. He was intellectually disabled, he offered no resistance and he couldn't fight back. I believe several men raped him. I was also told that on one of these occasions, to teach him a lesson, a steel pipe was forced up his anus into his bowel and a length of barbed wire was poked up through the centre of the pipe. The pipe was then withdrawn, leaving the flesh to gather around the barbed wire. Any bowel motion would cause the barbed wire to tear into the wall of the bowel. It was barbaric treatment. Rufus was taken to surgery and took a long time to recover from his trauma.

He was released after about eight months and when we found him, shifted him into one of our community units. He was a trembling, shaking, thin weed of a man. One day I thought I'd better catch up with Rufus. He had been on my mind ever since I had heard about his trauma inside the prison. I found out where in our units he was living and called in to see him.

He met me at the door of his unit, having called out 'Who's there?' several times. I had responded, identifying myself and making sure he realised it was safe to open the door. The door was opened. There was Rufus thinner than ever with a straggly growth of beard around his face. He was walking with the aid of two aluminium sticks, the kind that grip your arm below the elbow.

He invited me in. He was very unsteady on his feet. One leg threw out sideways when he tried to walk and his arms seemed to be uncoordinated. It was just as if he was spastic. This was totally different to the last time I had seen him before he went to prison. Something happened to his brain. Some physical spasticity had set in. Maybe because of the bashing on his head in prison - I don't know. All that I do know is that Rufus will always be a victim. He is permanently crippled. His mind has been horribly scarred. I doubt if any treatment could make any difference to him. After a few years, I was not surprised to hear he jumped into the path of a train and was killed.

Sex offenders cause so much trauma and so much long term hurt to their victims that I have no hesitation in believing that they should be gaoled and should pay for their crimes. But our prison system doesn't seem to be the kind of gaol where these mentally sick people should be punished. When they are caught they also suffer much trauma and at the hands of the system their punishment is very severe.

Some people say that is the justice of God. It eventually catches up with them. They say, 'The mills of God grind slowly, but they grind exceeding small; although with patience He stands waiting, with exactness grinds he all!' I don't agree with that. But I do know that justice for the sex offender is usually long and hard and sometimes out of all proportion. When people offend everyone suffers.

Marriage

I have stood before over two thousand individuals to declare them man and wife. Before the wedding service there was two or three sessions of helping them with details, counselling them to improve their chance of the marriage lasting and counselling on difficulties they faced. My experience usually cut through the difficulties and outstanding marriage services resulted. By teaching over a thousand teenagers each week at Cheltenham I was inadvertently allowing hundreds of teenagers to get to know me, which led in turn them coming to me to marry them. Even late in life, as a Parliamentarian, I am approached to marry, bury, counsel and conduct family celebrations of all kinds.

Beverley and I purchased a magazine, *Marriage Works,* edited by Jim and Grace Vine; to publish every three months by outstanding professionals to help thousands of young marrieds cope with the issues they face. This is a unique aid to improving marriage for thousands of couples.

One key function of a pastor is to be a priest on behalf of god's people, especially in praying for them. Beverley and I have spent time praying together for our members, people in the public eye and community leaders, as well as any known to us who are suffering or facing surgery. The role of an intercessor is one of our most important and consistent functions. Beverley's prayer list and journal records our concerns and God's answers to our intercessions.

Being a pastor opens people's hearts and homes and it is a great privilege to enter into both.

COUNSELLOR

Chapter Nine

One of the tasks I was looking forward to when I became Superintendent of Wesley Mission more than 27 years ago was providing some leadership in the field of counselling. Every city church has a huge load of people coming for counselling but Wesley Mission even more so. The Mission has always taken care for those people who are troubled, disabled, perplexed and confused, therefore the counselling load was high. But more than that, a few years earlier Sir Alan Walker had founded Lifeline, therefore we had an enormous stream of people coming to be counselled and other people who needed to be trained as volunteer counsellors.

I had developed what we call the 'Cheltenham Counselling Centre' in my suburban ministry in Melbourne and we brought together people with varying skills, backgrounds and training and established a one-on-one counselling service. I had also read very widely in the whole field of counselling and human psychology as I had undertaken some courses at the Cairnmiller Institute (a specialised institute for people who are going to undertake counselling).

I had been counselling boys I had on probation and parole from the juvenile justice system in the slums of Melbourne. Many of them had very poor self-esteem levels and I had spent much time in helping them sort themselves out. When I was a country parson I had many people in the rural sector who did not have access to quality counselling or psychologists of any kind in the community and when it was heard that I was working in counselling and was the chaplain in the psychiatric hospital, many people came for counselling concerning their personal and emotional problems. In the thirteen years as a suburban minister in Cheltenham we had built up an extensive counselling programme with hundreds of people from the community finding their way to our doors seeking to be counselled by one of our competent staff.

I discovered that from the earliest days I had the capacity to listen, to analyse peoples' problems and help them discover some answers. Because most ministers are compassionate people, those who came for counselling found that they were helped in an environment that they appreciated. And because we never charged people, there were many who were on very limited incomes for whom this was the only counselling they could afford. The opportunity to work in oversight of the training of counsellors for Lifeline was a wonderful opportunity bringing together the experience of the previous twenty years.

For 25 years I have spent almost every Tuesday Night training a counselling class of 60 - 80 young, enthusiastic trainees who were completing 24 weeks of serious training. Our trainers are mainly Psychologists and Psychiatrists although every week I open the counselling training by taking the theme for the night and using it to show how Christians can counsel with the insights of Jesus on that particular issue.

Over the years I've had more than 2000 people in my counselling courses. At the start of the twenty first century I found that those coming for counselling were quite different from those who first came more than twenty years ago. In general they are younger, more educated, most having completed their degrees in psychology at university and most intending to give us a short term of two years only service. In the old days we had some very fine counsellors who served us faithfully year after year, but these days most younger counsellors want to get the credit on their Curriculum Vitae and then get on with something else.

Apart from Lifeline I found it necessary over the years to establish a specialised financial counselling service, which we called CreditLine. Today it has grown, has a very large full-time staff with centres all over Australia and is the largest financial counselling service in the nation.

In the early eighties I was having so many people come to us for whom English was a second language that we established Ethnic Lifeline in order to provide counselling in half a dozen different languages. Eventually we got to about twenty different languages and the programme was taken over by the State Government who decided to set up an interpreter service.

We had YouthLine, which was a specialised programme of training young people to counsel other young people. That work continues to this day although others would copy the programme and set up a specialised Kids Help Line. There were hundreds of stories of the way counsellors helped kids in crisis. One I remember well was Melissa.

Melissa lived on our north shore with a respectable family. By nine she was a chubby child with a bright personality and was found to be sexually desirable by her father. She was abused and by ten she was drinking her father's alcohol to deaden some of the pain. The sexual abuse and drinking continued and each man she trusted, abused her. By fifteen she trusted no-one and had become a homeless street kid stealing and abusing alcohol and drugs. Melissa lived with other homeless kids beneath the Sydney Harbour Bridge. During the next six months she was regularly abused, raped, threatened, cold, hungry and constantly frightened. In her mess she contemplated suicide. She motivated herself to ring our YouthLine counselling service and came to see one of Wesley Mission's youth counsellors, Chris Varcoe.

Chris quietly and steadily talked with her for six months while she still lived on the streets, until she felt she trusted him. Wesley Mission arranged safe accommodation and long term support. Melissa Baker matured. She felt God calling her to Himself. She became a Christian. She then went to Morling College and studied to become a minister in spite of the fact she had dropped out of school. She graduated with her Bachelor of Theology, then did her Master of Theology. Today she is a lecturer at Morling and a candidate completing her Doctor of Philosophy! She is also today, Chaplain to the New South Wales Police dealing with street kids. Her book, *Jade's Story* has since been published.

One of the significant counselling service centres I established in 1985 was Wesley Gambling Counselling Service. This was a specialised counselling service to help gamblers who were finding increased opportunities to gamble because of the growing incidence of poker machines and casinos. We had enormous numbers of people coming for gambling counselling and that work continues unabated. Today Wesley Gambling Counselling Service is the largest in the nation. We are also responsible for providing advice to gambling organisations such as Star City Casino so that they can identify problem gamblers and so that there is a place to which they can be referred. All told my involvement in training people in counselling has become a major role in my life and my role as Superintendent of Wesley Mission.

What have I learned over the years concerning counselling?

For one thing, *patience*. I was troubled in the 1960's that in order to help some people I had to have an extensive number of counselling sessions. Sometimes I saw a person twenty or thirty times and it was troubling me that I was spending too much time on an individual, although the progress that individual was making made me realise that the continuance of the counselling sessions was vital.

One day I was attending a series of lectures by Professor Frieda Fromm-Reichmann, an outstanding American psychotherapist. She was giving lectures on 'The Principles of Intensive Psychotherapy.'

I thoroughly enjoyed that particular course and it opened my eyes in many ways enabling me to better counsel people who came to me. She was the daughter of Dr Eric Fromm, a German born social psychiatrist who like many other psychiatrists had travelled to the United States. He rejected Sigmund Freud's theory that behaviour is influenced primarily by our instincts particularly our sex drive. Dr Fromm said our behaviour is influenced by sociological factors such as the social and cultural environment in which we grew. I had read his books such as *The Art Of Loving* and others and really felt that he was giving great insights. His daughter was influenced by Dr Karl Menninger from Kansas whose work I'd also read. Consequently as I sat in her lectures on 'The Principles Of Intensive Psychotherapy' I felt that I had discovered an approach that would help in my counselling.

After one session I raised with her the problem I was having with a certain man named Don. Don was an intelligent man, married with three children and had a good job. The problem was that he was an extreme procrastinator. He couldn't make up his mind or move himself to do anything. The result was that his marriage was falling apart, his employers were threatening to sack him and his mental health was in a terrible situation. Don had come to see me about his problems. I had never met him previously. He told me that a well-known Melbourne psychiatrist Dr Gold had referred him to me as being someone able to help him. I had talked with Don for probably thirty sessions and felt that he was just enjoying my attention.

I kept giving him various tasks to undertake which he always completed satisfactorily. According to my understanding he should now be coming to a point of being able to make strong decisions for himself without procrastination. But that wasn't happening. I spread the case before Professor Fromm-Reichmann and then asked her 'How much time would you spend counselling a man with this problem?' Dr Fromm-Reichmann looked at me and said, 'I do not believe I can help him under 200 hours of intensive psychotherapy.' That floored me. I would have to be a lot more patient if I was really going to help change the life of a person like Don. It also made me realise that *I* was not the person who should be spending 200 hours with one person while I was minister of one of the largest protestant churches in Australia and a church, which was growing on all fronts. It was a wrong use of my time to be giving so much time to one individual. Having learned the issues I saw my role should be to teach other people to provide the counselling to him. I would need to multiply myself if I was to be efficient in my use of time. In coming to Wesley Mission and being involved in weekly lecturing trainee counsellors I was fulfilling this wise use of time.

The second thing I had learned from counselling was the value of confrontation. Most of us in our counselling were brought up on the values of listening and reflecting upon what the client had to say. One of the hardest tasks we had was to teach our counsellors not to give advice which so many of them were always ready to do, but instead to really listen to what the person had to say, to help them clarify the issues and enable them to come to some conclusions themselves. We believe that our clients would encode their feeling one way or another and that what we had to do was reflect back to them what they were saying in such a way that they could understand what it was that they really felt.

We followed the philosophy of Professor Carl Rogers. We trained our counsellors in the skills of listening and reflecting, paraphrasing and summarising. The primary role of a counsellor is to listen. By listening to what the client says we can help them sort through the complexity and confusion of their situation, understand their feelings and explore the options available with them so that they feel something useful has been done.

It was at this time that I was introduced to the American psychiatrist Dr Frederick Perls and 'Gestalt Therapy'. I was taught how to confront certain people with issues in their lives. Instead of merely reflecting what they thought, I would confront them with the issue so powerfully that they were shaken to their roots and their carefully built world of security was rattled. Professor Carl Rogers had said, 'Listening, rightly done, is the most significant thing you can do for a person.' Now I learned that for some people, on a rare occasion, total confrontation with them about themselves and their situation was the only way to break down carefully erected walls that gave them security.

I realised that this was what Jesus was doing when he was talking with the woman at the well. She kept asking him questions about where to worship and the difference between Jews and Samaritans. Jesus suddenly said to her, 'Call your husband and come here' the woman replied, 'I have no husband.' Then Jesus said with perception, 'You are right when you say you have no husband because you have already had five husbands and the man you are living with is not your husband.' That really shook her! She opened up to him in the most amazing way so that her whole life was completely changed through his incredible counselling skill.

Over the years on occasions I have needed to confront people with an accurate evaluation. I have found that this shattered their carefully constructed defences and they saw themselves and their situations clearly, for the first time. Confrontation rightly used can be the real means of helping heal a person.

A third value that I learnt was the influence of compulsion in an addictive sense. I had met compulsive drinkers, compulsive gamblers, compulsive eaters and compulsive dieters and with all of these you also meet compulsive liars. Breaking down that compulsion is often difficult. The famous Sydney psychologist Dr Lyn Barrow who did so much to help us understand how we can live more effective lives was the person who first helped me understand compulsion. It was out of learning from Dr Barrow that I initiated the development of our Wesley Gambling Counselling Services because gambling is one of the most compulsive habits that people can have, leading to stealing from their spouses, mothers, workmates and employers. Compulsive gamblers, compulsive liars and compulsive fools. Until the compulsion is treated there will be no healing.

The final thing I have learnt in counselling over the years has been the invidiousness of co-dependency. I think the first time I ever realised the significance of codependency was with a lady who was a member of my church in Cheltenham. Lydia was a courageous woman and joined in many of our activities despite the fact that people gradually came to understand that she was an abused wife. Her husband Morris was a brute of a husband who physically and sexually abused her, who kept money from her and would not allow her to join in many church activities. All the women knew Lydia and they pitied her greatly. In meetings people would pray for her and give her great encouragement. She always had a wistful look upon her face and people were moved greatly to support her. Some gave her money when she was short and others went and visited her with gifts during the daytime when Morris wasn't around. Some diligent people prayed that God would somehow send a thunderbolt from heaven and strike Morris.

I had followed the pattern of my predecessor. I pitied Lydia greatly and went to visit her during the daytime and she constantly asked me to pray for her husband. We all thought Lydia was a saint. This went on for years with nothing happening. We visited Lydia and prayed for her husband. Then one day after reflecting upon her situation I told Lydia that I was no longer going to come and visit her. What I intended to do was to pray for her earnestly that God would work a miracle in her heart. And instead of praying for Morris I intended to visit him at his work and speak to him during his lunch hour. I intended to visit him on a number of occasions and confront him with the way he treated Lydia. I was sick of Lydia being abused while we visited and supported her and all we did was pray for Morris. Now I was turning the situation around. I was going to pray for Lydia and I would go and confront Morris. She begged me not to visit him. She was frightened that he would blame her for the fact that I had visited him and he would then later take it out on her. It was a powerful argument but I was sure I was right.

I went and visited Morris at his work. He was surprised when someone called him from his office to see me just as lunch hour was beginning. I asked if I could eat lunch with him wherever he ate at a bar of a pub if he went there for lunch or out of a paper bag. Whatever he did I would do but I wanted to have an hour talking with him. I was surprised. Morris seemed a fairly decent bloke. He readily agreed and we sat down together in the work canteen and I had a good hour-long chat. We spoke about Lydia and I was amazed to see how caring he seemed to be for her. However I knew many men who were abusers were also people who could put on a good story. Often after abuse they were most apologetic and sought forgiveness. So I wasn't taken in by Morris' good presentation to me.

The following Tuesday lunchtime I was again at his work and again spent an hour with him and the following week another hour. I gradually began to realise there were two sides to the story. In point of fact, Lydia enjoyed playing the part of the abused wife and receiving the consolation, attention and pity of all of the other women and contrary to what we had been told, it didn't seem as if Morris was in fact an abuser. Now having built the personal relationship with Morris I asked him if I could visit him one night at home together with Lydia.

Lydia was around to my home like a rocket as soon as she heard that I was going to visit her and Morris together one evening after tea.

Well I'll let you guess what happened. But the fact was that Lydia was co-dependent upon Morris and she had built up a persona in the eyes of other people that was not factual. She had enjoyed the attention, the pity and the support of other women. Morris actually deeply appreciated the visits and it enabled him to say a few things to Lydia that he wanted to say but could never get across. My visits continued until Morris made a commitment to Christ, was baptised and became a member of the church. Now Lydia was faced with an incredible problem. She had to change her attitudes! They were harder to change than Morris's and I had to have long counselling sessions with her before she became the Christian that she should be.

One of the most exciting aspects of ministry is to spend time helping people make the most of themselves and become the people that God intended them to be. The only thing better than actually counselling people is the work of training counsellors who will be able to multiply our effectiveness in helping people grow. Today 2000 counsellors help people because of the lessons I have learned.

At Wesley Mission, this one church has over 3,000 volunteers, headed by a great Adventist Christian, Mr Alan Bates. They contribute 8,000 hours each month of quality service, not counting any contribution to Parish service. This means 120,000 hours each year, which if done by staff would increase our salary bill by $1.5 million, which we could not afford! In Christian work the volunteer brings much more than personal help, financial support and physical labour. The volunteer also brings personal care, interest, prayer support and the fellowship of the whole church. The spiritual commitment of volunteers adds something beautiful to all your work.

Volunteer telephone counsellors, such as our 400 trained Lifeline Counsellors, who are on the telephones every hour of every day, accomplish what professional psychiatrists and psychologists never can do. This has been documented in medical journals. *American Health* (Mar.88) proclaims, 'in the body/mind economy the benefits of helping other people flow back to the helper. New research shows that doing good may be good for your heart, your immune system and your overall vitality.' Dr James House and colleagues of the University. Of Michigan have followed 2,700 adults for ten years and found that doing regular volunteer work in the community 'more than any other activity, dramatically increased vitality and life expectancy.' Men who did no volunteer work were 2 times more likely to die during the study period than men who did volunteer work at least once a week.

Dr Eileen Rockerfeller and Dr Allan Luks write, 'We could see a sudden rise of volunteerism. Good Samaritans might cease to be a rare breed. Just as people now exercise and watch their diets to protect their health, they may soon scrape peeling paint from their elderly neighbour's house, collect money for local charities, teach illiterates how to read, or clean up trash from a public park - all for the same self-protective reasons. Doing good for others is good for you.'

Volunteering is not a substitute for paid work and is undertaken without coercion. Organisations who are involved in the recruitment and referral of volunteers have noted that 52% of unemployed people placed in volunteer positions without coercion, go onto paid employment because of the benefits that they have derived from their Volunteer effort. These benefits include increased self esteem, improved or maintained skills, the learning of new skills and in the case of the long term unemployed youth, the development of a work ethic culture.

Every superintendent at Wesley Mission has had a huge load of experience in counselling troubled and distressed people. Often because the Superintendent has a high public profile, people come to him from all over the city in order to talk confidentially about their personal issues.

When Alan Walker was Superintendent he was overwhelmed by the amount of personal counselling that came to him and an idea came in 1961 to use the telephone to allow a 24 hr per day counselling program manned by volunteers to provide someone who could always be there when a desperate person needed help. The idea of a Christian counselling service received enthusiastic support from members of the church who undertook a training program in counselling. The re-construction of a Flinders street, Darlinghurst property began in 1961 and became the first Lifeline centre. The title of the service was given to it by the sub-editor of the Sydney Morning Herald who called this new telephone counselling service 'Lifeline'. Volunteers trained for 6 months in order to equip themselves to counsel people in all kinds of personal difficulties. Alan Walker opened the Lifeline Centre on Saturday 16th of March, 1963. Immediately the telephones began ringing. Each telephone counsellor worked a four-hour shift once a fortnight and summarised the details of every conversation. The following morning a small committee examined the reports and determined if any follow up support was needed. In the first year there were 11,600 calls.

The second call was answered by Ivan Reichelt, an elder from the 7pm congregation who was one of Lifeline's longest serving counsellors, having served for 26 years. He took the second call in and a man with a query in his voice asked, 'Do you know how many holes are in a crumpet?' The man was not a practical joker. He was a mentally sick man who desperately needed help and he was trying to describe his own feelings about himself. Alan Walker continued to be involved heavily in the training of counsellors from 1963 to 1978. Over 15 years he trained hundreds of counsellors.

The genius of Lifeline was that it had about it an anonymity people could ring without revealing who they were. It also had confidentiality because they knew that whatever they said to the counsellor would be kept strictly confidential. There was also the ubiquity of a telephone. People could turn to that phone wherever they were. Soon the 11,000 calls had reached 25,000 when I became the chairman of the Lifeline board and in 1979 took charge of the workings of Lifeline Sydney.

COUNSELLOR

By this time we had a large number of Lifeline centres around Australia and oversees. Today that number has grown to 270 cities in the world where there are Lifeline telephone counselling services. When I took over the leadership of Lifeline there were two very serious problems. The first was that the type of counsellor that had been trained in recent years which had come into Lifeline reflecting a Christianity that did not truly represent the evangelical commitment of Wesley Mission members. The result was that some of those counsellors were leading Lifeline away from its Christian basis. It was becoming a secular humanist advice line. The second problem was that Lifeline Sydney was running with poor management. This needed urgent attention.

The second problem was handled quickly. I terminated the existing management and appointed committed Christian management without personal problems and baggage that was complicating the previous management. And to help overcome the secular humanist thrust, moved the Lifeline centre from Darlinghurst , where it operated as an independent unit into Wesley Centre in Pitt Street where it was under our eye 24 hours per day.

With new staff, new enthusiasm and the direct oversight of Wesley Mission, Lifeline Sydney soon began to break all records for the numbers of people effectively helped. Soon we had topped 60,000 calls per annum.

By 1981 I was taking time to examine the nature of those who were calling Lifeline and the kind of problems that people were facing. Out of that we developed a whole series of new ministries. The greatest reason for people calling Lifeline in those days was what we described as social isolation - people who felt utterly alone, who had no one with whom they could relate or talk. Quite a number of these people were repeat callers who found a friend who was willing to give support and encouragement to them. We quickly learned to encourage those people to come to Wesley Missions Singles' Society or to become involved in some of the other activities of the Mission where they could meet with others. This had an interesting impact upon the life of the congregation because we very soon developed a large number of people attending services, groups and activities who could be described as being socially inept - good people but just unable to relate well with other people. This group of people rapidly increased as a percentage of the congregations particularly in the 3pm and 7pm services where our members were understanding and accepting of people who were different.

This was going to be very demanding upon the elders within the life of the church to provide support and encouragement for those who needed one-on-one support. A second group of callers were those who were so depressed with life that they could see no reason for continuing. These people were potential suicides. Some of these people did in fact commit suicide after ringing to give a final call and unfortunately in those days their number was unable to be traced. It is always distressing for a counsellor to counsel a person who suicides. I remember receiving a letter at home from a man who simply told me where he had left his will and possessions and asking me to explain why it was he was killing himself to the de-facto. He explained where his body would be found and requested me to go and speak to his partner who had been living with him and explain the facts to her. By the time I had received that letter the following day he was already dead. I notified the police about the location of the body.

Then I went and told his partner who was worried because he had not been home all night. She was so supported during the time of the funeral and thereafter that when I looked up on the first week of the next training course I saw her sitting in the front row. She became one of our regular and very reliable counsellors.

There were many other reasons why people rang Lifeline in those days. Some days there were family issues with people unable to cope with children and we often were able to refer these to our Dalmar Child and Family Care and provide volunteers who would come to their home and help them with the business of bringing up children. Others were suffering from mental illnesses such as Schizophrenia and severe depression or anorexia and we were able to tell those people that help was available in spite of the fact that they had no financial resources. We made it possible for those people to become patients within Wesley Hospital, a mental health hospital run by the Mission. Others suffered Post Traumatic Syndrome (such as former soldiers from the Vietnam conflict). We were able to give these special attention. Talk to any of our supporters and you will find an inspiring story of gratitude and hope.

Jim Tully's story began with traumatic nightmares until Wesley Mission helped change his life. Jim was only a boy of 15 when he joined the RAAF and later went on to serve in the Vietnam War. But in 1997 Jim began to relive the trauma of his war experience with the onset of Post Traumatic Stress Disorder or PTSD. As Flight Engineer Jim took more than 50 flights in an RAAF Hercules over Vietnam between 1966 and 1971. 'We flew in supplies and returned with wounded and dead soldiers. Many of the soldiers had no limbs because they'd been blown off by mines. After five years of that, it really got to me,' Jim said. The flights back and forth were very dangerous and according to Jim, there were some nasty incidents. 'I was lucky to get out of the war alive,' he said.

But it was not until almost 30 years later that the memories of his experiences became chronic. It was the recurrent nightmares that Jim found most difficult and in 2000 he sought help through the Wesley Veterans Health Services program. The program helped Jim using Cognitive Behaviour Therapy and Group Therapy. 'They went to great effort to explain what was going on, the effects of PTSD and what was to be done to help me handle the situation,' he said.

Jim's hobby for restoring 1940's era motorbikes was the catalyst for healing. He was asked to picture himself riding past the disturbing images in his mind and his nightmares ceased. 'I'd focus on getting on my motorbike and riding past the dead bodies to meet up with all my mates. There's been no recurrence of the nightmares since. I really love not having to wake up to something horrible,' he said. The bike that got him through his trauma was an antique British BSA J12 1936 model 500cc with green petrol tank. The bike has won six trophies. Since then he has rebuilt two more and is currently working on a 1929 model.

To show his thankfulness, Jim has become a Wesley Mission donor on a regular basis. 'Since the program, I've been told I am a changed man,' Jim said. 'One friend told me I had sparkling eyes. I feel reborn in a sense.' 'I believe donating regularly is the least I can do to support the good work of Wesley Mission'.

But I found another group of people who had consistent problems with their money. These were people who were running into debt, who were unable to control the new credit cards that were so freely being given out by banks and those people that were losing money because of increasing gambling on poker machines. I realised if Lifeline was to effectively continue its work it would need to develop a subsidiary series of specialised services.

We had YouthLine a programme that was organised and run by youth for youth. Eventually YouthLine handed over most of its activities to the Kids Help Line where it continues strongly to this day.

CreditLine was established to help use specialist counsellors with training in financial management, such as accountants, tax experts and bank managers. People often rang with very deep problems and then came with bundles of unpaid bills and accounts to work out their situation one-on-one with one of our face-to-face financial counsellors. The task of credit counselling is today an enormous one and the work has now spread to cover the entire nation. Every credit counsellor throughout Australia has access to a special hotline into our CreditLine when they have problems and need advice. Today, CreditLine is the largest financial counselling service in the nation. All the work with those who are deep in financial trouble is free.

In 1981, there was concern with the large number of immigrants in the community who were suiciding. I decided to establish Ethnic Lifeline, a service where we trained people from a score of nationalities and provided counselling in more than twenty languages plus a free interpreter service. This service took off like wildfire, not so much from people who wanted to commit suicide from different ethnic backgrounds but from people who wanted someone to translate the instructions on a new washing machine that they had purchased or to understand the ingredients in a packet from a supermarket. This free Ethnic Lifeline counselling and interpretation service eventually was taken over by the State Government and is run as a free government service providing interpretation to new arrivals who do not speak English.

In the middle 1980's a chance conversation with the then premier, Barry Unsworth, alerted me to a growing problem. Barry Unsworth indicated that his advisors had told him that gambling was going to become a major issue in society over the next ten years. He encouraged me to set up specialist counsellors just to deal with compulsive gamblers. These people needed strong psychological training as well as general counselling skills. I employed Mitchell Brown as the first full-time gambling counsellor in the nation. Today he has built up an enviable record as being the father of gambling counsellors throughout the nation. We have been responsible for training most of the gambling counsellors in the nation. We likewise provide a nationwide telephone service for counsellors in remote and rural areas. In recent days this work has expanded into various ethnic communities and we provide Korean and Chinese gambling counsellors to deal specifically with the problems from those communities. With the opening of the casinos not only has the number of compulsive gamblers increased, but also the State Government levy upon casino turn-over has meant that the Government (through the Casino Community Benefit Trust of which I have been a trustee since its incorporation), has been able to fund up gambling counselling across the state.

The old problem of suicide stayed with us. By 1990 I began to despair at the continuously increasing number of people who killed themselves each year. Because of the effectiveness of a campaign the Wesley Mission had run in 1979 to introduce seatbelts, .05 random breath testing and several other preventatives, the road toll in Sydney was being reduced year by year. The time came when suicide was the major cause of death outranking that of even road death among healthy Australians. Today 2800 people every year commit suicide and about 14 times that number contemplate or attempt it. That led us to set up a national strategy called Wesley Lifeforce Suicide Prevention Service.

Today in conjunction with local community groups we have conducted hundreds of seminars training tens of thousands of ordinary Australians to identify the signs of suicide and to take practical steps to help a person who may be a future victim. We recently conducted seminars in 64 country towns throughout Victoria and are at the moment completing hundreds of seminars covering every community in NSW.

The final area of work, which became a specialist support service to people in need, was the establishment of Wesley Legal Service. This is a service which has brought together a group of qualified barristers and solicitors who work for Wesley Mission and who take up the cause of people who have lost their homes, jobs and personal self worth because of their own stupidity in gambling. The numbers of people who lose their home and who face court because of gambling debts is enormous. Frequently their families are very severely disadvantaged because of the sickness of compulsive gambling.

Recently one of our solicitors reported to me that she had been preparing with a QC a fraud case where the client stole $900,000 from her employer and lost it all on poker machines. She is only a young woman who had a passion for tennis and loved walking her pet dog. Now she is in jail for a long period of time.

Our solicitor is also working with a prisoner at Emu Plains who stole $76,000 from her employer and put all of her money into poker machines. She is now doing two years prison and we are conducting an appeal on her behalf. Our solicitors also appeared on behalf of a young father who has three children under the age of five who received an over payment of $60,000 from Work Cover and did not return it. He spent the money on the poker machines and was to be sentenced to a prison term. Our legal team were eventually able to have him released on a 2 year bond and he went home tearfully to spend Easter with his wife and three young children.

We have been to court for a significant number of very elderly women all of whom have been aided by unscrupulous bank and club managers to mortgage their homes in order to get more cash to gamble in poker machines. Those managers were successfully taken to court, the gambling debts cancelled, the homes returned to the very foolish elderly women and the managers concerned both from the clubs and the banks were dismissed.

For 25 years every Tuesday Night I have been involved in training over 2000 people for our telephone counselling services. My name is in the telephone book with my telephone number prominently displayed because I believe that I should be available for people to ring in times of crisis. Consequently on many nights of the week I have calls at 2 or 3 am from people wanting to tearfully tell their tales of woe or of contemplated suicide or of a ruined life. I am glad that I am able to refer these people on to our counsellors who are available 24hrs per day and who have specialised training to help them at their point of deepest need.

Sir Alan Walker realised that the telephone was a powerful tool when it was linked to trained committed counsellors. Wesley Mission has provided free counselling services to more than 3 million people who have come to us for counselling through the telephone in the first instance but then in increasing numbers in face-to-face supportive work. We do this because it is part of our calling to provide a mantle of care over the streets of Sydney.

Pastoral Counselling

During my ministry at the Cheltenham Church of Christ, the load of people desiring counselling grew and my appointment book was filled up weeks in advance. I started making case notes of scores of people on 6′ x 8′ cards who had come to me for help. These notes were not for the use of anyone else but simply to record my approach with them and to enable me to ask myself questions such as when was I best able to help them? What were their common symptoms? What passages of scripture brought best results?

Everyone who came for a counselling session was sent away with an assignment. They had to work at a relaxing therapy, which I would write out for them or they had to undertake confidence-boosting exercises or they had to write lists of personal and hidden sins which were then destroyed. At the same time that they were watching the list of sins being flushed down the toilet, they had to take into their own soul the fact that their sins had been taken away from them through God's forgiveness. I wrote on cards spiritual exercises for people to undertake and then the following week at the next interview they would bring me their assignments completed. Many people found that they needed to do something like this in order to concentrate the mind and not allow the lessons learned in an hour of counselling to evaporate. I needed it as well so that I wouldn't fall into the trap of being just a giver of advice.

Preaching With Insight

As the workload in counselling developed I realised that I would need to develop new approaches to counselling. The first was what I called ' counselling as preaching'.

This was something totally new to me but which had been suggested by a study of the sermons of Norman Vincent Peale. People who don't know this amazing American's pastoral record tend to think of Norman Vincent Peale simply as the person who put together the *Power of Positive Thinking* and a dozen other best sellers. But Peale was a past master at taking common problems and then preaching on those problems so that hundreds of people could be counselled at the same time. In fact through his television and radio talks each week he was counselling more than a million people at any one time on a common issue. He built a wonderful centre combining techniques of psychology and religion headed by Dr Smiley Blainton.

As a suburban minister I started to develop my sermons along the line of counselling as preaching. I would take a common experience - say, the sense of inferiority or a person's lack of confidence, or a person's uncertainty about how to cope with stress - then develop the symptoms for causes, then look at the scriptural passages concerned with such issues and then reveal from the scripture how we could cope with such an issue. I suddenly found these sermons really gripped people. Hundreds of people wrote letters and made comments about how they had been personally helped. I also found that brought a deeper relationship between me as a minister and my members. They knew what they told me was kept in confidence but that the issue would be seriously considered as a common problem among people.

I brought a great deal of insight from the pastoral care of the church into the role of preaching, developing scriptural passages and looking at how the scripture guides us in coping with our deepest needs. Letters began to arrive in great numbers saying how for the first time people saw the relevance of scripture, saw their lives being changed because of what the scripture had to say in their particular hour of need. I preached sermons on how to control fear, calm anxiety, handle anger and aggression, dissolve frustration, defeat depression, strengthen inner weakness, cope with pressure and so on.

Rev. Dr Gordon Powell who was in St. Stephen's Church, Macquarie Street, Sydney, wrote a most encouraging letter that inspired me to go on. I then brought together some of these sermons and published them as little booklets. Thousands sold every month. Soon a hundred and fifty thousand of them had been sold. I then wrote the book *The Secret of Confident Living* to which Alan Walker wrote the foreword and Dr Norman Vincent Peale wrote to me, 'I have read with admiration your inspired book *The Secret of Confident Living* and I am impressed by the wisdom, sound guidance and the creative inspiration which it contains. This book has the thought substance and the motivational quality to make it a truly indispensable aid to successful living.' My preaching found wings. People asked me to preach on various topics and requested that I show from the Bible further practical aid to Christian living.

I followed this by a series of sermons on how to create a positive personality, looking at the issues of self-esteem, self-control, self-motivation, self-image, self-discipline and the like. Little booklets on these subjects sold by the tens of thousands and the book *Be A Winner - How to Create a Positive Personality* soon sold out. This was followed by another series called *Confidence in Time of Trouble* and so on. That book also sold well. As a result a professor at Oxford University wrote to tell me how his life had been improved simply by reading that book.

I had discovered, as preachers had before me, that the Bible is living when it is applied to the personal problems faced by people. I also found that as a counsellor much work could be done not just one-on-one but by talking to hundreds of people about the same issue. The answers then crossed all lines of denomination and geographical area.

The Cheltenham Christian Counselling Centre

One day one of the local doctors whom I'd met two or three times in the course of visiting people stood at the study door. Dr Rockford Stewart, a brilliant young physician in our community who was studying for his Fellowship for the Royal College of Physicians said simply, 'I've come to ask you a favour. I've heard you've had some training in psychology and that you counselled many people when you were at the Aradale Mental Hospital. I'm wondering if you could help some of my patients. They come to me for counselling and I recognise their symptoms but we physicians have only had about half a dozen lectures on psychology. For me the problem of influenza or tonsillitis or appendicitis is easy but some of this human psychology is just sheer guess work. I'm wasting my time and their time trying to help them out. I'm wondering if I could send some of my patients to you who need some counselling?'

I told him I would be happy to counsel any of his patients whom he thought might be helped by being sent to me but in return I wondered if he would take some of the patients I was seeing who needed some good old fashioned tender loving care from a physician. He agreed to do that and very soon we had a fine cross referral of patients going on.

Then Dr Gerald Duff, a long serving Catholic Doctor in our community asked me if I could discuss questions of the ethics of contraception with some of his patients. He said, 'All of my patients know what they can do but the real issue is whether they should; they want to talk out the issues of being Catholic and using contraception. Father Bracken would kill me if he knew I'd advised them to use contraception. But I don't suppose that would matter if they came and spoke with you.' So without meaning to I spent a lot of time counselling Catholic couples who had a conscience on the issue of contraception but nevertheless did not have any confidence in their ability to cope with additional children.

In those days when there were no medical benefits or Medicare such as we have today, Doctors did a lot of honorary work for the poor and I traded off some of the people who came to see me from Dr Gerald Duff with the comment 'I'll do a deal with you Dr Duff. I'll talk to your couples if you'll do some calls on some of my elderly who need some medical care.' Dr Duff readily agreed and so I handled the conscience issue of contraception and he handled the issue of tender loving care.

I then encouraged the church to buy a large house nearby and established in 1977 The Cheltenham Christian Counselling Centre. Mr Bill Fowler, a scholar principal gave educational guidance, other specialists gave vocational counselling, marriage counselling, emotional counselling and so on. Twenty years later a new Cheltenham Premises, headed by Mary Dewbury, marriage counsellor and Registered Psychologist, opened for business.

We have built Wesley Hospital and purchased Wandene Hospital and expanded into Wesley Mayo at Taree, the only free standing psychiatric Hospitals conducted by the Protestant Church anywhere in Australia and assembled one of the largest teams of psychiatrists and psychologists to provide professional services to people in need. I would meet regularly with these doctors to provide continuity of Christian service with our values being fulfilled through the professional skills of the medical team.

'The work of saving peoples' lives at our counselling and health services, goes on day in and day out. In fact I know of literally hundreds of people who have been saved from suicide and death because of this work.

Recently I interviewed a former patent Jean Loo on my television program. She said:
'My eating disorder had its roots when I was growing up and chose not eating to make a statement or as a cry for attention. But during the time I was 15-18, anorexia took over my life completely. I guess over the years my self-esteem began to erode, due in part to uncontrollable things that happened to me and perpetuated by the bad choices I made.

I tried to salvage this self-esteem through achievements – I thought that these could make me feel better and give me some semblance of self-worth. But one year I had everything

COUNSELLOR

– I was at the top of my school, I got my piano diploma and played in a national piano competition. I took part in a ballet performance and I was even featured in the newspapers for a paper I presented on gambling… You'd think, 'Wow, Jean… You must have been very happy then!'

Actually, I felt the lowest then… I had everything and they didn't satisfy… I grabbed on tighter to self-injury and anorexia to vent my frustrations, to exert control on the chaos I felt in my life. Anorexia was never about dieting; it was my voice, my silent rebellion against all the world. And then I came to Sydney to start Uni at 16 and all alone, without my family or friends, I took the chance to starve myself more. I got thrown into hospital again and again and eventually Wesley Private Hospital for the eating disorders program.'

'But even while in hospital, I felt I didn't deserve to be there, that I was just taking up someone else's space… Each time the doctors made me eat I would do so just so I could get out, but I would run into my room in tears and cut myself as a punishment. Each time I was thrown into hospital, I started planning how I would escape… in fact, I have such a bad track record of checking myself out of hospital soon after each admission!'

'It wasn't that the hospital was bad or anything – in fact, my team of health care professionals led by my psychologist Professor Touyz is as good as it gets and I really appreciate all they did, it's just that I was running away… I kept running away… from myself. Just had such a low self-esteem I didn't want to believe anyone cared anymore. I didn't want to believe I was deserving of life, or even of help anymore…'

'During one of my hospital admissions, a nurse called Pam lent me a Christian book on eating disorders. I found a Bible verse in there that spoke about my situation – Psalm 107:18-20 says, 'They hated all kinds of food and drew near the gates of death. Then they cried to the Lord in their trouble and He saved them from their distress. He sent His word to heal them and delivered them from their destructions.' I couldn't believe it… this book, this Bible, written more than 2000 years ago, had this strange description that seemed to summarise my life! It said God could take me out of my living hell… was that true? I believed in it for a while and cried my heart out… but the next day, as per usual, I checked myself out of hospital.'

'I was in and out of hospital another 2 times after that… on the very last time, on the day I ran away from hospital, I didn't feel like going home. I had to go by the Town Hall train station to get home and so decided to stop at Wesley Mission across the road. I ended up in Wesley Theatre, I looked across at the rows of seats and spotted some people I knew, having attended church before.'

'These were people with such peace in them, such love overflowing to others, such confidence… Because I've grown up going to church, I knew exactly why they were like that… Such peace, such love, such assurance could only come from their relationship with Jesus Christ… I wanted that so badly… I finally decided that more than anything else I wanted to be at peace, to have a life worth living, to be able to make an impact on this society…

If Jesus was the only way, then from that day on He could take away all my guilt and be the leader of my life.'

'I made my commitment to Christ in an evening service. Not that it was all smooth going from that day on. I didn't self-injure or throw up or starve myself, but I often ended up crying and crying, curled up alone on the floor. But then, on the floor was the best position for me to get on my knees and cry out to God and even though I thought every day would be my last day following Christ because it was so hard, God was faithful and pulled me to my feet the next morning.'

'I got involved in church and for the first time in my life I wasn't doing it out of duty, but because I really wanted to! I attended every church service I could and at every opportunity took my Bible out so I could read about who God was. I soon discovered that who I was did not depend on what I did but on what Jesus Christ has already done by dying for me on the cross. I realised that He loved me so much, the value He put on my life was His own life... If He thought that was how much I was worth, it didn't really matter how much I weighed or whether I got a High Distinction on my uni exams! And when I finally realised that, I could chuck out my weighing scales – I was free at last! Free to eat chocolates! Free to enjoy life! Free to be me!'

'I guess my message is that no one is too far, too hopeless for God to help. I thought I was pretty badly off and kept telling my doctors, 'I don't care anymore... I'm gonna die from my eating disorder. So what?' I never expected to survive past the year, what's more to be living without an eating disorder! But the Bible says that God's hand is not too short to save and if He could do it for me, He can do it for you too – God is no respecter of man that He would do it for one person only. If you cry out to Him, if you decide to acknowledge Jesus as your Lord and Saviour, He promises to take you out of the pit of despair and make you new.'

It would also be my task to train others in the arts of counselling. My series of twenty four lectures, 'Counselling with the Insights of Jesus' has now been conducted more than thirty-six times, each of these courses taking more than five months and attended by an average of 70 to 80 trainee counsellors. I have trained more than two thousand counsellors in Sydney.

But volunteer counsellors need leadership by serving professionals. At Wesley Mission we employ scores of Psychologists, Psychiatrists, marriage guidance counsellors, family therapists and so on. It is my responsibility to get have the vision to see new areas requiring development and to raise the resources to employ professional staff at proper rates of pay.

Because of continuous media exposure (40 years on television and radio), I receive a huge amount of mail from all over Australia. They contain an amazing and complex series of personal problems. Most weeks I receive over a 1000 letters a week addressed to me. We employ one woman just to open envelopes and decide where to direct the letters. I have three secretaries to help me write replies.

They write personal introductions and conclusions and them incorporate the most appropriate of many responses I have written on that particular theme. One man, a trained counsellor of thirty years standing, does nothing else except answer the hundreds of e-mails and internet letters that come from all over to world. On radio there is further opportunity for counselling.

There is probably no better opportunity for a counsellor than through the anonymity of talkback radio. Done seriously and well, a late night program has powerful effects. Although I only allow one hour of my four hour weekly program for such counselling, I do take other time, each week, to touch one of fifty issues a year, thus, I cover in an introductory statement. fifty significant issues. For twenty years Sunday Night Live was the most listened to religious program in Australia. I have invited several psychologists and psychiatrists to do segments with me, but although their professional skills were great, I have not yet found a psychologist who is a good broadcaster.

In the late 1980's I experimented with preaching, teaching and counselling every week, on radio through a true story of how I dealt with some presenting problem, which I knew statistically would be in the personal experience of several thousand listeners or their family members. Their stories are quiet, positive, affirming and insightful. One book of them has been published. My stories, set in a pastoral context are the single highest rating half-hour on 2GB for any day, morning, afternoon or evening, by any presenter. People love stories. They concerned real people (but not their real names), their problems, how I responded to them and the ensuing result - often with a surprising twist!

When Jesus was to be born it was said by Isaiah 'His name shall be called Wonderful Counsellor, The Mighty God, The Prince of Peace.' In all the years of teaching *Counselling with the Insights of Jesus* I have come to realise what a wonderful Counsellor Jesus was, how practical his teaching is at helping people handle daily pressures and stress and what a difference this Wonderful Counsellor can make in the lives of people who turn to him in times of trouble.

FUNDRAISER

Chapter Ten

Billy Graham once told me that if I were absolutely honest, God would allow a lot of money to pass through my fingers- provided none of it stuck to them! Yet, when I commenced as Superintendent of Wesley Mission, following my appointment in December 1977, the first challenge that stood out was debt. Debt was written everywhere.

I had previously learnt to cope with debt in church life. In fact in each of the churches where I had ministered (the slums, the rural sector and the suburbs), the churches had debts. The big debt at Cheltenham when I started, which was equivalent to 10 years' total income, was so big that I indicated to the Board that I saw I would do nothing else in my ministry except to work to build up the church so that we could pay our debts. I indicated that if nothing else happened I would at least leave the church debt free. That would happen of course, but in the mean time the church grew so large that we spent several million dollars in development, growth and new buildings. None of it 'stuck' and God allowed the money to flow.

At Wesley Mission the same old problem of debt raised its ugly head. The only problem was it wasn't as easy to see and realise as it had been in the simple accounting systems of the other churches. The accounting system at Wesley Mission was horrendously complex. There was nothing about it that was not true and accurate but that it was just so complex that no one seemed to be able to understand the total picture. Certainly members of the Wesley Mission Executive did not understand the problem.

I knew we had some debts because of our new building for the homeless. It was built to get them out of the smelly rabbit warren where the homeless lived in huge dormitories on Francis Street. The debt on our new centre to house homeless people in Darlinghurst had reached $1.4 million by the end of my first year. This was due to extremely bad weather, a complexity of construction that was not foreseen by the architects and a very large number of disputes with our builders. We didn't have the cash on hand to be able to pay the bills. Fortunately face-to-face meetings with Mr Alan Kell of Kell & Rigby saw the builders write off many of these charges. Alan was a good man, but I argued as one with his back to the wall.

There was also an old debt on Wesley Centre of one and a quarter million dollars following its rebuilding by Alan Walker. Then I discovered he had lent a quarter of a million dollars to the Lyceum Property Trust, which had no hope of ever repaying! This trust was in debt and it owed Wesley Mission a quarter of a million dollars - money we would eventually write off.

There was a very large debt and future potential debts within our Aged Care Division for heavy maintenance on our hostels and nursing homes, some of which had not been upgraded for years.

There was also an operational debt, which simply meant that we were spending more money each week than we had coming in. This debt reached a crisis the week I began. We had a cash deficit. We were able to pay the next round of salaries but could not pay the salaries of our staff in two weeks time. That was an instant cash flow crisis. An immediate decision was needed. I ordered our staff to sell an orchard at Galston, the house at Gordon and the campsite at Leura. That helped an immediate need and kept us going the first year.

The financial accounts were extremely complex and confusing. In spite of having done some study in basic accounting and broadsheet accounting, I could not make head nor tail of them. What was more troubling was the attitude of senior management. Their answer to everything was simply to cut expenses by slashing staff. This meant staff other than themselves. There was a huge outcry when I suggested that we keep everybody on staff but that we all take a salary cut of an equal percentage. The answer of the Senior Staff was that other people had to go.

To make matters worse I saw little hope of raising money quickly. The records were poor and many of the donors on our records were, in fact, dead. I checked on our addresses and data file and found them to be so out of date it was useless. The first couple of weeks at Wesley Mission saw the word 'debt' come up time and again in conversations. It was a very worrying moment. We had bank overdrafts but we were not sure how much money we had actually drawn down. The books were in bad condition. Alan Walker wrote and apologised for the bad state of all of our records and account keeping.

In those first weeks I also found I had to face the resignation of some key people. Mr Peter Tebbutt, who had negotiated our call to the Mission, had resigned from his position as the Honorary Secretary. The Senior Minister Rev. Alan Jackson, on whom I was relying greatly to help us settle in to our ministry, had resigned from his position to accept a call from Alan Walker to head up his World Evangelism Ministry, which was also going to be headquartered in Sydney.

A new Honorary Secretary, Keith Walkerden, who had just been appointed, was then appointed by his company to become the Chief Executive of Olivetti, United Kingdom, and would be required to shift in the near future. Only Dr Jim Pendlebury, our Honorary Treasurer, remained. Even some members of our Board indicated that they had served with Alan Walker over many years and they felt that it was time that they too should resign. I felt abandoned!

Little did I know it but that was the best thing that could have happened for me. It meant that I had to immediately get to work, meet people I had never met before, sum them up and build a new team of leadership who would work with me. What an opportunity to start with a clean slate. Most of the new people whom I then appointed have served with me ever since.

I had a couple of basic principles concerning debt in my mind. The first one was that the Church should not be in debt at all. The second one was that the only way we would ever get out of debt was by hard work. I remembered my mother when she took over the business following my father's sudden death when I was aged eight. She had four little children, the youngest having just been born. The business was heavily in debt. She organised other people to care for her children and she worked night and day in order to turn the business around. I grew up sitting at the table with my widowed mother counting the day's takings from the bakery business and listening to her talk about her plans. I counted all the coins. I learned that lots of small pieces of money could make a large amount to go to the bank.

I realised the first thing that I should understand was the true financial picture of Wesley Mission. I needed to get someone who was extraordinarily good at understanding financial pictures of companies. Several people recommended to me Professor A.H. Pollard of Northwood. Professor Pollard was the Professor of Economics and Actuarial Studies at Macquarie University. My soon to depart, newly elected Honorary Secretary, Keith Walkerden, took me to his home and I took with me a huge box containing all the financial statements, annual reports and other relevant financial information. I had never met Professor Pollard before. After introductions I told him my predicament and asked if he could work through the financial reports of Wesley Mission and tell me the true financial picture. He willingly agreed to do so and indicated a time when we could meet a week later. I was impressed with Professor Pollard's sharpness of mind, of the questions he asked me and of his genial spirit.

A week later I met with him alone and he returned the big box of financial papers. He looked at me with a twinkle in his blue eyes and said, 'Do you want the good news or the bad news?' I looked back at this man; my heart had already warmed to him. Little did I know that we were to commence the most personal deep friendship that could exist between two people that would last for the next 23 years, until his untimely death.
'Well', he repeated. 'Do you want the good news or the bad news?' I replied to

him, straight forward, 'Give me the bad news. I can cope with the good news at any time but right now I have to get to work on the bad news.' Professor Pollard replied, 'Well, Wesley Mission is technically bankrupt. You have not got enough cash in hand to pay the salaries of your staff and your work is heavily in debt.' I said to him, 'Well what is the good news?' He replied with his eyes twinkling, 'Your books are in such a bad shape that no one will ever know!' That was the good news. We were broke but no one knew it. I said to him, 'What must I do first?' He replied, having already worked out an answer, 'You must get a loan of at least a quarter of a million dollars to pay your staff salaries. I have already gone ahead and made an appointment for you on Thursday with the Chief General Manager of the Commonwealth Bank on the corner of Martin Place and Pitt Street. I have told him about your need but you will have to tell him your terms and conditions.'

On Thursday I nervously stepped out with Professor Pollard down Pitt Street to the great imposing columns of the bank's head office. Although new to Sydney, I recognised this building instantly. Every child in Australia once had a tin moneybox with the picture of this huge building on it. I was going to meet the Chief General Manager.

He welcomed us into his office. He was benign and genial just like bank managers used to be in that era before banks became so unpopular. He settled me down, personally served a cup of coffee and after some warm chitchat came round to say, 'Now how can I help you?' His smile and warmth of character made it appear like the bank was in business to do nothing else but to help its customers.

Professor Pollard had told me that I was the leader of the work and it was up to me to tell my story and to do the arrangements. He held no position at Wesley Mission and was merely a friend who was trying to help a young man come to grips with his future. I cleared my throat and looked at the Chief General Manager. 'I want to borrow a quarter of a million dollars. We have a cash crisis, which I believe we will overcome. We have plenty of assets in buildings, nursing homes, hospitals and children's homes but I can't sell any property because we have very vulnerable people living in them. If I can get a loan of a quarter of a million dollars, without the normal security for a number of years, I will promise you that every cent will be repaid as soon as I can get this Mission back on its financial feet.'

The Chief General Manager smiled broadly. 'Is that all, a quarter of a million dollars?' I suddenly realised I had the money and with the courage that's only found in a very young man, I added, 'Yes, a quarter of a million dollars, but I want you to lend it to me at no interest whatsoever.' He smiled from behind his chair and tapped the tips of his fingers together. 'I am prevented by legislation from lending it to you without charging interest. But the bank normally helps charities with a donation or two from time to time. If you are prepared to accept the fact that the Commonwealth Bank of Australia will not give you any donations for your work I am prepared to lend you a quarter of a million dollars at 1% for the next 10 years.' I could not believe my ears. We had a quarter of a million dollars at only 1%!

I was able to get the financial position of the Mission straightened much more quickly than I anticipated and within three years we had generated enough surplus to not only clear out our debts but we could even pay that quarter of a million dollar loan. Again, Professor Pollard gave me advice which I will never forget. 'Repay it? Repay a quarter of a million dollar loan, which you have got at only 1% for another seven years? You will not! No, although you can pay the bank the quarter of a million dollars, you should take that quarter of a million dollars, go down to the bank and place it on deposit with them at 8%.' Professor Pollard was teaching me, one-on-one, a few lessons in economics.

After we had left the bank on that day when I first borrowed the money, I asked Professor Pollard would he consider giving the time in all of his acute busyness to becoming the Honorary Secretary of Wesley Mission. I explained to him that we were not in a position to pay any expenses and yet the job would involve him with more than ten hours of work a week. He replied with a typical response, 'No expenses and ten hours a week? All my life I have been looking for a job like that!' So Professor Pollard became our Honorary Secretary and with Dr Jim Pendlebury, our Honorary Treasurer, we met together on a weekly basis in the closest of friendships for the next 23 years.

So we were in the position to pay our staff their salaries, but the underlying problems were not yet solved. I didn't believe you solved the problem of a cash shortfall by terminating staff. That was the view of the then General Manager. My approach was to find ways to raise more income. So we were in conflict. I was deeply troubled with the thought of staff being terminated, the personal and family difficulties that they would face upon being dismissed and the mortgages they had to face.

It came home to me in a most personal fashion. We hadn't been long in the Mission when my daughter developed a friendship with a young administrative assistant who worked as administrative assistant to Dr Keith Suter. Ron Schepis and Jenny became close friends. I had first noticed them in the restaurant having lunch together. I realised that the enthusiasm that Jenny had showed coming in to visit her father at head office was not just to see me. They were in love and eventually they got engaged.

It wasn't long after their engagement that I found out what happened next. It followed the annual general meeting when I reported that the debts were still in existence and that it was taking a little time to financially turn the Mission round. The General Manager at the time brought me a list of staff members who should be dismissed in order to cut costs and at the head of the list was the name of Ron

Schepis. He said with a shrug of the shoulders as though to test me, 'The last one on should be the first one off.'

I knew I couldn't allow my daughter's love for the young man stop me making a right decision. I called Ron into my office and told him that because of the financial position he would either have to be terminated or else I would do my best to relocate him in another area of our Mission work. Ron, with characteristic good nature, understood and accepted the situation. It was a much more difficult task to announce and explain to Jenny at the tea table that night. I explained to her and to the other children as best I could the trouble we had with our finances and how I was working to overcome them. But in the meantime I had to cut our head office costs and this meant that some staff would either have to be retrenched or else moved to another section of our work where there may be a vacancy. It was not a very happy tea table discussion. The children naturally thought that because I would have to make the decision I could favour Ron, whom they all loved greatly. They didn't realise that in leadership one has to show fairness and impartiality, even when someone you love is involved.

As it happened I was able to place Ron in our work with the homeless. The young administrator now began to work with social welfare. Ron was to eventually go to TAFE to do night courses and graduate in the field of social work. This was a much better outcome than working as an administrative assistant in head office, but Ron had no sooner graduated in social work than he felt he wanted to be closer to people and so started studying nursing. He graduated from his general nursing course at Concord Hospital as a registered nurse. He worked at Concord Hospital and now had dual qualifications in social work and in nursing.

A couple of year's later Ron felt the call to train for the ministry and with my son David went to the Carlingford Theological College of Churches of Christ. Over the next three years they studied together, worked as student ministers and eventually graduated with their university degrees in theology. By this time Ron and Jenny married, shifted to Keilor in Melbourne, where they undertook a ministry in a local parish, returning later to serve at the Church of Christ, Pendle Hill, and is today ministering in a dual role as a psychiatric nurse and a chaplain to our Wesley Hospital and Wandene Private Hospital and in our mental health counseling services.

I never knew the end of the story until just before their wedding about the year when we were in so much debt at Wesley Mission that I had to move staff to other positions. Shortly before their wedding Beverley said to Jenny, 'You remember your bankbook we gave you when you turned 21? Where is that now? I am wondering how much money we have saved over the years?' Beverley and I had started the bank account for each of our children when they were born. Throughout their early childhood we had put money into the bank accounts every week. They also saved their school bank money and put it into the same bank account and as the years went by, with accumulated interest and regular deposits throughout their teenage years from their own pocket money and from other gifts that we had placed there, the bank accounts had grown substantially. Now Jenny was about to be married and as her parents our great delight was to be able to see that the money saved over the previous 21 years would help in the start of their married life.

Jenny mentioned she didn't know where her bankbook was, it was just somewhere in her room. Beverley insisted that she find it, and find it she did. When Beverley opened the book her expression changed. Stamped across every page was 'cancelled - account closed'. What happened? Jenny blushed and appeared very embarrassed. Ron explained, 'Do you remember when Wesley Mission was in such dire financial stress that you had to cut back on staff?' I nodded. 'Well, Jenny told me that she had this money in her bank account. We talked it over and she has decided to give it all to the Mission so that the poor and homeless would not suffer. It was not much compared to the need but...'

We couldn't believe our ears. We had hoped that they would be able to start off their married life at least having a substantial amount in the bank so that they would not have to scrape and save as we had when we were married. We were immensely proud of our kids. It was her money and she had decided to give it to Wesley Mission to help us out of our financial need. It was only through the sacrificial giving of many people that we eventually turned our financial position around. I got a cash flow going through hiring myself out to speak to corporations. We improved our congregational support by running a stewardship campaign. We built a better image through our radio, television, magazines and videos sold. We also sold our services: those things that we could do well in caring for people.

I also developed a program to encourage people to leave us something of their estate through their wills. And I wrote many letters asking people to donate to our work. As our teenage family grew over the years, they were quite used to Dad sitting of a nighttime in the lounge room while the family watched television, personally signing hundreds of letters. Because I always used a fountain pen and ink I would lay out each one so the signature would dry without being smudged.

Beverley also did her bit to help us out of the financial crisis. She became the honorary President of the Spring Fair Fundraising Committee and built a body of 400 volunteers who knitted and sewed, made and cooked to sell goods to raise money for every part of our work. Over the next 17 years she and her team of dedicated and wonderful volunteers raised more than three and a half million dollars to help us meet the needs of people in Sydney.

The work at Wesley Mission continued to flourish and grow. I remember well the year we reached an income of $5 million and it has continued to grow every year until this current year our income has reached $160 million. We have built Wesley Centre and redeveloped the whole of our Pitt Street and Castlereagh Street properties at the cost of $300 million and opened them debt free. We have built more than a hundred million dollars worth of retirement villages to house retired people in our community and we have opened them debt free. We have bought and built and leased more than 400 buildings and we have no debt on any of them.

We are today the largest provider of community services to people in New South Wales and our work stands debt free. The fear of debt made my mother work hard and I absorbed her commitment to be debt free. I believe that responsible debt such as for a house is OK, but as for the rest I prefer to pay cash!

I have always been proud to be called 'one of Australia's greatest fundraisers', for fundraising is an essential part of ministry. We live beneath the trinity of corruption: money, sex and authority. A willingness to give holds the answers to negating all three. Money no longer holds us if we first give our money to God. Sex no longer dominates our thinking if we first of all give it to God. Authority no longer makes us its slaves if we submit our lust for power to God. When we learn to give to God, we discover our inner resources of poise, peace and power.

Our world's strategy is built upon the necessity of us gaining more and more things. The advertising industry is built upon the premise that we must be persuaded to purchase what we do not want, with money we do not have, to satisfy a hunger that does not exist. When we consider how to fund the Christian cause, the great temptation is to concentrate on more ways of raising money rather than in considering what is God's call to responsible giving. Our concern is with the mechanics of getting instead of the motivation for giving, for slicker strategies of fund raising rather than for the spiritual significance of our stewardship.

One of my sons kept homing pigeons. The pigeons were born in their coops but the day came for them to be released. It takes a great act of faith to release birds that once were featherless and bare in your hands, but it is the nature of pigeons to fly free. He released them from their coops and they circled in the sky, coming down, not to re-enter their coops, but to sit on the rooftops, the fences and the trees. From every vantage point the pigeons watched as I considered ways of recapturing them and placing them back in their coops. I thought of large fine nets strung between long poles, of setting bird traps, of climbing roofs to frighten the birds down...and while I was thinking of more sophisticated and complex methods to recapture the pigeons, my son scattered some food inside the coop and they all flew in!

He gave and the birds returned to him faithfully. I was spending my efforts on structures, strategies and systems. I had failed to remember: 'Give and it shall be given to you, pressed down, shaken together and running over.' Stewardship is not a matter of strategies to get, but of remembering to give God's food. Many fundraisers concentrate on strategies: direct mail, appeals by media, special solicitation, telephone appeals, estate planning and deferred giving, stewardship dinners and the like, but here, I want to start by considering God's call to responsible giving.

Jesus understood the seduction of things and of the liberation that comes through a right handling of the things we possess. That is why sixteen of his thirty-eight parables were concerned with how we handle our money and possessions. That is why one out of every ten verses in the Gospels (288 in total) deal directly with how we gain, save and use our possessions. It is said that the Bible has about 500 verses about prayer, 500 verses about faith and about 2000 verses on how we acquire and use our money and possessions. That is one of the great tests of our spirituality.

The one saying of our Lord that Paul taught the young church that was not recorded in the Gospels was, 'Our Lord Jesus Himself said, 'It is more blessed to give than receive.' (Acts 20:35). The scriptures indicate how giving provides us with freedom. Giving denies materialism its illusion.

I was driving down a toll-way towards the tollgates when I was passed, fast, by a red Ferarri. It took me miles before I caught him! But at the tollgates I read the bumper sticker: 'He who has the most toys when he dies wins'. Right? Wrong! I have conducted funeral services for more than one thousand people and I have never seen a hearse followed by a 'U- Haul' trailer. You cannot take it with you! One hour after death other people are fighting over the red Ferarri.

Materialism is an illusion, giving a feeling of permanence to a transient generation. Materialism is the ultimate misuse of God's gifts. Stewardship is using God's gifts. Our giving places our living into perspective and breaks the illusion of materialism. Giving denies acquisitiveness its seductiveness. When you learn to give, you free yourself from the seductiveness of acquisitiveness. By nature we are hoarders and our primal insecurities demand that we gather more and more things, as if ultimate security lies in the piles of possessions. But Jesus cut through the seductiveness of things, telling us of a successful man whose whole life was spent in the acquiring of more and more symbols of his success. He built bigger and bigger barns to store his hoard, saying, 'Take life easy; eat, drink and be merry'. But one night God said, 'You fool, this very night your life will be demanded from you. Then who will get what you have prepared for yourself?' This is how it will be with anyone who stores up things for himself but is not rich toward God.' (Luke 12:20)

In the ruins of Pompeii, archaeologists found the body of a man who, instead of fleeing from the ashes of Mt Vesuvius, had waited to gather his gold and was suffocated reaching out for gold coins that had fallen from the bag clutched in his bony fingers. He couldn't take it with him, but further, it had stopped him from escaping and cost him his life. He choked, not on volcanic ash but on gold dust. Jesus had said, 'What good is it for a man to gain the whole world and to forfeit his soul?' (Mark 8:32)

Giving denies greed its pleasure. Those who gain do so because of the pleasure in greed. The scriptures never hide the pleasures that exist in sin for a time, but turn people to the longer view of the lasting values. The satisfying of immediate hungers is a sign of our instant age: instant food, instant coffee, instant mashed potatoes, fast food, fast cars, fast sex, drugs, alcohol, nicotine-gratification now!

The quick fix is followed by despair and hunger until the next quick fix. But when a person learns to deny themself and to give of themselves and what they possess, they discover the lasting joy of giving. Giving denies greed its short-term pleasure for lasting satisfaction. Paul said, 'For the love of money is the root of all kinds of evil. Some people, eager for money, have wandered from the faith and pierced themselves with many griefs.' (1 Timothy 6:10)

Responsible giving is our response to the calls about us. We face the reality of poverty. Poverty in Third World countries assails us from television and magazines as we see pictures of children with thin legs and bloated bellies. But poverty is real in the USA, Australia and other developed countries and in the inner cities and the rural areas. A 1994 Gallup Poll discovered that 23% of adults always have difficulty in meeting their monthly repayments and another 27% frequently have difficulty meeting their commitments, so over half the adult population cannot make their monthly commitments without a serious struggle. Christians give to relieve poverty. From the very first days of the Church, giving to aid the widows and orphans became a practice. We are called not only to words of salvation, but deeds of service.

We face the need of ministry. Every one of us knows the need that exists for an expanded ministry in the name of Christ: in worship, health, welfare, education, mission, witness and proclamation. The needs of the world become more pressing and we must give to meet the needs of an ever-expanding ministry. We face the cost of opportunity; to fund the Christian challenge is to face the cost of opportunity. Visionary people can see what can be done in the name of Christ and so we joyfully count the cost.

Faced with the reality of poverty, the need of ministry and the cost of opportunity, Wesley Mission Sydney uses all means to fund the Christian challenge. No one method dominates. We are responsible for the largest Christian welfare ministry among the poor undertaken by any one church in the world. Each year, in round terms, we fund it by raising $2 million by direct mail, $4 million through wills and estates, $2 million through tithes and offerings, $1 million through auxiliaries and fund-raising groups, $10 million through the sales of our services, $2 million through corporate donations, $1 million through television and radio programs, $2 million from the sale of orange juice from a citrus orchard we run,

$1million through sales of video and audio tapes and so on and the rest on selling our services in caring for people, reaching a budget of $150 million. Yet our earnest commitment and business endeavours have enabled us to build and pay for $340 million of building extensions; plus $100 million in hospitals and aged care facilities and $300 million in our Church and office block.

Throughout my ministry, I have given leadership to the raising of about $600 million to enable a local church to complete its ministry. By God's grace and the people's faithfulness, we are meeting the reality of poverty, the needs of ministry and the cost of opportunity. During my past twenty-six years in the one church, we have had a total income in excess of one billion dollars, more than any other church in the world.

Rarely have we been given large benefactions. Once, a businessman became impressed with the earnestness of our ministry and sent me a cheque for $5000. He was so overjoyed with my response and delight that he sent a second for $95,000! Twice, people who never attended my church listened to me faithfully on my weekly radio programs and they gave two large donations – Jack Richardson gave over $11 million in two cheques and Barney Horne gave us $11 million in his will.

Once I visited with a Board of a large steel manufacturing company, BHP and presented them with plans for ways in which they could help us with a donation of $30,000. The Chairman eventually agreed and indicated it would come to us over three years. I explained why that was an inadequate gift for such a great corporation and I couldn't accept it. When asked why, I explained I would be embarrassed to say such a big company could give so little. I was asked what would be a reasonable gift, so I replied, '$30,000 a year for 3 years.' He said he couldn't make it $90,000, but agreed that $100,000 over three years sounded better.

In my early ministry I organised large dinners, with the largest number of people possible attending, and ask them all to provide the funds for the Church's ministry. For twenty-five years in each of my four ministries I used the banquet format to challenge people to give. Then Professor Alf Pollard suggested he organise small lunches of a dozen or so corporate leaders. This was to introduce me to the significant leaders of the Sydney business scene and to allow me to present our needs. I would follow up each luncheon with a call and a visit and hundreds of thousands of dollars were raised by our partnership.

For fifteen years I then used the boardroom table that I had designed for the new Wesley Centre. It seated twenty-two. Our restaurant did the well-presented catering. The boardroom was hung with five original artworks. Our own Wesley Centre staff demonstrated the art of waiting on tables. I wrote and invited each person to come. About eight were leaders of business who already financially supported us. In between them at the table were another eight whom I was hoping to impress to support us. Scattered about were five of my key general or group managers. The luncheons began and finished exactly on time. I would open with grace, then tell everyone this was part of our long term fundraising strategy but that no one would be asked for a commitment then and there. I would ask, seemingly at random, those who were already financial supporters to explain their business. Without being asked they would always go on to talk about what they do to help Wesley. They typically praised us without reservation and spoke of how their social responsibility was exercised through Wesley. I would invite four or five to just talk on while we ate. Then perhaps the appropriate staff member to explain the difference that support meant to them and the people we helped.

I would ask then a few who were not financial supporters to tell us about their work. They would talk up big their achievements and how now they were in a position to give back to the community and, of course, it was intended to be through Wesley. I would describe two or three needy areas and before the luncheon desert was served these needs were met. I wrote and thanked everyone. Our existing donors liked others hearing of their support, the non-givers liked their peers to hear of their promises of support, our staff were brought into a personal contact with companies they would now visit and I would rather smugly note the results. Fundraising is fun! The newly appointed head of one of Australia's largest banks wrote to me after last month's executive luncheon: 'In my work I have attended hundreds of executive luncheons and fundraising dinners, but yours was the most enjoyable one I have ever attended. You can count on our support and I hope you will invite me again.'

But we rarely have large sums given to our work. The profile of our donors rests heavily on the faithfulness of little old ladies, who give their mite, and businessmen, whom I reach by a continuous round of business conferences and seminars. Responsible giving is God's response to us. 'God so loved the world that He gave His only son.' (John 3:16; Rom 8:32; 2 Cor. 9:15). The giving of His Son was the ultimate gift of many that God in his grace bestows upon us.

'For you know the grace of our Lord Jesus Christ, that though He was rich, yet for your sakes He became poor, so that you, through his poverty, might become rich.' (2 Cor 8:9); 'Every good and perfect gift, is from above.' (James 1:17)

But what other gifts does God give? The satisfaction that comes from honest labour is one mentioned in scripture. 'That everyone may eat and drink and find satisfaction in all his toil - this is the gift of God'. 'Moreover, when God gives any man wealth and possessions and enables him to enjoy them, to accept his lot and be happy in his work - this is the gift of God.' (Eccles. 3:113; 5:19)

Salvation is another gift of God mentioned in scripture. 'But the gift is not like the trespass, for if the many died by the trespass of the one man, how much more did God's grace and the gift that came by the grace of the one man Jesus Christ, overflow to the many. Again, the gift of God is not like the result of one man's sin; the judgement followed one sin and brought condemnation, but the gift followed many trespasses and brought justification. For if by the trespass of the one man death reigned through that one man, how much more will those who receive God's abundant provision of grace and of the gift of righteous reign in life through the one man Jesus Christ'. 'For it is by grace you have been saved, through faith - and this not from yourselves, it is the gift of God.' (Rom 5:15- 17; Eph 2:8).

Eternal life is another gift of God mentioned in scripture: 'Jesus answered her, 'If you knew the gift of God and who it is who asks you for a drink, you would have asked Him and He would have given you living water.' 'Whoever drinks the water that I give Him will never thirst.' (John 4: 10,14) 'For the wages of sin is death, but the gift of God is eternal life in Christ Jesus our Lord.' (Rom 6:23)

The Holy Spirit is another gift given by God: 'You will receive the gift of the Holy Spirit.' (Acts 2:38, 10:45) Jesus said, 'If you then, though you are evil, know how to give good gifts to your children, how much more will your Father in heaven give good gifts to those who ask Him.' (Matt 7:11)

Through the Holy Spirit, we are also given gifts and graces - charismata - that equip us for our Christian witness, worship and work. Those gifts and graces are necessary for us to complete the Christian challenge ahead of us and God gives us the resources that will be required. 'If God is for us, who can be against us? He who did not spare His own son, but gave Him up for us all - how will He not also, along with Him, graciously give us all things?' (Rom 8:32) Responsible giving is our response to God.

We are to give of ourselves wholeheartedly: 'Therefore I urge you brothers, in view of God's mercy, to offer your bodies as living sacrifices, holy and pleasing to God - this is your spiritual act of worship.' (Rom 12:1)

God desires our offerings. The comments Jesus made about the Jewish practise called 'Corban', was not about making an offering, but about people who put restrictions upon their offerings. (Matt 23:18-19). Our responsibility was to give to God our offerings without strings attached. Responsible giving starts with our tithes and offerings.

That is God's by right. The first fruits belong to him. Tithing started when Abel commissioned it, Abraham commenced it, Jacob continued it, Moses confirmed it, Malachi commanded it, Jesus commended it and Paul communicated it. Tithing was God's key to your successful personal finances. Tithing puts God first, makes you budget in discipline, involves your family as a team, frees you from the great dollar hang-up, proves the reality of your faith and releases the promises of God. 'A tithe of everything from the land, whether grain from the soil, or fruit from the trees, belongs to the Lord; it is holy to the Lord. If a man redeems any of his tithe, he must add a fifth of the value to it. The entire tithe of the herd and flock - every tenth animal that passes under the shepherd's rod - will be holy to the Lord.' (Lev 27:30-32).

Christians live under grace and therefore their tithing is not a legal requirement, but a response of grace to God. Jesus Himself fulfilled the Old Testament Law including tithing, but he never revised the law downward. Christians are expected to tithe and then give offerings as they respond to other needs. Every single member of my church tithes. Some bring their tithes to the church and place them in the offering plate. Others decide to spend their tithes on themselves and cheat God by giving only a token offering at this moment. But I have noticed that God still receives his tithes, even though he must collect it from them! God owns everything. When Howard Hughes, the billionaire died, naked and terrified of flies, someone asked how much did he leave? The answer was, 'All of it'!

The ultimate measure of a man's wealth is how much he is worth when he has lost everything. Naked we came into this world and naked we depart. Our wealth consists not in 'the abundance of our possessions', but in whom we have become as a child of God. How we must remember, 'The earth is the Lord's and everything in it, the world and all who live in it.' (Ps 24:1). We may possess things, but God owns them.

A friend of mine, the Managing Director of one of the largest chemical companies in the Southern Hemisphere, recalls how from 1960, he led the way in providing for employees shorter working hours and better conditions and wages. Each year he would send with every pay slip a letter that said: 'We do not wish to preach to you, but we want you to know that we believe this business has prospered because, having faith in God, we seek to serve to the best of our ability. It may not be always easy to believe that it is more blessed to give than receive, but this is just as true today as when Jesus first told it to his disciples. It is because we know something of the joy of Christian giving that we now desire to increase your wages by 10%. We make only one request that you refrain from thanking us. If you find it in your heart to do so, you should thank God from whom every good gift comes.'

Responsible giving is the fruit of our prayer. Our prayers are based upon the promises of God. 'I am the Lord, the God of all mankind. Is anything too hard for me?' (Jer 32:27) God promises resources to those who pray in faith. 'Therefore I tell you, whatever you ask in prayer, believe you have received it and it will be yours.' (Mark 11:24) 'This is the confidence we have in approaching God, that if we ask anything according to His will he hears us. And if we know that He hears us, whatever we ask, we know that we have what we ask of Him.' (1 John 5: 14 - 15)

That fruit of our prayer is powerful in its effect. He gives us power to become. $E = mc^2$ is a formula known by college students but understood by very few people.

Most of us know it had something to do with Einstein and was the formula that led to the release of enormous power and to the atomic and nuclear eras. It was the key to the discovery of a new thrust in power. Students know that 'E' stands for energy, 'M' stands for mass, 'C' stands for something I always forget except it has to be mixed and squared! I cannot understand Einstein but I agree with him completely!

In funding the Christian challenge, 'E' stands for 'Every', 'M' stands for 'member', 'C' stands for 'commitment' and the '2' stands for the effort multiplied by itself. The fruit of that kind of prayerful effort is powerful in its effects. 'If you believe you will receive whatever you ask for in prayer.' (Matt 21:22) Jesus promised it. I believe it. That settles it!

Our responsible giving comes in response to God's call. We have to be sure of God's call to us. God called Isaiah and he was sure of that call (Isaiah 6:1-10). God called Jeremiah and he was sure of his call (Jer 1:4 - 10). God confirmed his call upon the life of Jesus at his baptism, in the temptations and at the mount of transfiguration. When God calls, we can trust him to provide the resources. As Hudson Taylor proved, 'God's work, done in God's way, will never lack God's resources'. We must live certain of his call and confident in his resources. 'Is anything too hard for the Lord?' (Gen 18:14). His resources are infinite: 'For every animal of the forest is mine and the cattle of a thousand hills.' (Ps 50:10)

Responsible giving, or stewardship, is not man's way of raising money, but God's way of raising people. He is at work making us to be the people he wants us to be through how we give. A fundraising campaign may be the Church's most significant spiritual teaching. An emphasis upon stewardship is not something to be left to a special Sunday of the year, but like the Church's mission, witness, education and worship, it must be part of the fabric of its everyday life.

The Church's budget is not a list of its expenses, but a record of its vision. It is not a list of expenses to be met but a program of ministry to be achieved. We have a responsibility to expect responsible giving. The pastor, fund-raiser, or Christian executive concerned with fundraising has a responsibility to teach and to expect that the believers will fund the Christian challenge. 'Command them to do good, to be rich in good deeds, to be generous and willing to share. In this way they will lay up treasure for themselves as a firm foundation for the coming age.' (1 Tim 6:18-19) We must teach our indebtedness to God.

Part of that teaching must include our own dependence and indebtedness to God. For 'you are not your own; you were bought at a price. Therefore honour God.' (1 Cor. 6:19). Jesus had commanded: 'Store up for yourselves treasures in heaven.' (Matt. 6:20) and we are to teach our indebtedness.

We must realise that God rewards our faithfulness. We never give because of the expectation of his return. That is a faithless prosperity doctrine that abuses the promises of God. To give knowing that God blesses the giver is an act of Christian knowledge, but to give in order to induce God to bless us further is an act of unchristian blackmail. Amy Carmichael said, 'Scripture supports three methods of raising funds: asking God's people for money; tent making by earning your living to support your Christian service; and trusting God to supply your means by making them known in advance only to him. A fourth method is not scriptural: to profess to walk by faith in God alone and simultaneously to hint for funds or to manipulate people into giving.'

That fourth method is unworthy but widely practiced. That approach indicates that we lack the trust that God expects of us. God calls us to have the marks of his own character carved into ourselves and that includes our faith in his provision. Rather, 'Bring the whole tithe into the store house that there be food in my house. Test me in this, says the Lord Almighty and see if I will not throw open the floodgates of heaven and pour out so much blessing that you will not have room enough for it.' (Mal 3:10) Or, as Paul experienced it, 'Moreover as you Philippians know, in the early days of your acquaintance with the Gospel, when I set out from Macedonia, not one church shared with me in the matter of giving and receiving, except you only. For even when I was in Thessalonicia, you sent me aid again and again when I was in need. Not that I am looking for a gift, but I am looking for what may be credited to your account. I have received full payment and even more; I am amply supplied now that I have received the gifts you sent. They are a fragrant offering, an acceptable sacrifice pleasing to God.' (Phil 4:15-18).

That is a fundamental law of life: they who give receive more than they have ever given. St Francis put it succinctly, 'For it is in giving that we receive.' The miser does not believe it and so never experiences it. The widow gives her mite and receives joyfully every day. Even a Hindu proverb says: 'They who give have all things. They who withhold have nothing.'

Jesus is so clear: 'Give and it will be given unto you, a good measure pressed down, shaken together and running over will be poured into your lap. For with the measure you use, it will be measured to you.' (Luke 6:38)

'God is able to make all grace abound to you so that in all things, at all times, having all that you need, you will abound in every good work.' As it is written: 'He has scattered abroad his gifts to the poor; his righteousness endures forever. Now he who supplies seed to the sower and bread for food, also will supply and increase your store of seed and will enlarge the harvest of your righteousness. You will be made rich in every way so that you can be generous on every occasion and through us your generosity will result in thanksgiving to God.' (2 Cor 9:8-11)

On the memorable day in 1955 when the five martyrs died in the jungles of Ecuador, Jim Eliot wrote in his diary: 'He is no fool who gives what he cannot keep to gain what he cannot lose'. We who would fund the Christian challenge by our responsible giving to God's call, must be like the Macedonian Christians, 'Who gave as much as they were able and even beyond their ability. Entirely on their own, they urgently pleaded with us for the privilege of sharing in their service to the saints... they gave themselves first to the Lord and then to us in keeping with God's will.' (2 Cor 8:4-5).

When I commenced my ministry, I decided there were some people I would not ask to give to our ministry. No use seeking money from unresponsive soil. In that letter of apology sent to me by Alan Walker stating our rolls were dreadfully out of date, I soon found the truth of the matter. My first letter to donors using the Mission's existing rolls resulted in hundreds of letters returned marked 'deceased' or 'left address, forwarding address unknown'. If I wanted a harvest there was no use sowing seed there!

I was also aware that my predecessor Rev. Dr Alan Walker who had established an office in Sydney to support his new work of World Evangelism, had taken our donor lists to approach them for funds for his new work. I realised that people who had supported Alan in the past would give to him in the new work. People give to a person not an institution. They give to a person they can trust and Alan was certainly known by many people, whereas I was unknown to most donors in Sydney, having just arrived from Melbourne. I felt our donor's lists were virtually useless. No use approaching any of them.

I wrote down in my diary that Wesley Mission had some urgent needs, which had to be addressed within the next weeks. I realised we needed large numbers of people, good hearted, generous members of the public, in their tens of thousands, to support us. They were our needs. The question was, how we were going to achieve this?

In my diaries I wrote down solutions as they came to me. For example, I could immediately start visiting churches, preaching everywhere like a wild fire through Sydney. I knew there was not enough time to do this and even if I did it, it would generate little cash but much resentment from local ministers who would feel I was coming to take away either their members or their money, which was due to their local parishes. I dismissed that solution. In fact for the next 20 years I basically accepted no invitations to preach this side of the Blue Mountains.

Another solution involved us in building a mailing list where I could write to people, state our needs, in the belief that the average Australians who saw an honest attempt to help a genuine need would respond. But how was I to get people to give me names and addresses?

I decided the only way that could be done with integrity was to become well known. I immediately accepted an invitation from Chris Brammall, the Manager of Radio Station 2CH, to start presenting radio spots. I told Chris I had been preparing for years to do spots and had actually been writing spots every day for years before I had come to Sydney. I had more than 4000 scripts at hand. I commenced doing spots on 2CH the next day and continued for years.

I also approached Barrie Unsworth, the General Manager of Radio Station 2KY, described how I could fit in with their country music format and he granted me a one hour program on Sunday nights called 'Country Gospel'. That proved so successful it was relayed to other stations throughout Australia and extended to three hours every Sunday night.

I did, however, place on the radio and television programs a very important limitation. I would not use the media to ask for money for Wesley Mission. I did ask for support for all kinds of organisations that I promoted, but never for ourselves. My belief was that Australians would not support radio and television programs that were always asking for money but that if I could only earn people's trust they would both support me with money and be willing to come on to our mailing lists. The media was simply to allow me to become known.

We also needed a good magazine and I immediately went to work to upgrade the small broad sheet that Wesley Mission had produced, known as Impact, and later added a second magazine, *Frontlines*. These have been powerful tools for letting people know what we were doing. When people know what you are doing, they support it. I would offer free subscriptions for one year to everyone who wrote to me. That way I would build a database of tens of thousands for my mail appeals.

The negatives, however, were quite obvious. What I was suggesting would be slow to actually return money to us. It would take at least two or three years before we would see an upturn in our finances through any of those approaches. Further, a lot of people and organisations would be very suspicious of a clergyman asking for money. Thirdly, I was running a charity, which was in financial strife, and I don't believe people give to sinking ships. The fourth negative was the work at Wesley Mission demanded all of my attention in order to turn it around.

I was opposed to selling any of the Mission's assets, apart from a small fire sale of useless property, in my first month or two. I did not want to sell any of our buildings which would have brought us in quick cash to get us over the crisis, but as all of our buildings were occupied by people in real need such as children and children's homes and aged people in hostels, we would need to put out people in dire need in order to sell the property. I wondered what other assets we had.

I decided that we had skills as an asset that could be sold. Whose skills? My skills. What skills did I have that I thought were marketable? I believed I had three. The first was that I had a lot of experience on radio, television and in public speaking to communicate with ordinary people. Over the years my work on radio, television, in the press and speaking to large crowds of people, had given me a skill in communication that did not depend upon scripts and meant I could speak freely without notes.

I had a second skill - the gift of motivating people. This was not only in motivating Christian people but also business people. In Melbourne, a senior manager of the AMP Society had prevailed upon me at a time of difficulty to motivate his sales force. I had addressed his sales force that year with extraordinary results. He wanted me to do the same every year. I was not paid for doing this but I did say I would motivate his sales persons if he would agree to me being allowed to sit in upon one of their management training courses, because I needed to improve my management skills.

That was my third asset I could sell. I had built up over the years good management skills. After all, no other suburban church in Australia had undertaken such large building projects as we had at Cheltenham. We had spent in one year more than a million dollars on new buildings and over a period of years had built five retirement villages. I had built a strong staff and managed them well. I had gone along to management training courses at the Mount Eliza Administrative Staff College and undertaken courses with the Australian Institute of Management. I was to continue taking and learning management training programs until eventually I was elected by management peers through various levels until I became a Fellow of the Australian Institute of Management and a Fellow of the Australian Institute of Company Directors and was actually lecturing in management principles. I had been invited to look at a number of companies, examine their weaknesses, and advise their Chief Executives. An idea was born.

If I could combine the skills of communication, motivation and management and put that into one package and offer corporations my skills in communication, motivation and management I was sure they would be willing to pay for my time. This was a unique thought at the time. There were some communications experts out of the radio and television industry who taught Chief Executives how to present annual reports at the Annual General Meeting of a company and to shareholders. There were motivational experts who addressed sales conferences but mostly they only addressed them once, because they had a single story to tell of how they sailed around the world, won a gold medal or played in a premiership team. Once they had told their story they wouldn't be invited again. There were also management gurus who lectured managers on how to manage but I didn't know of one who had excellence in communication, motivation skills and management insights.

I set a fee of $2,000 for a corporation to invite me to examine its problems, to prepare a presentation to its staff and to present to the widest number of people in the company possible. The income from these talks would all go to Wesley Mission, not to myself personally. I didn't want to have any tax problems. Often at the meetings I would be given far more than the speaking fee. On these occasions I kept the fee and passed on the larger donation. Apart from that I needed the Mission's accounts office to keep a good account of the income and be able to chase up any slow payers. I even thought that these talks would pay for my own salary as well as providing needy income to support our work among the poor and the disabled. In years to come, my business addresses paid my salary and that of my secretary as well.

I had no sooner outlined what I proposed to do when the phone rang with the General Manager of AMP Australia asking me if I would speak at a business conference of his senior managers to be held at Wentworth in the Blue Mountains. This was to be repeated to another group at Surfers Paradise, to a wider group, which would fill the Sydney Opera House and to all their New Zealand staff in Rotarua. I accepted that and received wonderful responses wherever I went. Over the next 12 years I was to speak at more than 40 AMP conferences covering every state, New Zealand and overseas and every talk was completely different.

I had just started on this series of talks when Ron Tachi and Associates asked me if I would be a keynote speaker to be attended by two and a half thousand businessmen in the Sydney Opera House. He had previously brought out Norman Vincent Peale and he believed that I could take the famous Dr Peale's place in a new series being held in the largest auditoriums in Australia. I would accompany the other keynote speaker, Commander Neil Armstrong, the first man to walk upon the moon! I spoke in each of these gatherings and developed a warm friendship with the famous Astronaut.

The phone rang again; it was John Nevin asking me to speak in a series of conferences for World Book Encyclopedia, an encyclopedia that I had purchased and updated many times. This was shortly followed by Encyclopedia Britannica, who wanted me to meet with all of their managers in Australia and then later to take my wife and four children to Hawaii to address a World Conference of Encyclopedia Britannica managers. Constan Industries asked me to go to the Philippines. The phone rang again with Keith Walkerden, a former Officer of Wesley Mission, Sydney, asking me to address the Olivetti managers of Australia and New Zealand. That was successful and it was followed by two invitations to address all the managers of Olivetti through the United Kingdom and Europe. Shortly after that Australia Post was undertaking vast changes and I gave about 10 major addresses to Australia Post employees in every state of Australia. I was to also make for them a film explaining what was happening in society and how they had to cope with the changes within Australia Post. This film was screened hundreds of times in every little outpost of the nation, wherever there was an Australian Post Office.

This was the time when there were a large number of computer companies just expanding and I became known within the industry and addressed companies like Compaq, Wang, IBM, Hewlett Packard and so on. It wasn't long before I had spoken to more than 200 of the top 500 companies in Australia and all told over a period of about 10 years spoke to more than 400 top corporations.

The impact of this was instant. Wesley Mission had additional cash flow. The knowledge of Wesley Mission among people in the business community and among people who were likely to help fund our work spread across the nation. Everywhere I went I carried heavy parcels of our magazines and gave them out freely, indicating that those who returned filled in subscription forms before the day was over I would send that magazine free for the next year. I would come back to Wesley Mission with the side pockets of my suit coat bulging with new subscriptions. The database was expanding every couple of days. I sometimes spoke to twenty corporations in two weeks covering five different states. Aircraft seats became my bed and meal table. But the database grew with those who knew me.

The people who heard me in person also seemed to want to now watch me on television. Many letters were received from people who now said they had discovered our television programs. Others became regular attendees at the Sunday evening church services held in the Lyceum Theatre. But the greatest thrill I had was the unique opportunity to speak to tens of thousands of Australians every couple of months who would not otherwise have gone to church. In all of my presentations I was not only true to the Christian Gospel but I used the remarkable insights of Jesus to illustrate good management practices, much to the amazement of my listeners. Many a secret Christian came out and told other people with pride afterwards that was why he followed the way of Jesus.

Three or four years earlier the Central Methodist Mission had depended almost entirely upon good-hearted Christians within the Methodist denomination to support its work. I saw nothing wrong with that except there were not enough of them and they did not have enough money for what I wanted to do. Today Wesley Mission receives less than 1% of its income from the three denominations that make up the Uniting Church. We had set out a pattern of receiving funding from the community and from corporations at large.

There were three significant developments in this work. The first came when I was invited to speak in North Sydney at a rather unique convention. It would be attended by 700 people who organised conferences for their companies. They were told they would hear the six best speakers in the nation. I was the last speaker. Everybody ran over their time and the presentations were an extraordinarily high level. As the evening wore away every half hour I decided to shorten my address. At long last I got up at ten minutes past eleven to give the final address of the night. It was billed the keystone to the whole evening. I wasn't feeling like giving a top line address. Late that afternoon I had a wisdom tooth extracted which I had not expected. The dentist had trouble and eventually the tooth was out. It left me with a numb face and a lot of pain in my jaw. I did not feel like giving a significant public address.

With the other speakers going too long, I kept shortening my address until when the time came at ten minutes past eleven I delivered a very brief, very punchy and very funny address and wrapped up the evening. The impact was electric. I got the longest standing ovation I had ever received in my life. As people crowded around afterwards there was a very dignified blonde lady who kept looking at me. Her name was Christine Maher. She introduced herself as being the Chief Executive of Celebrity Speakers and on the basis of my performance that night she invited me to join the very exclusive band of Australia's best speakers. They would arrange my speaking engagements. They would charge more to cover their expenses, but I would have no worries because they would handle all travel, accommodation and other details. For the next 15 years I enjoyed being part of a group of Australia's 'celebrity speakers'. My colleagues in the 'stable' of speakers were the best in the business. Among them were the most famous achievers in the nation.

The second thing that really helped develop our work was that I needed to expand our staff to handle the mail that was generated from television and from radio. I found a wonderful young woman, Christine Johnson, who had been working with the American Television Evangelist Rex Humbard, who took over the responsibility of organising hundreds of replies every week to those who wrote to me following presentations on television and radio. Before long I was receiving a thousand letters per week from those who heard me. Christine has headed up our media office and staff ever since.

The third development was the establishment of Wesley Film Corporation in 1984. Backed by a number of Rotarians and business people who put up more than a million dollars, we were able to produce films throughout the middle-east and the Mediterranean on the life of Jesus, the life and teachings of the Apostle Paul, the growth and development of the early Church, the history and development of the country of Israel and many others. These were produced in different languages and sold worldwide and screened on television in prime time.

The development of our written material on the internet opened up another amazing market and this year we would anticipate about ten million downloads of material or hits on our website. The result of all of this was that Wesley Mission became one of those places that came to mind first whenever people thought of an effective and efficient charity. We became the largest provider of community services in New South Wales and number three in the whole of Australia, although our work is primarily in 450 suburbs, regional and rural centres and we are now known internationally. People constantly come from overseas to study our church and its ministry to people in need.

The result was that our debts were paid. Our income rose over the years, I remember it reaching $5 million in one year. Last year it was $150 million. And many of those corporations with whom I had made contact became long-term partners of Wesley Mission. Great corporations like the Commonwealth Bank and National Australia Bank, Ansett, Qantas, BBC Hardware House and the Housing Industry of Australia, Blue Haven Pools, Ford Motor Company, Sydney Water, the Copper Industry, the Payroll Association, CSR, HomeWorld, Telstra, Daily Telegraph, Westpac, LendLease, TCN9, 2UE, St. George, LG Electronics, AM Corporation, Darling Harbour Authority and so on joined with us as partners in helping meet human need.

Over that time the number of staff increased dramatically and today we have more than 3,500 paid staff, with another 3,500 voluntary, unpaid staff.

With the growth of the work there was no longer the same need for me to speak at so many large public meetings in corporations. I had already been voted by Rostrum and Toast Masters, the public speaking organisations, as the Australian Public Speaker of the Year. I slowly withdrew from addressing companies and rarely do it these days. Instead I invite the Chief Executives of major corporations to come to a Board Room lunch in Wesley Centre to hear about the work that we are doing and of course we added staff in the whole area of fundraising and corporate relations. The work today is led by three great General Managers and a team of Senior Managers. Many of these people have been with me for 15 to 20 years and we have an incredible personal relationship and an effective ministry to the community.

The problems I faced back in the 1970's with Wesley Mission were the same problems that are faced by many small businesses today. We had a cash flow crisis; we had management which was bogged down in too much detail. We had steadily rising costs, which were escalating beyond our income; we had communication problems and lack of clients to support us in our work.

Churches also, like small businesses, face these same problems and they have these problems because the Theological Colleges of various denominations do not train ministers to make churches grow. I have never known of one lecturer in any Theological College of any denomination who was competent in the fields of communication, motivation and management expertise. In fact many of them despise these competencies and continue as if the local church will forever fund them in their training program.

Leaders are called to lead. They are called to skill themselves and to give total commitment to build a team to multiply their own effectiveness. I also had one other watchword: I believed I had to work as if everything depended upon me and I had to believe and trust in God as if everything depended upon him.

One important area of fundraising is deferred. I had designed and run a wills and estates program in the 1970's. There was much mistrust by some of my members who did not understand. Now in Sydney I had a second chance to develop such a program, but at the other end of the scale was the need for services to improve the lot of aged and frail people. We had built retirement villages, hostels and nursing homes, but money was always short, so we established the Aged Persons Welfare Foundation. We had a very pleasant little ceremony in the Board Room of Wesley Mission one Friday when an anonymous donor handed over two cheques, one of $1,000, to open the trust upon which we must pay stamp duty, then the first contribution to the Trust which was the magnificent sum of $9.75 million. Apart from this there were two very large parcels of blue chip shares that needed to be sold when the price was right. When they were sold the total value of the donation to the trust was $11.6 million. The interest from this money is now used both in Wesley Mission and for churches beyond Wesley Mission who are involved in Aged Care.

While the Trust is independent of Wesley Mission, half of each year's distribution goes there. This has been a most wonderful gift, for which we praise God. It has also been the outworking of our policy of investment in 2GB, whereby we raised our community profile and attracted this donor who had no church background, no previous connection with the Uniting Church and no connection with Wesley Mission, save hearing of our work via radio.

He had previously given $250,000 to Rev. Harry Herbert of the Uniting Church Synod to be used to benefit older persons. A year later when he checked to see how the money was used, he found it was still sitting in a bank account. He asked for it back, but Rev. Herbert refused to give it back. The donor, Jack Richardson, believed he had been betrayed twice. There ensued a long battle to get the money back and use it for older people. Jack regarded the Rev. Harry Herbert's acceptance of the money, then its non-use, then and his unwillingness to return the donation as absolutely unethical. He determined never to give anything again to the Uniting Church Synod. Then he came to me whom he had heard for years on radio 2GB. He was distressed that we were part of the Uniting Church and so resolved to go elsewhere. But I convinced him we could set up an independent Trust outside of the Uniting Church with himself, his lawyer and accountant as trustees and myself as an advisor for the distribution of funds.

My personal relationship with Jack Richardson was the reason he trusted me. For the previous three years my wife and I had picked up Jack, a widower, and taken him with us as we visited our various aged care centres. He loved these outings. We praise God that we received this gift because of our patience and understanding of the donor's particular needs when previous organisations approached by him, including the Uniting Church's Board of Social Responsibility, treated him poorly and he eventually came to us. Although our donor had apologised for not coming to us first my response has been 'we made sure that we were the last'. By 2005 we were holding $15.5 million in trust, we had given away $4 million and have plans for this year of giving away almost another million. Deferred giving has become an important part of our financial stream and every year we receive between three and four million dollars from estates. Upon my retirement, we had information from lawyers that they had written in our favour future estates valued in excess of $45 million that will come to us.

When Jesus gave us the Great Commission to go into all the world and preach the gospel He gave us a command that has never been repealed. Every Christian in every church has to be interested in taking the message of the gospel to people who have not heard it. Wesley Mission has always been committed to the support of first the Methodist Church and then of the Uniting Church of its ministry to people in other countries. Every week, a portion of the total offerings given in all congregations are sent to the Synod in order to help in the ministry of reaching overseas people with the gospel. The Uniting Churches overseas ministries cover about thirty different countries of the world. Not only are funds sent to help local congregations but skilled people are sent to help, not only in the proclamation but also in the work of education, agriculture, village development, teaching, orphan support and many other programs. This is some of the best work the Uniting Church does and it divorces itself from the sexuality debates of other parts of the Church.

At Wesley Mission we have also adopted a number of programs to help people in other countries by additional giving by the congregation. For example some time later, after returning from USA, I wrote to supporters:

'I have been slow getting to write simply because we really hit the ground running. Every day has been packed. I received over 3000 letters while in the USA and although I have two letter openers and sorters and three secretaries to help me answer them, the ones they couldn't answer, or which they wanted instruction in answering, were in three large piles on the desk. Then there were many meetings held over and catch-ups of all kinds. But it has been a very satisfying three weeks at the Mission. Our first day back was our 'Thank You Lord' special offering and the people gave $37,000. I made 6 TV programs and spoke at a number of community meetings. I gave a talk at Rotary and they gave me $25,000 to purchase medical bracelets for a whole bunch of our elderly to aid in time of emergency. They were so willing to give I asked for another $10,000 at Christmas to cover some more!

'Our Home for Hope that we sold for $550,000 profit was the forerunner of three others we are building at the moment. There was lots of planning to get all this together, but I held a corporate lunch, made a pitch and came away with $140,000 towards our next target. One of my Rotarian friends at an evening meeting I addressed last week was impressed and sent me a cheque for $17, 000. Then I attended a Casino Trust where I insult the gamblers of the community and to shut me up, they gave me an additional $86,000 for our Gambling Counselling. So it has been a good time financially since I returned.'

I continued in my letter to supporters:
'Last Thursday I opened two new blocks of flats adjacent to others we have for housing

homeless alcoholics while we work on them. We have 52 men in this community of four blocks. The opening was an inspiration! Man after man gave his testimony of becoming a Christian, becoming sober and drug-free and now being useful. Twelve could not be present because they now all are regularly employed.

'Wesley Mission won the 'Environment Australia Partnership Award' for the GreenSmart Village at Kellyville. Our partners and sponsors in this great project included Australand, Wincrest Homes, HomeWorld, the HIA and The Copper Development Centre, CSR, BBC Hardware, The Daily Telegraph, Landcom and Fantastic Furniture, who all share in this important national award. I was honoured to accept the award together with Dian Ball, our Senior Manager, Corporate Development. Our partner Copper Development Centre also won an award, so our development won 2 out of the 7 awards. Our second GreenSmart Village was built in Brisbane, which was Queensland's first GreenSmart Village.

'On Friday evening August 31, 2003, at the National MBA Awards (Master Builders Association) Wincrest Homes - the Smart Wired Home - won the 'Display Builders House of the Year Award' value $160,001 to $200,000. This was also one of our houses! Wesley Mission was acclaimed as one of the top builders in Australia! You can see that fundraising can also be a lot of fun. Those who dislike raising money miss out on so much.

'Every year the Captains and Legends Cricket Challenge takes place at the Allan Border Field in Brisbane. This exciting fundraising event series is produced in partnership with Rotary's Australian Corporate Alliance Program, The Bradman Foundation and Wesley Mission. The Corporate teams who compete for the Sir Donald Bradman Trophy include North Lakes, Elm Financial Services, PATHE Partners, Ansett and St George Bank. Each team was led by a celebrity Captain and these included Craig McDermott, Merv Hughes, Ray Bright, Trevor Laughlan and Scott Prestwidge. The Bradman Foundation operated their famous cricket bal -bowling machine to entertain the younger members of the audience.

'We have raised significant funds with this match. Since 2002 our corporate matches are held at the spectacular Bradman Oval in Bowral. Penrith Panthers rugby league players Ben Reynolds and Scott Sattler signed autographs and distributed posters at the Quakers Hill Family Centre as a part of the Club's support for Wesley Mission's work with families and children in crisis. The players were among the Club's representatives attending an afternoon tea that we organised to acknowledge a recent $10,000 donation made by Penrith Panthers. Also present on the afternoon was Dalmar Patron and Mission Board member and former Wallaby Captain, Nick Farr-Jones. The money was used to expand the Stretching Your Wings program, which is run by Wesley Dalmar Child and Family Care.

'Stretching Your Wings provides support and care for young children who have witnessed or experienced domestic violence. As well as the donation to the Quakers Hill-based program, Panthers has also agreed to support Wesley Dalmar with a further $

50,000. This money was used to support drug and lifestyle education programs throughout the community.

'In all of our fundraising I seek to develop a partnership with individuals, sporting teams, government departments and corporations. Wesley Mission brings all of the pieces together. As an example, recently I announced a major new development that would bring together a wide variety of our resources to create a cohesive multiple resource program to work with dysfunctional families whose multiple problems require a total response.

'Wesley Mission spend 168 hours every week for nine months with families in what is the most intensive and extensive intervention according to family need, ever in Australia's history. The aim of the Family Makeover Centre is to take in damaged, at risk, homeless, single parent families and help them to discover skills for independent living in the community. Multiple resources are made available to cover each area of disadvantage. This is I believe a classic example of co-operative endeavour to meet a desirable outcome, involving all the major community stakeholders.

'Most fundraising is of a planned, regular nature. But some of the most challenging occurs when I swing into action upon first hearing of disastrous losses caused by a Tsunami, an earthquake, a famine, drought, flood, or bushfire. We have responded to all of these in the last decade and some of these every year. In total millions of dollars in cash and kind has been raised and sent and spent by responsible people. We receipt everything given and report back later.

'Here is an example of what we did when disastrous floods inundated a vast area of our rural community recently. The floods came to end a three-year equally disastrous drought. Within three hours of the disaster announcement, I announced, 'We have the 'Wesley Mission Flood Disaster Counselling Line' up and operational. The telephone no is 1800 777 045. It is manned 24 hours. Let us know your needs.'

'Within 12 hours the Commonwealth Bank had responded as a partner with Wesley Mission. They had printed posters and newspaper ads, promoting the flood appeal, opened every branch in Australia to the appeal and gave any staff member time off on full pay to go to the flood areas with Wesley Mission volunteers to help victims. In response to my appeal the Macquarie Bank sent a cheque for $7,500 to help the victims of the flood disaster.

'Others to respond very generously included: Amcal, Woolworths, Cancer Council, Golden Circle, Captain Snooze, Goldwell, Dilmah, Kleenex, Kelloggs, Darrell Lea, Goodman Fielder, Windsor Farm Foods, Kimberley Clarke and Allied Transport and National Hire. These companies responded to my request for food, toiletries and cash for hundreds of boxes for each family. All companies also agreed to give various donations. After four days we estimated that we had over $135,000 worth of products and cash. Teams of trauma and family counsellors were flown in to meet those who had lost their homes in flood-affected NSW. In the same way as we supported people after the Thredbo disaster, Wesley Mission was available to help those under stress or struggling to cope with this tragedy.

'Semi-trailer loads of parcels of food, toiletries and other goods arrived in the flood-affected areas. Meat, milk and vegetables were all purchased locally where stores were still able to operate. Other forms of support pledged by Wesley Mission to the NSW flood victims included distributing bales of clothing from Wesley Clothing, hosting camps for the children of families affected, as a way of giving both parents and them a much needed break away from the area; providing electrical white goods to replace damaged ones, providing respite care for any aged person or disabled person from the area, to allow families to concentrate on the cleanup and the saving of ravaged crops, providing bus loads of volunteers to clean up the mud, shift stock, hand feed lambs and straighten fences.

'Finally, I went to scores of farms identified by the local authorities as the hardest hit, on behalf of our members, supporters and donors, presented each family with cheques of $10,000 to enable them to purchase new grain to allow them to get a new crop in. I will never forget the tears of appreciation for these gifts.

When I returned home, I sat down and wrote personally to every major donor telling them of what happened to their gift. As I posted each letter I knew the recipient would say, 'Don't hesitate to ask me again in future if you need help'.'

That is what makes fundraising so enjoyable.

FAMILY MAN

Chapter Eleven

After I had been a student minister in the Newmarket and Ascot Vale for three years, the church invited me to stay on as a young married man. I was married in the Christmas vacation and after returning from a rather unusual honeymoon on which I ended up violently ill and had to be hospitalised, we settled into the first of six houses, which would be our future homes.

Our first house was at 15 Vine Street, Moonee Ponds, just down the road from the famous Dame Edna Everidge. It was grandmother's home and she had lived there all of her life. Like the houses of Newmarket nearby, it was a workman's cottage built in the very poor days at the turn of the century. The house was eighteen feet wide and ran the width of the block except for a narrow sideway two feet six wide down on one side, which then was joined by the wall of the next house. It was a weatherboard house with a corrugated iron roof and one long passage running the entire length of the house opening from the front door right on the street down to the end. Opening immediately inside the front door was the front room, which was always reserved for best and immediately behind it the main bedroom out of which my grandmother shifted for my new bride and I to have as our own. The middle room of the house was the lounge room and off it a very small single bedroom into which Grandma shifted. The passage then opened into a bathroom/laundry with a big brick surrounded copper in the corner, two stone wash troughs and a bath with a wooden chip heater. It served its dual capacity as bath and laundry. The kitchen was a rectangle in which people ate and was dominated at the far end by a large wooden stove, a sideboard for crockery and an ice chest. The' Ice-man' came every two days.

The only other building on the property was an outdoor toilet down the end of the narrow block of land with its back to the alley. Up this lane for several generations the night cart had come. This toilet had fond memories. One day when I was two years of age my Nanna was minding me for the day and while she was in that toilet, I slid across a door bolt, which locked her in. All morning and afternoon she was locked in, as my small fingers could not loosen the bolt. Neither could her shouting until my mother returned. At least she had a place to sit! But in Moonee Ponds in our day we had sewerage connected and a cast iron water closet sat at the top of the toilet with a chain dangling within reach. There was a small vegetable garden and a woodshed attached to the back fence. I was reminded that in this tiny little cottage my grandmother and grandfather had raised nine children.

Nanna had lived alone for a number of years and it was a concern of my mother and my aunt that she was becoming very forgetful and it would be good if the young married couple could move in with her. I was still a student at university and the low cost accommodation was a great boon to us, particularly as both the church and the university were not far away. We lived there for the next two and a half years with the lounge in the centre doubling as our common room, my study and our family room together. Very soon I had some bookcases moved in, a desk, typewriter and it was here that I used to counsel many of the young boys that I had in our Youth Club and the first of the boys that came on probation.

My grandmother felt she owned the piece of street immediately outside her front fence and as our house was adjacent to the Moonee Valley Racecourse there were always race goers parking their cars outside. On every race day she would stand outside the front gate with her arms folded across a very ample chest, glaring at any car who dared to park in front of her house. She would place empty wooden boxes on the road with pieces of timber across them so that no race goer could park there. The fact that she did not have a car and we did not need it for parking was quite irrelevant. That was her piece of road. She paid rates on it and if the Council allowed people to park their cars in front of her house on her road, then they would soon hear about it!

Living with my Nanna was very difficult for my young bride. Unfortunately Nanna's memory was failing and although her daughters had not seen it and I was too young and inexperienced to realise it she was well advanced in a stage of dementia, suffering from Alzheimer's Disease. Very soon we began to notice a lot more symptoms than the loss of memory. She would occasionally bring home from the greengrocer's large boxes of berries and a huge bag of sugar and start mixing pounds of jam on her stove, or bottling dozens of bottles of preserved apricots. Whenever I would ask her why she needed so many she would always reply, 'If you have a large family you must do the bottling! It is jam time now and I've got to get the preserves in.' She had so much happiness making jams and preserving fruit even though she no longer had children round about to eat them, that I took to a rather tricky subterfuge to help her. As soon as her preserving cupboard became full and she started to complain she had nowhere else to put the bottles of preserves I would sneak out bottles of preserves and jams and give them to deserving people in the community whenever I visited or else to some of the ladies from the church who would run a street stall. Nanna was never the wiser about where they went but when she noticed the cupboards were down by a few bottles would make comments about how she would soon need to get some more sugar in because 'those kids have nearly finished all of the jam'. When the time came to leave, she suffered a stroke and we rushed her to hospital. After a short time she passed away.

The second house we lived in was really the first manse we ever occupied. The little church at Newmarket and Ascot Vale had not had a house for a minister since the early 1930's and had relied upon student ministers to supply over all the years. After three years of student ministry and now another two-and-half-years of part-time student ministry, the churches were showing signs of vitality and great growth. The Sunday school was booming, boys and girls clubs were at good strength, we had a teeming teenage group and church attendances had reached the highest they had been for forty years. It was obvious that we needed to move into full-time ministry and that would require the purchase of a manse. To those poor people living in the inner areas of Melbourne, the purchase of a manse was a huge undertaking.

I broke down the cost into units and encouraged people to buy one unit representing part of the total cost of the property. We encouraged other people to give some interest free loans and very shortly we had sufficient money to purchase our first manse at 85 Athol Street. It was a moment of enormous pride in the life of the church. They had achieved what people had talked about for forty years. It was a lovely house, one of the best in the street. Unlike almost every other house it was solid brick and painted white. It had a little patch of lawn in the front, but like all the other houses still had only a very narrow frontage. This time however, we had gone from 18 feet to 25 feet in width. It also had a door opening at the front leading into a passage that ran the length of the house with one front bedroom, then a lounge room, then a kitchen and dining area and finally a second bedroom and, opposite a laundry. This time we had a toilet attached to the house even though we had to go outside the house to enter the toilet.

On one side of the house we shared the common wall with the family next door, an Italian family who covered their backyard with trellis growing grapes and who squashed the grapes for wine in the family bath.

On the other side we had a narrow sideway and our one lounge room window opened directly opposite the lounge room window of the house next door. They had a large family and the mother and father were always shouting at each other and engaging in physical fights. In our young married life we would often be astounded to hear the shouts, the swearing and the physical assaults that were taking place. There were times when we would just sit on our single lounge chair looking out the window at life size shouting and fighting and carrying on next door. We referred to it as our 'life size television'. It was really quite a soap opera. On one occasion Mr Lake fled out the front door of the house closely followed by Mrs. Lake who was brandishing a broom taking swipes at him. He managed to get out the front gate and started running down the street with Mrs. Lake in hot pursuit. As they reached the front of our place she caught him on the back of the head with the end of her broom and he fell to the ground like a stunned mullet, completely unconscious. Mrs. Lake looked at him lying there, rolled him over with her foot and taking her broom under her arm, calmly walked back inside knowing that he would recover and come home for his meal.

Our first baby was born while we lived in this house. We did a lot of work in establishing gardens front and rear and in building a carport at the back, a brick barbecue and a tool shed. We had not been there long, however, before long many of the community's derelicts came to know our address and our house became the most popular one in the street for people who dropped in for meals and handouts from my young wife who would meet them at the door.

The third manse in which we lived was in the country town of Ararat, Victoria. 90 High Street, Ararat, was right opposite the busy Ararat railway station. Here, all night during harvest time the trains would be shunting the huge open carriages of wheat backwards with front and rear talking to each other with systems of whistles signals. Beside us was a plumber who manufactured large round rainwater tanks and the hammering of the tanks night and day made sure there was always plenty for us to listen to. We had not been called to this church and they were not expecting a minister. It was a church that had been riven by strife and factions. A series of young ministers had left broken-hearted. While preparing to go overseas for some graduate study the Conference of Churches of Christ of Victoria and Tasmania asked me to go up to this little country church, to sort out the differences and settle it down so that a minister might be sent and have a fair chance of having a happy ministry.

All of our furniture and belongings had been sold or else sent to America in preparation for our arrival. We had nothing at all except what we stood up in when we arrived at the door of the church manse. The church people knew we were coming and knew that we had no furniture of our own but they had guaranteed that they would furnish it. The house itself was an absolute disgrace. The iron roof was totally rusted, having not seen a coat of paint since the First World War. The timber walls were all cracked and the paint had long since disappeared leaving the boards exposed to the weather. There was a rusty iron fence outside and an unmade dirt track up the side of the house. On my first day I painted the rusty iron fence with zinc chromate, turning it bright yellow. The following Sunday, people certainly knew we had arrived.

The church had promised to furnish the manse but we were surprised with what greeted us. There was a nondescript old wooden bed in the front room with a wire that sagged almost to the floor. A kapok mattress full of lumps on this weighed down the wire. It was more comfortable to put the old kapok mattress on the floor than on the wire. The rest of the house had an odd assortment of mismatched chairs and tables and an old lounge suite that had been in somebody's garage. We had been furnished with people's second hand furniture that was not good enough to give to St. Vincent de Paul.

The toilet, as with country toilets, was outside and down the back. There was a slow combustion stove that was very slow and was without a firewall, which meant that it was completely useless. The hot water service was supposed to run off the stove and so it had to burn night and day, but as the tank was out in the open and not insulated we had lukewarm water even at the best of times. The old wooden house had huge rooms with high ceilings. In the heat of the summer the house was an oven by day and in the cold of the evenings, freezing by night. There were no carpets but odd pieces of congolium were tacked to the floor. It was an absolute hovel.

But here we turned some back sheds into some fowl houses and started keeping some chooks, brought home sleepers from along the railway sidings and split them in the backyard to keep the slow combustion fire burning, laid out gardens in the front and along the side and at the rear and made for the first time a level lawn. It was here that our second child was born in the local country hospital. We ended up staying two years because the church experienced the nearest I have ever seen to a Rev. ival, with large numbers of new members joining it. The church property itself was demolished in part and new buildings were erected and the whole life of the church became vital and expanded. By the time a new minister was called and willing to come, arrangements were made to purchase a new manse.

Our fourth manse was 101 Chesterville Road, Cheltenham. We had struck another winner. It also was an old wooden house but better painted with asbestos sheet walls. The church had once possessed a very nice manse for its minister but had sold it in order to buy the block of land next door to the church upon which this old house had stood. They explained to me when I came that they were thinking of building a new manse. We stayed in that manse for the next ten years and it was always the same. Every time the wind blew the carpets would all rise up. The lounge room carpet would rise nearly three feet in the centre on a windy day. The lathe and plaster walls and ceilings were in very bad shape because of movement in the foundations from the rumbling traffic that screeched to a halt at the major intersection right outside our door. There were 36 traffic lights outside our front door on a major 13-lane highway and the rolling of the heavy trucks and sudden braking at a red traffic light always caused the house to vibrate. The stumps had gone and the walls were sagging and as the walls moved huge cracks appeared across them. Lumps of plaster would regularly fall off the ceiling roof. But this house had an inside toilet and it was in this house that two of our children were born in the next ten years. It was here Beverley's mother came to live in a tiny room at the back of the house during her last illness as we nursed her towards her death.

Once more we built gardens, both flower and vegetable gardens and a chook shed for ducks and chooks. In the large backyard we had a sheep, a tortoise, a dog, a cat, 56 white mice, a gander, several drakes, a flock of ducks, a rooster or two, some hens and, at various times, other additional members of the family.

The problems of the dropping floor, the sagging walls and the pieces of ceiling that kept falling in the various rooms of the house, was overcome by the Officers after a great deal of opposition. The time for building of a new manse was not now, but as it was impossible to live with the plaster falling down about our ears, a practical solution was reached. A false ceiling was put in throughout the rooms and sheets of masonite were nailed up over all the walls to stop the plaster from falling.

After ten years that church had grown to be a very large church with huge properties with the first of three retirement villages being built and by now a large staff. When I had come I was the only person on the payroll but now we employed an office secretary, a minister of education, a minister of visitation, a minister of evangelism, a minister of administration, a social worker, a part-time nurse, a retirement centre receptionist and so on. The time had come to replace the old manse. The church quickly gathered the money to build the new house. Plans were drawn up and the old house was demolished while we lived a little distance away. I took our children to see the last day in the life of the house as a bulldozer pushed it all into a heap and set fire to it. Our children were absolutely devastated. I did not realise the traumatic effect because for four of them it was the only house they knew as home.

Six months later we moved into the new manse, large, light airy, beautifully presented. It was the first time we had ever had such comfort and convenience in our life and just after we were shifted into it the call came to leave to come to Sydney.

And so we came to 16 Corona Avenue, Roseville, our fifth manse, a grand old home that had been the home of Superintendents since 1930 with large rooms and high ceilings. But after the new modern house it felt dark and depressing. The laundry was outside the house up behind the garage and had no hot water connected to it. The hot water had to be carried from the kitchen in buckets.

The carpet was original 1930 and had holes in many places and had split at the joins. The Officers were apologetic and immediately set about building a new laundry and enlarging the kitchen and installing hot water to the laundry. As for the carpets I looked inside hall cupboards and, sure enough, found that the carpet layers had even carpeted inside the cupboards in those extravagant days of the 1930's. So those pieces were cut out, the holes were patched and the split seams were re-sewn and they lasted us another ten years until they were replaced when we added a fine study in the lofty roof space. But once more we had the old plaster walls cracking with each drought as the walls moved and the plaster came unattached. Sand and dust came in the cracks, covering the furniture.

The unusual thing in all of this is that from the early days of our marriage my wife and I struggled to get enough money to put a deposit upon a house of our own. Eventually in 1971 we bought our own house and it has followed us wheRever we have been, but we have been unable to live in our own house because the church where we served insisted that it was proper that we should live in the church residence. So our own house has been for us a refuge, one day a fortnight when we would mow the lawns, do the painting, clean out the gutters, do the gardens and pay the rates like any other couple.

Our experiences of church manses, in spite of the fact that we have ministered in two of the largest and most significant churches in the nation, have been as I have described. And yet we hear people say, 'But aren't you lucky, having the church provide a house for you.' They never realise that ministers rent their manses from the churches and the rent is taken out of the salary before it is even paid to them.

But over all the years we have never complained and we have never asked the church to do anything major about our manse believing that it is the church's responsibility to provide a convenient and comfortable residence at the level of its own concern for its minister. God has blessed us with great happiness in the houses in which we lived. But on the whole the church members who were given the responsibility of seeing the Church manse was kept in good condition failed to carry out their responsibilities. But I must admit that where we were going to live never consciously figured in our minds whenever we heard a call to minister anywhere and never once have we actually visited a manse prior to accepting a call. The heart of each home in which we lived was Beverley. Since a deep friendship began when she and I were both thirteen, she has been much more than wife and mother. She has been in full time ministry too.

No other woman has raised so much money anywhere in Australia using only traditional methods and volunteers to aid the poor than Beverley. Today thousands of Sydney's poor, needy, homeless, derelict and ill have been helped by Beverley and her remarkable band of volunteers. When we shifted to Sydney in 1979, Beverley was appalled at the plight of the homeless in inner Sydney, especially the more than 100 derelict men who slept in deplorable conditions in squalid dormitories in Francis Street's 'Night Refuge for Men'. While I worked to complete a new high-rise for them in Bourke Street, she realised that second-hand clothes, food and companionship were not enough, but that large sums of money were required to provide decent accommodation and basic care.

A quiet and reserved person, she did not find it easy to mix with the men nor to start raising money. Her four teenage children needed all of her attention. It would have been easy to forget the needs of the inner city. She started immediately to care for them and to raise funds to improve their conditions. Then in November 1980, several boats with Vietnamese refugees landed on the north coast of Western Australia including 30 children whose parents had been shot and raped by pirates in the China Sea.

Wesley Mission was asked by the Commonwealth Government to care for them.

However the Government provided only $5000 as a one-off grant for their care. Beverley decided to help provide care for the 30 boys. A huge residence with 30 bedrooms was found and in five days it was cleaned, painted and renovated. Beverley purchased hundreds of plastic bags that she labelled 'VIET-KITS'. Each included a list of requirements either for hygiene, educational, medical, or clothing needs. Over one weekend they were distributed to hundreds of church members who each filled one bag with specific requirement for one boy. From appeals on television and radio I was offered 120 truckloads of bedding for 30 children, furniture, books, sporting equipment and school requisites. Health-care, cooking, language interpreters, staff and volunteers all had to be recruited and organised and with the help of others from Wesley the children were all adequately provided for.

Over the next six years each boy completed the Higher School Certificate and every one went to university, or institutes of technology, except three, one of which commenced a motor engine repair business and the other two opened their own restaurant. She became a foster mother to the boys in the grief of their own loss and the difficulties of establishing themselves in a strange land with different language and culture.

Beverley saw how much could be done by organising volunteers and in 1980 accepted the task of raising money to help provide for Sydney's homeless, the Vietnam orphans, aged people and children in care. Working with a group of mainly elderly ladies, she organised craft stalls, cake stalls, dinner parties and the like and raised in her first year $72,000.

When she saw what that money did in providing personal comforts, buses, furniture, holidays for the under privileged, relief for inner city families and the like, she commenced working full-time in an unpaid task of raising money. She has organised concerts, garage sales, book fairs, garden parties, dinners, dances, hundreds of stalls to sell cakes, food and hand-crafts, organised radio and TV ads, distributed handbills, gained the presence of personalities from the media, political and ceremonial life including Hazel Hawke, Lady Stephen, Lady Rowland, Lady Cutler and a host of others. The leading celebrities in Australia accepted her invitation to open special events.

The personal pressure was enormous. It has been a united family effort with each of her children helping their mum. Apart from this, she has supported me in all of my work as head of Australia's largest Christian welfare organisation and as minister's wife in Australia's largest church where she works as an Elder.

Beverley used her own home to type letters, sew bedspreads, cushions and aprons, bake cakes and made floral arrangements. She constantly soaked tens of thousands of used postage stamps and packaged them. She organised letters to hundreds of companies requesting donations of outdated stock, off-cuts and factory seconds, which she then distributed to others who made goods for sale.

At the same time over 400 volunteers were recruited and organised through monthly meetings, which she chaired. Soon help was being provided to fourteen childrens homes, a sheltered workshop, nine aged care centres, two hospitals and sixteen homes for the intellectually handicapped, mostly in the inner suburbs of Sydney - a total of 122 centres of care.

A retired lady jeweller offered to repair fashion jewellery so Beverley set up in George Street on the footpath, a stall where she personally sold the jewellery each week. While organising hundreds of other volunteers, she led by example becoming involved in all areas of fundraising. Others joined in to help selling the stock, especially Ivan and Alice Reichelt and Maria Burns.

In all of this practical Christianity, Beverley maintained an enthusiasm even when fulfilling tasks that were taxing and against her natural inclinations. She would not accept methods of fundraising that would violate the Christian conscience of some and so no form of gambling, raffles, bingo or alcohol was used. Yet without these she had raised as clear profit after expenses a total of over three and a quarter million dollars. Beverley worked voluntarily and never claimed any expenses.

Beverley Moyes (nee Vernon) was born in Mont Albert, Victoria. She was educated at Mont Albert Central School and Camberwell High School. After secretarial studies she worked for seven years with an English textile-importing firm. Beverley attended the Box Hill Church of Christ and was a member there for eight years until her marriage. During her time with the Box Hill Church of Christ she taught Sunday School, led a junior girl's Club and held leadership positions in the Box Hill Church and in various youth organisations.

Beverley and I met at the Box Hill Church of Christ at the age of 13 and we have been together ever since. We married in 1959 and now have four married children and their spouses and ten grandchildren.

In 1966 we commenced ministry at the Cheltenham Victoria, Church of Christ, where we ministered for thirteen years. During our first three ministries, Beverley taught Sunday School, led youth groups, taught Scripture in school, led women's groups, was a member of two choirs as the accompanist, played organ or piano for weddings, funerals and church services and performed all the other tasks necessary in a minister's home.

During our Wesley Mission ministry, Beverley was more than a voluntary fundraiser. Beverley's activities have been many and varied. Whilst still seeing herself as a minister's wife and all that entailed, she has led prayer groups, a home Bible Study group, spent much time counselling and giving pastoral care to Wesley Mission church members and the now paid staff at Wesley Mission. She counselled troubled people, provided food for transients and took into our home an elderly lady who needed nursing and a young drug addict.

In recognition of Beverley's voluntary work, both in fund raising and in other areas of work at Wesley Mission, in 1988 Beverley was honoured by the Bi-Centennial Women 88 Awards, as one of the twenty outstanding women achievers in Australia and was listed as one of the ten major award recipients. Thousands of women were nominated through Australia's premier women's magazine, *Australian Women's Weekly* and to be judged one of the Nation's ten most outstanding women was a great achievement. Majorie Jackson who was also in the final selection, became a friend when Beverley was elected as one of Australia's ten outstanding women.

Also, in 1989 Beverley was the recipient of an Australia Day Citizenship Award given by the Sydney City Council for voluntary service to people of the city of Sydney.

Further to that, in the 1989 Queen's Birthday Honours List, Beverley was appointed a Member in the General Division of the Order of Australia (AM). At this time we were the only couple in Australia to be separately honoured. In recognition of Beverley's work as a volunteer amongst the people of Sydney, the Rotary Club of Sydney awarded her a Paul Harris Fellowship, one of Rotary's highest honours.

Family life has always been of greatest importance to Beverley and has always been and remains her top priority, along with her strong commitment to God and service to him. She is an elder in the Church at Wesley Mission and she actively works in a caring and counselling role to the hundreds of people involved with Wesley Mission. She leads in public prayer and for years has led a good Bible study group in her home.

The program of the Australian Bicentennial Authority was really a wonderful one. They called for nominations for Australia's most outstanding women in every part of the nation and 1200 women were nominated for their outstanding permanent achievement to Australian society including Sallyanne Atkinson then the Lord Mayor of Brisbane; General Eva Burrows, then the world leader of the Salvation Army; Joan Carden, Opera Singer; Nancy Kato, author; June Dally Watkins, famous model; Caroline Jones, media presenter; Eileen Joyce, the great international pianist; Dame Leonie Kramer, the university professor just elected Chancellor of Sydney University; Senator Jean Melzer of Victoria; the athletes Shirley Strickland and Marjorie Jackson; Margaret Noff of the Wayside Chapel,;Nancy Bird-Walton the famous aviatrix; Professor Di Yerbury - Vice Chancellor of Macquarie University and so many others. Every famous woman in Australia was on the nomination list.

The aim of the Bicentennial year was to recognise the achievements of Australian women and to give public recognition of women who have a high personal quality that has been translated to significant achievement in their personal and community lives.

Beverley had been nominated by some men on our Church Board. The requirements were that the Australian Bicentennial Authority were looking for 'Australian women who have consistently shown such qualities as courage, tenacity, leadership, compassion, humanity, determination and creativity in the work in which they were involved. 'Beverley was told she had been a chosen among 20 such women to be the final representatives from across Australia. She and I were invited to fly to Melbourne to a special dinner of honour to be attended by hundreds of people in the Melbourne Hilton.

At the Melbourne Hilton, there were more than 500 of Australia's outstanding women. There were ten chosen as the outstanding achievers in Australia. There was Dr Patricia Brennen: doctor, missionary, reformer, leader of the movement to ordain women priests in the Anglican Church; Dr Helen Caldicot medical doctor and leader of USA's powerful group Doctors for Social Responsibility and well-known anti-nuclear campaigner; Kay Cottee the solo yachtswoman who was the first woman to solo circum navigate the world in a sailing vessel; Dr Jocelyn Scutt Australia's most academically qualified lawyer including 4 masters degrees in two different fields and her doctorate was done in the work of rape and prostitution and non-sexist law. There was Christine Milne a remarkable member of the Tasmanian Parliament. There was Marjorie Silver Weiss, the founder of Australia's Flying Nurses Service which pre-dated even the Royal Flying Doctor Service and who has given a long life time of serving the Far West Children's Hospital Scheme and outback nursing, Joan Winch, outback health worker of Western Australia, who was named the Aboriginal of the year, 1987. Among these top ten was Beverley Moyes, for 'a life time of support to people in need, using her own home and organising church women in raising millions of dollars for charity, the most successful in Australian history, using traditional women's methods of crafts, cooking, concerts and the like.'

The judges said of Beverley 'She rarely receives recognition for her extraordinary community service. This modest self effacing woman is truly typical of Australia's quiet achievers.' For us as a family, it was not new that this wife and mother should be elected as one of the ten most significant women in Australia. We all knew she deserved this honour. Beverley stood before those 500 outstanding Australian women being chosen in the top ten. It was such an honour but more was to come. Beverley was asked to speak on behalf of all of the women of Australia. Hers was the only speech given by the ten award winners. Beverley acknowledged her faith in God and what a privilege it was to help those people who can't help themselves. She thanked church members and others who motivated and inspired her and indicated that she wanted to go on helping others in the community as long as she was able. It was a beautiful speech and strongly applauded by the ten fellow awardees and the 500 guests.

The ten top awardees each received a gold, ebony and silver broach and $2000 worth of crafts of her own choosing made by outstanding Australian craftswomen. Beverley chose a magnificent quilted wall hanging, which hangs in our house to this day and a handcrafted leather handbag and some jewellery. At our table was Marjorie Jackson. Marjorie received a special commendation for her work, as not only an all-Australian, great athlete but for her work in raising more than $1 million for the Leukaemia foundation.

Because of a number of press conferences and media events in which they were both involved they spent some quality time together. We never lost contact with this remarkable lady. Now in her late 60's, Marjorie still lives in Adelaide where she is the greatly loved and respected Governor of South Australia.

In all of this Beverley was a busy wife and mother. Each of the children got married and grandchildren began arriving and she saw her role increasingly as being mother, not only to her family, but also to the many hundreds of people within the life of Wesley Mission. As an active Elder of the church she is busy caring and counselling people in the life of the worshipping congregations and was elected for this work 'Mother Of The Year'. The members of Wesley Mission were unanimous in choosing her and the announcement was met with cheering and appreciative acclaim.

That part of her life has evolved and changed leaving her a very experienced public speaker and mature leader. One aspect of Beverley's life and ministry in Sydney has been the exercise of a gift of hospitality. Hundreds of people have appreciated the meals that she has prepared and served in our Roseville home. The dining room table seats 12 so consequently dinner parties always have 12 present. She has cooked and prepared for hundreds of people over the years in these dinner parties. New staff, donors to Wesley Mission, members and visitors to this country have all been welcomed as guests to our table. She has also presided at meals or functions in which more than a dozen Governors General, Prime Ministers, Premiers and their wives have been present, as well as visiting dignitaries from overseas such as Sarah Ferguson, The Duchess of York. In turn Beverley has been a guest at many functions for distinguished and royal visitors. She has had conversations with the Queen and Prince Philip and other members of the Royal family.

In all of this Beverley remains a very humble person, loving her garden, always growing flowers and giving them every Sunday to other people or a carton of eggs from our hens or a parcel of vegetables from her extensive vegetable garden. But Beverley is never happier than when fulfilling her role as an Elder within Wesley Mission congregations; visiting the sick, leading the home Bible study group and home prayer group, welcoming visitors and caring for those who sit in the pews. Her gifts and talents in ministry did not come naturally; they have been acquired by hard work, careful preparation and a willingness to be uncomfortable as she tackles something new. She is a highly intelligent woman who listens to all major newscasts and understands contemporary issues well. It is wonderful to live with a woman of intellect and contemporary understanding.

Beverley and I have frequently been interviewed by journalists. City journalists were not like Chris Fisher in Ararat. We discovered a new breed. I also discovered that ethics was not a word to be associated with some journalists. There is a senior woman journalist writing for the major press who is known for her viciousness in attacking people. She never seeks to build up, only tear down. Her name is a by-word amongst public figures. I remember on one occasion when she wanted to come and interview. Many of my friends advised me to ignore and cancel the appointment. I hadn't found a vicious reporter pRev. iously and rather foolishly granted an interview in which I openly and frankly answered her questions.

Most of what I had to say was not news worthy and consequently didn't see the light of day. Instead she attacked my footwear, my ties and my appearance. She actually made mistakes on all of them. She declared that I was wearing extremely expensive silk ties from overseas. The fact was I had purchased three ties from the corner store of Market and Pitt Street, which had been closing down owing to a fire sale for the last three years and had been running a special on ties - 3 for $5! The image that she gave was that I was expensively dressed and possibly using money given to a charity on my own appearance. I discovered this woman over a period of time was incredibly vicious and seemed to want to destroy any person with a high profile within the community.

A senior male journalist I discovered had a deep-seated hatred of clergymen. I don't know where this hate began but I certainly know he turned the blowtorch on me with some of the most untrue and vicious lies I have ever encountered in my life. One of his often repeated insinuations made public was his quote 'He drives a gleaming gold Fairlane' as much as to say, I had the most expensive car possible and that again I was wasting charitable money. He also used to link me with American television evangelists in a way that was totally untrue and unfair. The bit about the gleaming gold Fairlaine, for those who knew me was a bit of a laugh. My car is a Fairlaine, a 1983 model. I guess there are not many people still driving 22-year-old cars on the road these days. And it is gleaming because both my wife and I are careful to wash it and wax it with the result that it has remained rust free over the whole period of its life. She's a delightful looking grand old bus and we enjoy driving it. But its insured value is less than $1000. But not according to the way this journalist wrote it. Apparently he has problems with cleanliness as well as godliness.

I discovered also in the mid-eighties, another kind of senior journalist who works for a respectable newspaper but whose articles I never now read. I discovered that he deliberately generated gossip in order to get headlines and news stories that were blatantly false but just dropped into obscurity with the next new story that came along. I remember him ringing me one morning as he was getting close to a deadline and asking me 'Is it true that Premier Neville Wran is putting together a group of people to take control of the Channel Ten television network and that you are one of his key players?' I replied to him, 'I don't know what

Neville Wran might be considering. All I know is that I have no comment to make. I have not spoken to Mr Wran in the last few weeks and I certainly have no intention of becoming involved in the ownership or running of a major television network.' That statement was translated into a major story much to the surprise of Mr Wran as well as myself 'Wran and Moyes to take over Ten TV' read the headline. I gathered he had asked Mr Wran whether he knew that I was considering him to be chairman of the board to take over Ten TV. I have never read his articles since discovering his techniques. Recently a leading politician told me of several similar incidences with the same journalist. You would think the newspaper Editor in Chief would call him to heel.

But Fathers Day 1986 was to introduce our whole family into the gutter ethics of journalism. I had always noted with some pleasure the very distinguished people who were chosen each year to be Father of the Year by the National and NSW Fathers Day Council. Usually I felt their choices were very well considered and appropriate. Never for a moment did I think that during 1985 I would be approached to consider being the NSW Father of The Year for 1986. I was approached by the Father's Day Council in the person of the President, Denis Cudworth. Mr Cudworth was a remarkably fine upright businessman with a good reputation within the retail industry. He organised a small luncheon with his personal assistant Mrs Margaret Wangman who handled most of the arrangements for the Father of the Year function and with Sir Ian Turbott, the previous Father of the Year (a diplomat of very distinguished international experience and the newly appointed chancellor of the University of Western Sydney).

At this luncheon I was surprised that the NSW Father of the Year Council had researched a number of suitable candidates very thoroughly. I was even more surprised when I discovered that the Father's Day Council had a very serious purpose in the promotion of the Father of the Year. That purpose was expressed in the 'Decalogue'. '10 Rules for being a good Father', which was promoted very widely at their luncheons and other functions. They also raised money for most worthy charitable purposes. At that first meeting with the president and former Father of the Year, I must say I was most impressed with their research, thoroughness and gentlemanly approach to the whole issue. Mr Cudworth noted I was wearing cufflinks. He then informed me that he was the leading importer of cuff links into Australia.

Consequently the NSW Father's Day Council had a luncheon of several hundred business and community leaders on Friday August 22nd at the Sheraton Wentworth Hotel when I became the 30th Father of the Year. There was a very distinguished gathering of community leaders supporting this programme, including the Governor Air Marshal Sir James Rowland and Lady Rowland, the former Governor Sir Roden Cutler and Lady Cutler, the heads of all the churches and the Chief Rabbi. There were also former Fathers of the Year including some whom I was pleased to call friends, such as the entertainer Bobby Limb, the Australian Test Cricketer Alan Davidson, the medical researcher Dr Brad Norrington, the former Chief Commissioner of Police Jim Lees, the former Governor General Sir Zelman Cohen, Broadcaster Gary O'Callagahan, Major General Alan Stretton, the hero of the re-building of Darwin and many others.

The presentation as Father of the Year was extremely well received by all of those present. In my speech I reflected on what my father had given to me. I explained my father's premature death from alcoholism and how that influenced my attitudes today. I said, 'I am different from my father in every way because I don't drink and he was never involved with the church. And I don't swear either and the only words I can ever remember my Father saying to me was, 'God Damn you Mick' (Mick being his nickname for me). My mother and I discovered him dead one night not far from my home where he had fallen down drunk and hit his head on the gutter. I was only eight at the time and I remember the doctor saying to me, 'You are the man of the house now, you are responsible for the family.'

His death gave me a very strong sense of responsibility but knowing what insecurity felt like at an early age made me very responsible. It also made me ensure that my four children had a strong sense of security. I believe that children gain this primarily by having parents who are happy and loving towards each other. So my wife Beverley and I have always demonstrated our affection for each other openly.'

As part of my duties it was expected that I would travel around the state and accept speaking invitations to support the role and significance of the family within the community. This I was pleased to do and it gave me a most enjoyable year-long experience.

On the morning on which the announcement was to be made, Denis Cudworth had warned me that we would have all of the television stations coming to our home for interviews, that there would be radio personalities and press reporters there by the dozen.

I thought that some of them would want to see me at work in my study, so I cleared up my desk and threw out a whole lot of papers with which I had finished. I then emptied my waste paper basket into our bin. Meanwhile Beverley was busy cutting sandwiches and preparing morning tea for the press. We did television interviews for all the major television stations and also for the radio stations. The press asked me some questions about my relationships with my children and my wife and I remember saying to one; 'The best thing a father can do for his children is to love their mother.'

Beverley and I did not realise it but some of the press were taking our children away by themselves. We didn't realise it because Beverley and I were being questioned by other members of the press about a conflict between being a clergyman and being a father. I regarded it as a privilege without any areas of conflict and

Beverley supported me on this.

It was only afterwards that I discovered that other reporters had taken our children off one by one on the pretext of asking to be shown to their rooms and quizzed very strongly. It became quite apparent that they had been charged by their Senior Editor with the task of finding dirt on my relationships with my children which would allow them to have a headline such as 'Child Abuser Father of the Year' or suchlike. I remembered Jenny saying with a horrified voice. 'They kept asking me, 'Does your father belt you? Does he abuse you?' Peter said that he felt like hitting one of the questioners who said to him in a very sneaky fashion 'How do you feel when your Mother and Father quarrel?' He replied with a great deal of strength that his mother and father didn't quarrel. David and Andrew were asked, 'Does your father show any interest in you or is it mainly in his work?' David said he didn't know how to reply to that question because we were all interested in my work not just me but my wife and children as well but at the same time I showed great interest in each of my children. David said, 'Then I remembered something you said Dad, that we should give first commitment to God, then to our family and then to our work. The family always before work' Afterwards someone said, 'There are papers all over the nature strip!' Apparently a couple of guys were going through all the copies of letters I had put in the rubbish bin. Someone had thought that if they investigated our rubbish bin they might find something that would incriminate me!

It was all to no avail. The chooks had scratched around every possible avenue and couldn't find anything except a well balanced, well relating family.

The public however responded in a magnificent way with hundreds of letters, telegrams and faxes of congratulations from people that I never thought would take the trouble. I received congratulations and invitations from Municipal Councils, Parliamentarians, the Lord Mayor, the Premier, from Rotarians here and overseas, from other church leaders and from book publishers.

My children responded with a great deal of affection and pride. They each sent me special Father's Day messages that year. I have kept them and only just now have looked back through them. There was one of my children, our only daughter Jenny writing, 'I cannot remember a time when you haven't been to us, the Father of the Year.'

'Father of the Year' was a great honour but there were those who were determined that that honour should have been turned into a story of abuse and conflict. Denis Cudworth was right. There would be a great interest by the media and the press but what I didn't realise was that there would be a few in their number who were determined to discover the Father of the Year had feet of clay. That their role was to pull down rather than build up and to get for themselves headlines over stories regardless of the ethics used or the truth involved.

I always regarded myself as a fit person. I never realised how that changed over the years. At 18, I was one of the top junior athletes in the state. At 35, I was still playing in a football team, training twice a week and competing in matches every Saturday. At 45 I still ran everywhere and leapt up the stairs two at a time. But the next twenty years would give me two major health scares because I was not fit and lived such a busy life.

In May 1996, I was invited, with the Governor of NSW, to join in the opening of a new Emergency Ward at the magnificent Sydney Adventist Hospital. I was asked to speak on 'Recollections Of A Former Patient.' What I said at the opening explains what for my wife, family and myself was the biggest crisis of my life to that date.

The best thing that has happened in my life, in medical terms, occurred in this hospital when I had heart surgery, in December 1993.

I was carrying a heavy load. I was managing Wesley Mission, which was on a strong growth curve. We had then grown to 1,750 full-time paid staff, 3,500 volunteers, 250 caring centres, hospitals, nursing homes, retirement villages and children's homes; I was senior minister of the largest church of any denomination in the nation with an annual budget of $70 million, host of a national weekly TV program, daily radio programs, had been writing, lecturing and counselling non-stop, preaching overseas and for 15 years had spent 35 weekends every year conducting small evangelistic campaigns in 400 small towns all over the nation-which meant, flying back to Sydney every Sunday afternoon to conduct afternoon meetings and evening church services before doing three hours of broadcasting until mid-night. December had us booked into 67 Christmas parties, more than 100 speeches and sermons and 50,000 people at our biggest service 'A Darling Harbour Christmas' which I would host on national television. It was the end of really great year!

The cardiologist was blunt. 'You are overweight. If you had been a drinker or a smoker like your father you would have been dead as he was at thirty-eight. At present half your heart is dead meat. It may never recover. You have already had two major heart attacks and you continued working. I want you in the Sydney Adventist Hospital immediately. If you have the slightest pain now, you will go by ambulance to the Royal North Shore Casualty. At present you are ten minutes from death.'

Safely transported to Sydney Adventist Hospital, I was given an Angiogram. The cardiologist and two surgeons explained, 'You have arteries blocked in five places. I am trying to book a theatre and a surgeon for first thing tomorrow. You are in urgent need of surgery.' The surgeon smiled and said to my wife, 'I have been looking at your husband's heart on the screen. He certainly presents a challenge.'

The operation took four hours, required five bypasses, and for 47 minutes my heart was stopped. The Sydney Morning Herald and the Telegraph announced it to the world. I was unconscious. My wife took a long and concerned call from the Governor. Then came assurances of prayer from prayer groups all over the nation. More than 1000 letters, faxes and cards came to the hospital from the Premier, politicians, church leaders, international Christian leaders, the Trade Union Movement, media personalities, church members and myriads of people who sent flowers and fruit.

My family gathered round the bed in the Intensive Care Unit while a nursing sister stayed at the foot of the bed monitoring the equipment over 48 hours. I remember nothing of that, except my family told me that when one sister left to get something, my son remarked she was a very pretty young nurse, to which I apparently replied, 'Yes, but she's a bit of a tart!'

When I arrived up in the ward, the bed had been stripped and a manufacturer of a new kind of mattress, on hearing of my hospitalisation, had visited the hospital, and had received permission to install a new kind of mattress so I could test drive it. The recovery days in the private ward were a wonderful experience of gratitude to God for growing recovery and wonderful appreciation for my wife whom I had courted continuously since we were both aged thirteen.

On the fourth day I rang my wife at 6am and asked her to bring my best cardigan, which would fit around the tubes. She came in at 7am and I had been up and was fully dressed. The Nurse Unit Manager arrived and scolded, 'Look at him, he's up and dressed like he's ready for church. He must think it's Sunday.' I replied, 'Not here Sister. It's the Sabbath!'

On the fifth day, I experienced the worst pain in my life for six hours while blood and fluid in the rib cage was drained off. Referred pain, at the point of shoulder ended completely as the catheter was withdrawn. I was walking one kilometre up and down the passage, each morning and afternoon.

At home I worked hard at breathing and developing my lung capacity, at walking every day, then swimming every day. I lost 17 lbs, was leaner, fitter and healthier than I had been for years. At the end of eight weeks I was back at work completely. I gradually resigned from the Presidency of five national organisations, stepped down as Chairman of more than a dozen committees including the Boards of Management of two hospitals. I continued as President of the Rotary Club of Sydney. I was going to have a narrow focus on my core work.

I thank God for five features of the hospital:

1. For the superb surgical teams and facilities;

2. For the excellence in caring by the staff, including escorting of my family

through the Intensive Care Unit explaining to them what would happen to husband and father;

3. For the promptness and generosity of my Hospital Benefits fund into which I had contributed for thirty years before I made a significant withdrawal;

4. For the Adventist friends I had known for years who made sure I received VIP treatment, including the CEO who arrived to welcome me with a bottle of non-alcoholic wine to toast my recovery; the Chaplains who made the Christian presence among the staff so real, the dieticians who reorganised my life-style and even the physio who pummelled my chest and made me cough had an ounce of compassion.

5. For the classes in diet, exercise, stress and life-style led by a young woman I had lectured in Wesley Institute.

It was the best thing of my life in medical terms and it occurred in a fine hospital.

There is that delightful chapter in Mark Twain's, The Adventures of Tom Sawyer (Chapter 17) when the three boys, Tom Sawyer, Huck Finn and Joe Harper are believed by the town to have drowned in the river. The following Sunday a funeral service is held for the three missing boys. Only they are alive and hiding in the church's gallery. They listen to the eulogies over their own lives and hear what people thought of them. So moved were they that they decided to come down from the gallery and present themselves to the public.

For two months I was in the gallery listening in at my own funeral service! It was a humbling experience. My dear friend, Vice President of the Boys Brigade Australia and fellow Rotarian Carl Harman, a year pRev. ious had felt a pain in his heart and had died immediately. For some reason, that did not happened to me. I felt no pain, suffered two heart attacks, had one portion of my heart turn to what my surgeon described as 'dead meat', had my heart and lungs stopped for forty-seven minutes, received five bypasses to the heart and within two months was back at work. Our whole family were grateful to God for such a positive outcome.

From the time we were teenagers Beverley and I knew we would marry. We knew we wanted to have four children – we even picked some of their names. We had four children, they have introduced to our family four greatly loved spouses and ten grandchildren. We are a tightly knit family that see each other frequently. Our children enjoy their own company without us and every year they go on holidays together with all the cousins joining in.

****

As our children came along, some principles have guided us as a family. Seeing Beverley has been awarded 'Mother of the Year' and I was 'Father of the Year' these principles may be of interest to others. In an era when family life is often denigrated and others claim it is an impossible dream, we have kept these principles to the fore.

Beverley and I pray aloud with each other every night for each family member. Of course we pray for others, for friends and world situations, but we pray for each family member without fail. Prayers are answered, concerns we have are remembered and decisions to do something about such concerns are made. Nothing has aided our marriage togetherness so much as that daily prayer.

Then we have been fairly strict with our children as they were growing. My experience in the juvenile justice system and my days as a probation and parole officer underscored this point. Once I examined the files of 104 serious offenders and every one of them mentioned 'little or no home discipline'. One day in a courtroom listening to another list of offences I realised the danger was greater with too little discipline in the family than with too much.

Beverley and I had an occasional need to smack a child but no child was ever beaten or spanked. We encouraged good behaviour continuously with praise and if needs be, disciplined bad behaviour by depriving the child of some luxury or freedom. Our grandchildren have also been brought up the same way. None of our children have ever been convicted, smoked or used alcohol or drugs even though they have been available.

We worked on the principle that our family did things together. We would spend time together and always holiday together and if one child brought home from school a swear word or concept that was not right, we explained that while their friends might speak like that or behave like that, that was not said or done in our family.

We held our breath when Andrew our youngest became a good musician and founded a rock band. We encouraged them to rehearse in our home, but were concerned when their only venue for 'gigs' was in large hotels and nightclubs. But the band played on and Andrew never did drugs or drank alcohol like those listening to them. To this day, none of the family are into alcohol or drugs.

We keep family celebrations. Everyone has a birthday party when their turn comes with every family member contributing. With grandchildren, that is twenty family celebrations per year, plus Christmas, Mothers Day and Fathers Day. Roughly every second week of the year we get together to celebrate. Other occasions like breakfast together after the Easter Sunrise service make for many happy family traditions.

Because Beverley and I lead a very busy life with hundreds of appointments and nights out each year, this would seem to be a scheduling nightmare. It is never an issue of scheduling. It is a matter of priorities. At the beginning of each new year I write into my diary, 23 family celebrations and around them over 400 other appointments. The family has priority.

Another principle we have followed is not to expect too much but to realise God is faithful. We have always had a very restricted income. We learned to budget, never to have debts (except for house mortgage) and not to live extravagantly. Our children understood we could not have all that others had. But God was faithful and we always had enough. I have had staff that also were on limited budgets but people gave to them very generously. I have known pastors to be given airfares, holidays, motor vehicles and even a house! We have never received such gifts. Nor have we expressed our needs to others. Our needs were between ourselves and God and he supplied them. God has given us good health. There is no reason why we should not work hard to achieve what we need. With good budget discipline we had enough money.

We have never been ashamed to wear second hand clothes or gifts of clothes. Beverley knitted for every member of the family every year. Her mother was a professional tailoress, who taught Beverley how to read patterns, cut material and make clothes. Our children were always well dressed. Then a lady whom I helped asked if we would receive gifts of clothing. She was head of the returns department in a large store that sold exclusive children's clothing. Many wealthy mothers returned clothing because a button was off, or a zip was broken or some stitching was unravelled. Every month to our home came a large bale of hardly ever worn, slightly imperfect goods. Beverley mended or repaired each one and gave them to families in our church or to our children. Result? The best-dressed kids in the street! Likewise I was given shirts and jackets that had been on store models in shop windows and therefore could not be sold. I purchased shoes that had been on store models for quarter price. Then, when I started appearing on television every week, a Christian tailor John H. Cutler offered to make me a suit every second year, which he did for twenty years. In turn, all our own clothes were handed on to other families or to the homeless. I have sometimes seen my former suits walking the streets!

Or take bread. For years Beverley would take the children in the family car at 5:30pm to a couple of bakeries where they would have large garbage bags full of unsold bread and cakes. Beverley would then drive on a 'bread-run' and deliver the bread and cakes to each of our retirement villages where everyone would take their pick, then onto some poor families and finally to a convent where a group of nuns would get their bread and cakes. And there would always be some for our table. God provided the bread and cakes but it took some friendly people in the bakeries, a family car, an hour just before the mealtime and some petrol, but the miracle of the loaves and cakes continued over the years. That was a partnership that meant more that the bread.

Partnerships were the key to the provision of other necessities in our family life. We all helped and when it was Spring Fair everyone supported Beverley and when it was Easter Mission everyone helped Dad because the children knew these things were important to us.

Another principle our family accepted was that just because I was on a platform speaking everyday of my life and speaking on radio and TV programs, the family could not expect to be promoted. I abhor preachers who include comments or smart things their children have said. Our family would not be praised or humiliated publicly even though what they said and did might make us very proud. In some ways this was unfair. Everybody else's children we praised for their every contribution and sometimes our children added more to the common good, but until now we limited the public exposure and praise. What needed to be said was said to them in private. We would not be a family of self-promoters.

Finally, we would help our children develop their interests and talent in directions in which they wanted to go. We guided their choices and encouraged them, but did not try to work out our interests, beliefs and desires through them. Consequently they all developed different interests yet abided by our family values of clean living, practising Christian beliefs, keeping clear of drugs, smoking and alcohol, speaking respectfully without swearing and devoting time to their children and the needy of the community.

Our first child was Jenny, born while we ministered to the people in the slums of Melbourne. She trained as a School teacher, teaching in a Jewish school which broadened her knowledge and then as a Personal Assistant to the General Manager of Corporate Services at Wesley Mission, Richard Menteith. She also trained as a Lifeline Counsellor. In recent years she has been Personal Assistant to Wesley Mission's Group Manager of Pastoral Services Graham Want, who has the oversight of all of our worship services, chaplaincies, ministries and pastors, youth leaders and pastoral carers. Her experience of ministry in local churches as a minister's wife certainly equipped her for this task.

She married Ron Schepis, a member of Wesley's staff. Ron worked in administration and in the welfare of homeless people. During their courtship they both served the homeless. After graduating with his Social Welfare certificate, Ron started studying and graduated as a Registered Nurse with extensive experience in nursing people with mental ill health. That led to further study.

Then Ron responded to my call for people to consider studying for Pastoral Ministry. He entered Carlingford Theological College and graduated with his Diploma of Ministry and Bachelor of Theology from the Sydney College of Divinity. Later he completed his Master of Arts. Ron and Jenny served in full-time Parish Ministry at Keilor (Victoria) and Pendle Hill (NSW) before accepting a call to be a specialised Chaplain to the Mentally Ill in two of Wesley's Hospitals and a trainer of Lifeline Counsellors for the telephone counselling service. Jenny and Ron both have loveable personalities. Ron lived in our home for quite some time before their marriage so we all became one family.

Ron and Jenny have three children, Michael, Rachael and Emma. Both of the girls are strongly into team sports and Michael is the leader of all the ten cousins at every family celebration. He also had a beautiful treble voice and travelled the world singing in concerts with an international choir.

Peter our second child, was born during our Ararat ministry and something of the love of countryside and animals has always stayed with him. Because of Peter's love for animals, our backyard at Cheltenham resembled Noah's Ark. He was always caring for sick and injured animals and birds. Once a Major Mitchell cockatoo, came walking up the drive of our Roseville house dragging a badly broken wing, as much as to say, 'Is this where the man who cares for injured birds lives?' That cocky still lives with Peter over twenty-five years later.

As a teenager, Peter operated the sound and lights in our old Lyceum Theatre during church services. This was a demanding job with early set ups. He was so good at that he was included in the Wesley Film Production Ltd crew that filmed throughout the Mediterranean and Middle East. His interest in animals, land care and horticulture led him into courses at Ryde Horticultural College and work as groundsman at a local Golf Club where he continued studies in pesticides and the operation of heavy machinery. This was soon to benefit his parents.

Peter married Trina, a highly talented Occupational Therapist who had learnt the arts of restorative massage. From the first visit to our home, we knew she would make the most wonderful wife and daughter-in-law. She related well with each of the other children as Ron had done. When they had built their home, on acreage of course with horse, cow, goat, hens, ducks, sheep, dogs etc, Peter had dreams of living off the land but his acreage was too small. Because Trina was able with her professional practise to earn more than Peter with his horticulture, after the birth of their third child Peter became the primary carer of the children.

When I added being a Parliamentarian to my otherwise overfull life, we faced a quandary. The house at Tumbi Umbi into which we would shift when I retired from Wesley Mission needed extensive alterations and additions and the acreage needed a great deal of upkeep. So while the children were in school, Peter came to our rescue as builder and estate manager.

I would never have been able to cope with all the demands if it wasn't for Peter who has overseen the renovation and extension of our house and who has built and maintained our property. Every one of his skills and background training has been used. I owe Peter a debt I can never repay.

Their three children are each accomplished swimmers: Cassie is a qualified surf life-saver who is regularly on patrol, Jack is an outstanding surf swimmer, second in the State in his age group in the gruelling 'Iron Man' events and Indy is a 'water baby' competing in events covering all styles of swimming. Between them they have scores of trophies and medals.

David, our third child, was born in Cheltenham. As a young teenager, interested in radio broadcasting, making movie films and in all things electrical, David was the centre of the biggest crisis in our young family's life.

Through no fault of his own, but due to some very old, faulty electric wiring in our Roseville Manse, David was one night electrocuted in his bedroom. Hearing his scream I rushed to his room to see him convulsing on the floor with the full 240 volts still going through his body. I grabbed a wooden broom and forced the wires from his body and the electric light that had become alive. A large hole was burnt in the flesh of his arm. He was conscious but incoherent. We turned off the power and rushed him to the Royal North Shore Hospital Emergency department. The doctors were amazed he was still alive. A long recovery with skin grafts was to follow. In the hospital bed and almost unconscious, the fourteen-year-old said, 'Thank you God for saving me. You must want me to be a minister.'

David never remembered this and Beverley and I never mentioned it, until four years later, in discussing his post school career David re-affirmed his commitment to becoming a minister. He trained with his brother-in-law Ron at the Carlingford Theological College and graduated with his Diploma of Ministry and his Bachelor of Theology from the Sydney College of Divinity. David has been minister of three very large churches: Epping Church of Christ (NSW) Monash City Church (Victoria) and senior pastor at Belconnen Baptist Church (ACT), one of the largest Baptist Churches in the nation.

He married Leisl, the beautiful daughter of one of the pioneer Church families in Churches of Christ. They have two daughters, Brianna who has represented two states in both soccer and basketball and Chelsea who is outstanding in her sports of physical culture and basketball. When all ten cousins get together you can imagine the sporting competitions.

David is a mature minister and a good preacher with a caring heart. At Wesley he and our other children grew up with children living in out of home care, with people from great social disadvantage, with the homeless, the mentally ill and the disabled. While David was at School a teacher said, 'We are introducing disabled children into mainstream schooling but we are having difficulties with most of our students. Only David has the capacity to relate naturally with disabled.' Those years at Wesley had prepared him and his members comment on that compassion and wisdom to this day.

Our youngest child Andrew was born at Cheltenham. He quickly developed an interest in music and was active in our youth groups becoming a good leader in youth camps and club leadership. He also trained as a Lifeline Counsellor. He formed his own band and played at local churches and at gigs. He entered banking after completing his schooling, started to move up the ranks very quickly, then left the bank to undertake University studies, only to return to the bank to continue his career in commercial banking. Today he holds a very high position in commercial banking being the bank's representative with major customers.

Andrew married Rebecca, a trained teacher who specialises in teaching children with developmental problems. She is a keen horsewoman and you see that in the youngest of their children, Scarlett who with her horse at the Royal Easter Show in 2005 won over a large field of competitors as the best in the State in her age bracket. Her older brother Tom is School House Captain and enjoys boating and fishing with Andrew. The family have built their own home on mountain acreage from a self-build home-kit.

That's our family. The joy of our life.

PARLIMENTARIAN

Chapter Twelve

In 2002, I added to my role as Superintendent. I decided to stand for election to the Legislative Council in the NSW Parliament. At a joint sitting of both houses of Parliament, I was elected to take the seat of The Hon. Elaine Nile, who retired because of illness after 14 years of working beside her husband, Rev. The Hon. Fred Nile MLC, the leader of the Christian Democratic Party. 6 months later I received in a general state election overwhelming support to win one of the 21 seats in the Legislative Council. There were 292 candidates.

This gives me the new opportunity of not only working to make life better for the poor, the under-privileged, the aged and all those who need help by proclaiming the Gospel and serving through leading the largest charity in NSW, but now of oversighting all Government Legislation to ensure it will benefit these people for whom we care. Mostly, charities provide palliative care to suffering people. Now I had a new opportunity to work in preventative care through more Christian legislation. Prevention, not just cure.

Over the years Wesley Mission has been greatly blessed by people in our political parties. On our Wesley Mission Board we had The Hon. Milton Morris, an ALP Minister, and The Hon. Bruce Baird, a Liberal Minister and former Deputy Premier. The Uniting Church has had a minister as Deputy Prime Minister (ALP) and another a Senator for the Democrats. The Christian Democratic Party is not a political party in the traditional sense but a significant group of Christians who seek government of our country, based upon the teachings of the Bible and the value of the family as the basic unit to society. I shared this invitation that came to me in 2002 with the officers of the Mission and the President of the Uniting Church in Australia, Professor James Haire, all of whom supported me.

The Christian Democratic Party has policies which really seem like a list of concerns from Wesley Mission: housing, especially of the homeless; aged care; defence; Aboriginal justice and reconciliation; family and community services; law and order; the environment; land degradation and water conservation; education and training; state and regional development; child protection and care; and disability support.

The Christian Democratic Party supports whatever party is in power on its major budget proposals. The former NSW Premier Mr Bob Carr rang me to congratulate me on my appointment and to say personally how thrilled he was that I was entering the Legislative Council and how much respect he had for the way the Christian Democratic Party has always supported the government of the day on these important matters. The great value to Wesley Mission of having the Superintendent working as a member of the Legislative Council is that we now had access to all ministers and senior public servants. I soon became Chair of an important social issues committee, which gives me the opportunity to raise all the important issues that our staff raises with me. I also have the opportunity of speaking out on the social justice issues, which have always been a significant part of our ministry. I have chaired important inquiries in NSW health (its hospital and medical operations), juvenile justice, the ambulance service and the insurance industry. The Prime Minister Mr John Howard, who in 1994 invited me to advise on matters of social welfare, requested me to stay on, which I did for the next ten years. I led the Christian Democratic Party in the March 2003 election for both the upper and lower houses and I was elected until 2011.

Back in October 1992, one Thursday, I had lunch at Parliament House with the Deputy Premier, Bruce Baird, the Minister of Health, Ron Phillips; the Minister of Community Services, Jim Langley, the former President of the Legislative Council, Johnno Johnston, and a few other back-benchers. During the meal the Deputy Premier asked me, 'Would you ever consider coming into Parliament?' I replied, 'No. I would never take one step towards coming into Parliament because I am an evangelist, called of God, and any step in any other direction is always a step downwards.'

I had already been asked that question by the Electoral Committee in Higgenbotham, Victoria, when The Hon. Don Chipp had stepped down from the Frazer ministry and had decided to launch the Australian Democrats. It was a 'blue ribbon' seat and I was assured a place in Federal Parliament if I agreed. My reply was the same: I was called to be an evangelist.

Why did I change my mind? Simply because my travelling ministry as an evangelist came to an end. I had announced that I would not accept a proposed extension of ministry as Superintendent of Wesley Mission beyond my 67th birthday, in November 2005. After twenty-seven years in leadership it was time to pass the responsibility onto another person. Giving three and a half years notice would allow time for the search committee to scour the world for the very best successor and still allow perhaps six months of overlap where we could work together before I closed my office door for the last time.

The timetable worked well. My successor was named, Rev. Keith Garner M.Th., of Rochdale, U.K., and he arrived in time for a good handover. My concern was to be able to introduce him to all of my community contacts, major donors, supportive corporations and members and to encourage their ongoing commitment to Keith and Wesley Mission.

I had no intention of ceasing ministry in the work of proclaiming the Gospel and caring for the community. I would do both. But with all of my contacts and understanding of society's needs, I was in a place where I could contribute in a preventative way to the making of a more just and Christian society. Many laws made by Parliamentarians are designed to overcome a problem, but are then found to create more. In our parliaments there is not another member who has a lifetime of experience in the field of social welfare. Most are lawyers, accountants and trade union officials.

If you ask any politician, 'Do you have an ambition to become leader of your party and the nation?' you only believe those who agree with the ambition to be leader. Those who deny their ambition are usually lying. Yet I have no ambition to be either party or national leader. Why should I be believed?

Two reasons. One, I have told my Party Leader and my Party Executive I will never accept leadership even if it were to be offered. Second, I have joined a Party that can never be in political power. My sole reason, after a long, fifty-year ministry, is to work to improve social welfare for the whole state. As stated earlier, Parliament is a place for many ambitious lawyers and trade union officials, but there is no one with extensive social welfare experience.

After being sworn in I had dozens of people saying to me that they were assured that at long last we have a person with hands-on experience. When I speak on the issues of homelessness, poverty, drug addiction, public housing, ageing, health care and the like, I am listened to with politeness and silence. On decisions impacting on these matters, my colleague Rev. Fred Nile and myself hold the balance of power. Our vote determines the legislative outcome on these matters, I am a tribal elder - and rejoice in that role.

I will always be a Christian spokesman in Parliament, but many people question the future of the Christian Democratic Party. For twenty years the supporters were good Christian men and women who were concerned about the moral drift in society and who worked hard to have Fred and Elaine Nile elected because they trusted them to uphold their views. But there was little success in building a national party structure based on a well-thought out statement of beliefs that could be easily communicated to the general public.

The party lacked an intellectual basis and sound political strategy. It existed primarily to ensure Fred and Elaine were re-elected. Today, smart young voters want a clear statement of political purpose and strategy. Every voter under thirty years of age can tell you in a sentence what the Green Party stands for. But they cannot say what the Christian Democratic Party stands for.

Will the CDP survive? It will not unless there is fresh blood in the Parliament representing the Christian vision, a well articulated political platform and a sound party structure based upon democratic principles, where each branch has input to policy and legislative decisions. That is going to require major changes that the long term supporters and leaders may not be able to make.

However, a major article in the Sydney Morning Herald, 'Getting Biblical not main thrust in Christian politics' by Linda Morris (March 29, 2005) spoke hopefully of the change.

'The party of morals campaigner Fred Nile wants to ditch its image as an anti-sex party and has launched a recruitment drive as it moves to compete for the Christian vote with the emerging Family First Party.

The Christian Democratic Party will re-brand itself to broaden its appeal across the Christian right and prepare for life after its founder. The move comes as Family First is to open its first NSW branch in coming months and its chairman, Peter Harris, says it is planning to mobilise an 'aggressive campaign' for the 2007 state election that could see a Family First candidate go head-to-head with Fred Nile.

The Christian Democrats' state director, Phil Lamb, said competition for the biblical Christian vote had the 'effect of pouring gasoline into the tank'.

The party was building a new structure, a database of supporters and had recruited 500 new members. Recently I invited 42 church leaders to provide feedback on the party's image and performance.

'We are changing from a Fred Nile support group and the many welded-on supporters to a grassroots-driven, Christian-based political party,' Mr Lamb said. 'Up until now, the party is perceived as being 'morals crusaders', however, that will have to change. Our party is simply not just the anti-sex party, a reputation that has stuck for the past 23 years.

'The truth of the matter is that anyone who sees Fred Nile and Gordon Moyes work in the upper house knows that they are genuinely engaged in the whole process of governing and have a much wider and balanced world-view than the press communicate to the public.'

The Sydney Morning Herald in an editorial expressed it cleanly:

'The Christian Democratic Party, born of the morality crusades of Fred Nile, finds itself in battle with the newcomer, the Family First Party. The Christian Democrat's NSW director, Phil Lamb, argues that competition will grow the cake and that the fallout will be multiplication of the conservative fundamentalist Christian vote. This seems more wishful prayer than political realism, at least in the short to medium term.

Mr Nile, a former Uniting Church minister, is the great survivor of NSW politics, having entered the NSW Upper House 24 years ago - only a year after the Reverend Jerry Falwell's Moral Majority helped Ronald Reagan's elevation to the White House. Mr Nile has kept his place by polling about 3 per cent of the overall NSW vote, enough for a state upper house seat but nothing like sufficient for a Senate seat, which he failed to attain last October despite outpolling Family First. Meanwhile, amid speculation that senators bearing the brand of Christian fundamentalism would control the balance of power, only Family First's Steve Fielding won a Senate seat and only then because of a complicated flow of preferences in Victoria.

So Mr Nile held the ground all those years without expanding it. Then along came a new generation of the same breed with a message promoting values in a broader context than the Bible. If either has the potential to lure substantial voting support from major parties, Family First is better positioned because its message is more attuned to blue-collar voters, while the Christian Democrats are caught between a rock and a pillow. They want to move away from morals crusading and to join the same path as Family First but are being held back by the public perception of Mr Nile, whose high profile also holds them together.

Christian fundamentalism holds more sway over American politics because it is more deeply rooted in the US and because, unlike Australia, voting there is voluntary. And there is little room here for Christian minnows to grow, given their need to bite into a Coalition already attractive to conservative fundamentalists.'

Although I was asked to fill the Hon. Elaine Nile's seat when she had to retire due to ill health, I am not sure she liked the change. I had asked the Parliament to build me a computer table in the Parliament Chamber. They did build it alongside the Crossbench where Fred and Elaine used to sit. This led Elaine to write for her page in 'Family World News'. 'We always used to say there were three of us on our seat: The Lord and Fred and Elaine. Now Fred sits alone with the Lord. Gordon is plugged into his computer on the Liberal's back bench, but wherever we are the Lord is with us.'

'The Love Seat' as it was known was too small for Fred, our papers and me and with Fred's outspoken views on homosexuality, it would give rise to perverted humor. Incidentally when the Parliament made me the computer desk with its direct line, I was able to notify my constituents that they could email me directly into Parliament House while issues were being debated and I would consider including them in my speeches. I would also reply to them immediately giving them from within the Parliamentary Chamber my views on the state of the proposed legislation. I became the first member of Parliament to become directly in contact with constituents electronically.

The Legislative Council, our nation's oldest Council of government and our State Senate, was the ideal place to do that. I would have the resources of the Parliament, my expert staff and a decent budget. Further, I had the unfettered freedom to raise in Parliament any issue I desired, to speak on every piece of legislation, to establish public inquiries, to Chair important committees and to deliver addresses – even sermons – on any Christian matter.

For example I constantly raise in Parliament questions to the Minister leading to tighter regulations on social problems. Their problems cost us all dearly. Gamblers with large debts commit up to 20 per cent of white-collar crime, often against their employers to continue gambling, win back what they have lost, or pay for living expenses. While drug addicts mostly commit crimes against property such as break and enter, purse snatching and so on researchers have found that problem gamblers turned to fraud and financial theft to feed their habit. One study of nearly 2,800 District Court and Local Court cases in New South Wales from 1995 to 1999 found that nearly one in five of those convicted of larceny or cheque fraud had gambling problems. Overall, 4 per cent of all crimes were found to be directly related to gambling. The gamblers, aged 17 to 71, had stolen and largely gambled away about $4.2 million from employers, shops and individuals. One 54-year-old woman, for example, had lost more than $425,000 taken from her employer over 10 years. Often it was easy for the gamblers to cash false cheques, falsify their employers' books or access the bank accounts of others and the studies warn that many companies had poor auditing and internal security arrangements.

One man forged his employer's accounts after loan sharks threatened him and his family. Another robbed a TAB so he could place a bet on a trifecta. Almost two-thirds of offenders with gambling problems received gaol sentences ranging from three months to six years, but few were ordered to undergo counselling or treatment for their addiction. In a sense the NSW Government is hindering compulsive gamblers. On the one hand, the Government relies on a budget that is based very largely on gambling-related income. On the other hand, the Government is seeking to help resolve gambling problems. I congratulate the Government on some of the major initiatives it has undertaken in recent times, including a statewide cap of 104,000 poker machines.

They also included the requirement that venues undergo a social impact assessment before new machines can be installed; that hotels and clubs with gaming machines being prohibited from shopping centres.

My experience in counselling people with personal needs and destructive habits comes to the fore in being a Parliamentarian, for there in Parliament I ask the questions of the Government Ministers on the issues that are faced by real people and get real results.

In a unique double sitting of both Houses of Parliament I was nominated by the leader of one party and seconded by the leader of another – a unique situation. The vote was unanimous. I would finish the term of the Hon. Elaine Nile MLC and then stand for re-election. With more than a million voters desiring that, I was re-elected for an eight-year term. The news was not greeted with enthusiasm by the Uniting Church hierarchy! The Christian public flooded me with letters and invitation to visit and speak to Churches, but the Synod bureaucrats were worried by two unexpected concerns that would never have occurred to me.

The problem was two fold: one, I would now receive two salaries, and that is unethical, and two, as Parliamentarian I can speak beyond the discipline of the Church and I would not be subject to the Church's methods of keeping its ministers in line. The second point is true and if the Church tried to silence me on matters when I speak under Parliamentary privilege, the Church could be held to be in contempt of Parliament. You may be horrified how many ministers are silenced by the decisions made by committees of the Church without proper evidence and without the presence of the person concerned. I was not present when my salaries were discussed. What was said was untrue and I had no opportunity to correct it. Hence I will tell you.

I have not been paid by the Parish of Wesley Mission for any of the work that I do when preaching, speaking on radio and television, providing pastoral care or home and hospital visitation. I voluntarily offered this to our congregations. I do get the equivalent of a Minister's salary for my administrative work but this I offered to raise for Wesley Mission every year from outside of the Church. For the last 15 years I have raised my own salary and that of running the Superintendent's Office, from sources outside of the Church, including raising $25,000 from auctioning donated goods, just as I write. The money I do receive from the Mission, I have given back to the Mission every month since my election, to supporting another person and to fund a Christian magazine, '*Marriage Works*', to help young couples improve their marriages. The offerings and donations Beverley and I have made far exceed that of any minister's total salary. So much for the integrity and honesty of people who speak to the press from Synod questioning my salary! As a former Labor Premier said to me, 'When I read that article I said to my wife, 'That Synod bloke only wants Gordon's job!''

I commend to my critics the practise of raising their own salary. They would cease to be a burden upon our congregations as they currently are, bring them into contact with people outside of the Church and enable other people to be employed. I have enjoyed raising my own salary without using anyone else's donations or offering.

Apart from this, the Trustees of Emmanuel School of Religion U.S.A., where I have taught Urban Mission over more than a decade have honoured me by appointing me Adjunct Professor of Urban Church Mission. It is expected that I will do no more than I have been doing in the past decade, but this will allow me to keep updated on the impact of city living on Christian ministry, so that I can not only pass on that knowledge to students, but also incorporate those insights into our ministry. Teaching and ministering at the same time is one thing, but what

of legislating and ministering at the same time?
My acceptance of this position with the Legislative Council is in response to the Uniting Church's Basis of Union declaration that 'the Uniting Church will provide for the exercise of men and women of gifts God bestows upon them and will order her life in response to his call to enter more fully into her mission.' I sought to use my gifts and experience to enhance the mission of the Church.

When the possibility of this election was raised, I discussed this with the officers of Wesley Mission, representing the Board, Council and members of Wesley Mission. I informed the Committee appointed by the Presbytery Pastoral Relations Committee to bring a recommendation for my extension of ministry of the possibility of being offered an important position in government. Later, I informed the Presbytery, of which I was Chair, in session, of the same possibility. I also met with and informed the President of the Uniting Church in Australia Assembly to gain his counsel. All persons so consulted were affirming that I should accept. The President at length expressed the view that he supported the proposition that Uniting Church ministers should use their talents in the political arena and in the light of the special time commitments of the Legislative Council, while I was still in placement as Superintendent of Wesley Mission. The President further suggested a UCA Church Service at which he would be willing to preach, to set me aside into this additional role.

I also approached the President of the Legislative Council and the Clerk of the Governments to see if a minister in settlement would be acceptable as a member of the Legislative Council. The President indicated that as the normal term of office was eight years, she saw beyond my present work commitment to my retirement from that position and my full-time involvement as a M.L.C. The Clerk of Governments indicated that as almost all of the members of the Legislative Council also pursued their professions as doctors, architects, graziers, lawyers and the like, he saw no difference in me being in settlement until retirement or a replacement was made.

The Clerk also indicated that in the next eight months only 23 sitting days were involved and in a full year 46 sitting days were required. There were some good reasons why the Superintendent of Wesley Mission Sydney should combine this role with that of being a lawmaker. The Uniting Church in Australia has always seen that ministry should go beyond the four walls of a church into the heart of a nation's educational, social, cultural, corporate and political life.

Being involved with the legislative program of the nation requires special gifts and abilities. I had long been involved on advisory groups to the Prime Minister and also to Ministers of the State Government on major social issues. I saw my appointment as similar to that of other ministers who are encouraged by their congregations to become involved in extending their ministry into community activities. Some ministers in settlements serve as local councillors and even Mayors of communities. Others have been Presidents of local service clubs and others active in political branches and State political organisations while in settlement. Others are chaplains to sporting teams and in schools, hospitals and industry. In the previous twenty years, I pioneered the extension of ministry into the corporate world and served as director and chairman of a number of significant companies in media, insurance, life insurance, film production, public and private hospitals and in the ownership and running of two of Sydney's major radio stations. My training and skills were recognised by the granting of fellowships at the highest level in the Australian Institute of Management and the Australian Institute of Company Directors. The fellowships are not awarded lightly and came as recognition of expert training and the experiences of my skilled leadership in those fields.

There are precedents for the Superintendent of a large Central Mission combining his ministry with that of service to the nation in the upper chamber of the Parliament. Rev. Dr Donald Soper, Superintendent of the great West London Methodist Mission, served as Superintendent for sixteen years after being appointed to Britain's House of Lords, where he made a remarkable contribution to the national life of the UK serving in both roles. Here, in NSW, the Legislative Council has found members from among the serving clergy in settlement since the days of Rev. John Dunmore Lang, who served the Legislative Council while minister of Sydney Presbyterian Church. They have included a number of bishops, archdeacons and even the Archbishop of Sydney, all of whom continued in office while a member of the Legislative Council.

The legislative issues that come before the Legislative Council are of particular interest. The Upper House does not restrict the budget bills from the Legislative Assembly, but closely reviews every bill impacting the lives of citizens, particularly issues of housing, especially of the homeless; aged care; defence; Aboriginal justice and reconciliation; family and community services; law and order; the environment; land degradation and water conservation; education and training; state and regional development; child protection and care; and disability support. These issues are many of the social objects of Wesley Mission and all have been part of my concern and interest over many years.

Besides all of this, I followed the tradition of my predecessors and have always spoken out strongly on social issues such as the Uniting Church's proposals for the treatment of asylum seekers. Now I have the opportunity of speaking out on the social justice issues that have always been a significant part of the Uniting Church's ministry.

Over the years I have thrived on extra activities while busy building one of the largest city churches in the world and the Uniting Church's strongest parish. I used to be on about 20 Boards and committees that involved me in more meetings per month than the Legislative Council does. For fifteen years I spent 35 weekends a year conducting small evangelistic programs in more than 400 churches round Australia, in every state, flying back every Sunday afternoon for an 8 hour afternoon and evening program of meetings, church services and radio broadcasting. Like many ministers in placement, I learnt the art of time management and using contacts outside the Church to build up the Body of Christ.

I waited the maximum time possible before delivering my maiden speech. Anticipation increased and at the appointed hour the House was packed. The Legislative Assembly emptied as members followed the Premier in coming to hear the speech. It was brief. I include it in full:

'My life has been a very simple one. My wife and I were born almost adjacent to each other in the same week and in the same community of Box Hill in Victoria. We did not get to know each other in the baby health centre, otherwise I would have proposed then, but we grew up in the same community and we have been together ever since. When I was a teenager I was greatly helped and blessed by some people who attended a church that my parents never attended. When I was eight years of age my father died as an alcoholic. He literally dropped dead in the street, leaving behind four young children, of whom I was the eldest. Through the influence of these kindly people from a neighbourhood church I eventually became interested in the Church. As a teenager I became committed to following the way of Jesus Christ and I have endeavoured to do so with whatever strength and capacity I have had since that period of time.

'Right from the earliest days I was challenged by a schoolteacher, my school principal. Once I earned his displeasure, he said to me that I had to make up my mind to either be part of the problem of this society or part of the answer. He indicated that I was not to leave the front of his desk, to which I had been called, until I had given him an answer. That man's name was W. M. (Bill) Woodfull, who was the captain of the Australian Test cricket team during the 'Bodyline' series. He was a great leader of men. I remember standing before him in tears as a schoolboy and making the decision that I preferred to be part of the answer than a continuing part of the problem.

'Consequently, my wife and I, as teenage sweethearts, volunteered immediately and we started to serve the churches in the inner slum areas of Melbourne - in North Melbourne, Kensington and Flemington.

'While I went on to university and theological college studies, we worked among the hopeless and despairing of the slum areas. I became the youngest parole officer and the youngest probation officer in Victoria's history. At one stage I had about 104 murderers and car thieves assigned to me. With my girlfriend, who became my fiancée and eventually my wife, I spent eight years trying to help these people through the difficulties that they had encountered in their lives. It was from these beginnings in the slums of Melbourne that we developed a life pattern of working with people who have particular needs and concerns in society.

'That flowed on to what was a very remarkable event that changed our life completely. It was the day that John F. Kennedy was shot. Traditionally people say they remember where they were at the time of that tragic event. I remember where I was very clearly. I was in the United States Consulate, here in Australia, where we were about to have our visas stamped. I had been appointed to do postgraduate study in the United States of America. When the shots rang out in Dallas, Texas, the doors at the consulate were shut and the United States Embassy went into high activity. People were thrown out the doors and papers went everywhere and with them went our visas, our work permits, our passports, our chest x-rays and a whole lot of other stuff. The result was that the boat upon which we were to travel, together with all our clothes, personal possessions and belongings, sailed to America - but we did not.

'In order to survive I went to a small country church where I used my background in psychology and ministry to become chaplain in a very large mental institution and my experience as a probation and parole officer to work in the psychiatric ward for the criminally insane. That experience in a small country church became a turning point in our life. I then went to a suburban ministry for 13 years. During that period I saw the development of very large-scale works, including building retirement villages - the first of their type built in Victoria - and other multimillion-dollar constructions in what was then arguably the largest Protestant church in Australia. From there I was called to Sydney – 27 years ago – to follow the remarkable Reverend Dr Alan Walker.

'I have had the best part of 25 years in that role working with the disadvantaged, the poor, the homeless, prisoners and the mentally sick and managing hospitals, nursing homes, retirement villages and so on. They have been very, very happy years. I bring with me a lot of background in caring for the underprivileged, which I hope will help me when I come here to speak on issues that relate to the people of New South Wales.

'I am a preacher. But preachers are called on not only to do deeds of goodness in a community; they are called on also to proclaim the Word. So I have sought to proclaim the Word of God. For the last 44 years, since being a teenager, I have preached. In the last 20 years I have preached on average nine times each week. I preach on television; I have five half-hour national television programs. It is a wonderful opportunity to get the message of God through to people. It is 36 years since I started preaching on television, back in the days of black and white television with four-turret cameras in BTV 6 in Ballarat, Victoria and then on to GTV 9 in Melbourne. The last 25 years I have been every week on TCN 9 in Sydney and on the Nine Network around Australia. That all developed into my speaking each week on a whole range of radio stations around the nation and that, in turn, led to me writing. If you are going to communicate, you use all the abilities and opportunities that are open to you.

'I have authored something like 50 books, which have been published in Australia, the United Kingdom, the United States and, most remarkably, China, where they talk in astronomical figures in terms of publication of our books. Whereas in Australia you might think a book does well if you sell 5,000 or 10,000 copies, in China 500,000 copies of each book have been sold. Honourable members might be interested to hear that when I address universities in places such as like Beijing, because of the number of books we have sold in China and because of the government oppression of religion in China I am regarded as a radical who is likely to turn the world upside down! We have been chased by religious police and political police. Part of my group has been arrested. One of my party was arrested when we were smuggling Bibles into China. My wife and I were more successful. It is quite remarkable that a middle-aged or older, plumpish, conservative, Anglo-Saxon should be hailed by student groups as a radical and a revolutionary, holding clandestine midnight meetings and working with the underground church.

'All that led to the Internet. The remarkable thing about the Internet is its power to connect with the world. We now have something like 4,000 addresses and editorials on the Internet that are read or downloaded by literally a hundred thousand people around the world each week.

'Some years ago I felt there was a need to produce films. Not Cecil B. De Moyes films but documentaries based on some of the strengths I developed through the study of history and archaeology. The film company that we set up has been remarkably successful. We have produced about 50 documentary films, which were made predominantly in the Middle East and dealt with archaeology, history, the development of the early church and Christian beliefs. We have recently made films in China. They have been released internationally. It is awe-inspiring to travel in America, where a series of programs has been broadcast on public television and to be recognised in airports by people who tell us they have watched our films.

'I am not an academic or an intellectual. I have described myself in other places as possessing a fair, average quality, second-rate mind. Given that, I need the help of researchers. I acknowledge those people who have the gifts and graces that provide us with the opportunity to communicate those truths and to present good, sound, factual material. I have been very impressed with the quality of the speeches I have heard in this House, recognising that often behind an honourable member's contribution is some very good research done by other people. I acknowledge those who have helped me in that regard over the years.

'Part of the role of a minister of the gospel is to manage resources. We have built up the resources of the Wesley Mission very well. When I started at the mission we had 23 properties. Over the past five years, I have opened a new building, on average, about once every two weeks. We now have 489 communities in New South Wales that have a Wesley Mission home, hospital, nursing home, retirement village, childcare facility, employment agency or whatever. My wife and I are at present visiting 62 rural centres in New South Wales to help with drought relief funding. Madam President, with your permission, at the end of this brief contribution I would normally ask for an offering, but if honourable members are interested in helping with drought relief, I can provide very practical opportunities for them to do so.

'My involvement in the Wesley Mission over the years has required me to learn management skills. I have gained that education since the 1960s and 1970s with the Australian Graduate School of Management, the Australian Institute of Management at Mt Eliza, Monash University and the Graduate School of Management at the University of New South Wales. One of the blessings that has come our way is to be elected a Fellow of the Australian Institute of Management and a Fellow of the Australian Institute of Company Directors because of the positions held on boards of a number of listed and unlisted companies in a variety of fields. As a result of that work, honours have come our way which often have not been deserved but which have always been appreciated. I am not an academic, but I have been honoured by a number of institutions of higher learning with degrees and positions and I have lectured for many years at a university and a seminary in the United States. I have developed a course that was originally unknown in that country, known as 'urban mission'. Earlier this year I was appointed on a permanent basis as the adjunct professor of urban mission, which gives me an annual trip and an opportunity to teach students in urban mission studies.

'Over the years I have been described by community-based organisations as the Citizen of the Year, Father of the Year and Public Speaker of the Year. All of those accolades are enjoyable. Recently, I was named the New South Wales Entrepreneur of the Year, which for a minister and a clergyman is a most unusual accolade.

'Beverley and I have also been honoured by the Australian Government. Beverley was elected by the Sydney City Council as the Citizen of the Year. She is also a member of the Order of Australia. During Australia's Bicentennial, the authority concerned nominated 20 outstanding women in Australia and Beverley was chosen as one of the 10 most significant women in this country- along with people whose names are known to all. It has been a wonderful experience as a husband to learn to walk just one pace behind when we go out together. For my part, in the mid-1980s I was made a member of the Order of Australia and at the beginning of this year I was granted Australia's highest honour as a Companion of the Order of Australia.

'I appreciate the fact that we sit in this very historic place, not only because a long line of clergymen have been here before me, including Reverend the Hon. Fred Nile, but also because, going back over the years, we have had members who were bishops and archbishops, back to Reverend the Hon. John Dunmore Lang, who was a member of this House. I hope to uphold the best of the traditions of those great leaders in the Church and the community.

'In 1964, while doing some research I chose to write on the history of what were known as the 'iron churches'. A small number of churches constructed in iron smelting works in the United Kingdom that were shipped primarily from Birmingham, although a couple came from Manchester, to Australia during the gold rushes. Church authorities in Australia wanted demountable buildings that they could get quickly to the goldfields. I decided to trace their history and discover where they were and how they were used. One was purchased by the Methodist Home Mission Department. Because it was felt that the iron churches - which had iron roofs, walls, uprights and supports - would blunt the teeth of termites, it was sent to Palmerston, which is the former name of the city we call Darwin. That church still stands, although it is not used. Iron churches are very difficult to air-condition. After well over a century of use it is still standing.

'I found another iron church in Ararat. It had also been purchased by the Methodists for use on the goldfields. On the side of this huge church were four big wheels 5½ feet high and made out of slivers of a huge tree trunk on which they were dragged by teams of oxen around the goldfields. The last goldfield it was taken to was Dunkeld in 1863. It was then dragged to Ararat and left temporarily in a vacant paddock behind the Methodist church. It was still there when I visited in 1965 and it is probably still there today.

'Another iron church was purchased by the Anglicans and on-sold at a profit for £1,200 to the people of New South Wales. Of course, that church forms the framework of this Legislative Council Chamber. We show visitors the steel structures behind the Chamber, the packing case walls and so on. I feel at home. Madam President, I have noted in my short time in this place that you occasionally have trouble with the more obstreperous members and you have to call them to order. You will not have a problem with me, because from early childhood I have been told how to behave in church.'

The applause as I sat after this speech, given without notes, was thunderous. A Hansard reporter later said to me, 'That was the best speech I have heard in Parliament in 25 years of transcribing them.' But applause from the Parliament was not echoed in the UCA NSW Synod offices. The NSW Council of Synod was not only disturbed by my parliamentary salary, which made me independent of the Church's financial ties (I had been independent since I started raising my own salary fifteen years earlier), but was concerned I would be independent of the Church's control and discipline. Scores of ministers had been controlled by the various Synods through secret committees called 'counselling' or 'discipline' committees. Their membership is secret, the proceedings are secret, the minister needing counselling is not allowed to be represented, the decisions may deprive a minister of his job, his professional standing, his house and his car – and no appeals are allowed. The Synod bureaucrats try to keep ministers in line through fear. One of the most obnoxious of these bureaucrats wrote to me criticising a question my colleague Rev. Fred Nile had asked in Parliament on a matter of public safety following a terrorist alert to the Parliament by the Australian Government. I replied as follows:

'I am not aware of any UCA Regulation that forbids any minister asking any question anywhere. Further, I am not aware that any part of his question contravenes any doctrines of the Uniting Church. I would believe that for people concerned with the tragedies of Moscow and Hamburg, in the light of the warnings delivered to the Parliament that day, that this question could be asked in the Council of Synod or anywhere else. The freedom to question has been a prized right since the Reformation.

'Parliamentarians have some protection while speaking in Parliament and every citizen has a right of reply to the Parliament.

'Parliamentarians who are Ministers of Religion, as have been many members of the Legislative Councils over the decades including high office Anglicans, Bishops and even an Archbishop and other ministers such as Rev. John Dunmore Lang, still are within the discipline of the Church. I know of no case where any parliamentary Minister has ever been questioned on clash of allegiance. I hold allegiance to the discipline of the Church and will for the rest of my life. I am also aware that there are immediate authorities and ultimate authorities. I guess, although I do not know, that Ministers of the Uniting Church who are members of the Masonic Orders have an obligation to their Order while in certain places and in matters of disclosure. I know that Chaplains of the Uniting Church when on the scene of an emergency must obey the directions of the Emergency Services. I know that military chaplains are under the control of the field commander while on service duty. School chaplains have a responsibility to obey school discipline.

'This does not mean they are no longer under the discipline of the Church. It is the same in parliamentary duties. There is an immediate duty to the Parliament. That involves telling the truth, behaving respectfully and listening to the Prayers that are said every day. The prayers acknowledge the ultimate authority of God. Members of the Council of Synod probably do not know that every day we pray: 'Almighty God, we humbly beseech Thee to vouchsafe Thy blessing upon this Parliament. Direct and prosper our deliberations to the advancement of Thy glory and the true welfare of the people of our State and Australia.' Then we together repeat the Lord's Prayer - and in my observation it is repeated by almost all Parliamentarians, including the phrase, 'Thy Will be done in earth, as it is in Heaven'.

'Parliamentarians acknowledge the Parliament is under the authority of God as found in Romans 13. That is why Ministers of State are called ' Ministers', because they are ministers of God in the expression of His will in the governing of the community. They may do it poorly, but that is the problem ministers of religion may also have.

'There is no issue of the discipline of the Church being in conflict with the discipline of Parliament. Both are under the authority of God and in the Christian

Democratic Party, we must always place the authority of God as our highest obedience. I am available every day if you have further questions.'

I heard nothing in reply. Not long after that particular General Secretary, Rev. Dr Chris Budden, resigned his position before the end of his term. His departure was not lamented. When the State election of 2003 was to be held, I took some leave owing to me to campaign for the election. How do Christians campaign for Parliament?

The Christian Democratic Party believes in campaigning in a different manner. Over twelve weeks, with only a couple of days off for Christmas, Rev. Fred Nile MLC, the leader of the Christian Democratic Party, who was not up for election, and myself, as leader of the CDP'S Upper House ticket, each spoke to over 150 political rallies organised all over the state and in every suburban area.

We visited every one of the 93 electorates and over 100 rural and regional towns, from Tweed Heads to Albury, Eden to Broken Hill and including places like Cobar and Walgett and all places in between. We each drove over 13,000 kilometres. No politician in the NSW Parliament addressed in those three months more public gatherings than we two. When passing through communities where we have Wesley Mission facilities, my wife and I would call in upon our staff. We addressed breakfasts, lunches and dinners and evening rallies every day without a break. These were arranged by a local committee and local candidate in every area.

They invited sitting members and candidates from all parties to attend. In one gathering four Liberal candidates were present, another Liberal candidate attended four meetings and ALP, National and other candidates attended. These 'opposition' candidates were given a chance to address the crowd. For them this was a new experience – they were applauded, not attacked!

Crowds gathered in large numbers - even larger than for the Leader of Coalition and the Premier! Crowds of 100, 200, 400 were common and on one occasion there were 800 and on another 4000 present! We gave countless interviews to the press, television and radio to wide coverage. In drought stricken areas, farmers were asked to come to speak of their plight. (During 2002 I had written to 980 farmers in drought areas and provided $140,000 in cash aid from Wesley Mission donors and members.)

Newspapers in the cities were concentrating on the Greens and peace marches as a political tool. The Christian Democratic Party has been pressing flesh, face to face listening and going to where the people are. Ours was old-fashioned politicking! It is no wonder at the election I received over a million first and second preference votes. The exact number is not known because when the first 21 candidates of the total of 290 are declared elected, the count ceases. I thank Kylie Lawrence, our Party Executive Secretary Phil Lamb our State Director, Linda

Munoz, my Legislative Lawyer, and Jonathon Flegg, my parliamentary secretary and my Personal Assistant, Blossom Vickers, for all their help in the election and since.

With all of our national problems, can the Christian faith influence politics enough? Our nation is facing a crisis. We live in a land of peace and prosperity, with sound, democratically elected governments, with growing accountability from those in positions of authority and a high level of personal morality. Yet such is the rate of change and the decline in personal ethics, we are now facing a national moral crisis. Can religion give Australia new hope?

Traditionally the Church has delivered that sense of national cohesion and reconciliation. But is the Church capable of delivering it today? Some mainline churches are divided over lack of commitment to the Scriptures as the only revelation of God. Their acceptance of immoral sexual standards among clergy without any expectation of change of behaviour is a denial of the discipline and beliefs of the Church over centuries. That denial is a heavy price for being thought trendy.

Some churches are politically aligned and spokespersons speak to every issue along predictable ideological lines, not supported by a majority of their members. The very organism that people should be able to turn to in confidence is itself in crisis. These churches are showing signs of wear and tear and lack of direction. They adopt a religious pluralism that believes no one can be ever wrong and a post-modernism which declares everything is subjective, open to your own opinion. What is important is not the Bible, nor what Christians believe, but what is your story. One view is as good as any other. Everyone does what is right in his or her own eyes. That church attitude will never help Australia.

For these Churches, Christianity has become a form, not a force. Faith is a performance, not a person. It is religion, not a relationship. They minister by remote control, preach by memory. They have no fire, no fervour and no friendship with the living Jesus.

A crisis abounds in nation and church. Where is an answer? Only commitment to Jesus Christ offers us hope. Jesus made the laws of Moses tougher and the standard of morality among his followers harder. He was marginalised because of his teachings and his close association with the poor, the rejected and the leprous, put him offside with everyone, from the Pharisees to the Romans. Yet Jesus Christ became, through the Cross and Resurrection, the Messiah of all. He will one day return to establish God's Kingdom and reign on earth, as in heaven. Our only hope lies in committed Christians, obedient to the scriptures, who pray for the governments and witness to their faith and who are willing to live under the authority of the Word of God. Will our nation continue to decline or can individuals find in Jesus Christ the deep answer?

I have had many opportunities to witness to and pray with Parliamentarians in both the State and Federal Parliaments. In one week, this 'Great South Land of the Holy Spirit' became the meeting place for the President of the most powerful nation on earth at the beginning of the twenty-first century and the President of the nation, which will be the most powerful nation on earth at the end of the twenty-first century. President George W Bush and President Hu Jintao flew into Canberra to address both Houses of Parliament in joint sittings. I was there by special invitation.

I sat in a reserved section for twelve people who had been invited by Prime Minister John Howard to meet Mr Bush personally to discuss issues on their minds. The twelve were an impressive group of Australian leaders. I was honoured to go to the Cabinet Room and to meet and discuss issues I thought were important with President Bush. Issues like Iraq, free trade, international relations, Australian prisoners in American prisons and agricultural subsidies were on the agenda.

When President Bush heard I was from Wesley Mission, he offered that he was a Methodist and attended a Methodist Church. I told him I knew that and many other things about his spiritual life. I encouraged the President to push through his reforms involving 'faith-based initiatives'. He replied that the legislation on faith-based initiatives was the most important on his domestic agenda and he was determined to use state funds to help churches and synagogues run social programs meeting community needs, a promise that he has kept with amazing generosity.

I informed him I had been reading a publishers preview copy of a new book *The Faith of George W. Bush* (Pan/Charisma) by Stephen Mansfield. He asked me how it had treated his faith. I told him and the First Lady that the author and his team of researchers had uncovered some fascinating and little-known information about Bush's conversion, his sense of divine calling and how faith helped him overcome his drinking habit. I guess I was the only person on his overseas visit that talked to the President about his drinking habits! But people are interested in the President's faith. They also have a lot of questions that need to be answered. He knew about the book.

I told him this book, due to be released the following November, included the fact that Bush first heard the call to run for president during a sermon by the Rev. Mark Craig at Highland Park United Methodist Church in Dallas. Craig described Moses' reluctance to lead God's people and Bush's mother, Barbara, turned to him and said, 'He was talking to you.' The First Lady, Laura, immediately informed me that was true. I mentioned that before Bush announced his candidacy, he invited Texas Evangelist James Robison to meet with him for prayer. That was also true.

George Bush is a close friend of British Prime Minister Tony Blair, also a committed Christian. The two have shared Scripture and prayed together. George W.

Bush has attempted to apply faith to presidential leadership. He asked me what I felt the book would do to his standing among Christians and I replied, much to his and the First Lady's delight, that it would help him get re-elected in November 2004. I stressed the need for more openness in his commitment to Christ.

Christianity is not a way of life; it is not Western culture. It is not conformity to a standard of living. Christianity is a relationship with Jesus Christ, who sends us as his ambassadors of reconciliation. We are facing a rapid deterioration of the Christian ethic. Jesus confronted the economic and political power structures of his day, out of his commitment to God. He died on a Cross, not because he dared to change hymn-numbers, but because he cared for the poor and was prepared to confront and change practices and policies of injustice.

Chuck Colson said, 'What we do must flow from who we are. Christians must contend for biblically informed morality and justice in the halls of power. That is the balance that keeps our ethics and our activism in proper perspective. I urge you to hold tightly to your courage and your moral convictions during the stressful days ahead. This is no time to wimp out!'

God knew when he had rescued the people of Israel from slavery in Egypt and brought them into their own land that they would prosper. With prosperity there comes complacency. With complacency there comes a decline in personal ethics and morality. People will accept anything. In the name of tolerance all standards disappear. They forget their heritage and what made them a people.

God knew that. So when Israel entered the Promised Land, He reminded them: Deut 8:7-14 'The LORD your God is bringing you into a good land-a land with streams and pools of water, with springs flowing in the valleys and hills; a land with wheat and barley, vines and fig trees, pomegranates, olive oil and honey; a land where bread will not be scarce and you will lack nothing; a land where the rocks are iron and you can dig copper out of the hills. When you have eaten and are satisfied, praise the LORD your God for the good land he has given you.

'Be careful that you do not forget the LORD your God, failing to observe his commands, his laws and his decrees that I am giving you this day.

'Otherwise, when you eat and are satisfied, when you build fine houses and settle down and when your herds and flocks grow large and your silver and gold increase and all you have is multiplied, then your heart will become proud and you will forget the LORD your God.' How relevant is that to Australia today!

Australia is changing. Many of the changes causes us regret, but thank God we are learning to regret our past sins and failures! We now need to commit ourselves to a new future, with committed Christians making the legislation for the future of our land. Regretfully the Uniting Church in Australia continues to be a battlefield. Tens of thousands of loyal members have left. I meet them in churches of every other denomination in which I preach. In 2004 over 5000 regular attenders left the UCA, yet the Church bureaucrats seem to think they are better off for their going.

There is spiritual warfare within the Church today. I have no proposals for others who do not live and behave according to Biblical standards. The church has adequate processes to deal with ministers through counselling and discipline. That is not my role, nor do I sit in judgement on others.

On many occasions I have indicated the use of vocabulary based upon war is inappropriate. We are not talking about war in the military sense, but spiritual warfare, which is a Biblical topic. Paul certainly used the metaphors of spiritual warfare. Of the nine occurrences of the noun 'war' in Revelation, eight are symbolic. The verb is found seven times and six of these are symbolic. The use of spiritual warfare is widespread in the New Testament, not only in Paul's epistles but also in John's - some 45 occasions. We do not fight according to the flesh, Paul states, but then speaks of spiritual warfare.

I always find it amusing that those who want to proclaim themselves 'inclusive' always want to threaten the exclusion of those with whom they differ. Many evangelicals know what it is like to be threatened and harassed. My language and conduct is entirely appropriate. It is my conclusions others may not like. I am a minister of congregations and have been so for fifty years, the last twenty-seven in the same church. I do not seek any position of leadership in the Church, nor in the agencies or groups of the Church.

I have always respected people of differing viewpoints. I am always polite and respectful. I seek to represent other viewpoints honestly but without gloss. My hopes for every minister within the Uniting Church is that we will be true to the Scriptures, that we will lead a devout and holy life, that our behaviour will reflect the holiness expected of those who are redeemed, that we will be active in doing the work of evangelists and we will show a care for the least, loneliest and the lost. I would hope all leaders uphold their ordination vows, that they are diligent in the study of the Bible and that they live a holy and a disciplined life, as our vows stated. My concern is that all ministers, myself included, place themselves under the judgement and mercy of God, as revealed in the Scriptures, as mentioned at our Ordination. I have sought to live a just, holy and disciplined life and I hope others do also. It is not a question of theology but of behaviour that many find objectionable.

I know all ministers are required to place themselves under the authority of the Holy Scriptures; we are required to live holy and disciplined lives, obedient to the expressed commands as found in the Old and New Testaments and in the light of the truths found in the confessional documents and the Basis of Union. I write this on a Monday evening. Today, I preached four different sermons from the Gospels following a busy Sunday of services. Since last Monday I have peached at 14 services. With 50 services every week, life is busy in a growing church. I have also had funerals and a wedding and well as all the normal pastoral and staff cares. Such is the life of a Church minister. What can I achieve through also being a Parliamentarian?

After 27 years of heading up Wesley Mission, the largest welfare organisation in New South Wales, employing some 3500 staff, I realised how much legislation works against families, against the unemployed, the poor, the homeless, the aged, the sick, the disabled. We need people who know, making a positive contribution to our laws. Governments never seem to get it right.

Strong family relationships are key to a stronger Australian society. We are concerned about the moral, social and economic impact that some legislation has on NSW families. We believe every person has a right to good health and access to quality health services. After years of being Board Chairman, running both public and private hospitals, I know the frustration that many people experience with our health system. I can ask the right questions to get the right answers for the people of NSW. Every citizen has the right to live safely within his or her home and community. The Christian Democratic Party is committed to ensuring the security of our citizens.

Rev. Fred Nile and myself helped defeat the Government's plans to sell Hunter's Hill High School and Erskineville Public school because we support parents' right to choose schooling that supports their family where they live. Likewise my colleagues and I defeated the Australian Democrats' attempt to remove Christian Schools from their current exclusion under the Anti-Discrimination Act. We defeated their attempt to remove the right of Christian schools and churches to employ staff of their choice.

We vote in support for all living humans from the beginning of biological life at fertilisation until natural death. Euthanasia will always be opposed by us. We are pro-life and support stem-cell research but never by the destruction of human embryos to harvest those stem cells. We believe governments must enact legislation to safeguard against abuse of air, land and water resources and to preserve our natural heritage. That is why we helped defeat Government legislation to sell Callan Park for more high-rise apartments by private developers. Public parks should remain public.

The Christian Democratic Party has achieved much through our Parliamentarians. We established the Royal Commission into paedophile activity, which uncovered society's dark side. We were responsible for banning tobacco advertising in newspapers and magazines. No wonder the press lampoon us - we cost them too much income! We were successful in prohibiting smoking in public places like clubs and pubs and I am sure you now enjoy eating out. It was the Christian Democratic Party that saved country jobs such as the Letona fruit cannery. I have visited 150 rural and regional communities in NSW to listen to local needs.

We strongly support the police force. We defeated the Greens when they tried to end practice of opening Parliament with prayer. We oppose all soft laws on illegal drugs, injecting rooms, brothels, gambling extension and the availability of pornography, issues that have been supported by both Liberal and Labour parties voting together. The Christian Democratic Party defends the rights of individuals, promotes quality family life, encourages small business, supports Christian schools and brings Christian ethics to bear within our society. We are a balanced, skilled team.

Many people are concerned for the future of our country. We are the only party committed to ensuring Australia retains our Christian heritage. We want Christian ethics and morality as part of the fibre of New South Wales and we will ensure Christian faith, freedom and values are protected within our government.

A number of newspapers reported on 31st of January 2002, a notice from Canberra. It made front-page news in every state of the nation:

'The Superintendent of Wesley Mission, Sydney, the Rev. Dr Gordon Moyes AC, has received the highest honour ever awarded to an Australian clergyman still in full-time ministry - Order of Australia Companion (AC) in the General Division.

'Dr Moyes, who was one of only six Australians who were awarded the AC on Australia Day, received the honour for 'service to the community in the delivery and expansion of social welfare and outreach services through the Wesley Mission, fostering networks and partnership arrangements with other agencies to make services more widely available and to religion.'

'He said he was surprised and stunned by the award, which he claimed was an acknowledgment of the work of Wesley Mission staff, volunteers and supporters. 'It is a recognition of the work of the Wesley Mission team,' he said. 'It is a wonderful honour and an affirmation of our ministry of word and deed conducted by our 3600 staff, 3000 volunteers who are supported by our tens of thousands of donors.' Dr Moyes arrived back in Sydney on 25 January after spending the previous three weeks lecturing at a major theological college, Emmanuel School of Religion, in Tennessee, USA.

'The honour was also due to Dr Moyes' involvement in building partnerships between charities, churches, governments, corporations, donors and people in need, to better serving the underprivileged. To this end he was a founding Board member of the Prime Minister's Community Business Partnership. For more than 25 years, Dr Moyes has promoted other organisations and their work every week, both on radio and television, seeking to raise funds for any worthy Christian or charitable activity.

'For some years Dr Moyes has been active in seeking support from politicians of all parties. He has built close relationships with our national leaders. One media reporter described him this week as being 'one of the most influential clergy in the nation, due to his direct contact with all senior Cabinet Ministers and, in particular, with the Prime Minister.'

'During the election last year, one prominent politician was asked by an audience member to get a certain message back to the Prime Minister. The politician, Ross Cameron, of Parramatta, replied, 'If you want to get a message to the Prime Minister, then you better work through Dr Gordon Moyes. He has more access to the Cabinet and the Prime Minister than I have.'

That highest of all honours has never been given to a minister in parish work or to any politician in any Parliament. It was a seal on my life's work. A number of colleagues approached me with the idea of researching social and community issues and then to do something about them. I suddenly realised that while all my life I had usually been the youngest to do this or that, I was now a 'tribal elder'.

No clergyman in a church has ever been so honoured as I was by being made a Companion of the Order of Australia. Usually only Governor Generals, Governors, Prime Ministers, Chief Judges of the High Court and a few extraordinary people have been so honoured. In England, this honour is equivalent to being elevated to the House of Lords.

I found out that if one has already been honoured by being made a Member of the Order of Australia, a second honour can only be conferred for a different kind of work. In my case, this meant for work in developing the concept of helping people by developing partnerships between corporations and employees, a welfare organisation, the governments and people in need, a concept that I carried into the special taskforce established by the Prime Minister on which I have served. The partnership programs Wesley Mission have developed have become national models. It is an honour that I will share with all who work with us. That honour brings instant recognition from key people in our nation.

Then in 2003, I became the recipient of the Commonwealth Government's Centenary Medal, struck to honour those people who had made a significant contribution to our nation during the previous one hundred years since we became federated as the Commonwealth of Australia.

In 2004, Beverley and I spent a week in Brighton England, with its stone beaches, for the world Convention of Churches of Christ. It was our 6th World Convention, but they were spread over 52 years. In our early married years, we could not afford overseas travel. We caught up with many of our friends we see only once every four years. 165 countries were represented. Every day there were main speakers, many seminars on a dozen topics and great evening rallies. I presented two seminars on ministering in the inner city, each running for 4 hours. I had two excellent groups of interested people from many countries.

One night I was greatly surprised during the evening service. It was announced that a new international citation was to be awarded each four years. This was named to honour Sir Garfield and Lady Todd, remarkable New Zealand missionaries to Southern Rhodesia for 72 years. They pioneered the education system in Southern Rhodesia. I had met him at my first World Convention in Melbourne 1952. Meeting him and other famous missionaries and church leaders made me feel, as a thirteen-year-old boy, that I was walking with giants. With the move for Independence, Garfield went into politics trying to move the country to a bloodless change to black power. He became Prime Minister for eight years, but the illegal coup of Ian Smith meant his fellow whites imprisoned him for 12 years. We prayed for him during this time. Eventually with the overthrow of the Smith regime, he was released and appointed a Senator in the new Government. Unfortunately, the new Prime Minister, Robert Mumgabe, was far from Christian, even though he was a former student of Garfield's. Garfield died earlier in 2004.

The recipient of the Garfield, Todd Citation, was for a person who had served the Church and the broader community of the Church, politics and commerce. It was then I heard that I was the first recipient. I was absolutely speechless and unable to believe it. Beverley knew but kept it secret from me. The president read an outline of my ministry and I was given a standing ovation by the thousands present. It was a highlight of my life, to be honoured by my peers from around the world. Every day thereafter, I had people greeting me and wishing us well.

Back at the 1952 World Convention, I carried an autograph book and sought the signatures of the great and famous. Now all of those memories came flooding back and some young boys and girls at the World Convention pressed their autograph books and Bibles into my hands, asking for my signature. I willingly signed each one, praying that each child would be as influenced as I was at my first World Convention, 53 years earlier.

Prophetic ministry is Biblical, but never fully understood by most congregations. The most controversial aspect of the ministry of Wesley Mission over the years has been its bold proclamation on matters of social justice. A city church is in a unique position to see the injustices of society and to have the ear of the public. Frequently social action has been the result of the strong presentation of the prophetic word to our country.

Just as the prophets of old spoke out the word of the Lord according to the social evils of their day, Wesley Mission has spoken a word of rebuke, of guidance and of witness to the Christian message. Earlier Superintendents did not exercise the prophetic ministry with as much controversy or strength as did Rev. Dr Sir Alan Walker, who very quickly gained a reputation for his controversial and hard-hitting stands.

Sometimes the Mission lost support because of his prophetic utterances and other times greatly gained. Under his leadership the Pleasant Sunday Afternoon, which provided musical and biblical content for people over many decades in the heart of the city, became The Lyceum Platform where, for a number of years, social issues were debated and examined by speakers from the Christian point of view. The message of this crusading platform was carried by radio to the people of Sydney. In recent years radio and television have become overpopulated with current affairs programs and people making utterances on the social issues of our day and the voice of the Church is only one of many competing voices. The Mission decided to continue its social issues presentation with a changed format.

Instead of finding fifty social issues each year to fight from the Lyceum Platform, the Mission chose to raise issues on television and radio where we have direct access to a large listening audience and instead of criticising what the Government had done, provided more materials for the Government by way of submissions during the decision-making process, rather than after it. Submissions are made to Federal and State governments on a wide range of social and moral issues and in one Senate Select Report a large amount of the Mission's submission was accepted ultimately as the Federal Government's report. Dr Keith Suter uses remarkable intellectual skills (he has two Ph. D's!) and deep Christian commitment to formulate new submissions on government policy.

However, public protests are still held when matters of importance are raised and the new Wesley Theatre is still open to the church at large to be used for significant Christian protest. One important aspect of the prophetic ministry is at the individual level. The church must speak on behalf of those whom society ignores or tramples. The poor, the confused, the hopeless, the homeless, the unemployed, the socially neglected, the physically ill are part of the constituency that is represented by Wesley Mission. These people have little voice in the community and against the bureaucracies and although their need is real it is seldom heard. Someone needs to stand alongside them and with all of its strength speak on behalf of the powerless. That is where since 2002, having a Superintendent who is also in the Parliament, Wesley Mission has an advocate for the poor sitting on the leather seats of legislation and speaking every day to the ministers of the Government.

Wesley Mission sees itself as the voice of the voiceless. Understanding, compassion, backed by specialist social research, provide the basis for Christian social action on behalf of those people in the community who have no muscle of their own. To represent the powerless in the community requires a city church ministry with muscle. A powerless church is only another ineffective voice. The weight and size and strategic strength of Wesley Mission has been effective in helping people in their battle against State and Federal government bureaucracies and on behalf of ordinary people caught up in legislative changes and political decisions. The Mission speaks to enable justice to be done. Only a church in the heart of the city with a city on its heart can do that! The powerlessness of ordinary people caught up in the machinery of government and the apathy of so many public servants make more urgent the role of Wesley Mission. Personal political lobbying at the highest level by senior staff, close personal contact with politicians and public service bureaucrats mean that ordinary peoples' needs can be helped, frequently by a simple telephone call to the right person. The progression to Parliamentarian was quite natural and I look forward to many years of service to God and humanity.

POSTLUDE

It has been an interesting life being a minister of religion. The twelve facets of my expanding ministry have all enlarged my capacities and competencies. They have all had freedom, while in ministry to God, in proclaiming the Word and in caring for people.

Traditionally, theology was the 'Queen of the sciences' and at graduations at Universities like Oxford, the Doctors of Divinity lead the procession in their scarlet robes. I was reminded recently as I walked in with the academics, fellows, and graduates of our Wesley Institute of Ministry and the Arts, to give the graduation address anything learnt in this life and offered to God for His service, can be used by Him.

May the dodecahedron shape of my expanded ministry be of encouragement to others to offer their interests and talents to God and to allow Him to expand them.

Rev. Dr. The Hon. Gordon Moyes AC, MLC
Superintendent
Wesley Mission, Sydney:
Member of the Legislative Council
New South Wales
Australia
2005

2005 Equity Trustees Not for Profit Australian C.E.O. Awards: Winner Long Term High Achiever.

2004 Appointed Adjunct Professor of Christian Ministry, Emmanuel School of Religion, Johnson City, TN, USA.

2004 Awarded the Inaugural "Garfield Todd Citation" at the Churches of Christ World Convention in Brighton, England, in recognition of services to the church and the broader community of the church, politics and commerce.

2003 Awarded Commonwealth Government's Centenary Medal for Distinguished Service to Australia.

2003 Re-Elected as Member of the Legislative Council at the 2003 New South Wales State Elections until 2011.

2002 Reappointed as Superintendent of Wesley Mission until the end of 2005 when Dr Moyes will retire from Wesley Mission after 27 years as Chief Executive and Senior Minister. (Superintendent)

2002 Winner Eastern Australian Entrepreneur Of The Year Award for Entrepreneurship In A Social, Community or Not-for-Profit Enterprise

2002 Elected as Member of the Legislative Council by Joint Sitting of both Houses of New South Wales Parliament

2002 Appointed Companion of The Order of Australia, Australia's highest national honour.

2001 Elected Chairperson of the Sydney Presbytery, Uniting Church in Australia.

1999 Member of Prime Minister's Community Business Partnership Board

1998 Reappointed Superintendent Wesley Mission until end of 2003

1996 Member, Community Benefits Trust

1996 Member of Prime Minister's National Task Force on Youth Homelessness

1996 Chairman of Aged Persons Welfare Foundation

1994 Rotary International President's "Distinguished Service" Award

1993 President, The Rotary Club of Sydney

1991 Vocation Service Award, Rotary International

1990 Chairman of the Board, Harbour Radio Ltd subsequently of Macquarie Network Pty Ltd

1990 Commenced lecturing in Urban Mission – the Church in the city, at Emmanuel School of Religion, Johnson City, TN, USA.

1989 Doctor of Letters, Milligan College, Tennessee. USA.

1989 Doctor of Laws, California Graduate School of Theology

1988 National President of Boys' Brigade, Australia

1988 National Chairman, Habitat for Humanity, Australia

1988 Chaplain to the Australian Olympic Team, Calgary

1987 Elected a Fellow of the Royal Geographic Society, London

1986 Elected Father of the Year by the NSW Father of the Year Council

1986 Elected a Fellow of the Australian Institute of Management

1986 Double awards for his 'Discovering Jesus' won in Book of the Year Awards.

1986 Communication and Leadership Award, Toastmasters International. Australian Public Speaker of the year Award.

1986 Australian Government bestows Member of the Order of Australia
1985 First Australian Keynote speaker at Million Dollar Round Table USA

1985 Doctor of Divinity, California Graduate School of Theology

1984 Australian Public Speaker of the Year by Rostrum

1983 'Sydney Morning Herald' named him in Our Top 50 Achievers

1979 Inducted as Superintendent of Wesley Central Mission, Sydney

1978 Paul Harris Fellow, Rotary International's highest award.

1977 Accepted invitation to become Superintendent of Wesley Mission, Sydney.

1977 Citizen of the Year, Moorabbin, Victoria

1976 Founded Christian Retirement Centres, Victoria

1974 President, Rotary Club of Cheltenham, Victoria

1964 Bachelor of Arts, Melbourne University

1959 Diploma of Ministry, Federal College of the Bible, Victoria

OTHER BOOKS BY GORDON MOYES

Further Reading

- Twelve Steps to Serenity: Basic Help for Living in a World of Pressure
- Mission on!: The story of the world's most amazing mission
- Discovering Jesus
- Discovering Paul
- Discovering the Young Church
- How to Grow an Australian Church

FILMS BY GORDON MOYES

- The Apostle who Changed the World
- Change the World
- The Church that Changed the World
- The Man who Changed the World

CONTACT WESLEY MISSION

Contact

wesleymission@wesleymission.org.au

Ph: (02) 9263 5555

Fax: (02) 9267 1022

Ph: (Int'l) + 61 2 9263 5555

Fax: (Int'l) + 61 2 9267 1022

Wesley Mission,

PO Box A5555,

Sydney South, 1235

NSW, Australia

220 Pitt Street, Sydney. (Opp Hilton)